vol.

8

GLEIPNIR

SUN TAKEDA

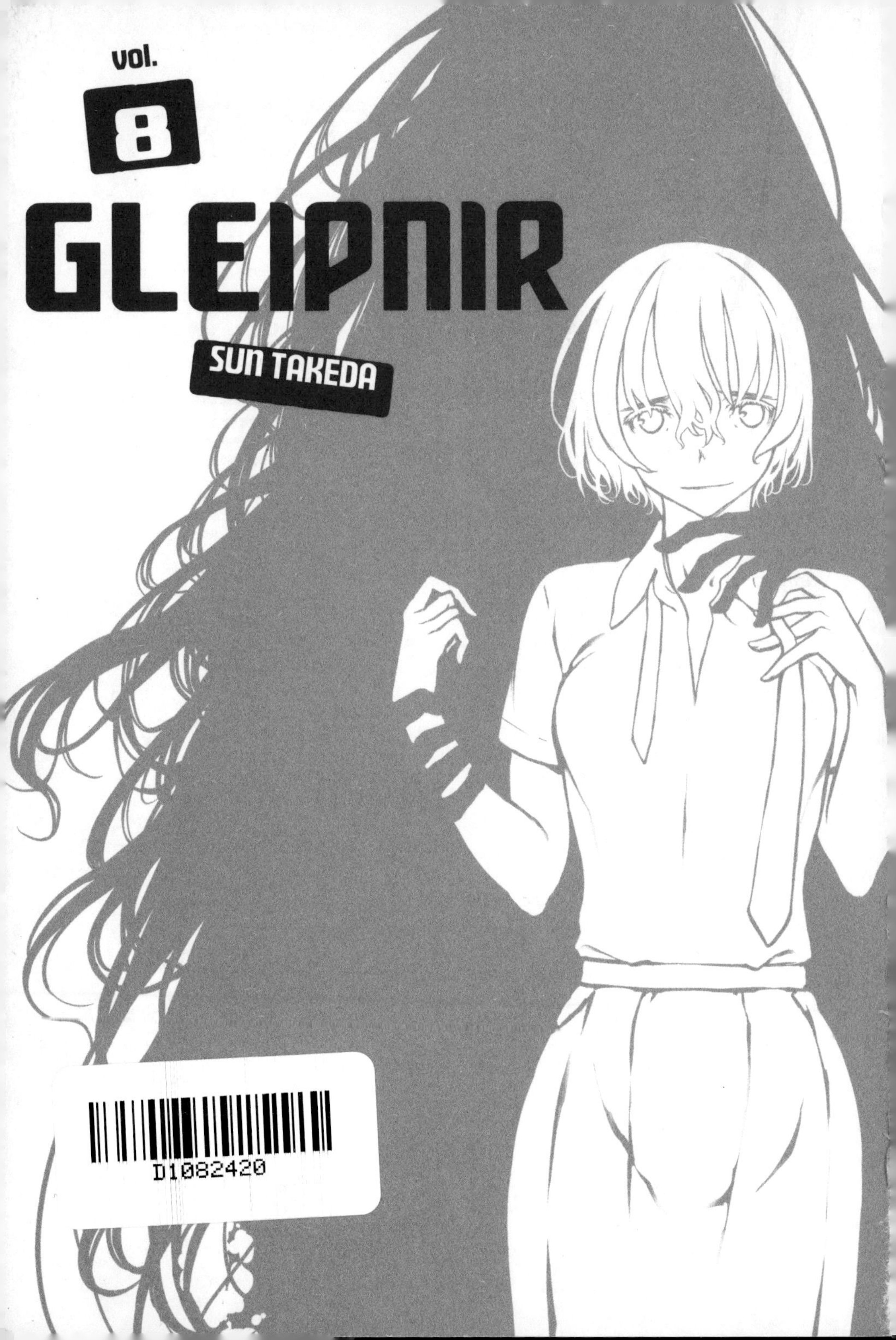

CONTENTS

G L E I P N I R

CHAPTER 47

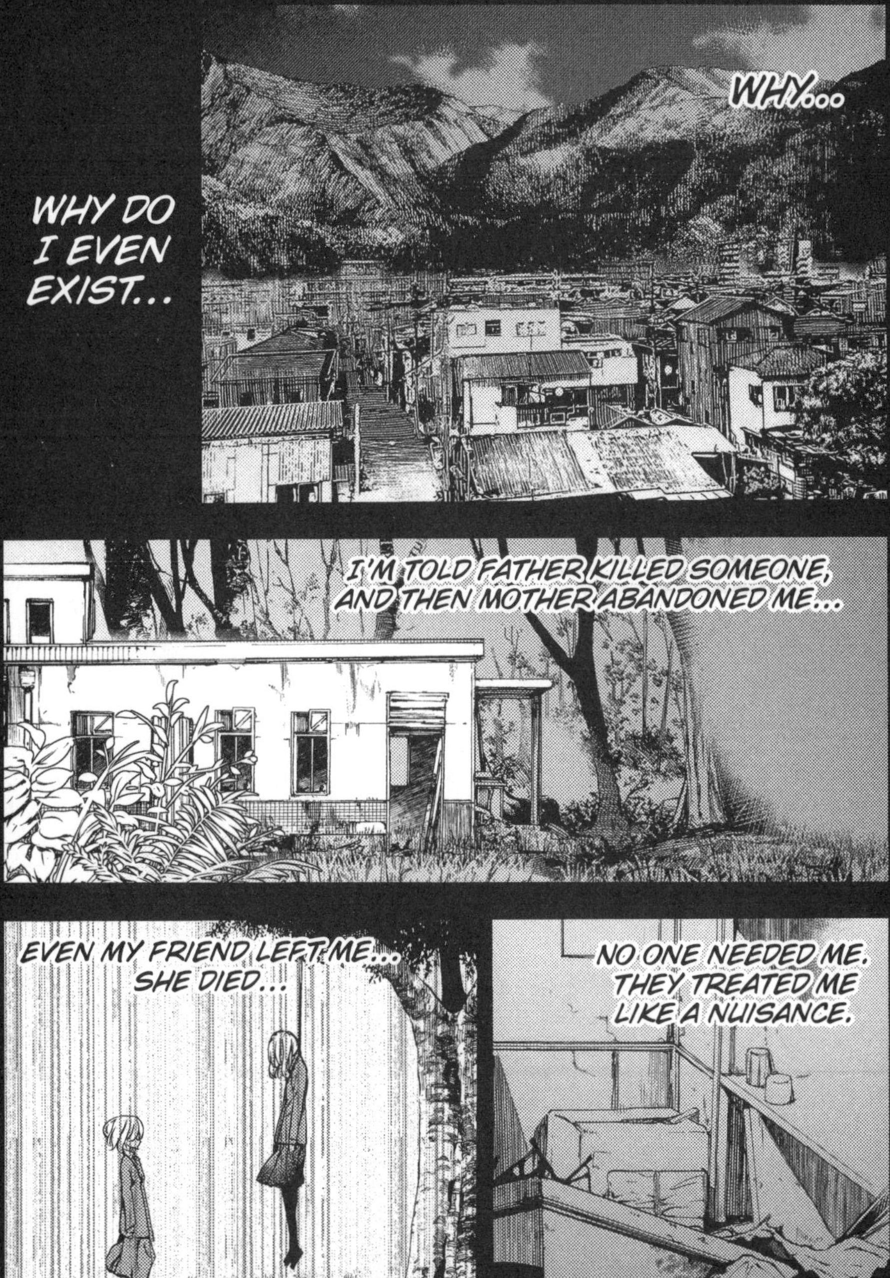
WHY...
WHY DO I EVEN EXIST...
I'M TOLD FATHER KILLED SOMEONE, AND THEN MOTHER ABANDONED ME...
NO ONE NEEDED ME. THEY TREATED ME LIKE A NUISANCE.
EVEN MY FRIEND LEFT ME... SHE DIED...

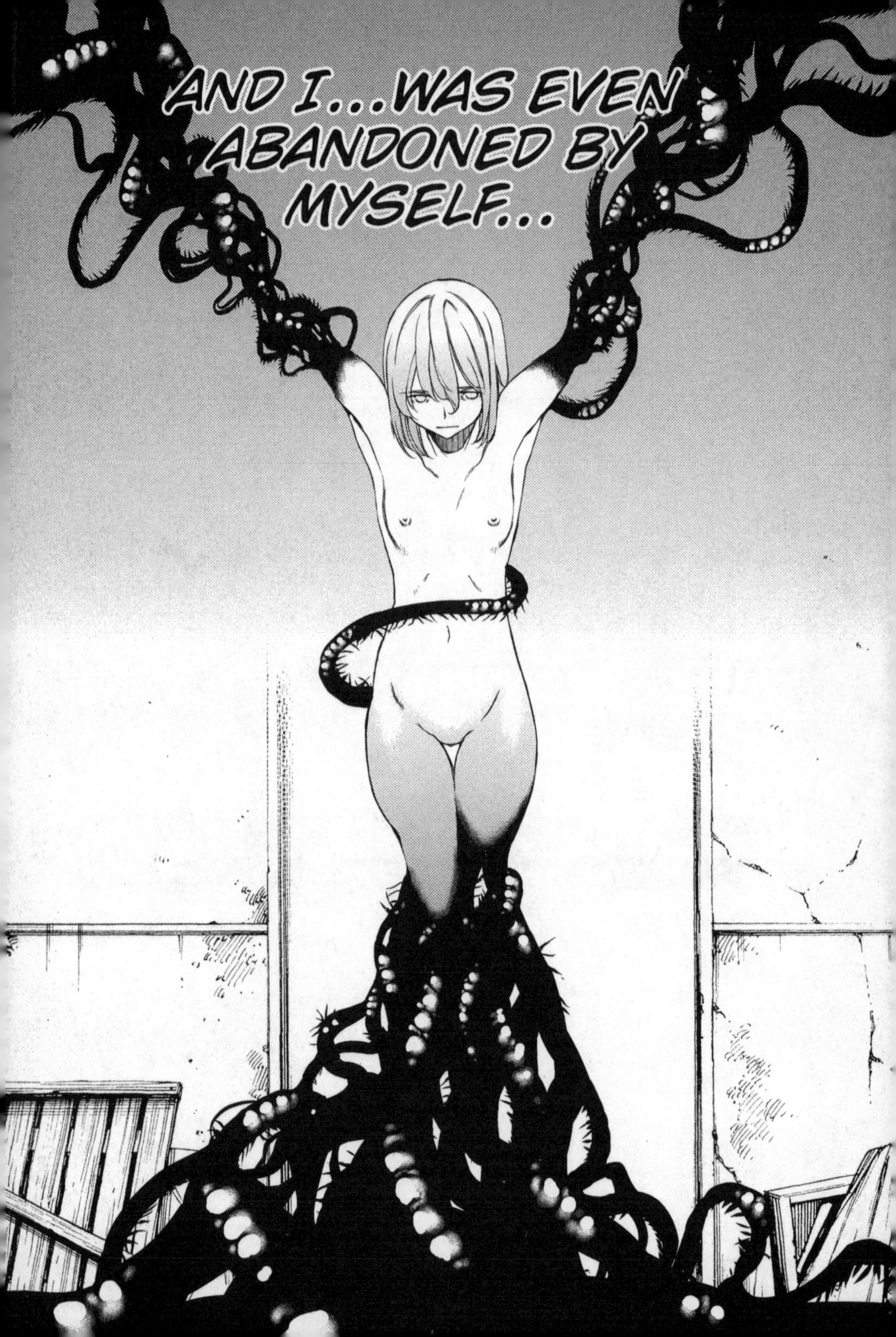
AND I...WAS EVEN ABANDONED BY MYSELF...

CHAPTER 47 ✚ UNTIL THE END

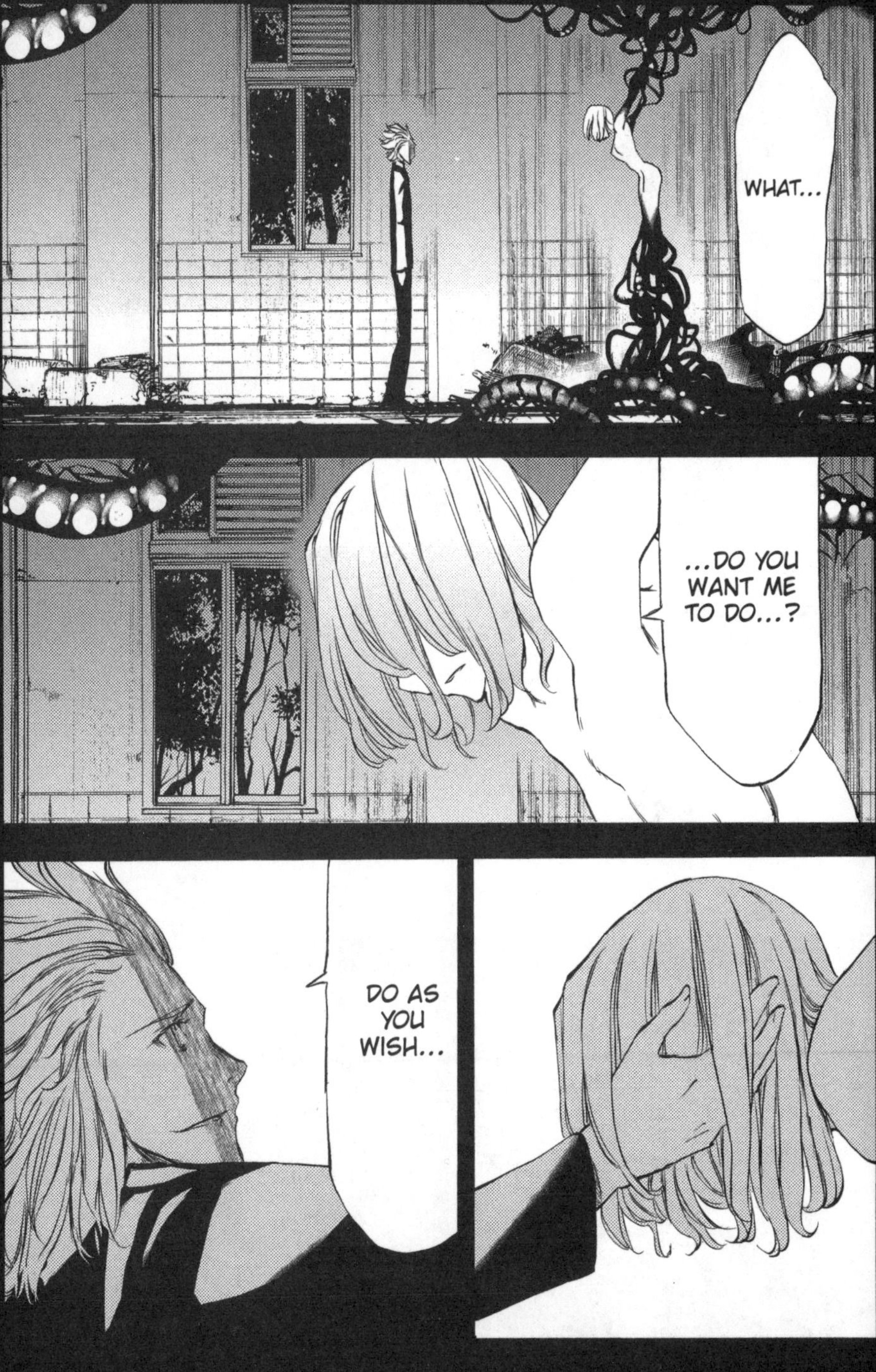
WHAT...
...DO YOU WANT ME TO DO...?
DO AS YOU WISH...

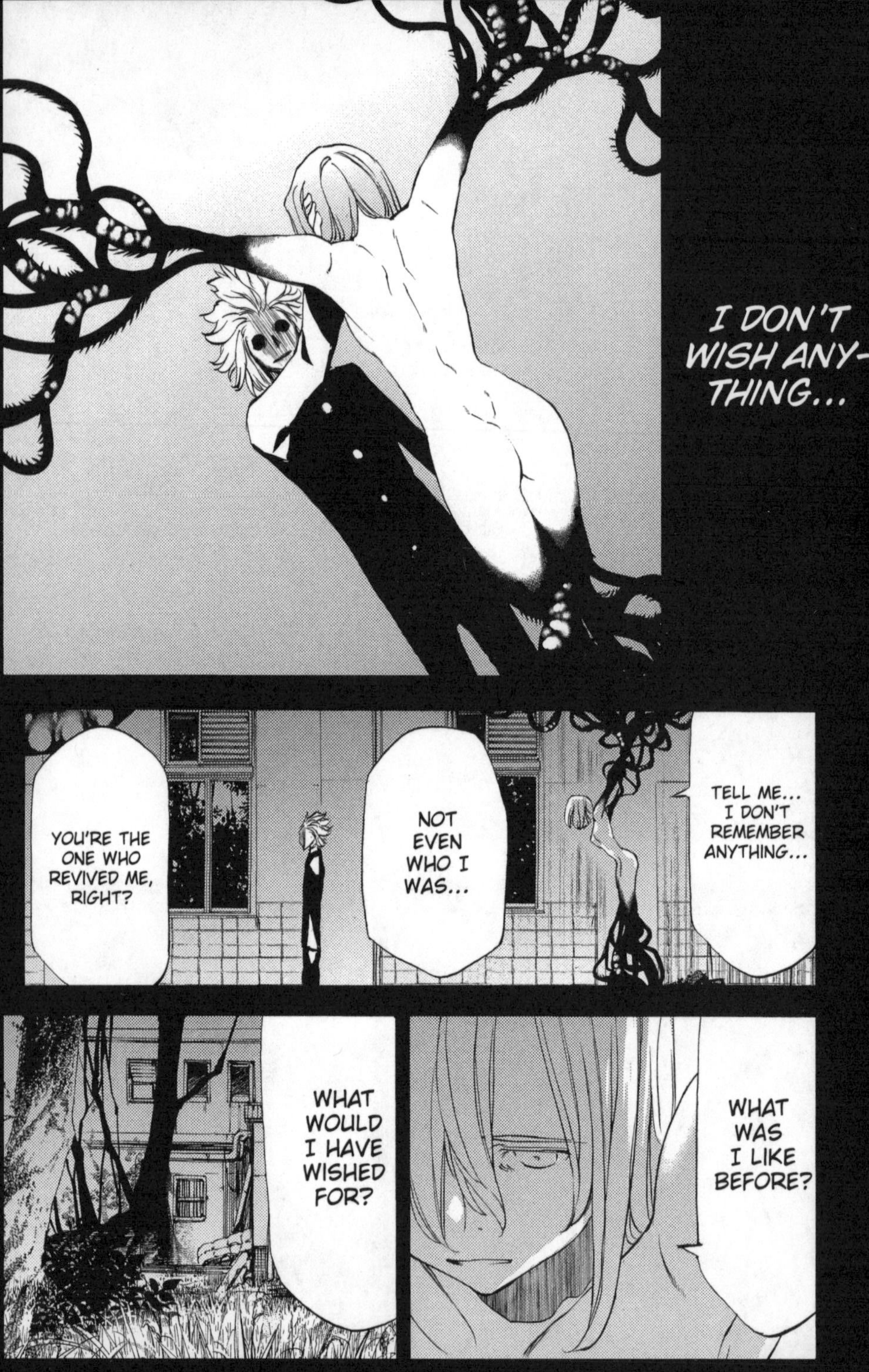
I DON'T WISH ANY-THING...
TELL ME... I DON'T REMEMBER ANYTHING...
NOT EVEN WHO I WAS...
YOU'RE THE ONE WHO REVIVED ME, RIGHT?
WHAT WAS I LIKE BEFORE?
WHAT WOULD I HAVE WISHED FOR?

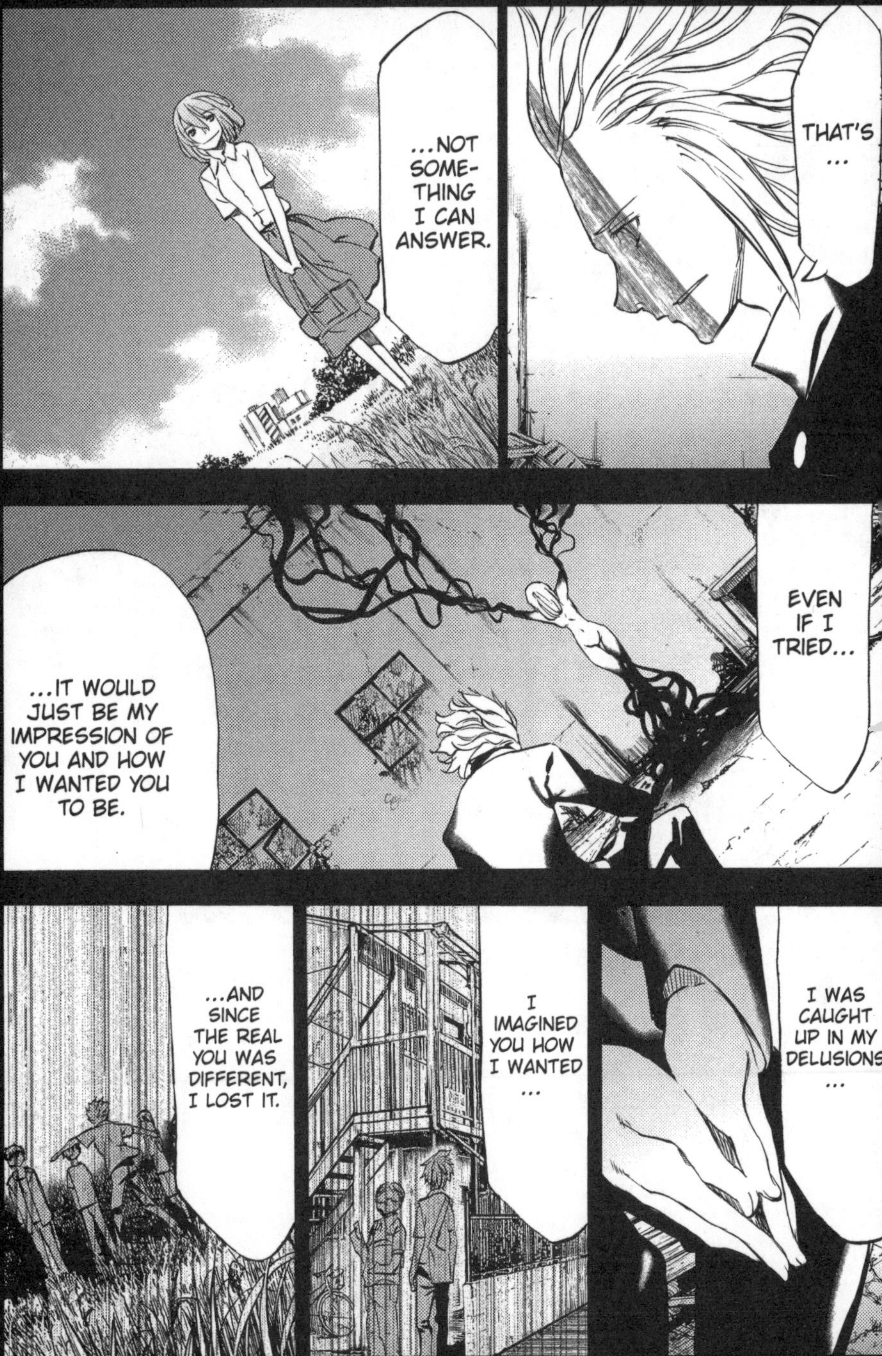
THAT'S ...
...NOT SOMETHING I CAN ANSWER.
EVEN IF I TRIED...
...IT WOULD JUST BE MY IMPRESSION OF YOU AND HOW I WANTED YOU TO BE.
I WAS CAUGHT UP IN MY DELUSIONS ...
I IMAGINED YOU HOW I WANTED ...
...AND SINCE THE REAL YOU WAS DIFFERENT, I LOST IT.

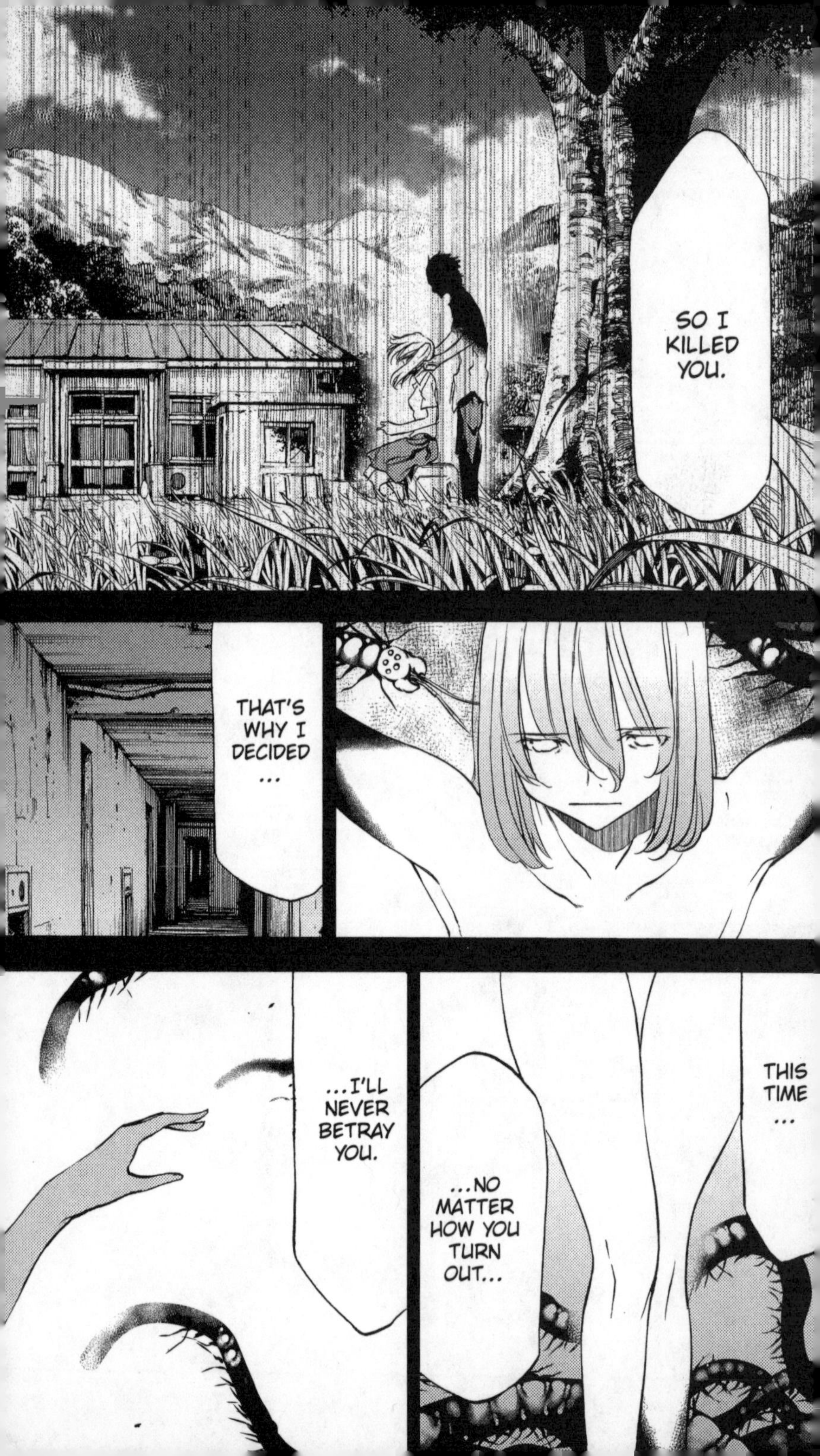
SO I KILLED YOU.
THAT'S WHY I DECIDED ...
THIS TIME ...
...NO MATTER HOW YOU TURN OUT...
...I'LL NEVER BETRAY YOU.

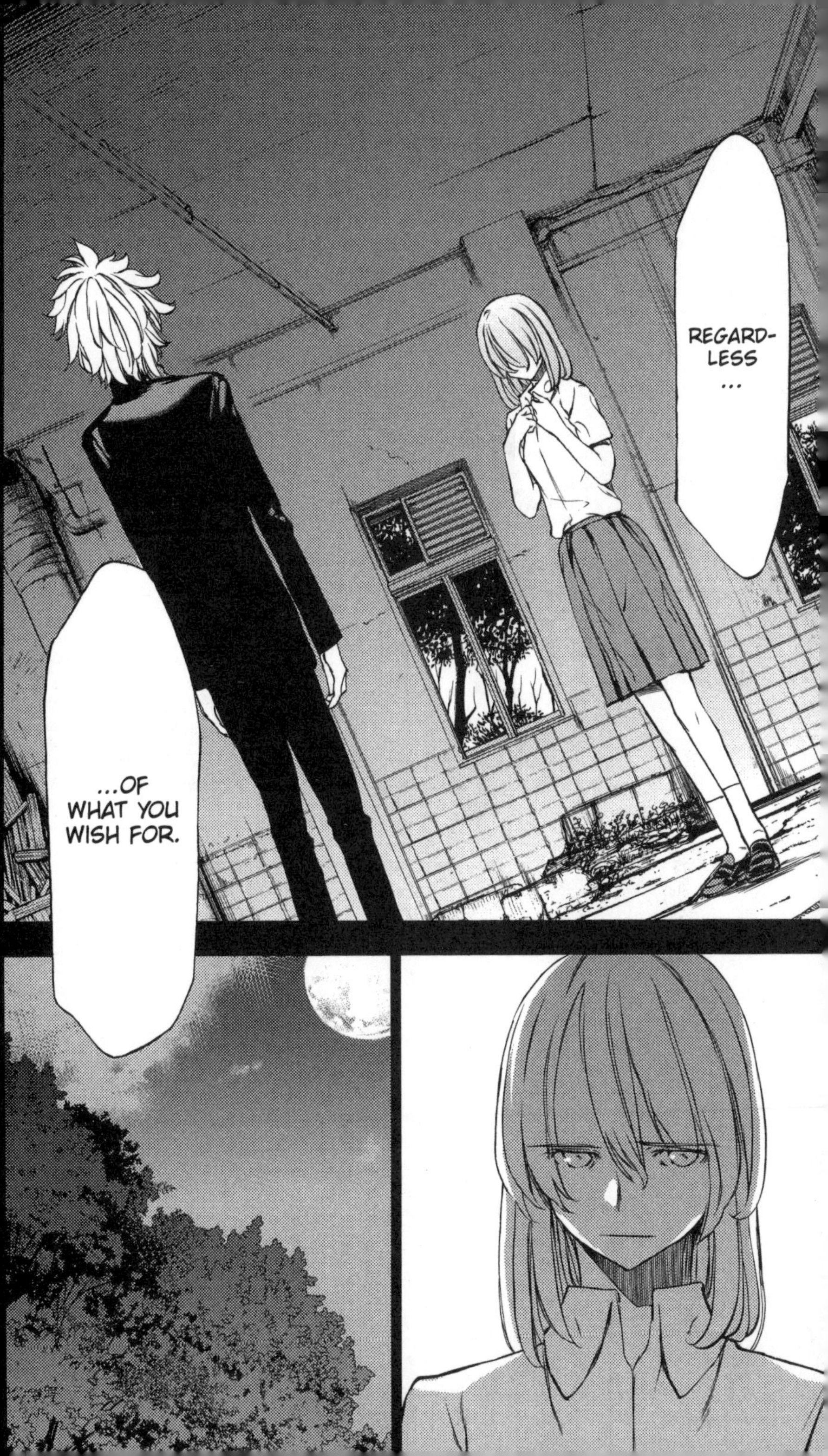
REGARDLESS...
...OF WHAT YOU WISH FOR.

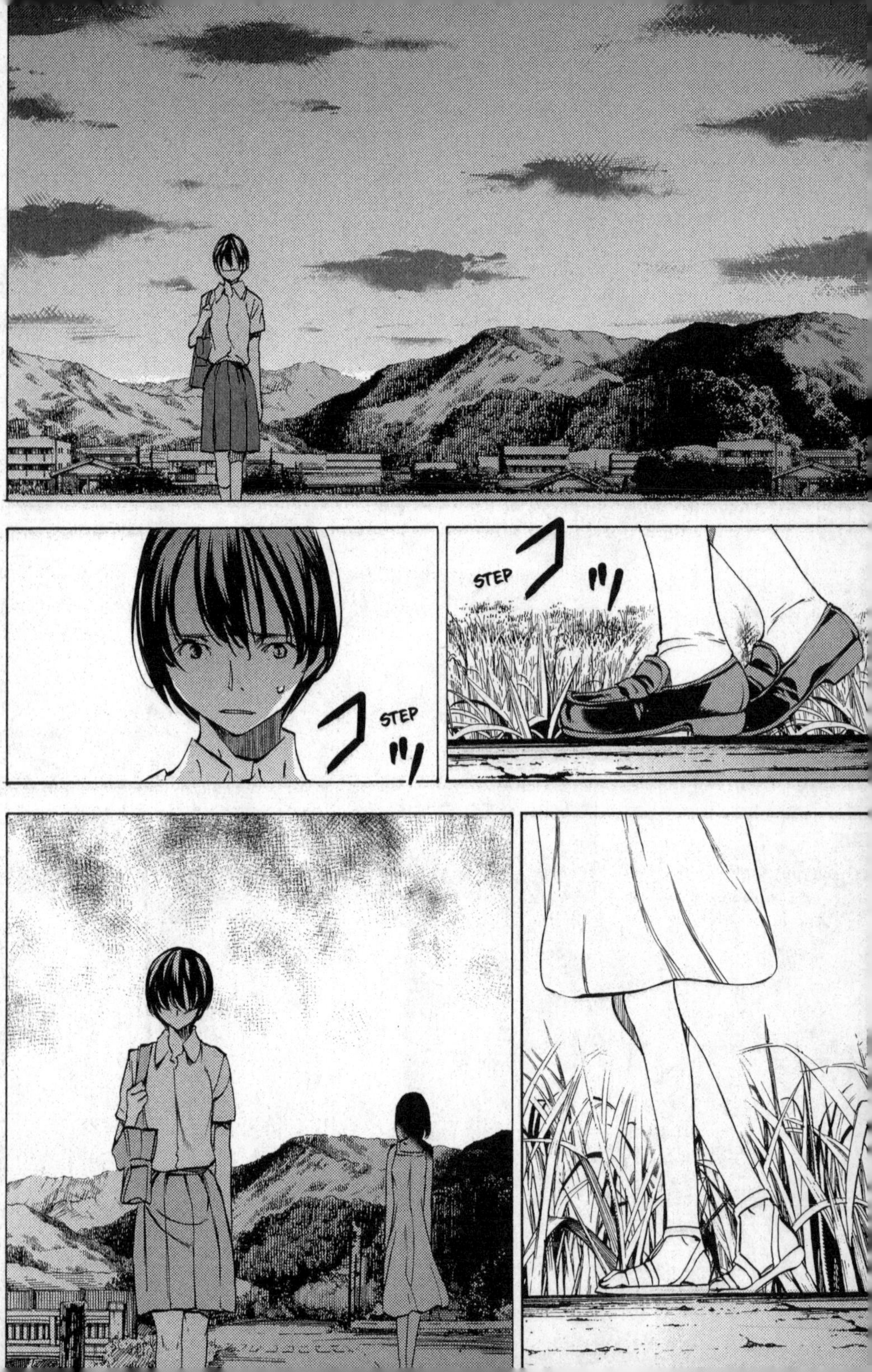
コツ
STEP
コツ
STEP

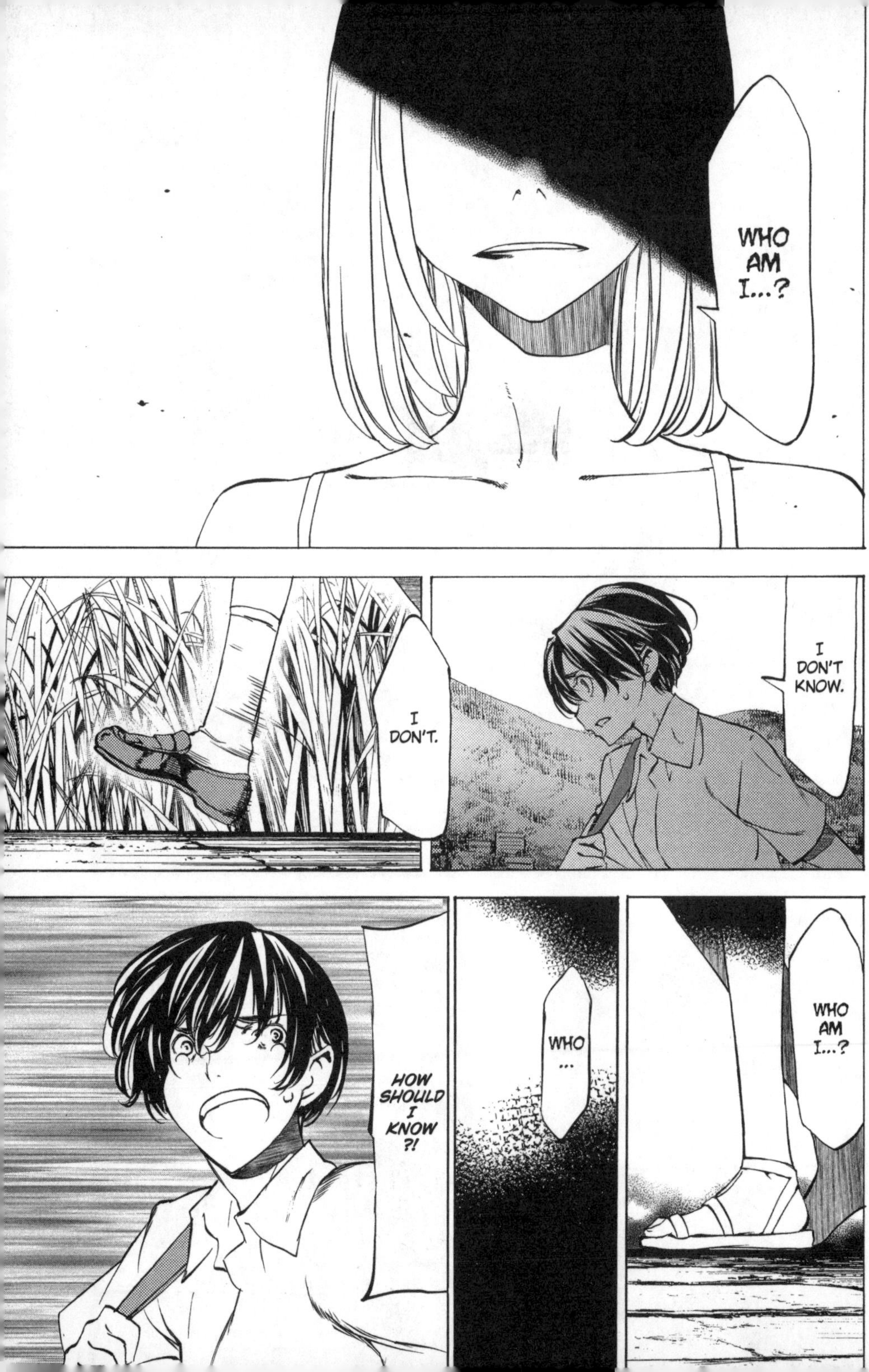
WHO AM I...?
I DON'T KNOW.
I DON'T.
WHO AM I...?
WHO ...
HOW SHOULD I KNOW ?!

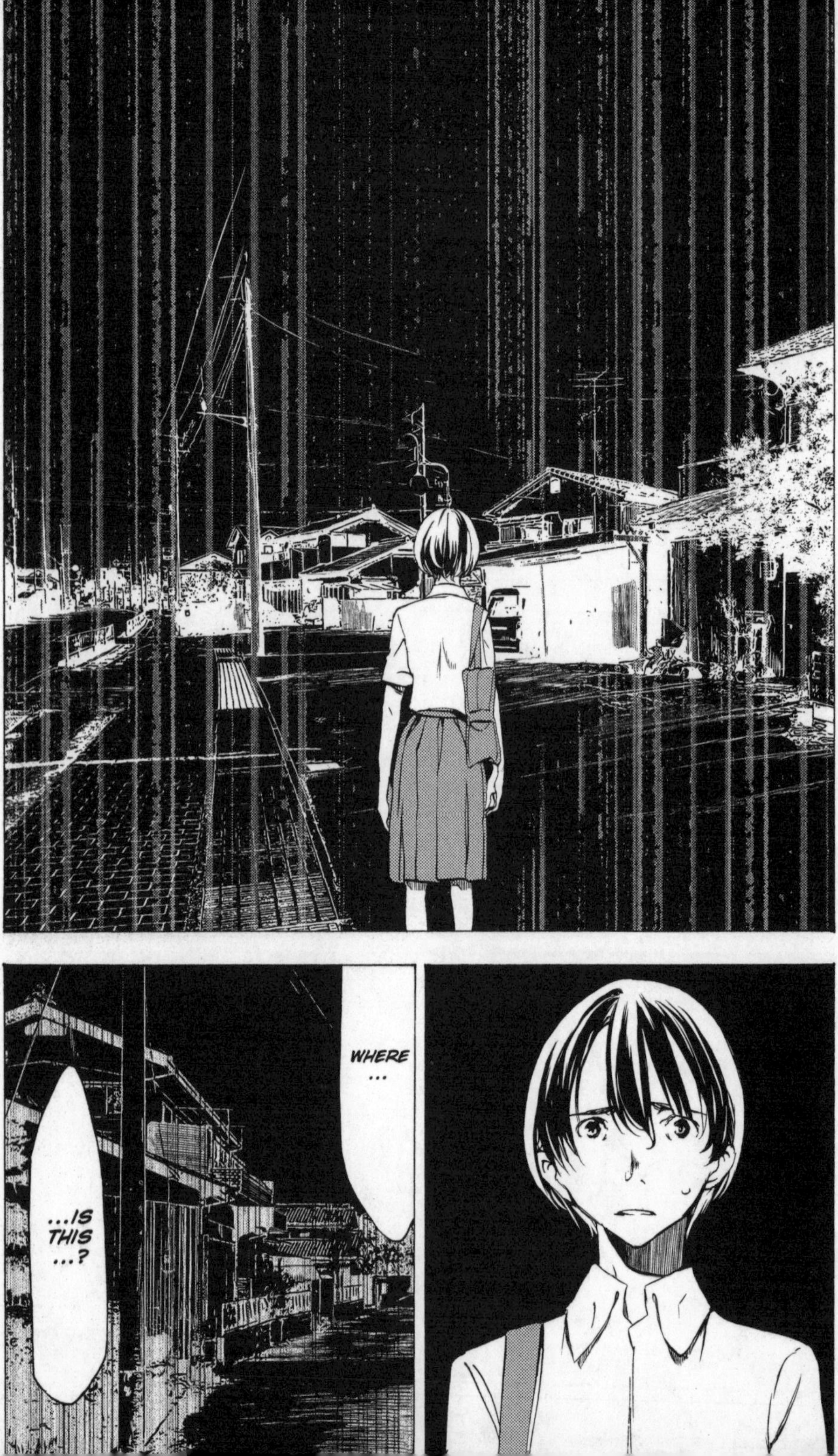
WHERE ...
...IS THIS ...?

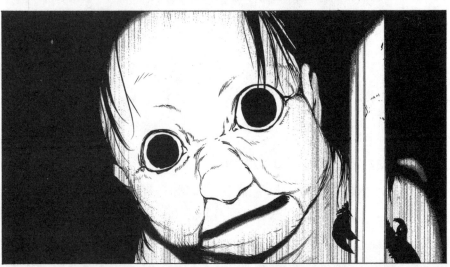

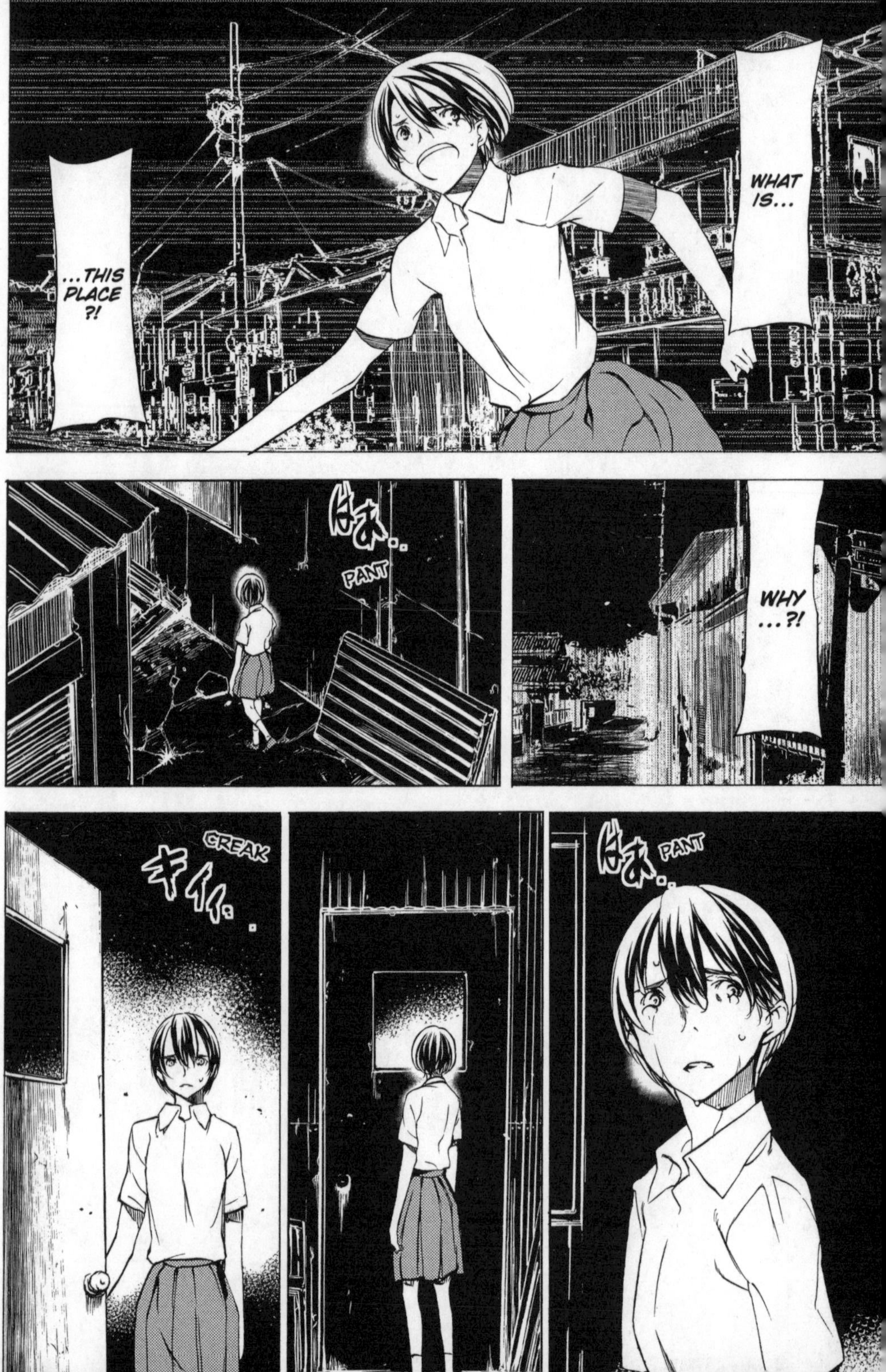
WHAT IS...
...THIS PLACE ?!
WHY ...?!
はぁ..
PANT
はぁ..
PANT
キイィ..
CREAK

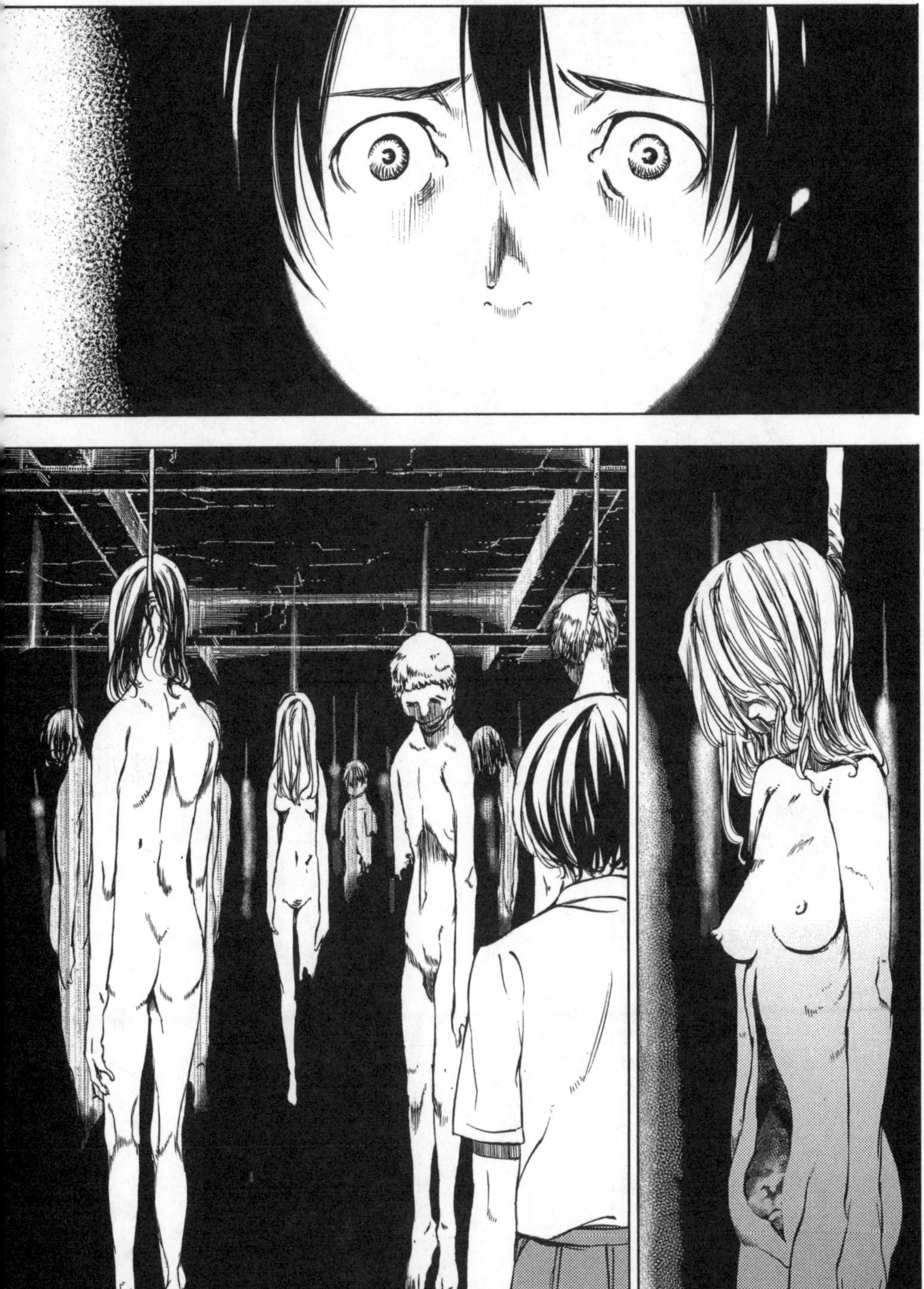

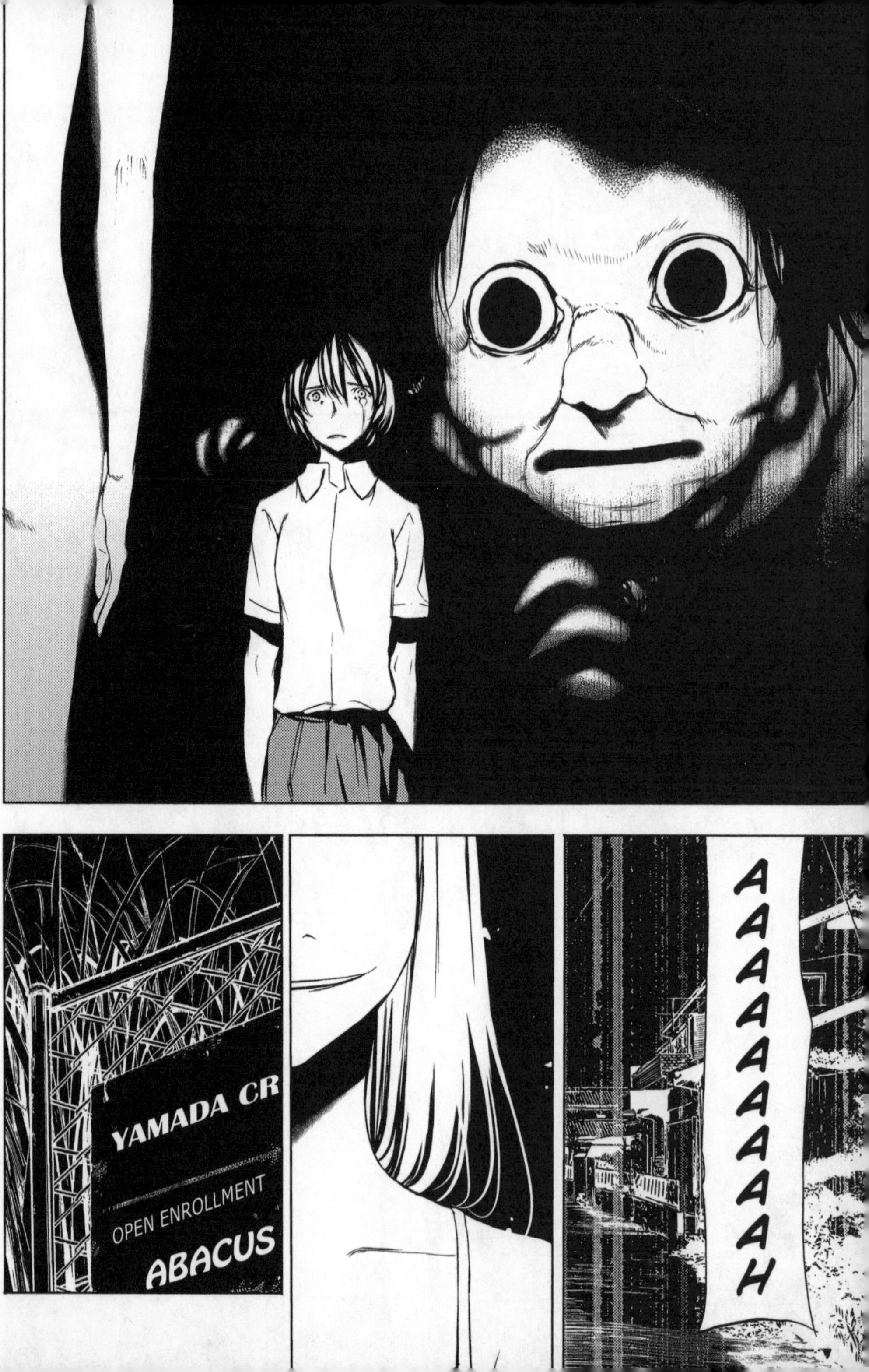
AAAAAAAAAH
YAMADA CR
OPEN ENROLLMENT
ABACUS

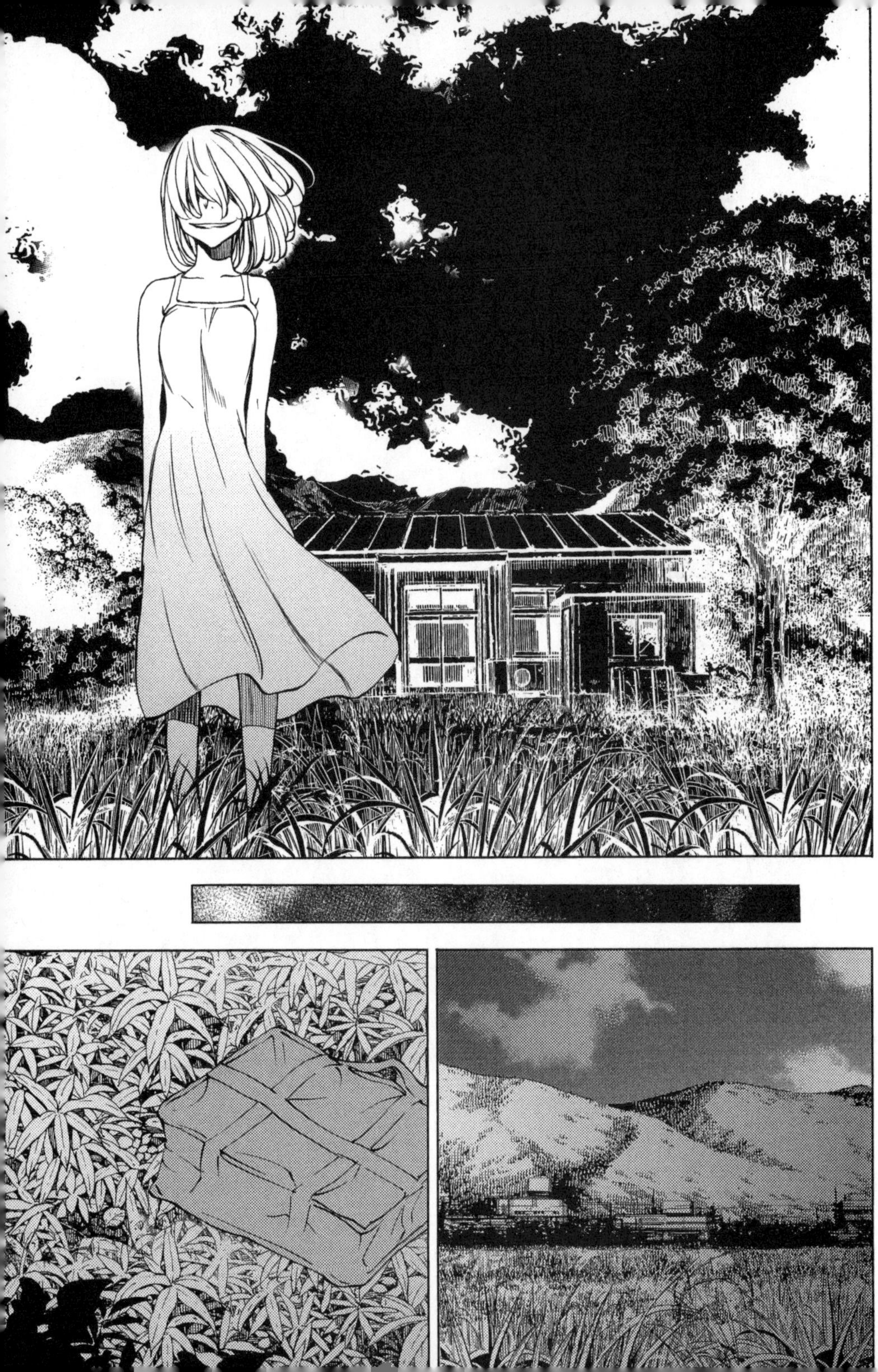

OKAY...

MY TURN.

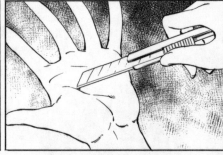

NO BUGS...

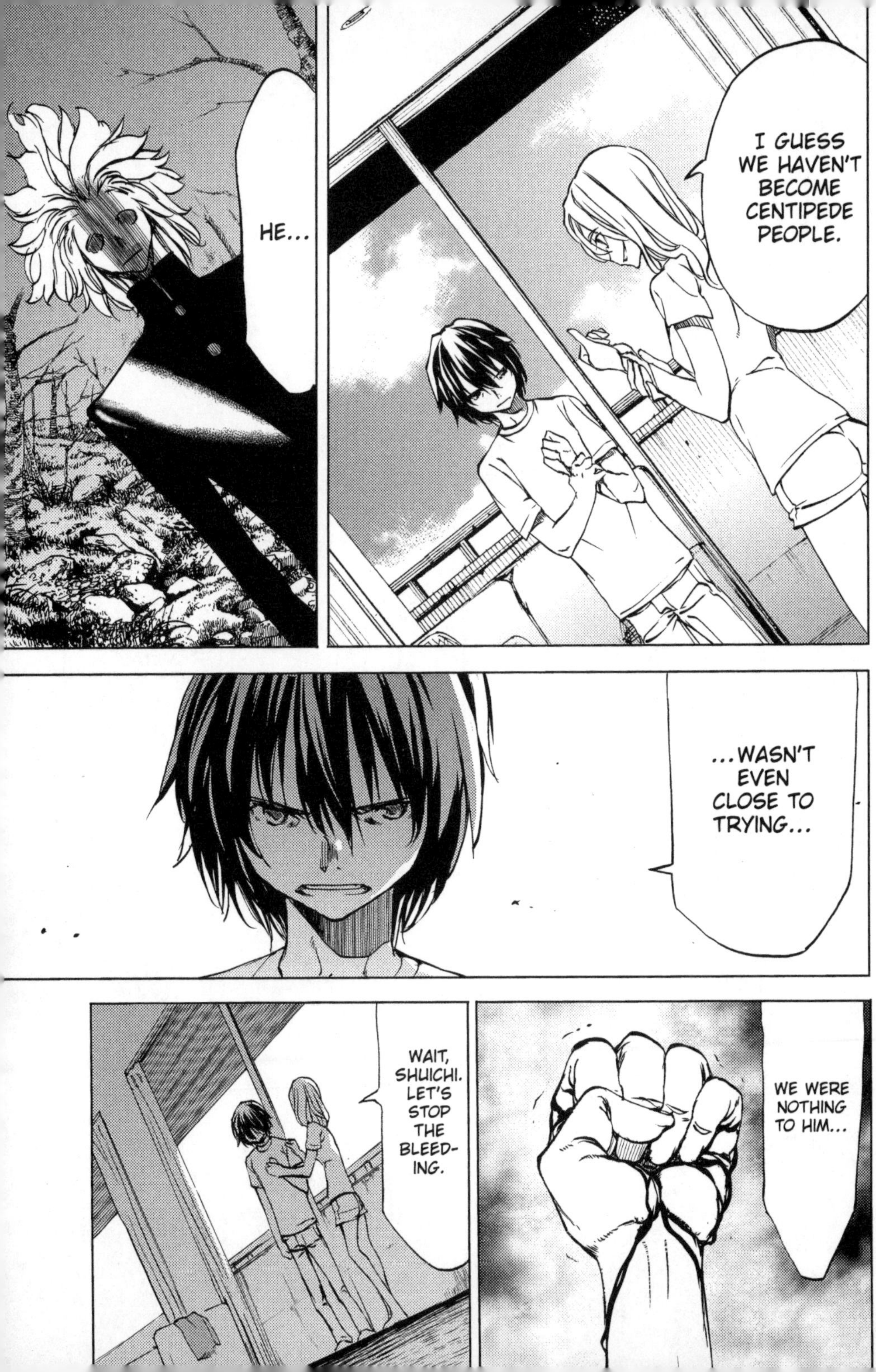
I GUESS WE HAVEN'T BECOME CENTIPEDE PEOPLE.
HE...
...WASN'T EVEN CLOSE TO TRYING...
WE WERE NOTHING TO HIM...
WAIT, SHUICHI. LET'S STOP THE BLEED-ING.

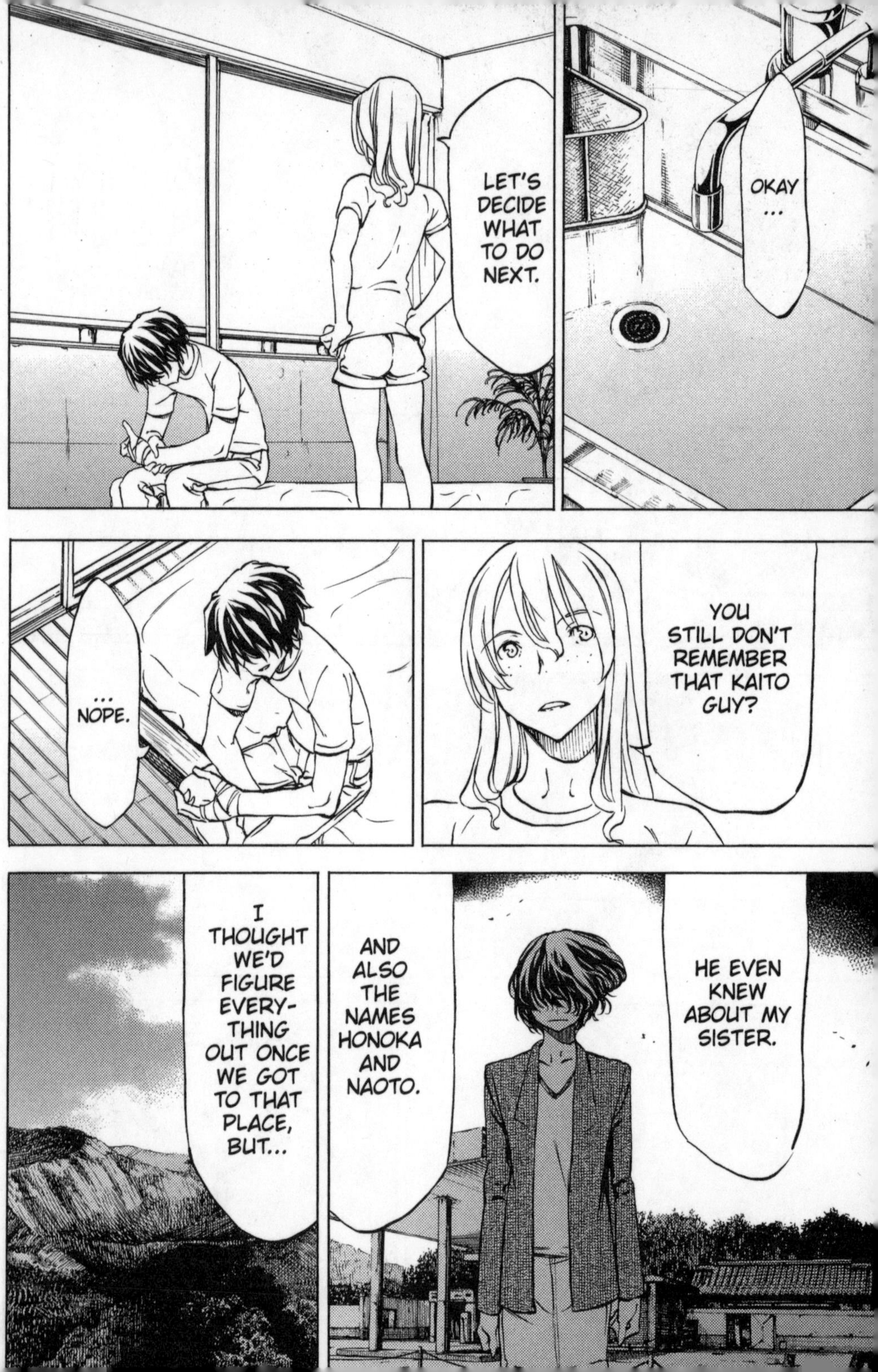
OKAY ...
LET'S DECIDE WHAT TO DO NEXT.
YOU STILL DON'T REMEMBER THAT KAITO GUY?
... NOPE.
HE EVEN KNEW ABOUT MY SISTER.
AND ALSO THE NAMES HONOKA AND NAOTO.
I THOUGHT WE'D FIGURE EVERY-THING OUT ONCE WE GOT TO THAT PLACE, BUT...

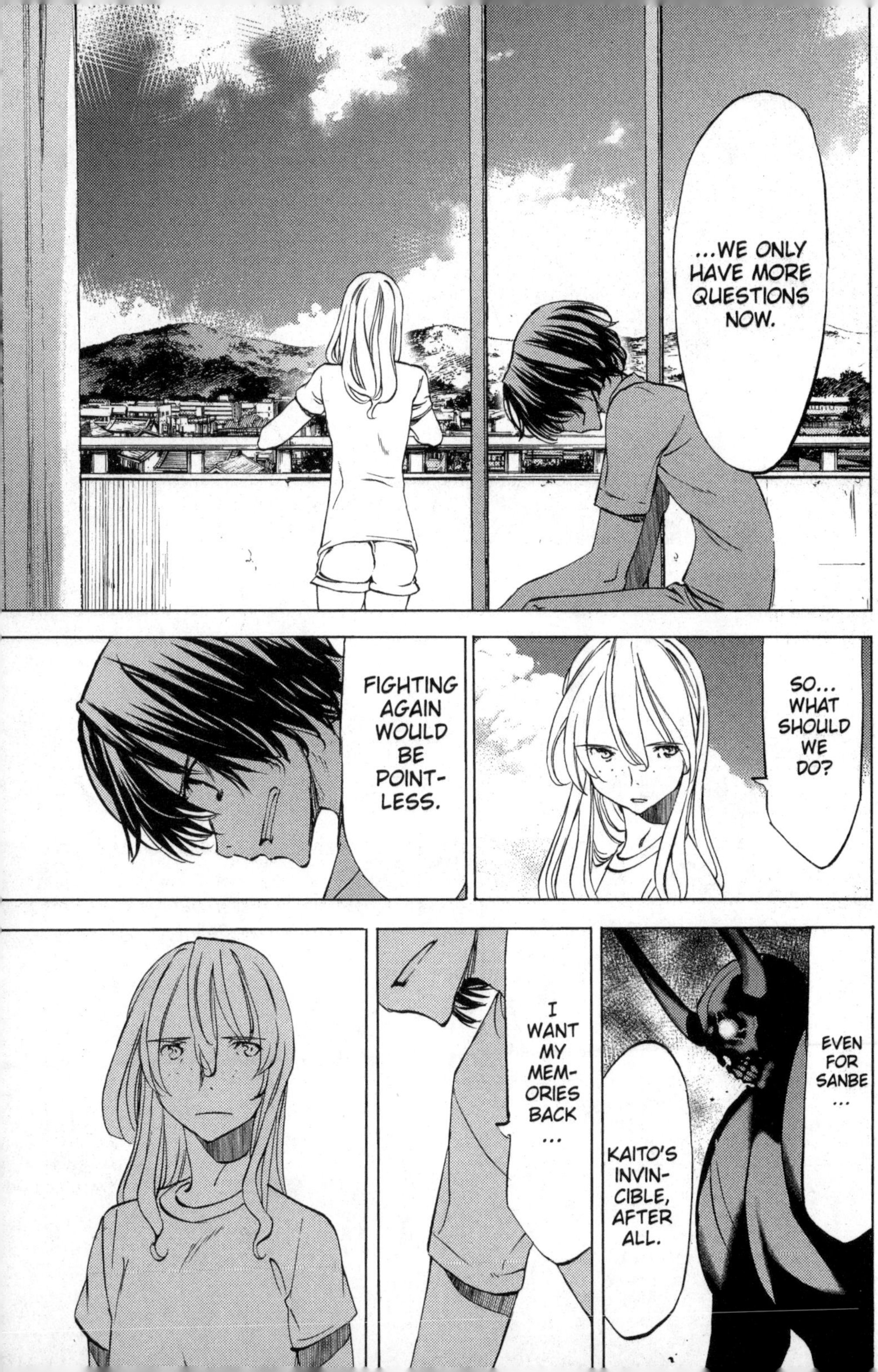
...WE ONLY HAVE MORE QUESTIONS NOW.
SO... WHAT SHOULD WE DO?
FIGHTING AGAIN WOULD BE POINT-LESS.
EVEN FOR SANBE...
KAITO'S INVIN-CIBLE, AFTER ALL.
I WANT MY MEM-ORIES BACK...

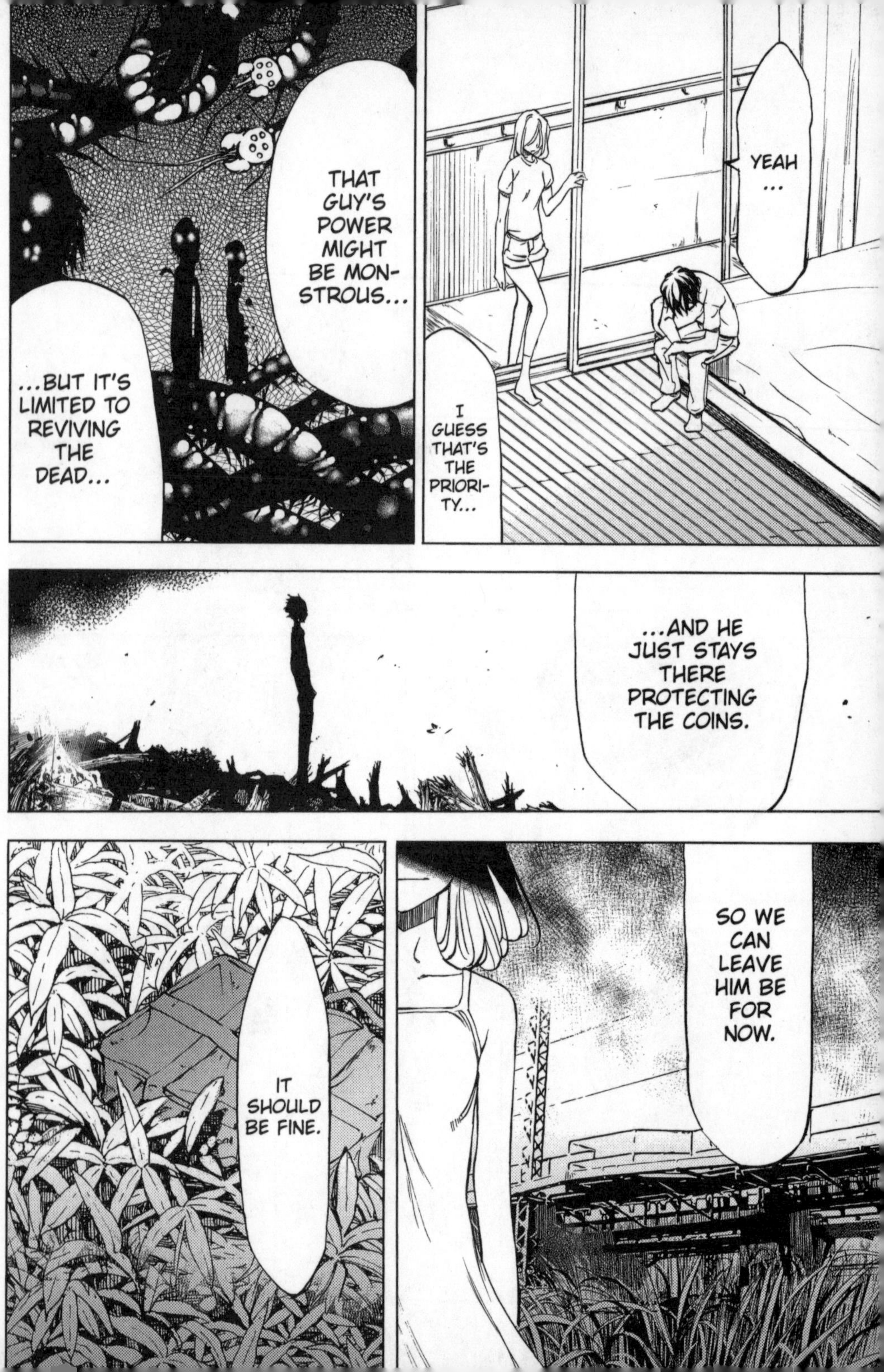
YEAH ...
I GUESS THAT'S THE PRIORITY...
THAT GUY'S POWER MIGHT BE MONSTROUS...
...BUT IT'S LIMITED TO REVIVING THE DEAD...
...AND HE JUST STAYS THERE PROTECTING THE COINS.
SO WE CAN LEAVE HIM BE FOR NOW.
IT SHOULD BE FINE.

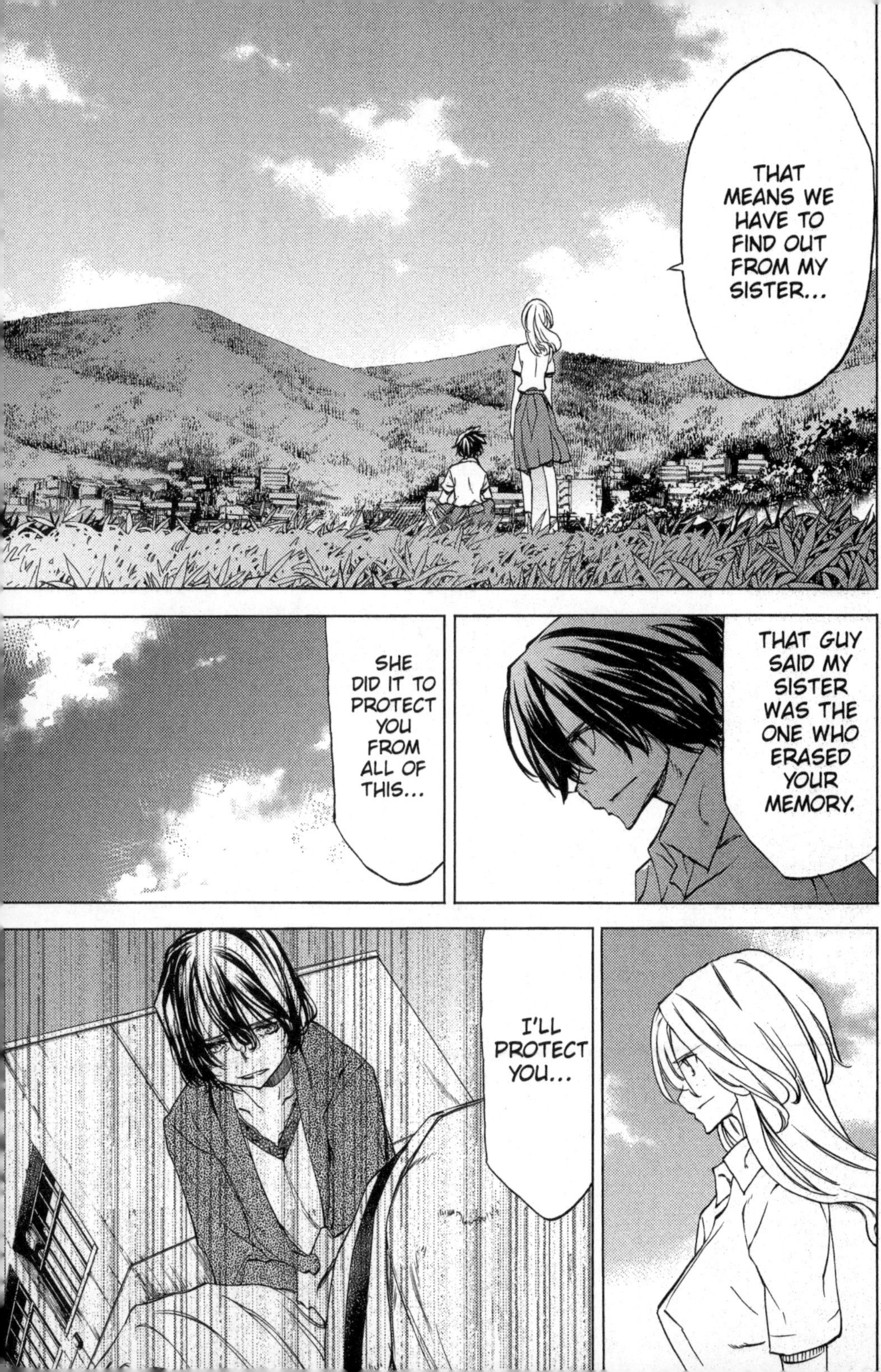
THAT MEANS WE HAVE TO FIND OUT FROM MY SISTER...
THAT GUY SAID MY SISTER WAS THE ONE WHO ERASED YOUR MEMORY.
SHE DID IT TO PROTECT YOU FROM ALL OF THIS...
I'LL PROTECT YOU...

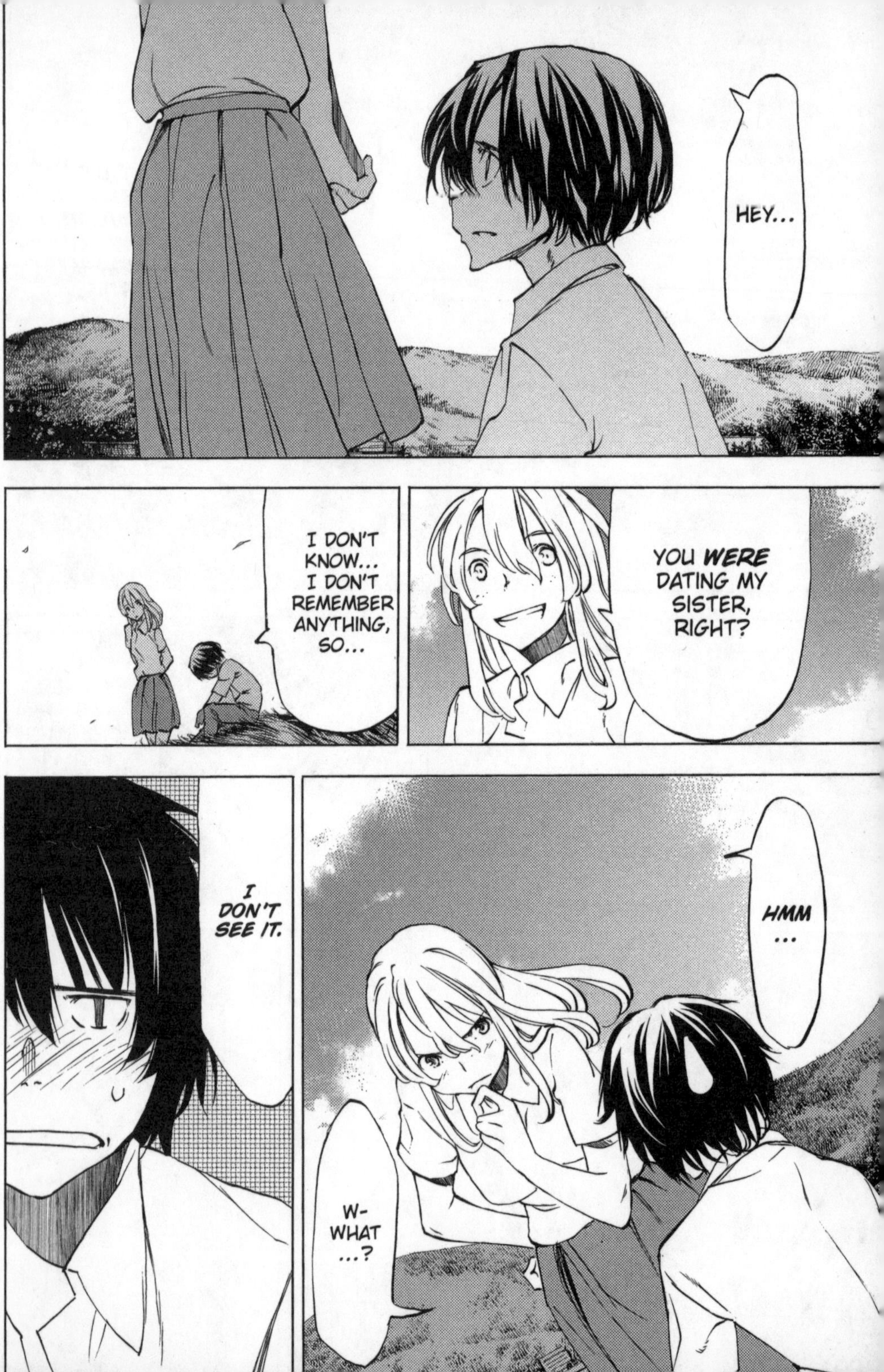
HEY...
YOU WERE DATING MY SISTER, RIGHT?
I DON'T KNOW... I DON'T REMEMBER ANYTHING, SO...
HMM...
W-WHAT...?
I DON'T SEE IT.

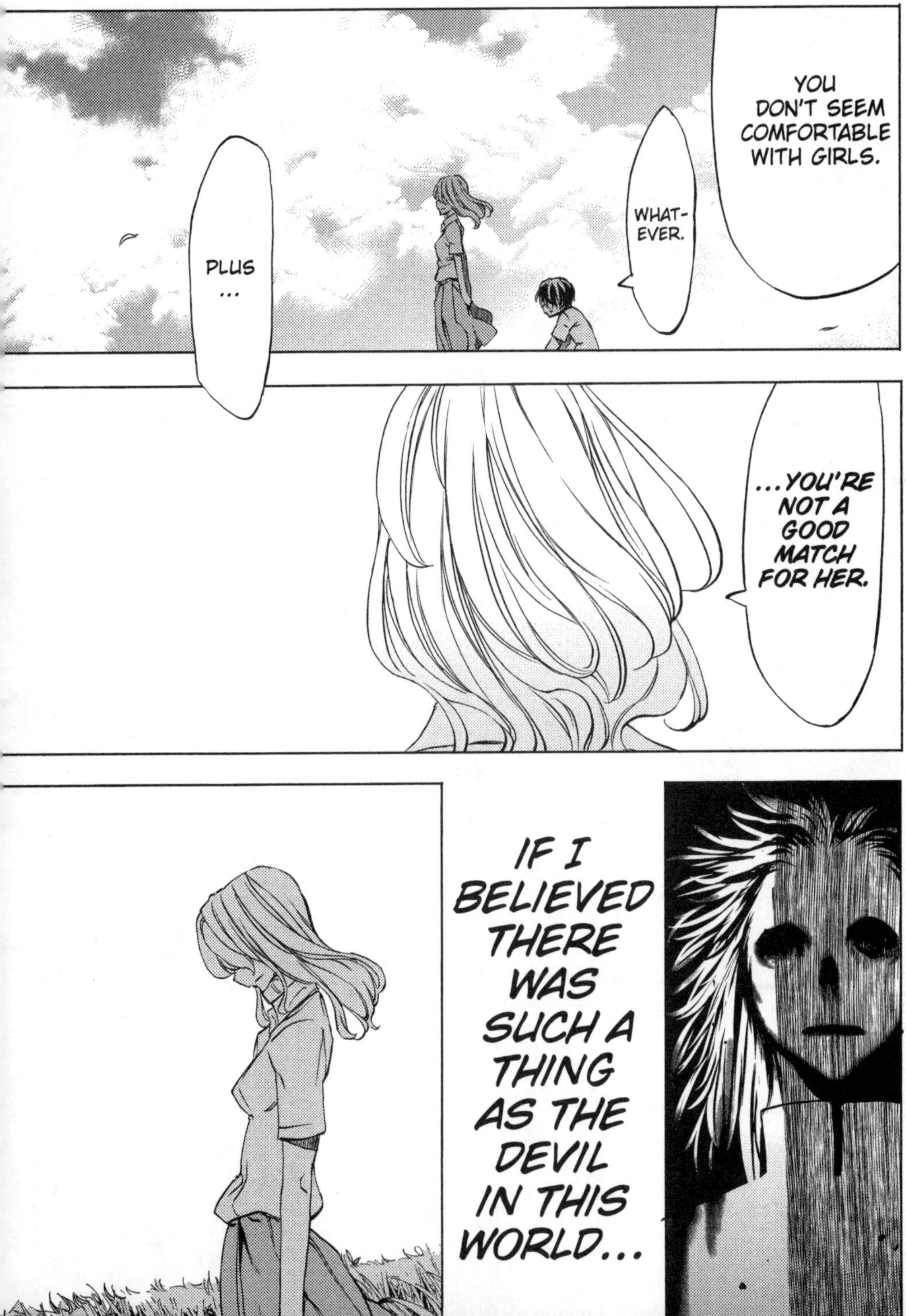
YOU DON'T SEEM COMFORTABLE WITH GIRLS.
WHAT-EVER.
PLUS ...
...YOU'RE NOT A GOOD MATCH FOR HER.
IF I BELIEVED THERE WAS SUCH A THING AS THE DEVIL IN THIS WORLD...

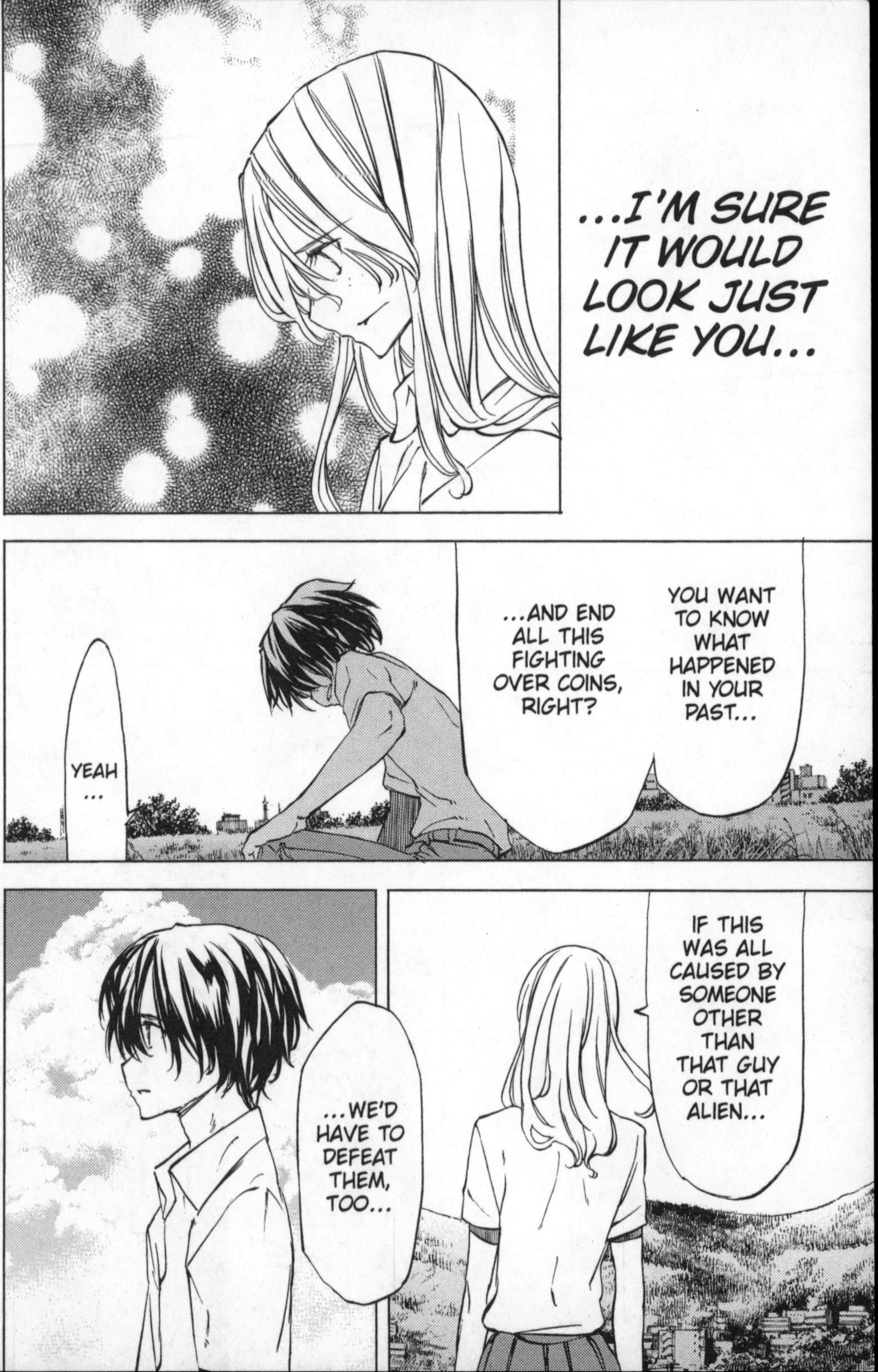
...I'M SURE IT WOULD LOOK JUST LIKE YOU...
YOU WANT TO KNOW WHAT HAPPENED IN YOUR PAST...
...AND END ALL THIS FIGHTING OVER COINS, RIGHT?
YEAH...
IF THIS WAS ALL CAUSED BY SOMEONE OTHER THAN THAT GUY OR THAT ALIEN...
...WE'D HAVE TO DEFEAT THEM, TOO...

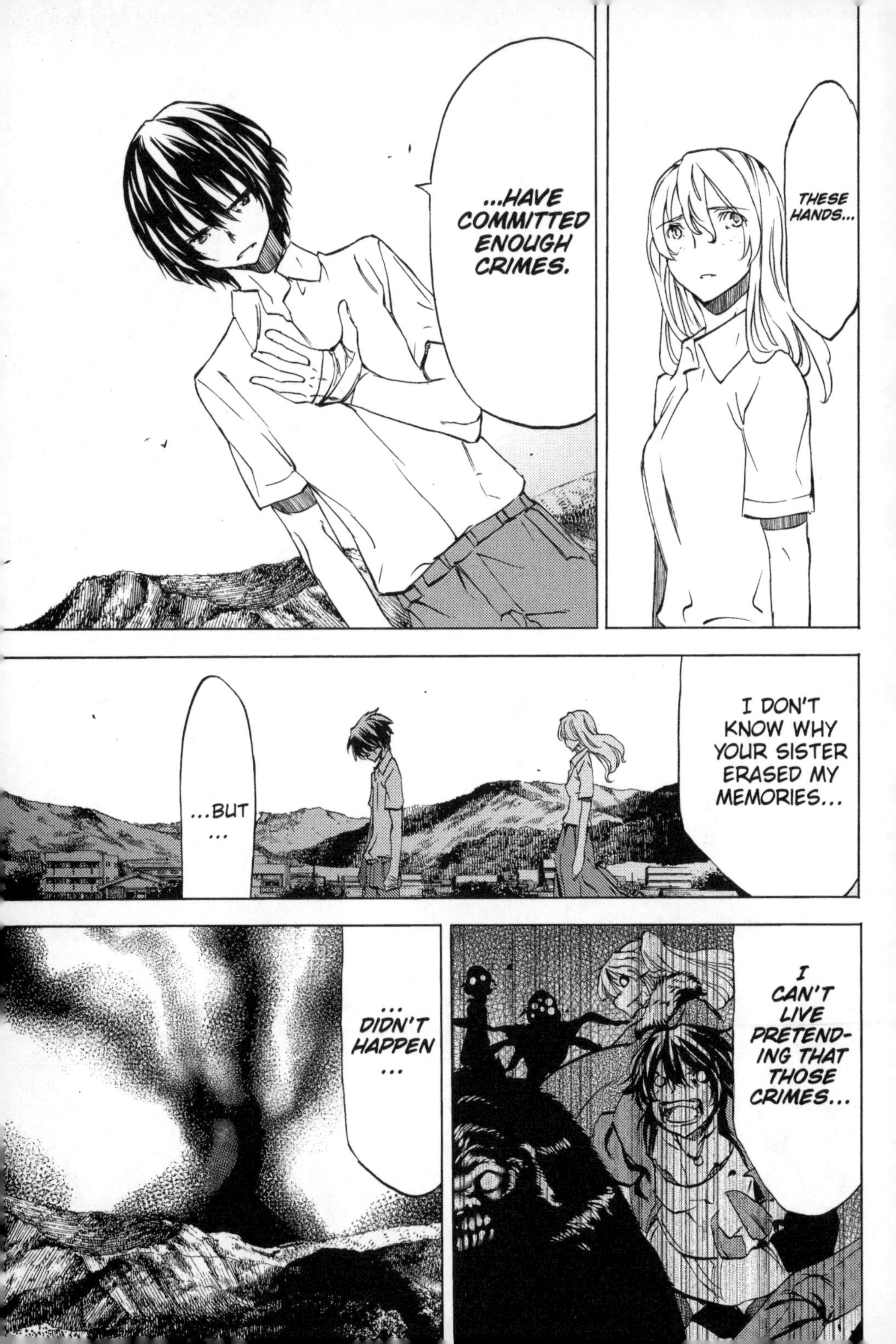
THESE HANDS...
...HAVE COMMITTED ENOUGH CRIMES.
I DON'T KNOW WHY YOUR SISTER ERASED MY MEMORIES...
...BUT ...
I CAN'T LIVE PRETEND-ING THAT THOSE CRIMES...
... DIDN'T HAPPEN ...

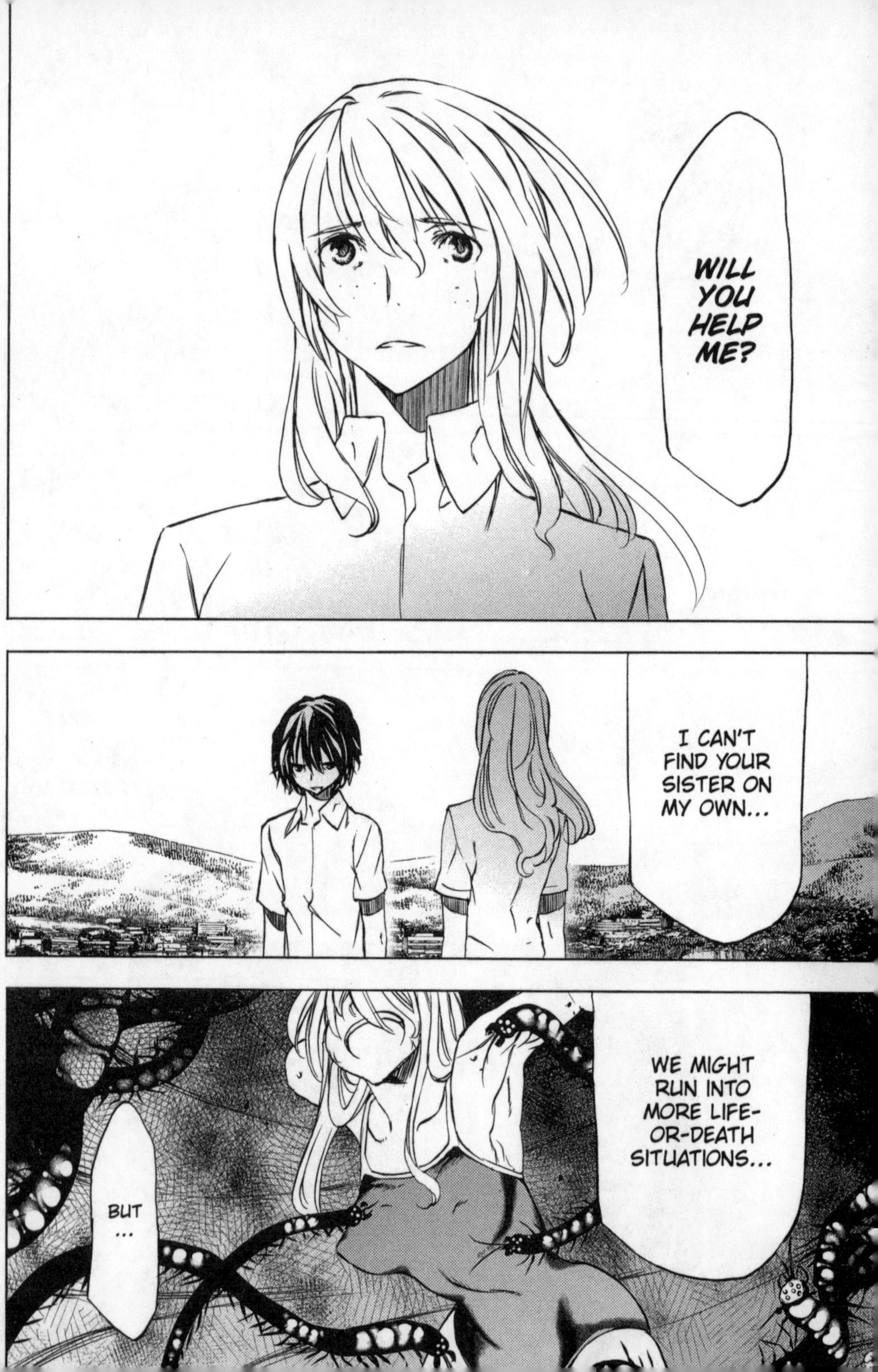
WILL YOU HELP ME?
I CAN'T FIND YOUR SISTER ON MY OWN...
WE MIGHT RUN INTO MORE LIFE-OR-DEATH SITUATIONS...
BUT ...

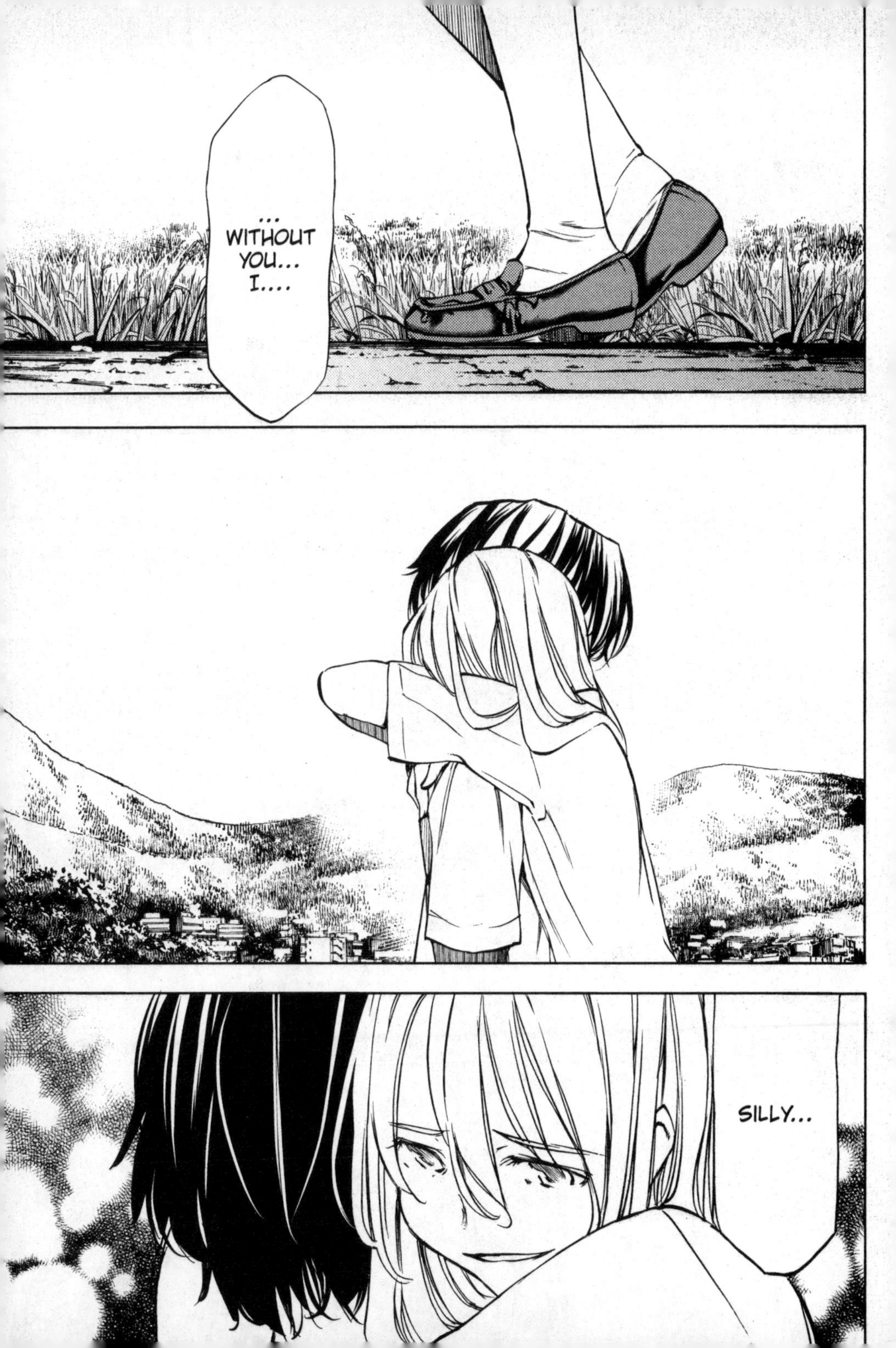
...
WITHOUT
YOU...
I....
SILLY...

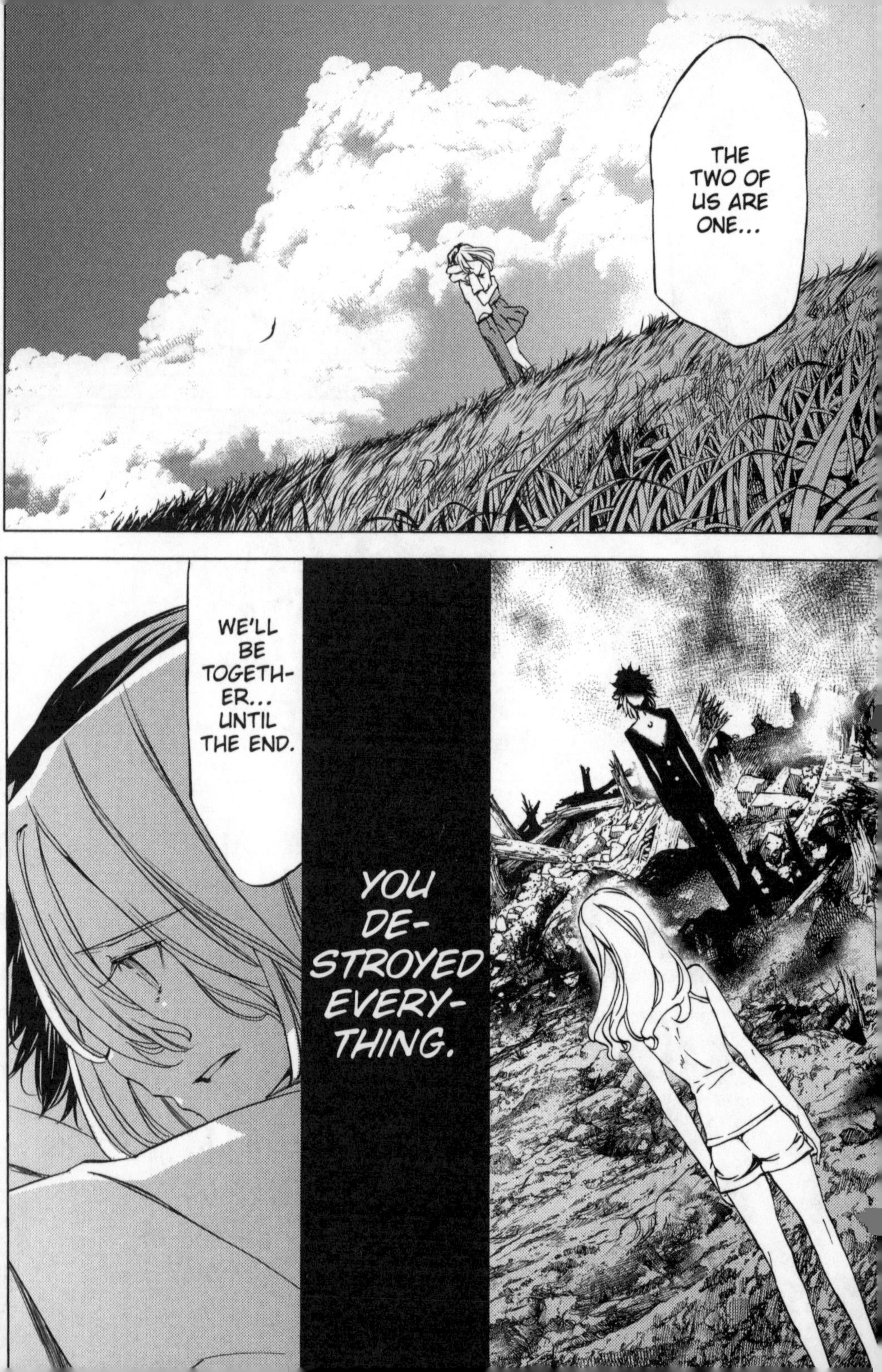
THE TWO OF US ARE ONE...
YOU DE-STROYED EVERY-THING.
WE'LL BE TOGETH-ER... UNTIL THE END.

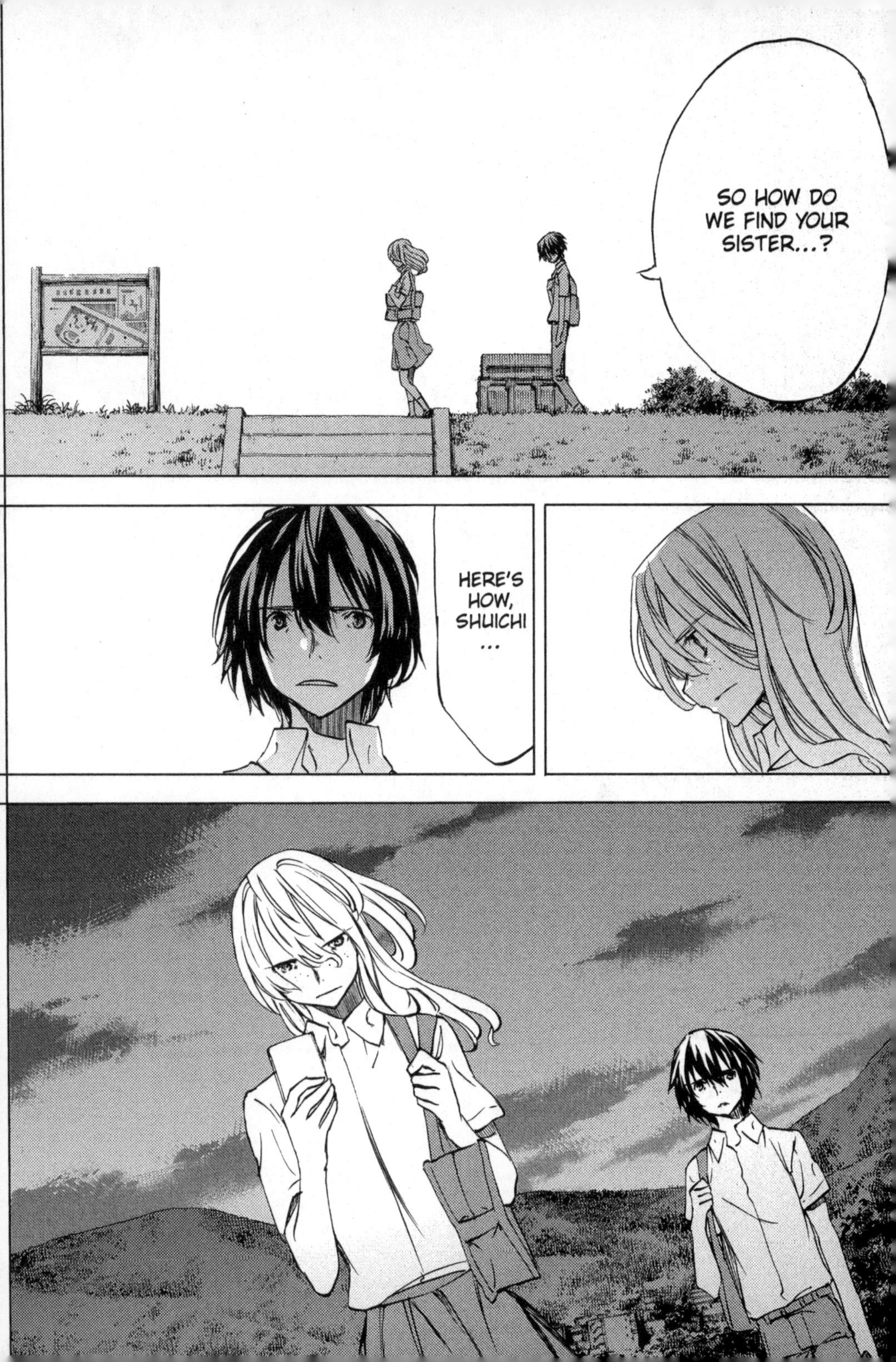
SO HOW DO WE FIND YOUR SISTER...?
HERE'S HOW, SHUICHI...

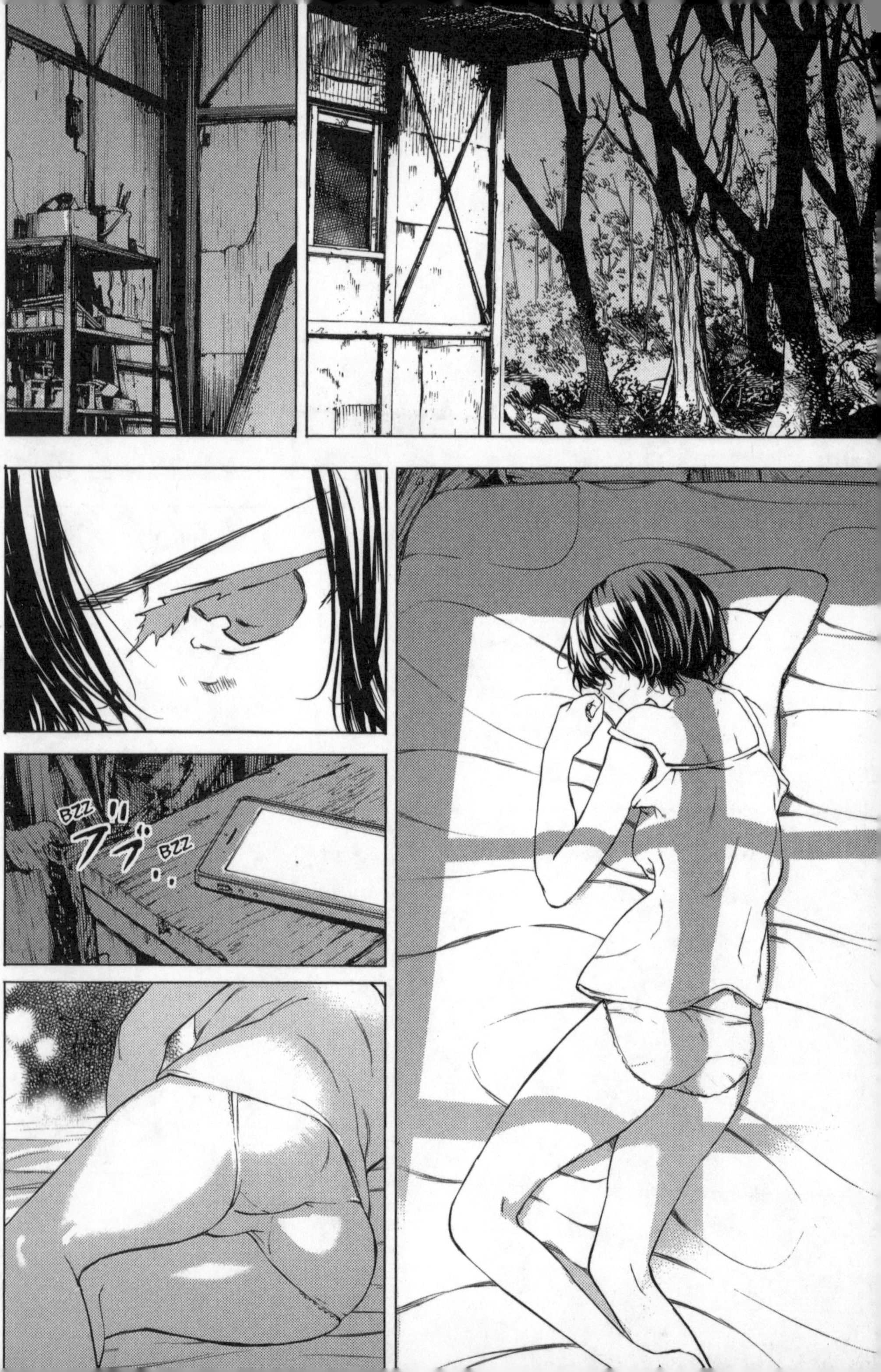
BZZ
ブブ
BZZ

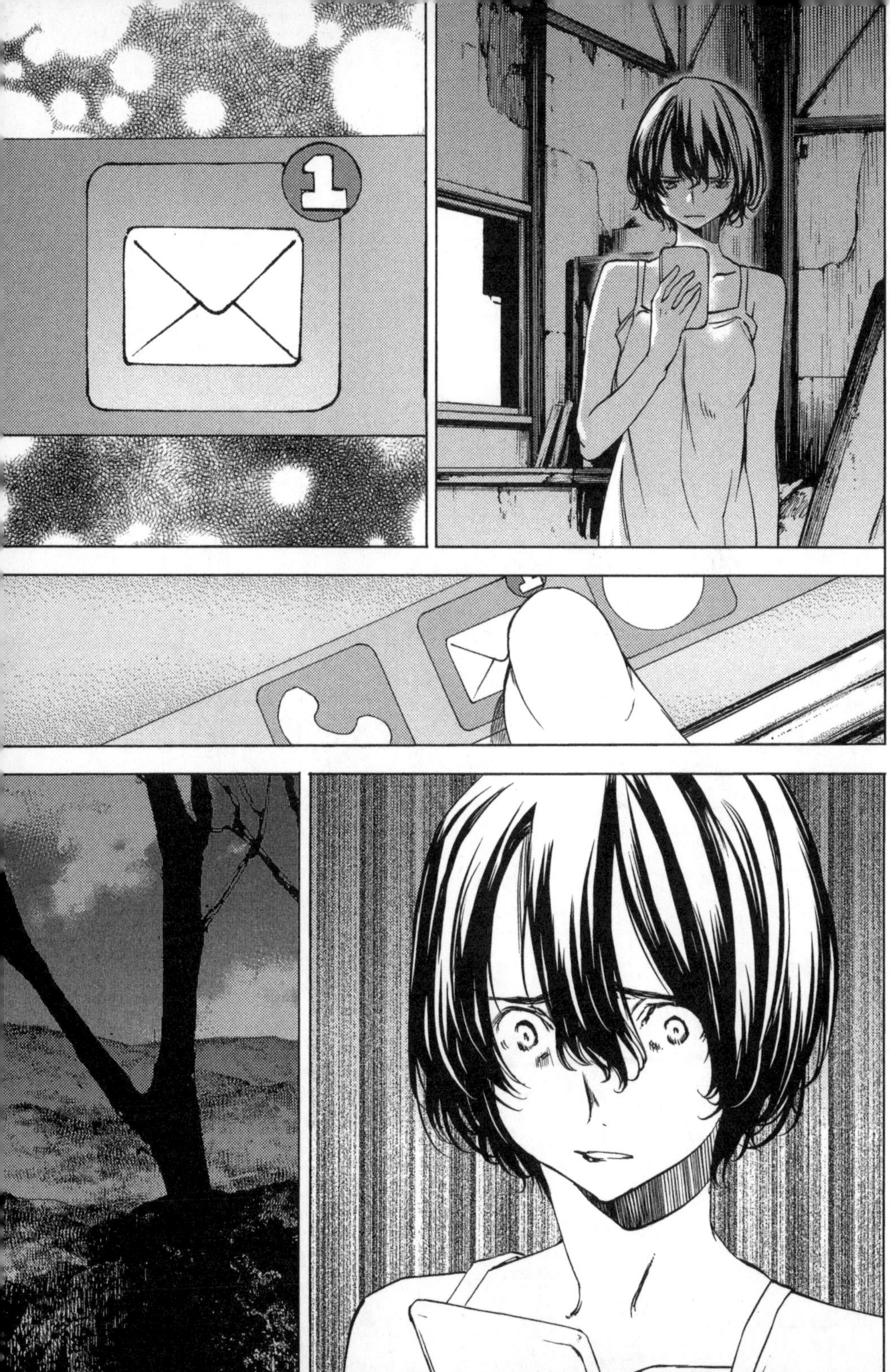
1

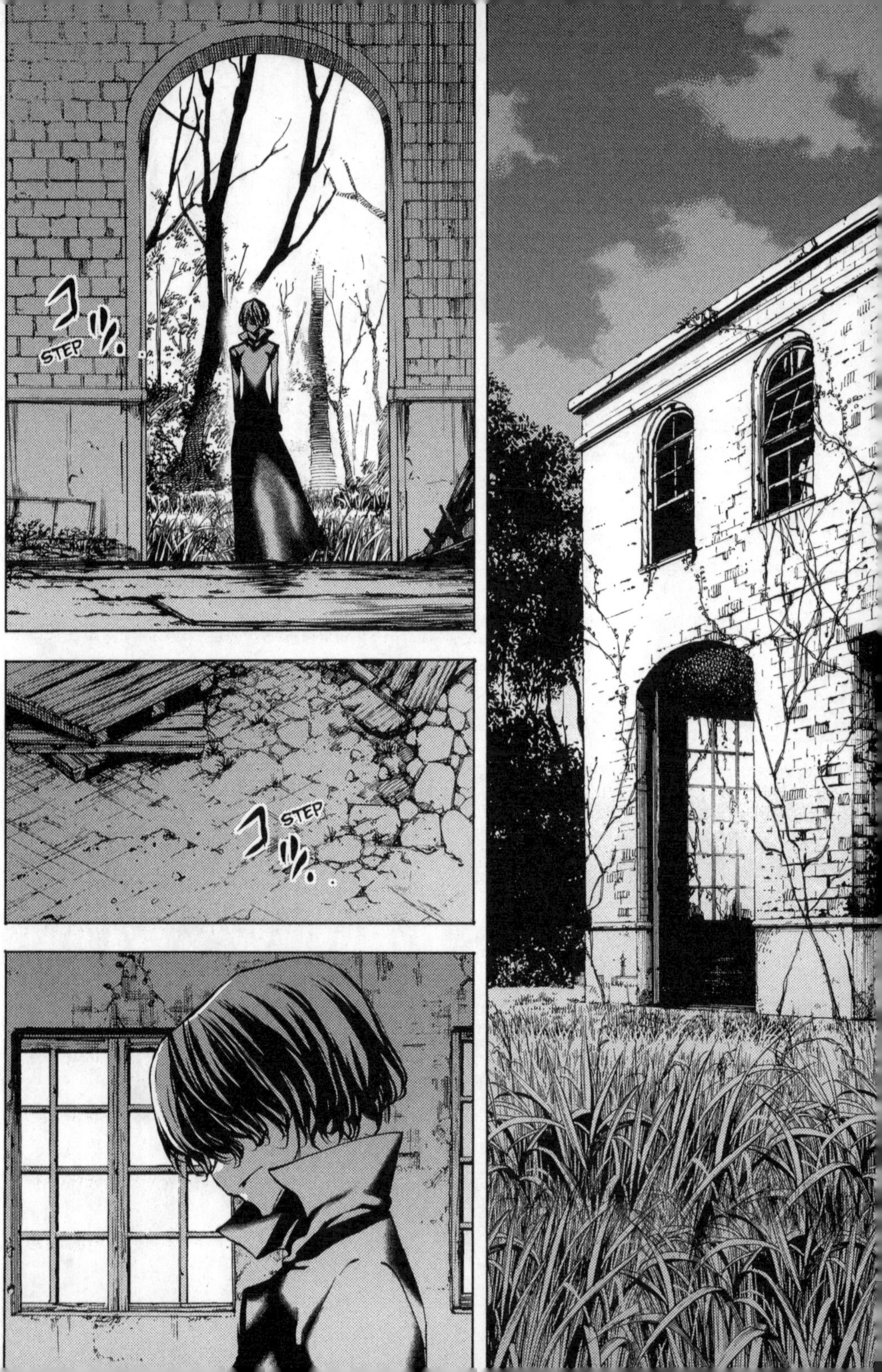
コツ..
STEP
コツ..
STEP

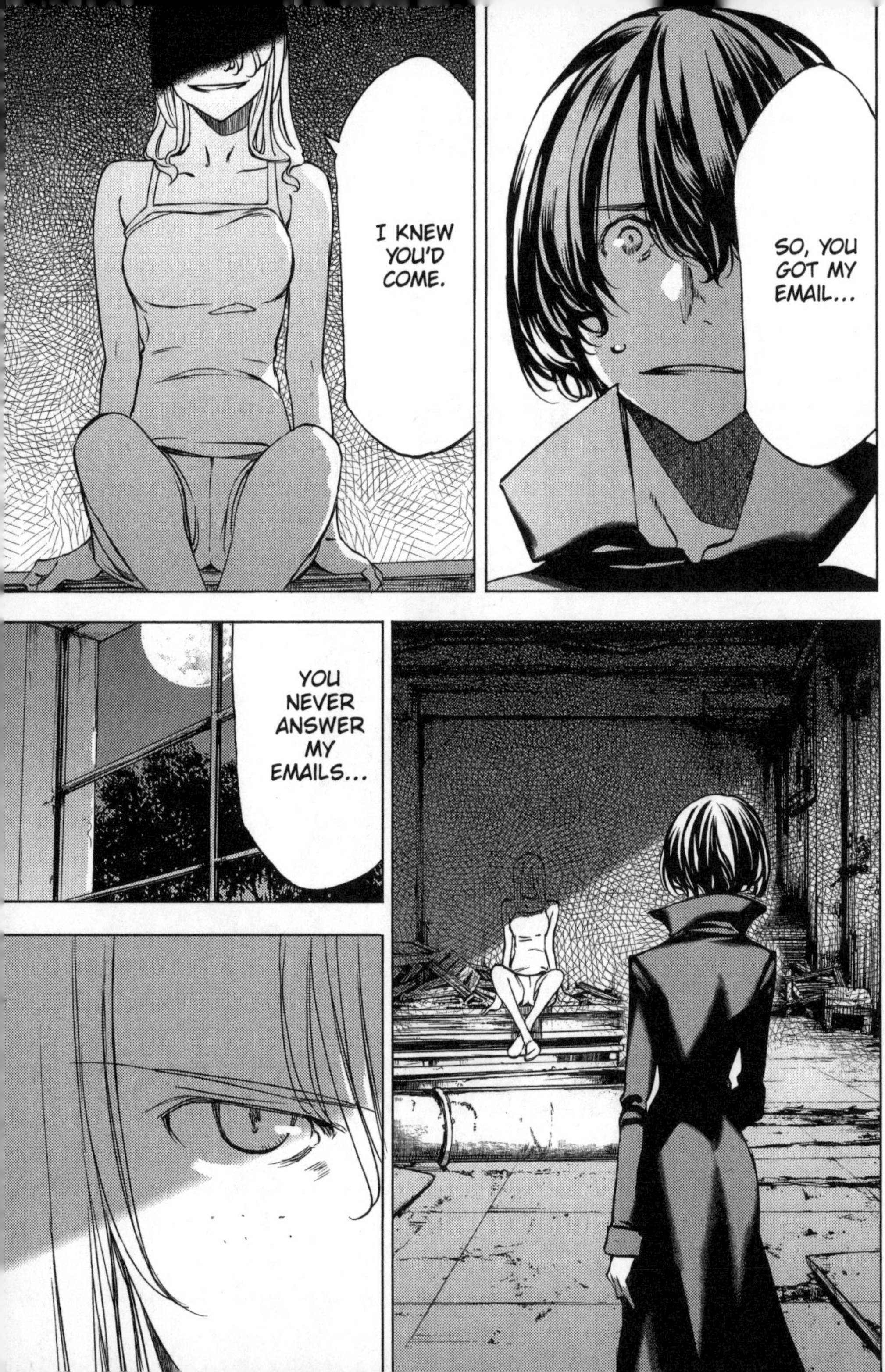
SO, YOU GOT MY EMAIL...
I KNEW YOU'D COME.
YOU NEVER ANSWER MY EMAILS...

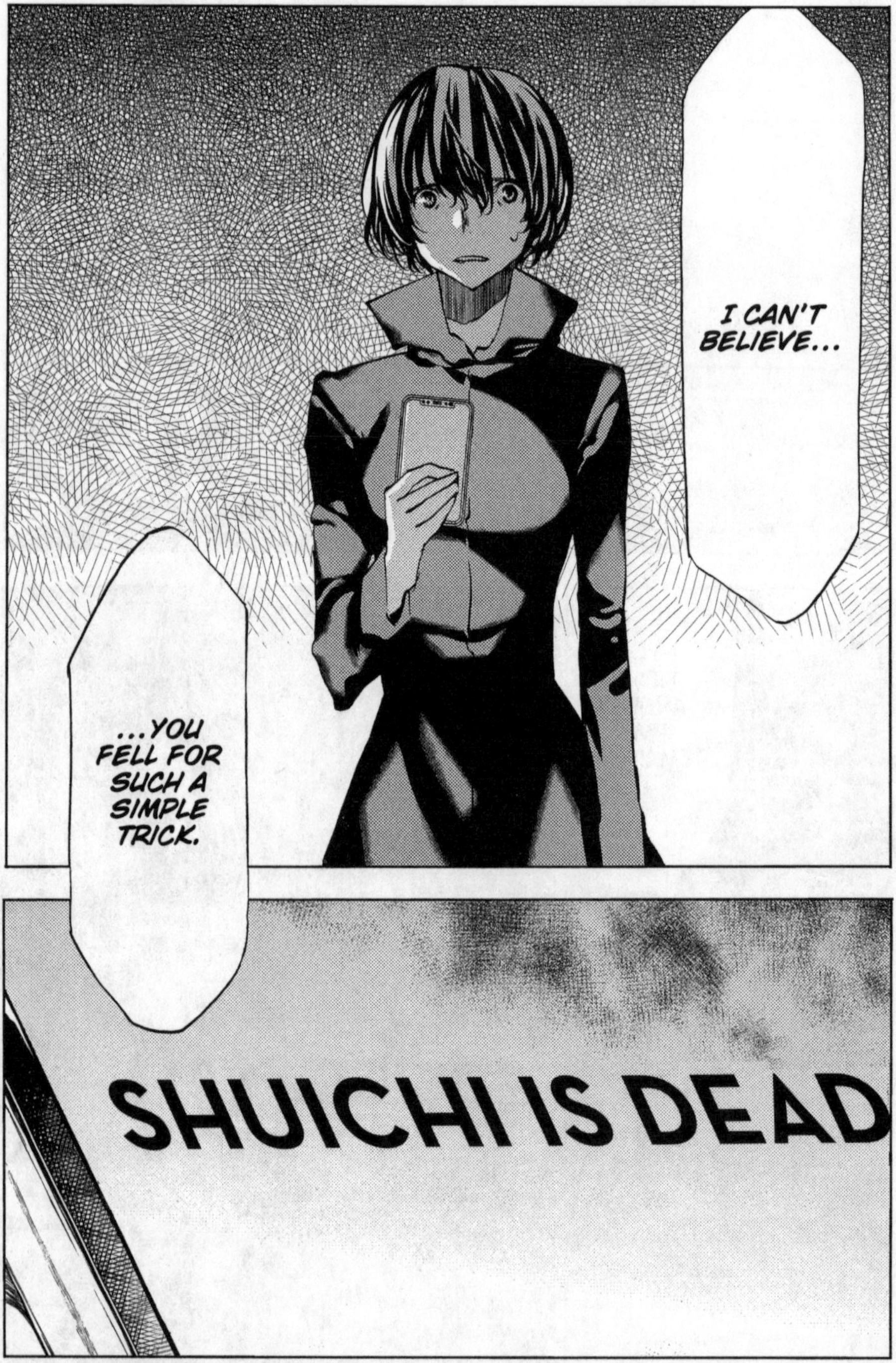
I CAN'T BELIEVE...
...YOU FELL FOR SUCH A SIMPLE TRICK.
SHUICHI IS DEAD

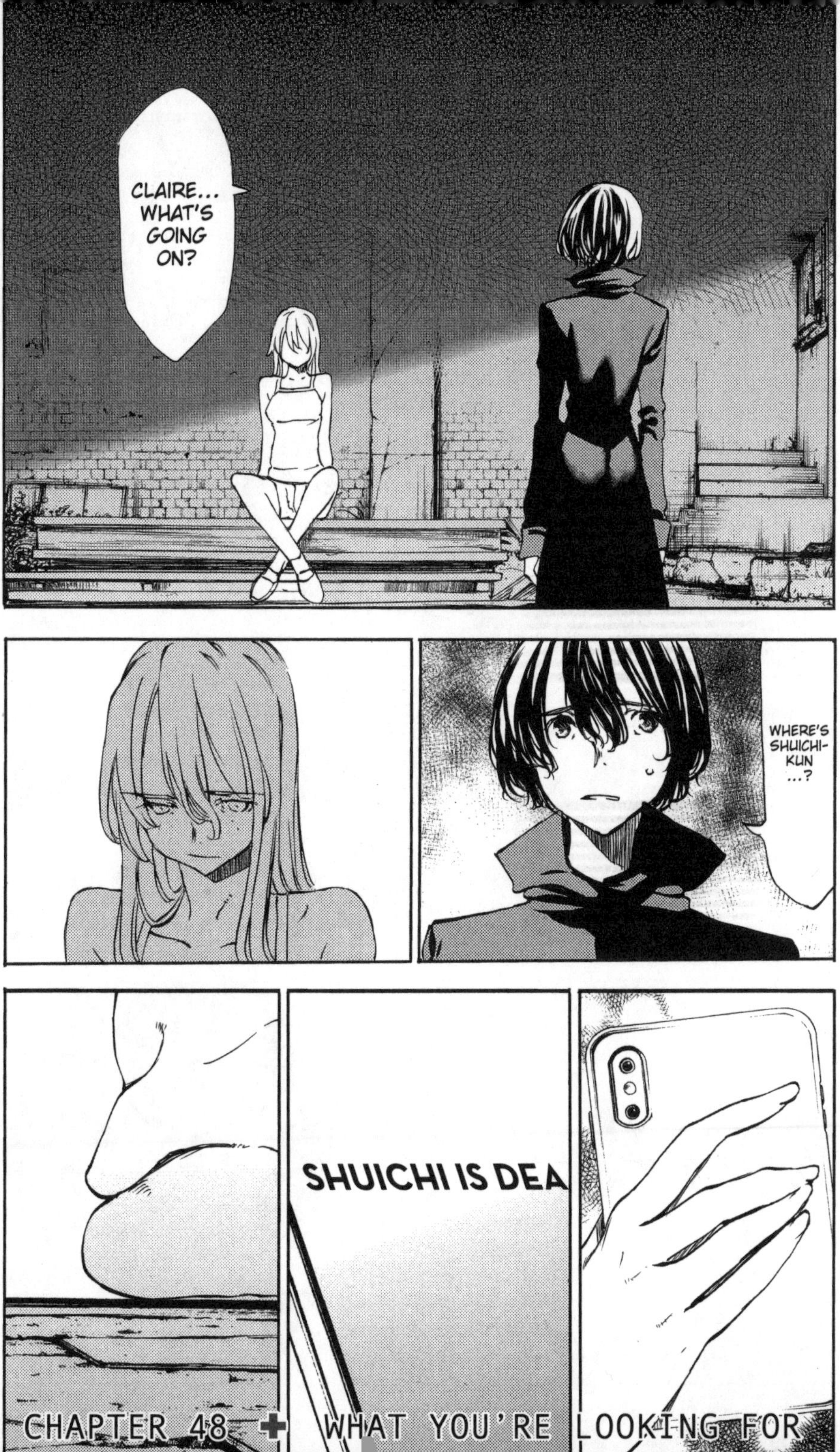
CLAIRE... WHAT'S GOING ON?
WHERE'S SHUICHI-KUN ...?
SHUICHI IS DEA
CHAPTER 48 ✚ WHAT YOU'RE LOOKING FOR

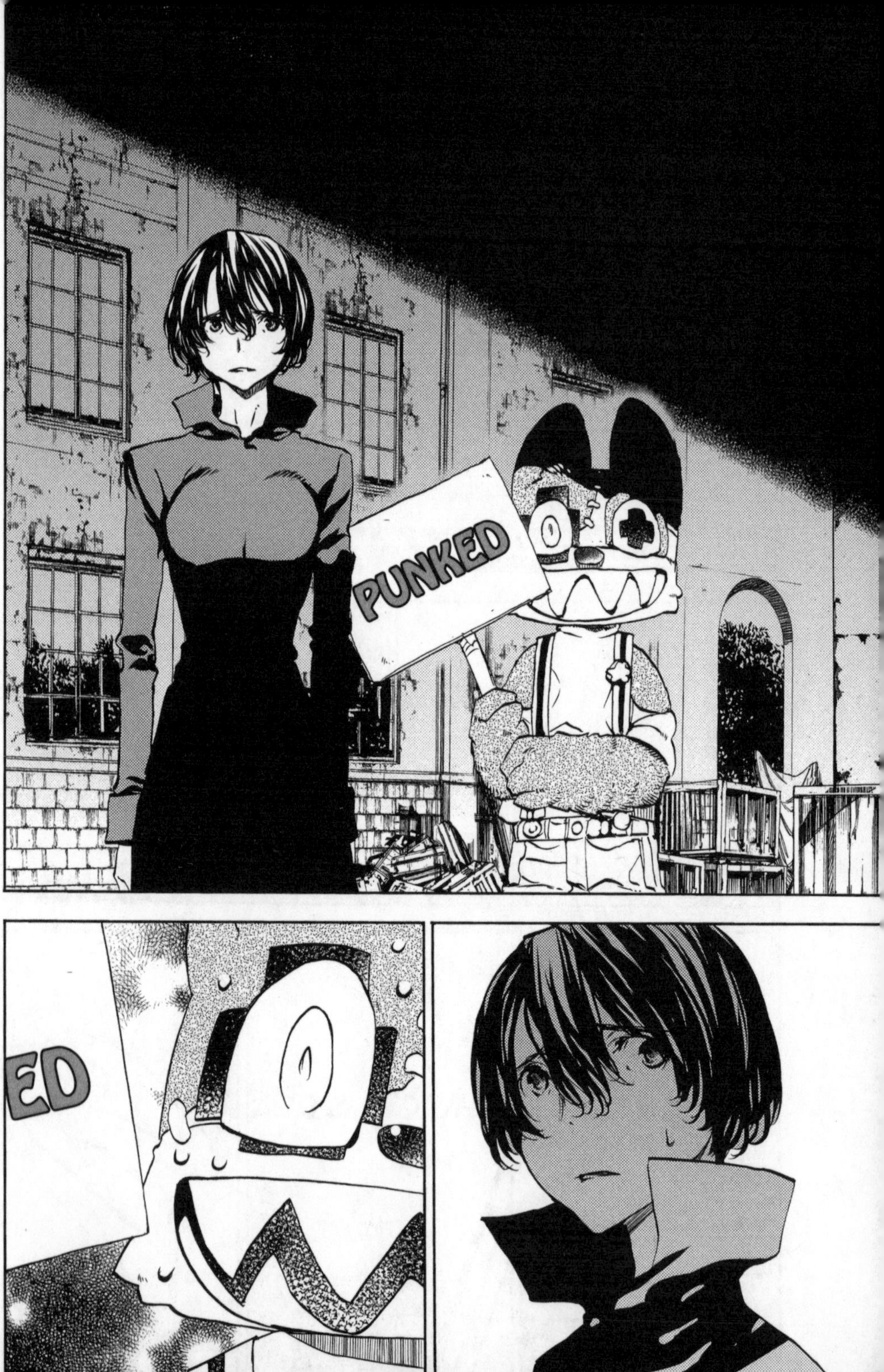
PUNKED
ED

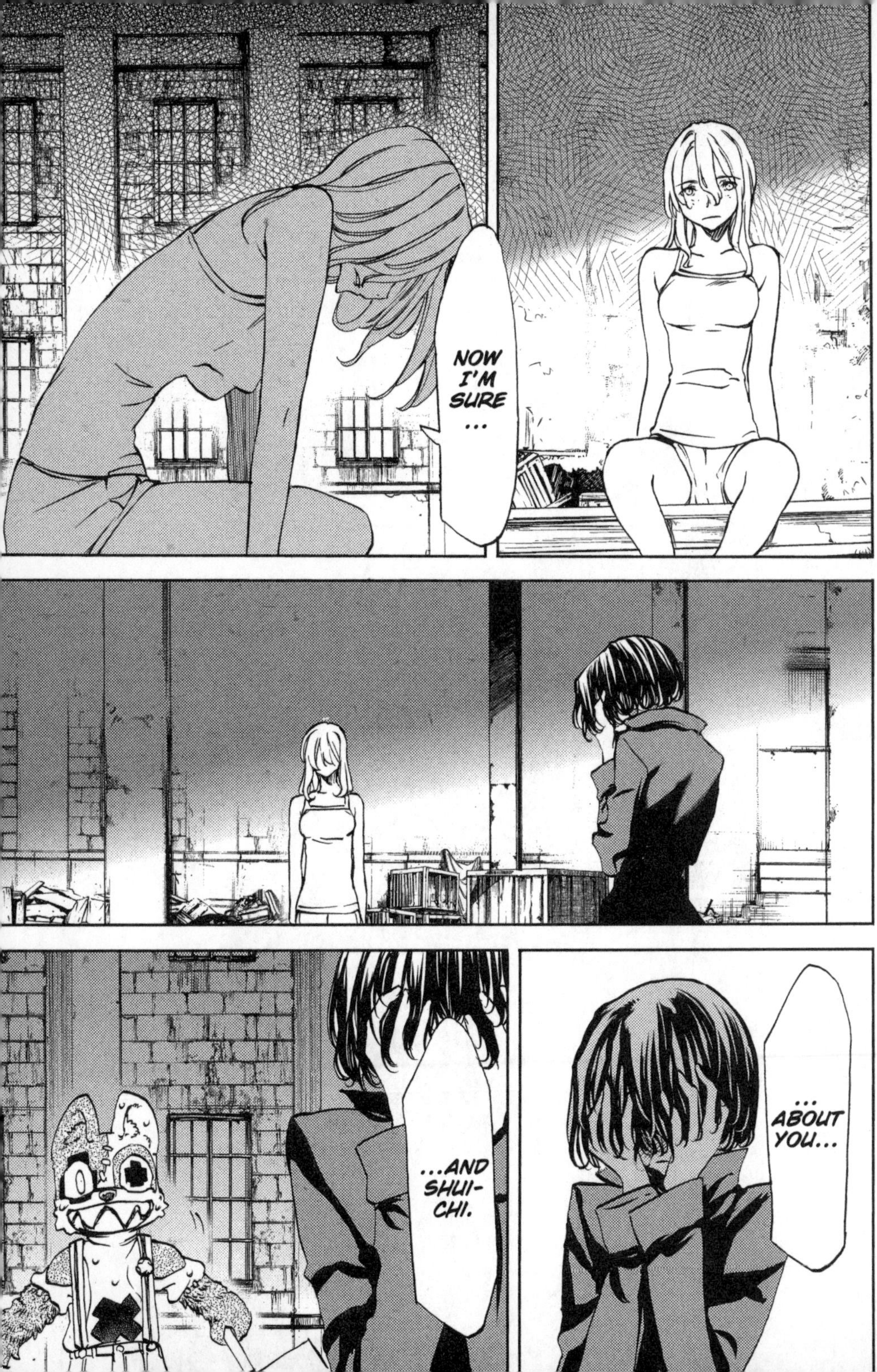
NOW I'M SURE ...
... ABOUT YOU...
...AND SHUICHI.

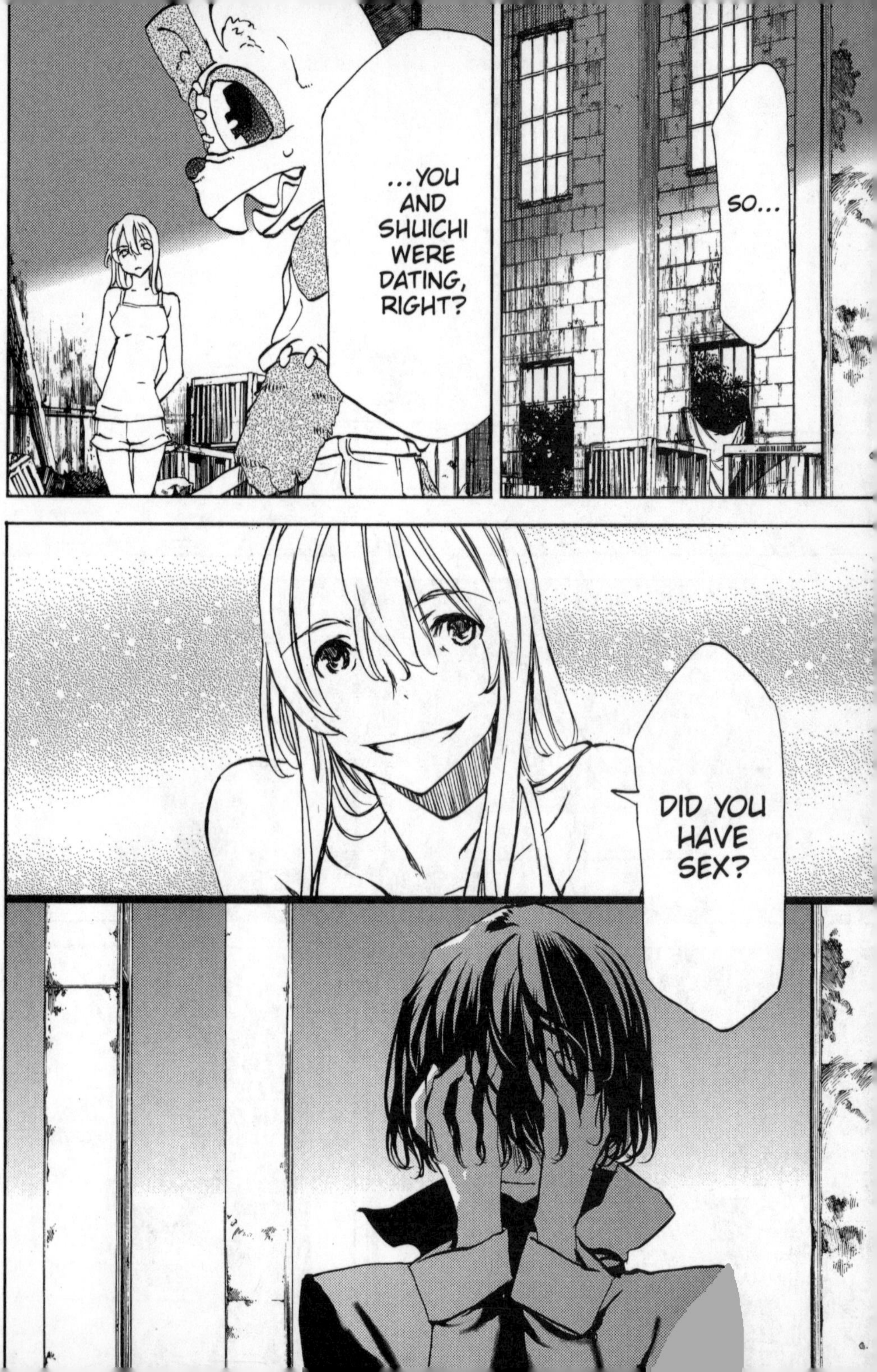
SO...
...YOU AND SHUICHI WERE DATING, RIGHT?
DID YOU HAVE SEX?

SHUI-CHI-KUN AND I...

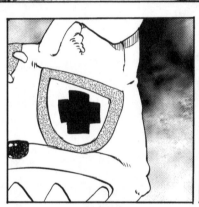

...WE WEREN'T IMPURE LIKE THAT.

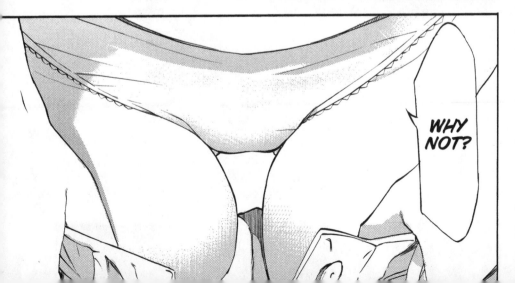

WHY NOT?

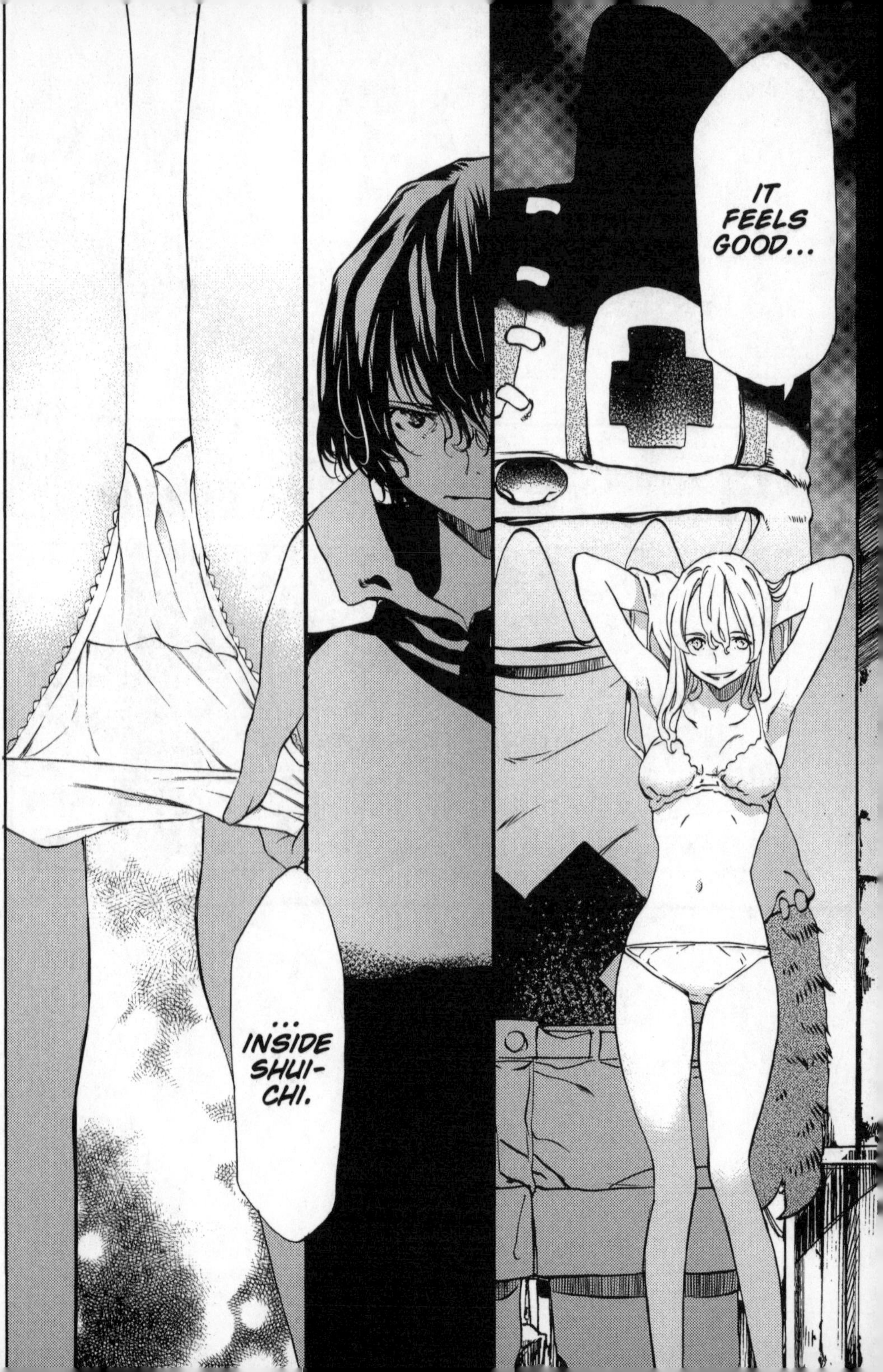
IT FEELS GOOD...
...INSIDE SHUI-CHI.

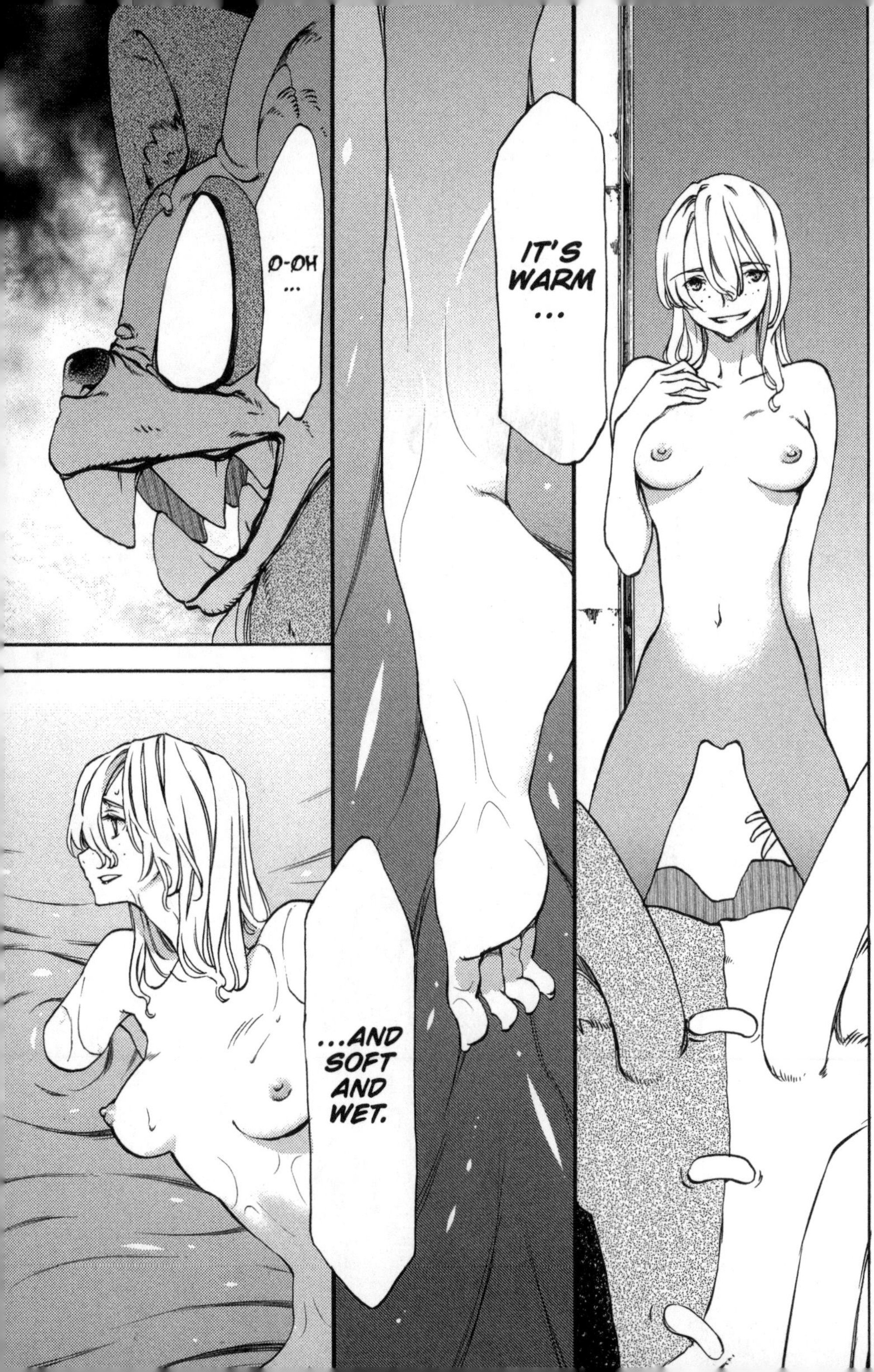
IT'S WARM ...
O-OH ...
...AND SOFT AND WET.

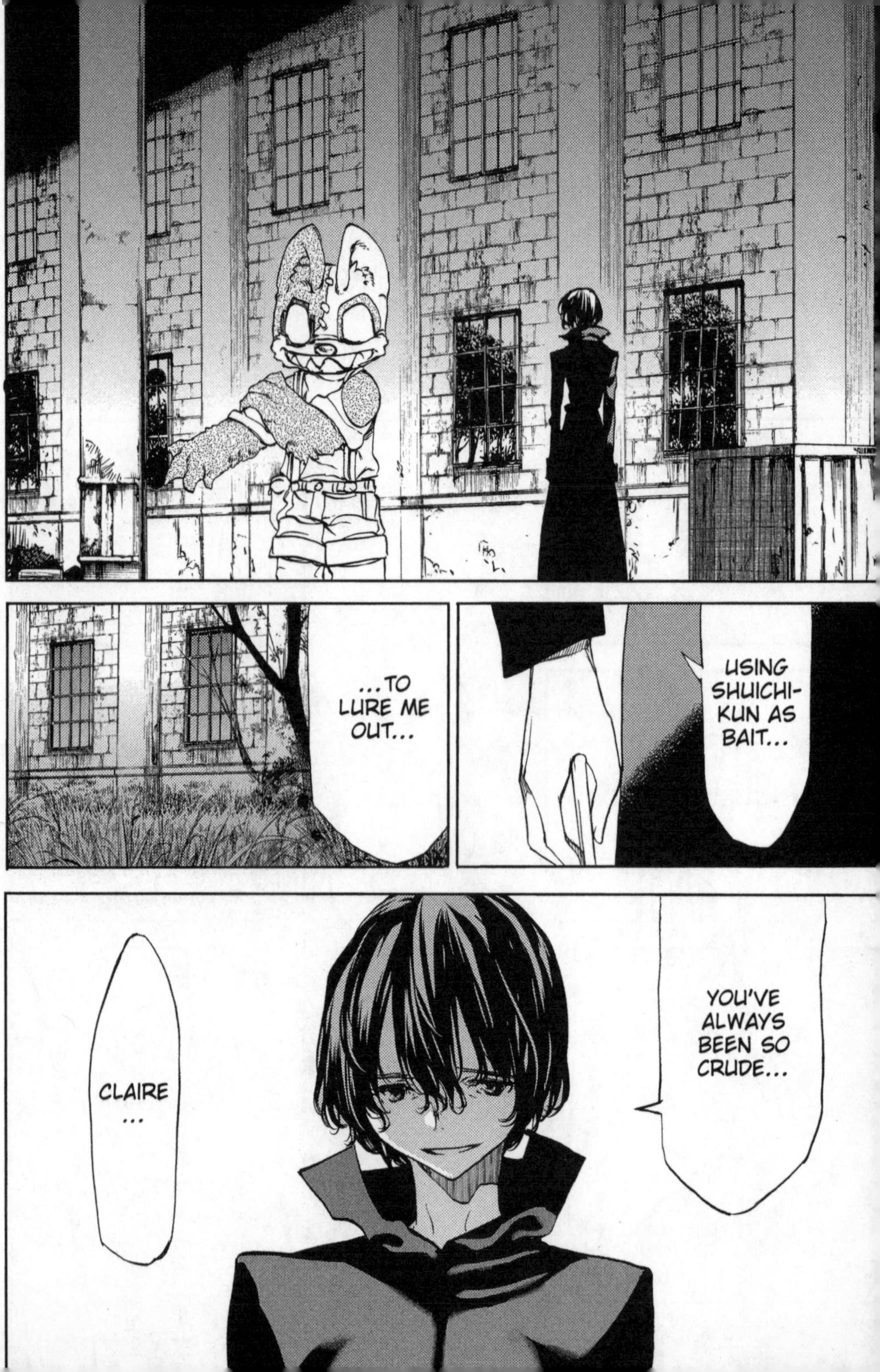
USING SHUICHI-KUN AS BAIT...
...TO LURE ME OUT...
YOU'VE ALWAYS BEEN SO CRUDE...
CLAIRE ...

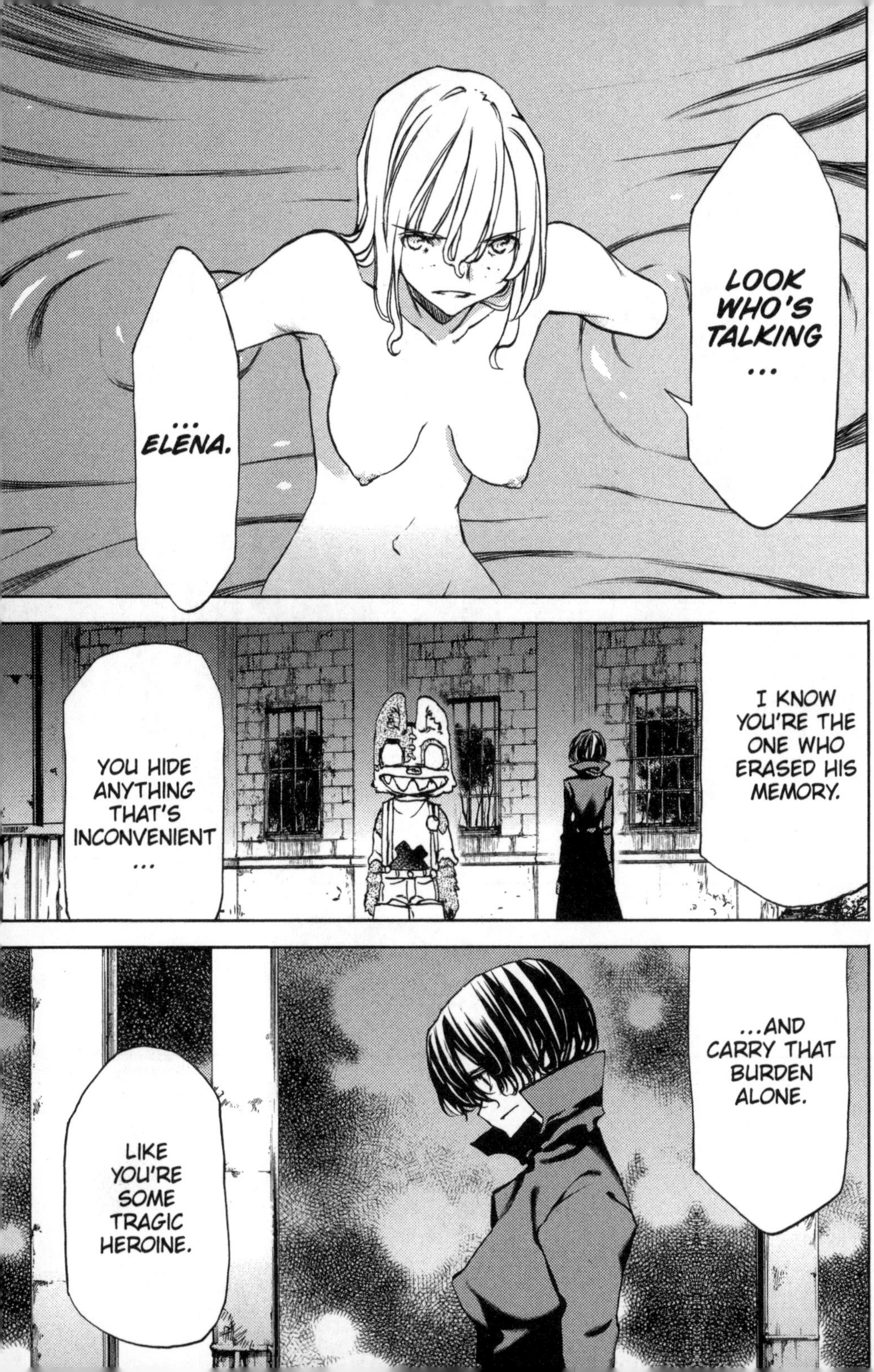
LOOK WHO'S TALKING ...
... ELENA.
I KNOW YOU'RE THE ONE WHO ERASED HIS MEMORY.
YOU HIDE ANYTHING THAT'S INCONVENIENT ...
...AND CARRY THAT BURDEN ALONE.
LIKE YOU'RE SOME TRAGIC HEROINE.

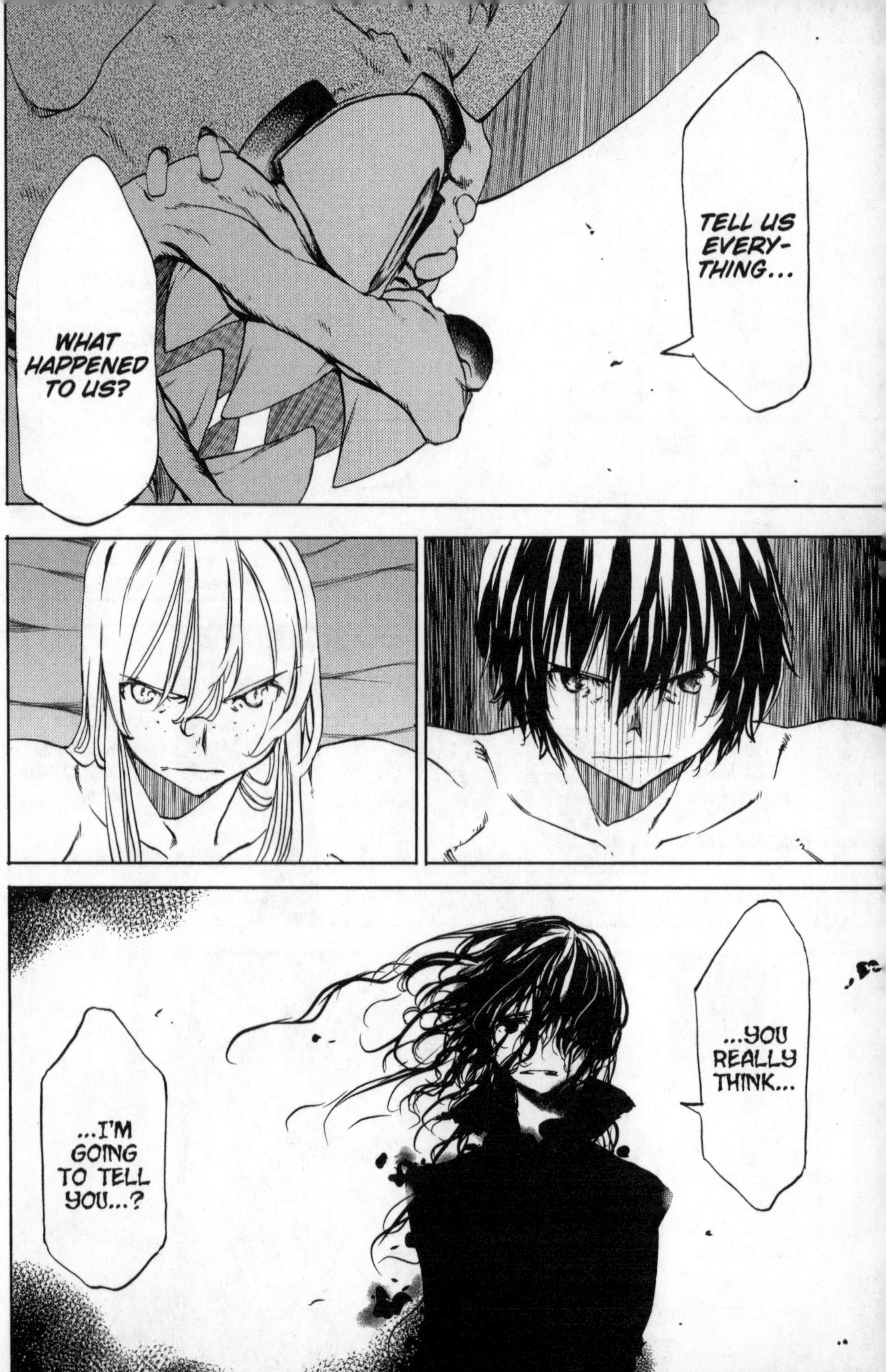
TELL US EVERY-THING...
WHAT HAPPENED TO US?
...YOU REALLY THINK...
...I'M GOING TO TELL YOU...?

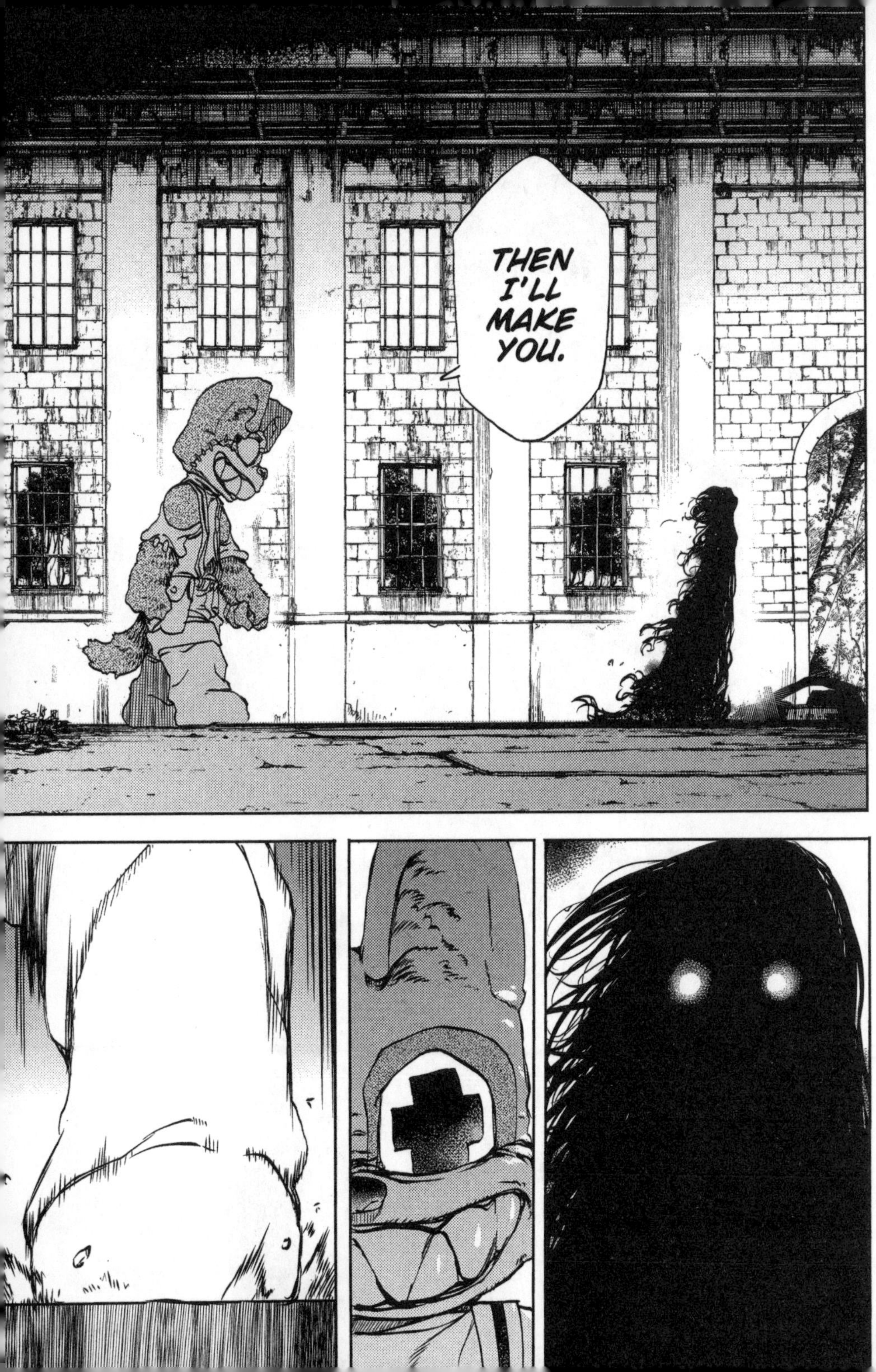
THEN I'LL MAKE YOU.

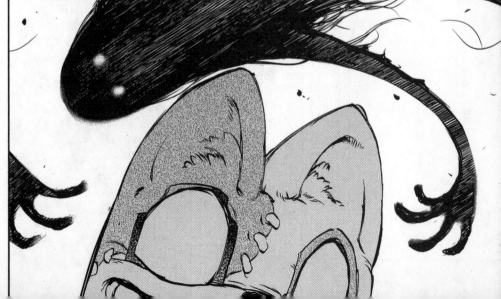

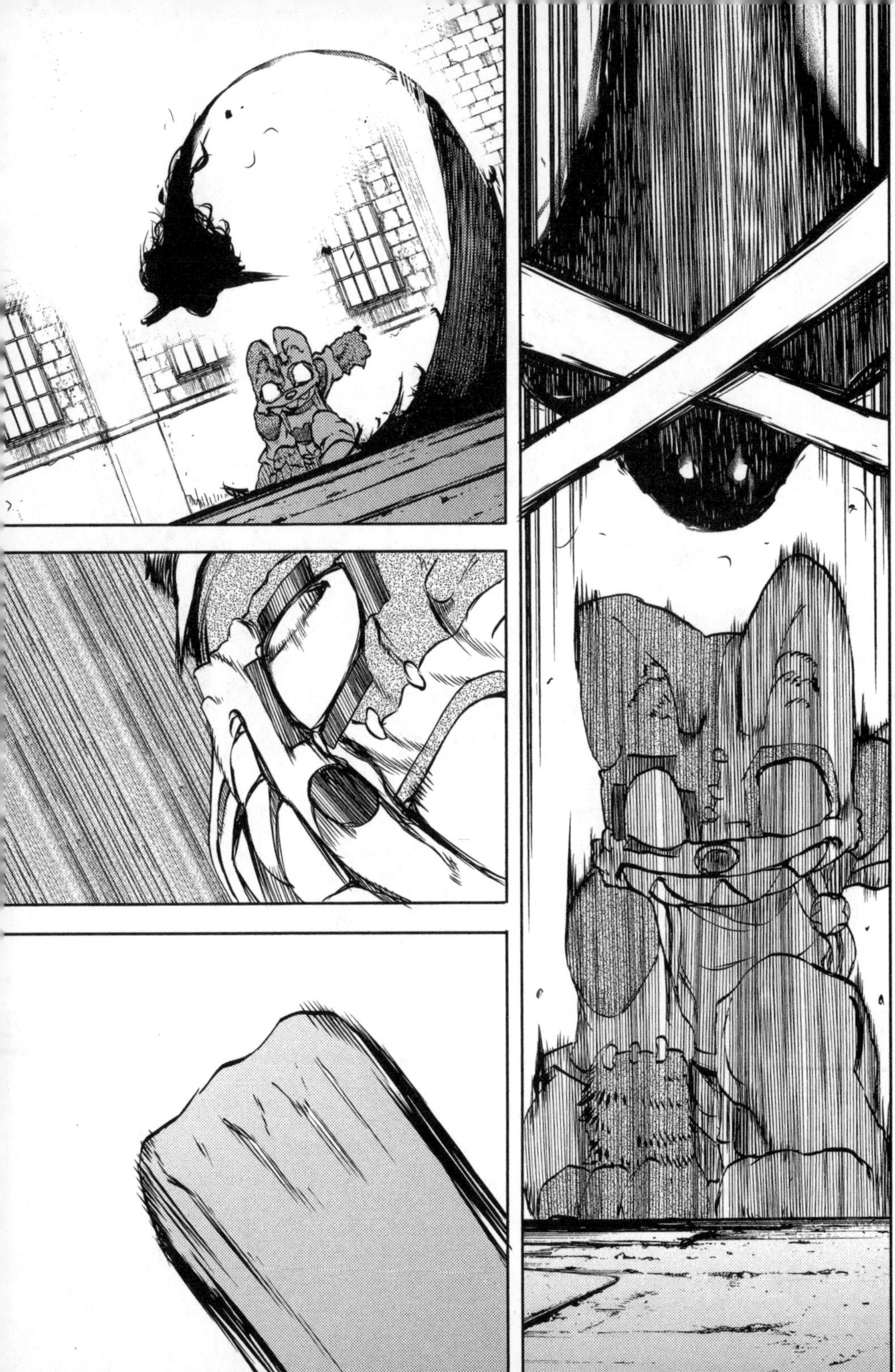

WHAM

STOP FUCKING AROUND.

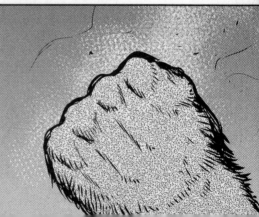

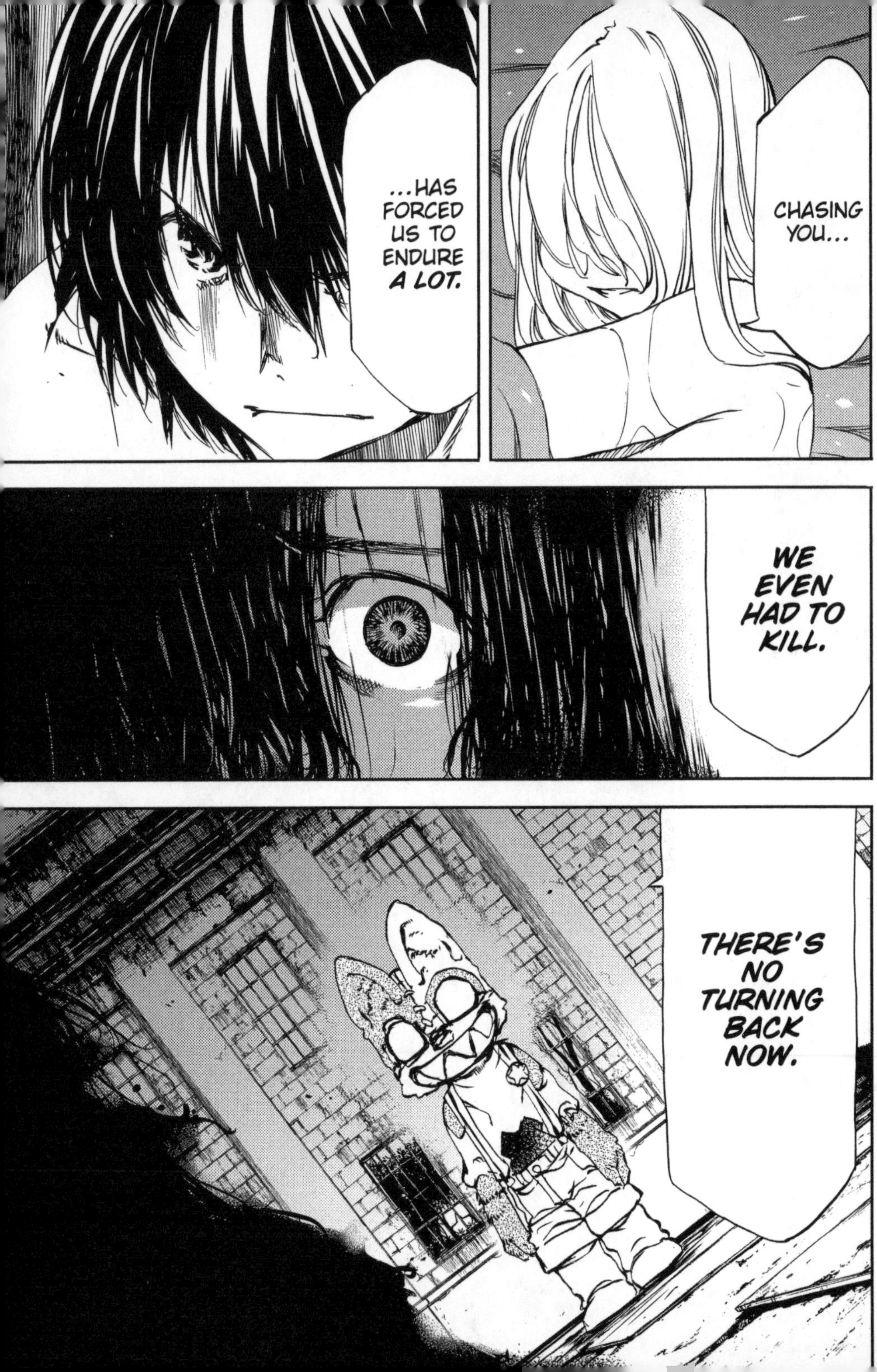
CHASING YOU...
...HAS FORCED US TO ENDURE A LOT.
WE EVEN HAD TO KILL.
THERE'S NO TURNING BACK NOW.

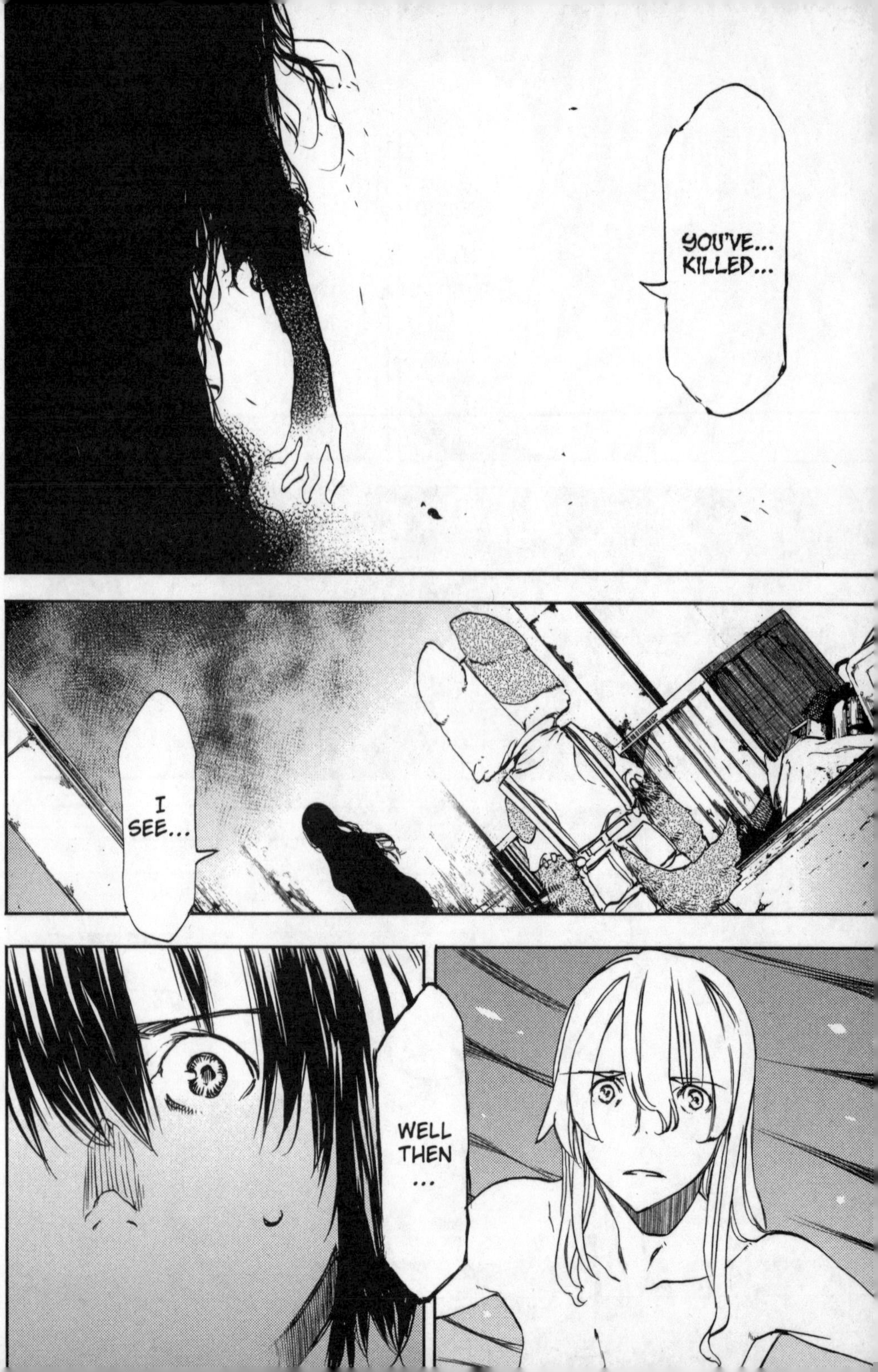
YOU'VE... KILLED...
I SEE...
WELL THEN ...

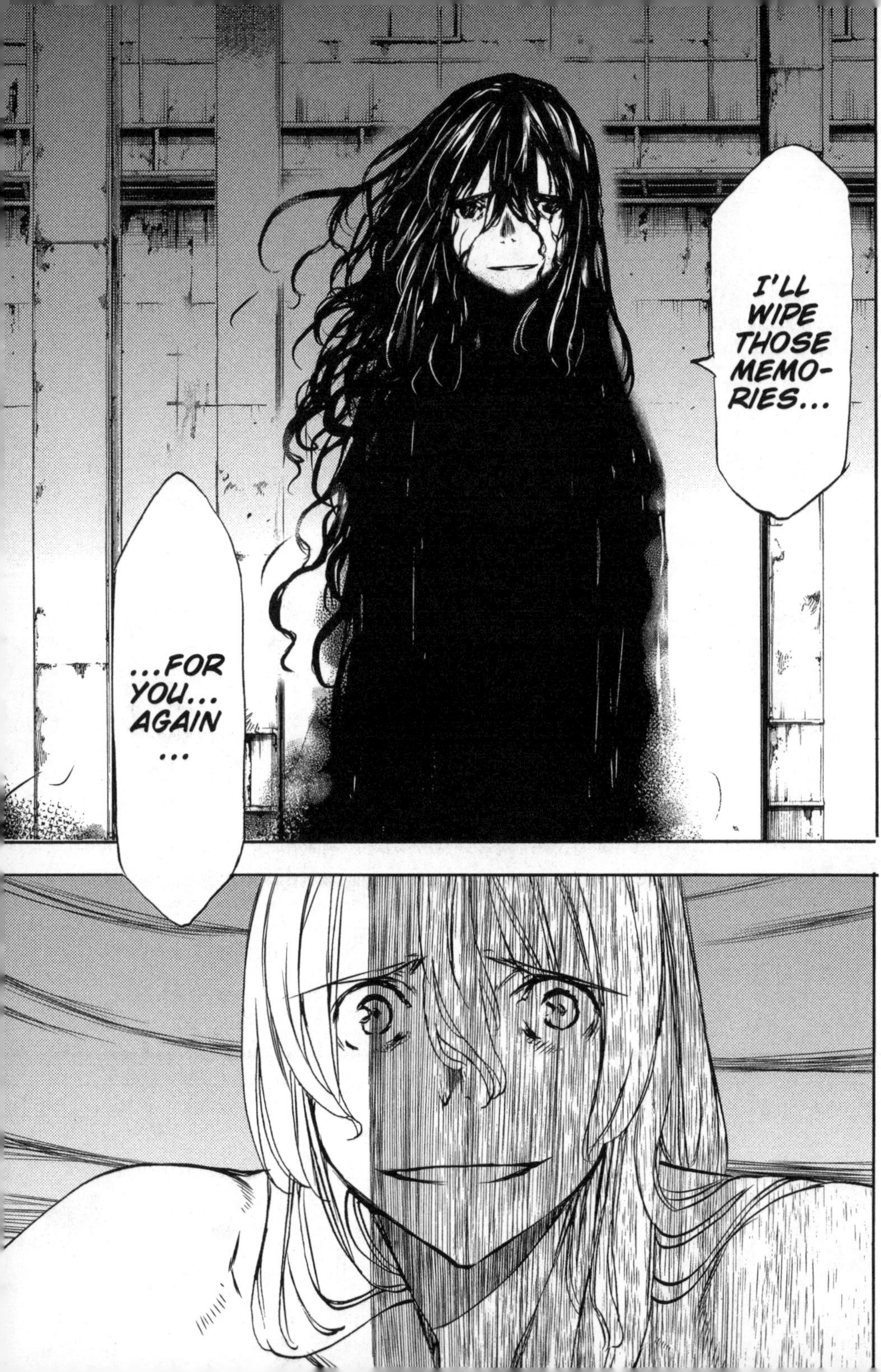
I'LL WIPE THOSE MEMO-RIES...
...FOR YOU... AGAIN ...

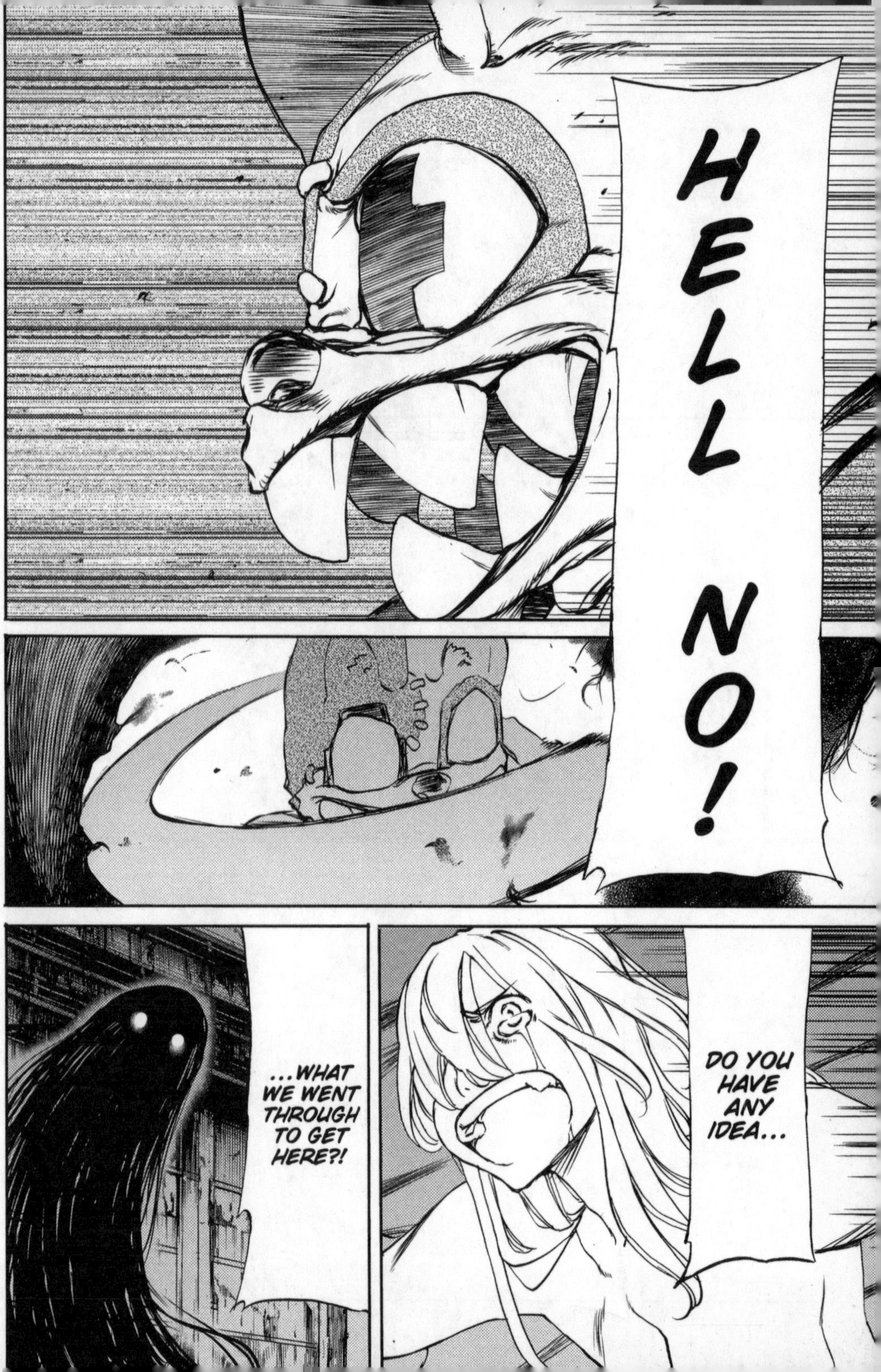
HELL NO!
DO YOU HAVE ANY IDEA...
...WHAT WE WENT THROUGH TO GET HERE?!

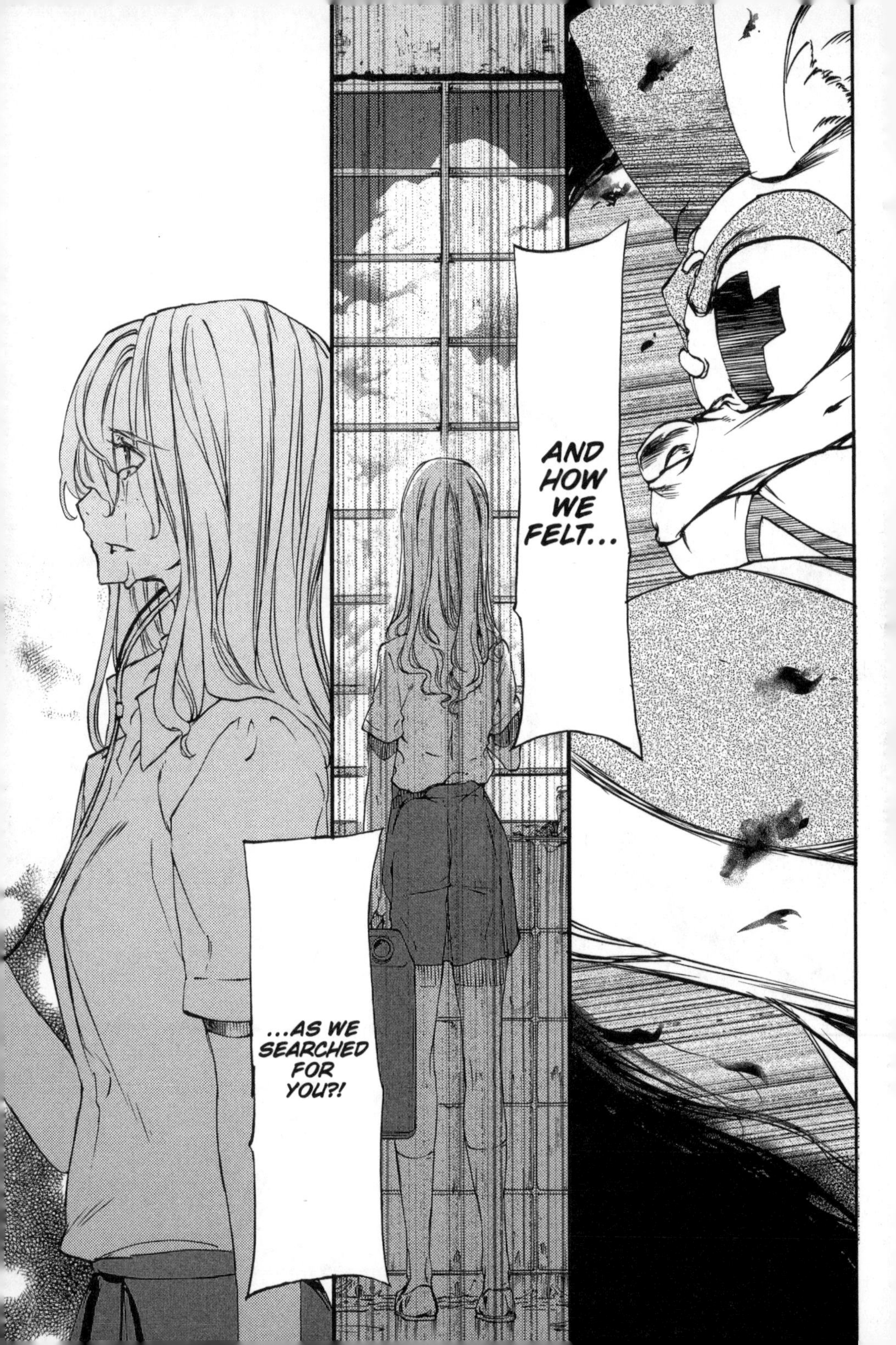
AND HOW WE FELT...
...AS WE SEARCHED FOR YOU?!

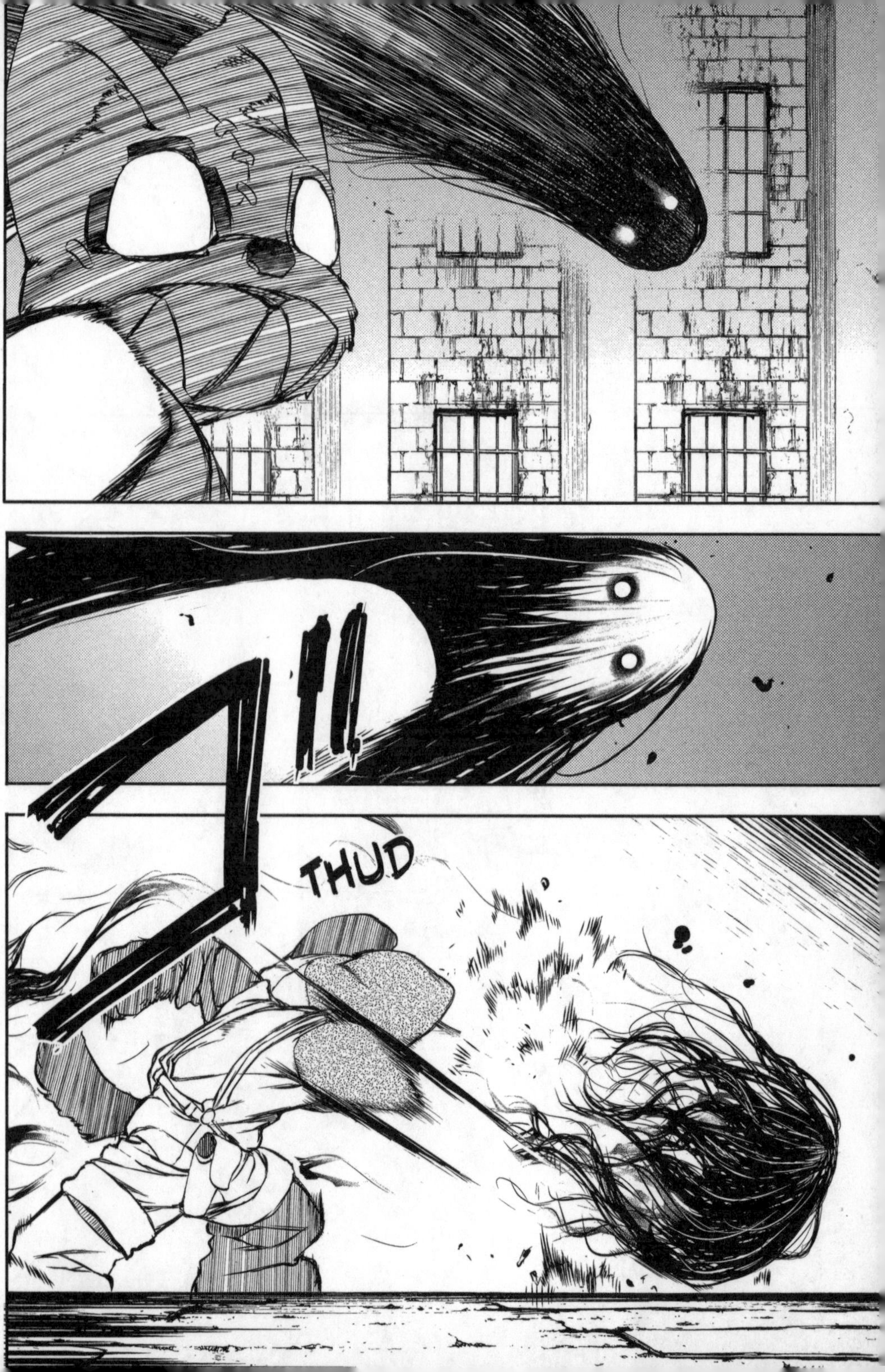
THUD

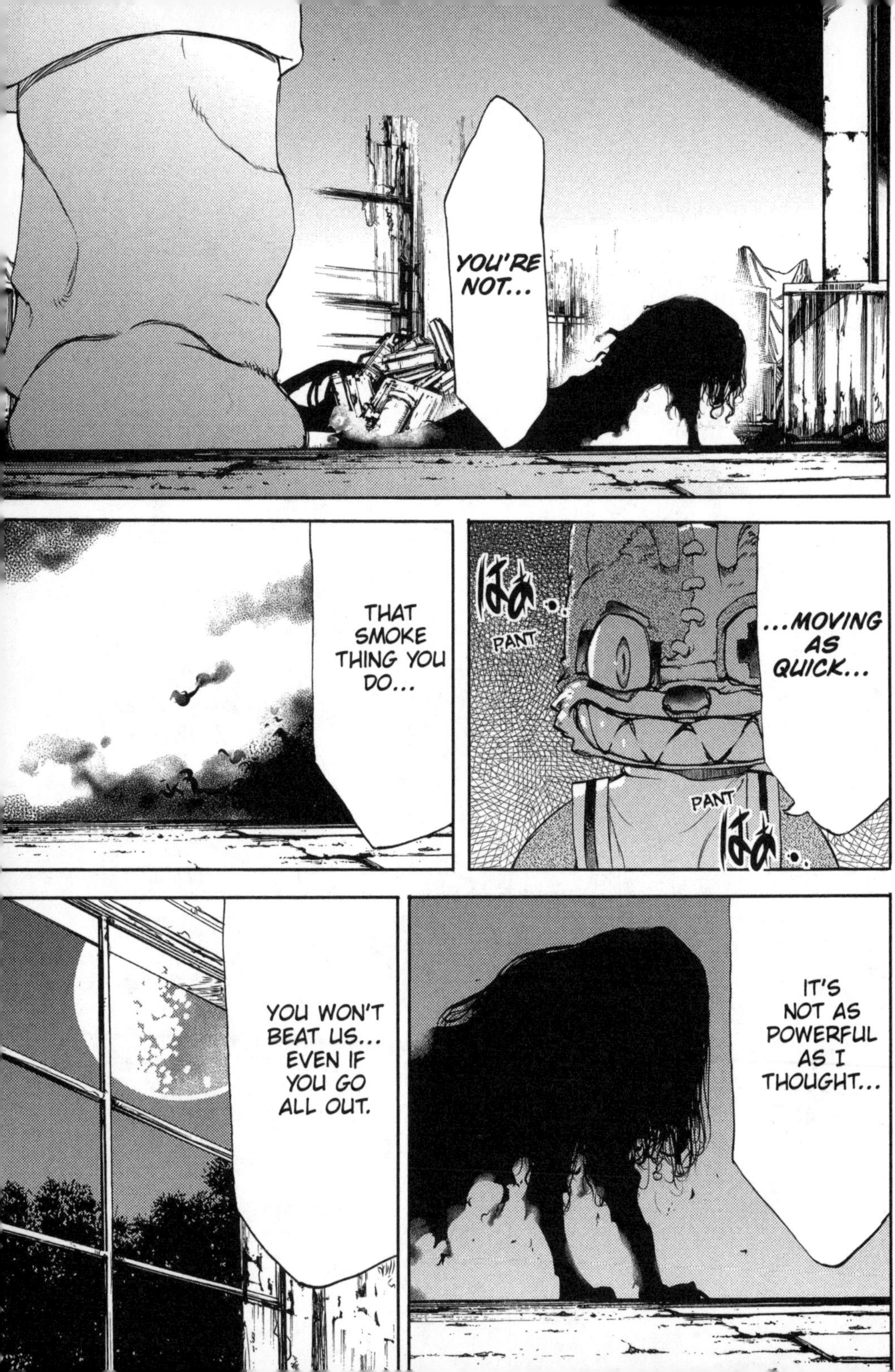
YOU'RE NOT...
はぁ..
PANT
...MOVING AS QUICK...
PANT
はぁ..
THAT SMOKE THING YOU DO...
IT'S NOT AS POWERFUL AS I THOUGHT...
YOU WON'T BEAT US... EVEN IF YOU GO ALL OUT.

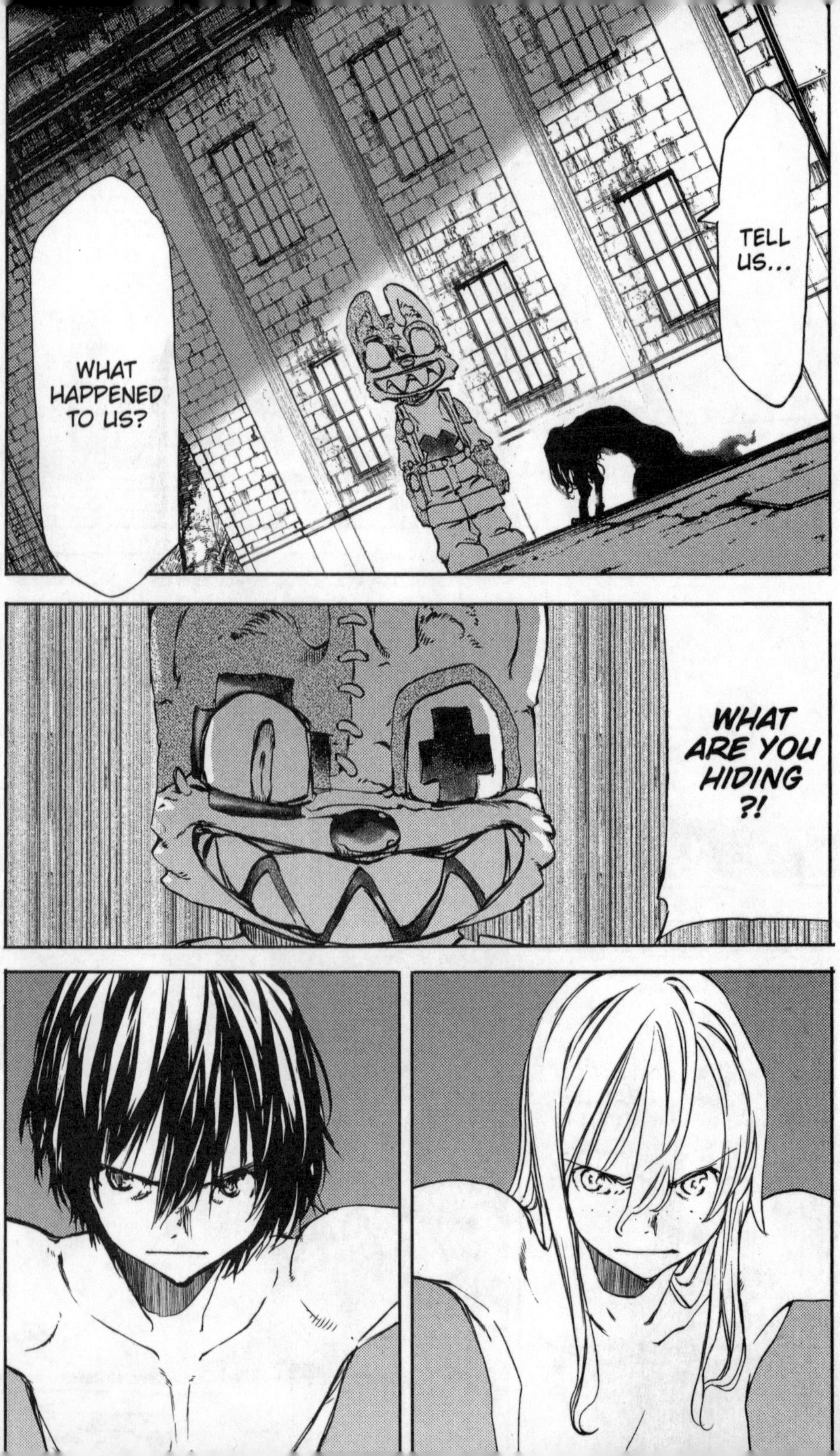
TELL US...
WHAT HAPPENED TO US?
WHAT ARE YOU HIDING ?!

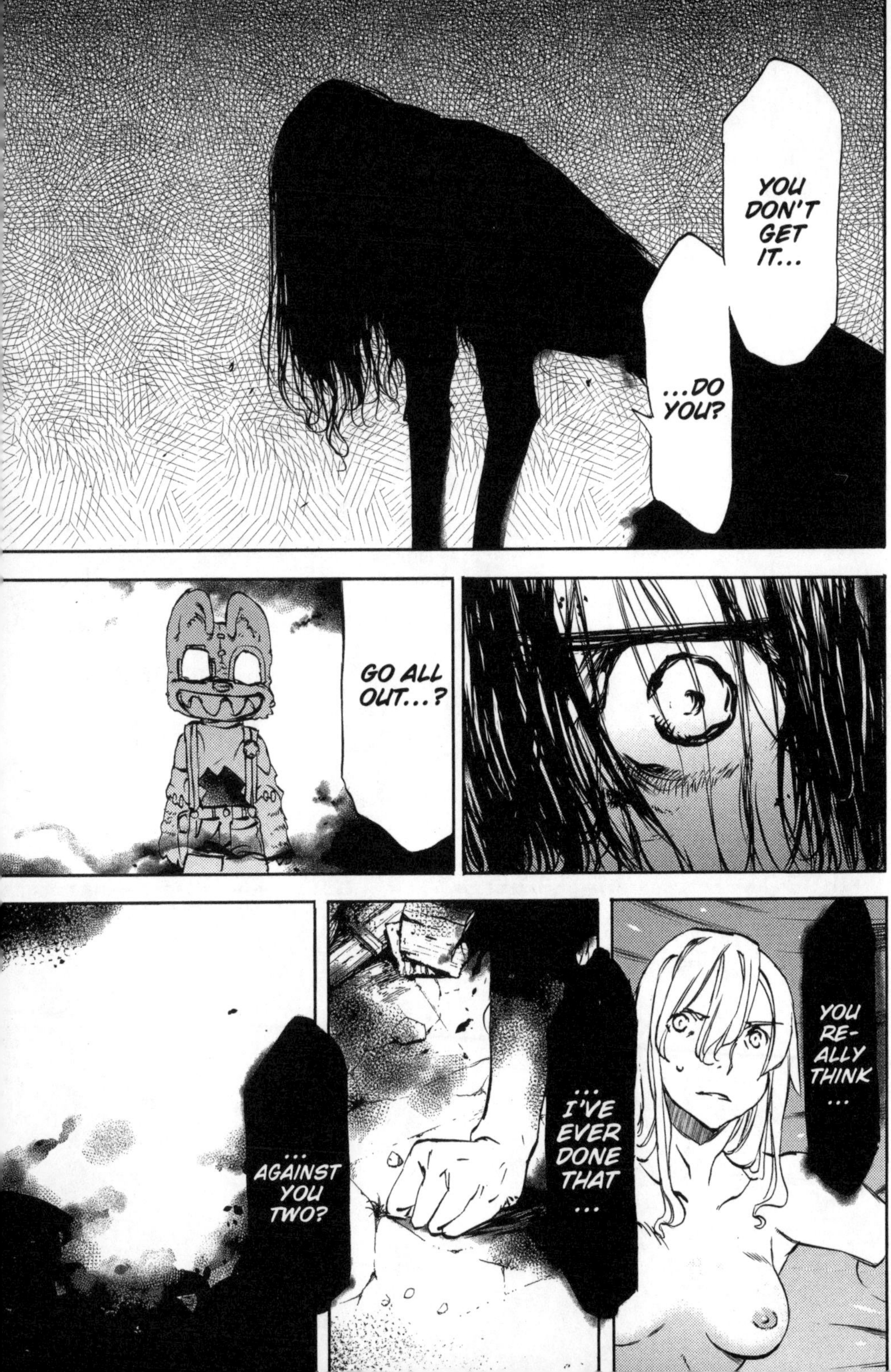
YOU DON'T GET IT...
...DO YOU?
GO ALL OUT...?
YOU RE-ALLY THINK...
...I'VE EVER DONE THAT...
...AGAINST YOU TWO?

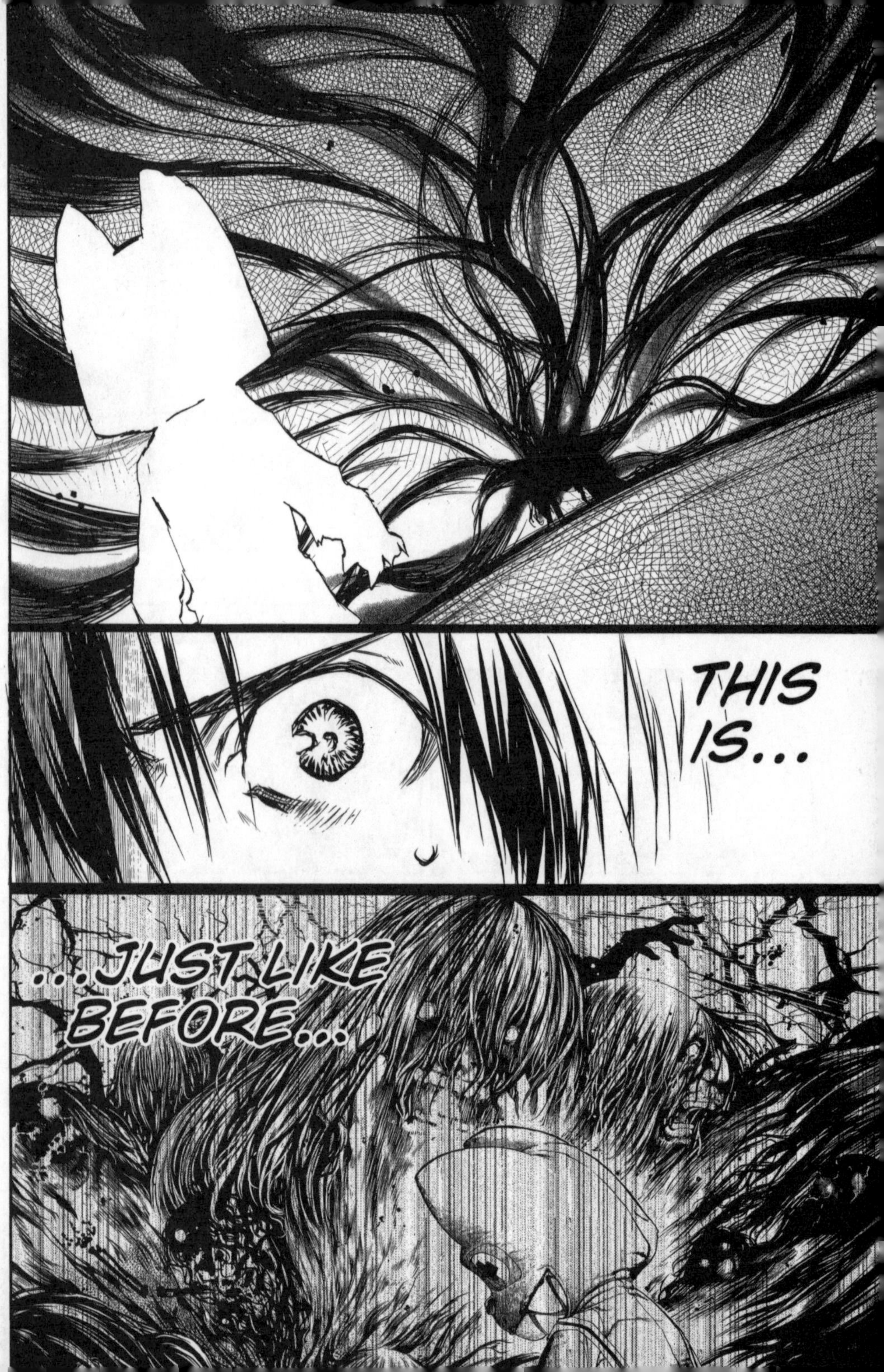
THIS IS...
...JUST LIKE BEFORE...

I SAID...

...YOU'D TRY TO...

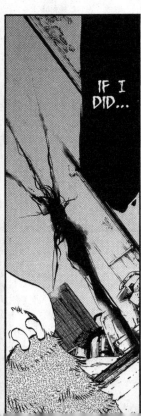

IF I DID...

...I'M NOT TELL- ING YOU.

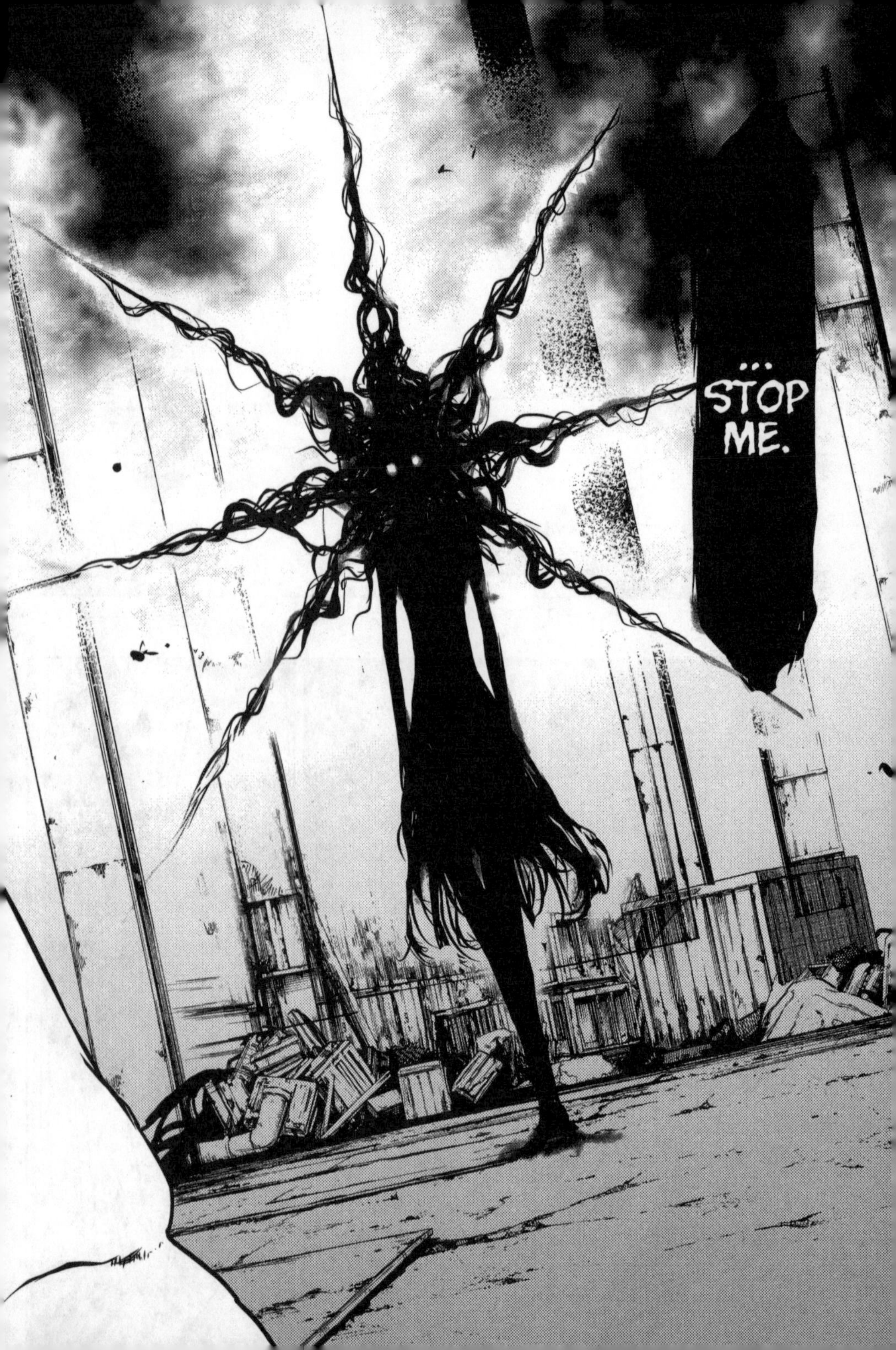
...STOP ME.

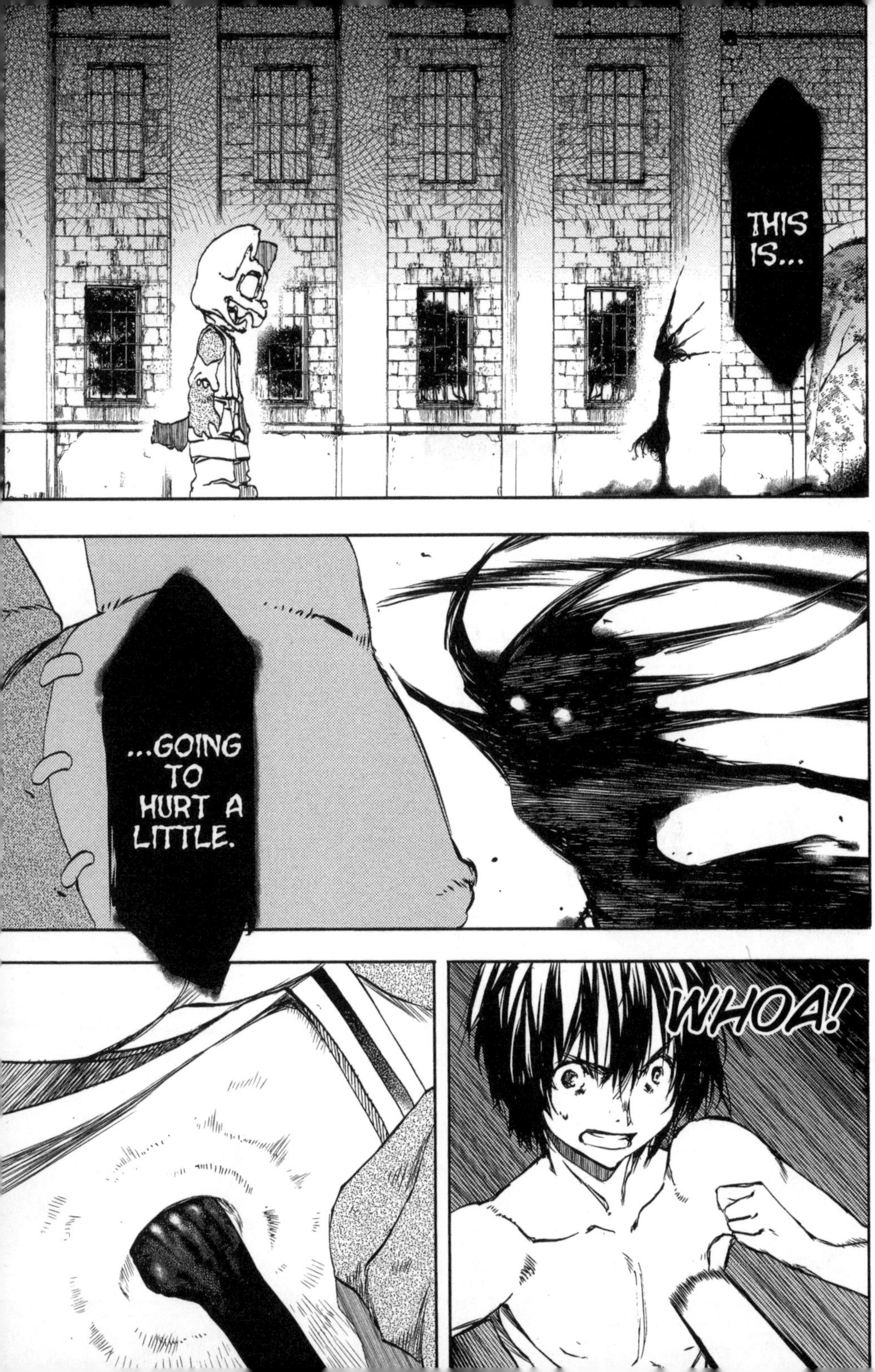
THIS IS...
...GOING TO HURT A LITTLE.
WHOA!

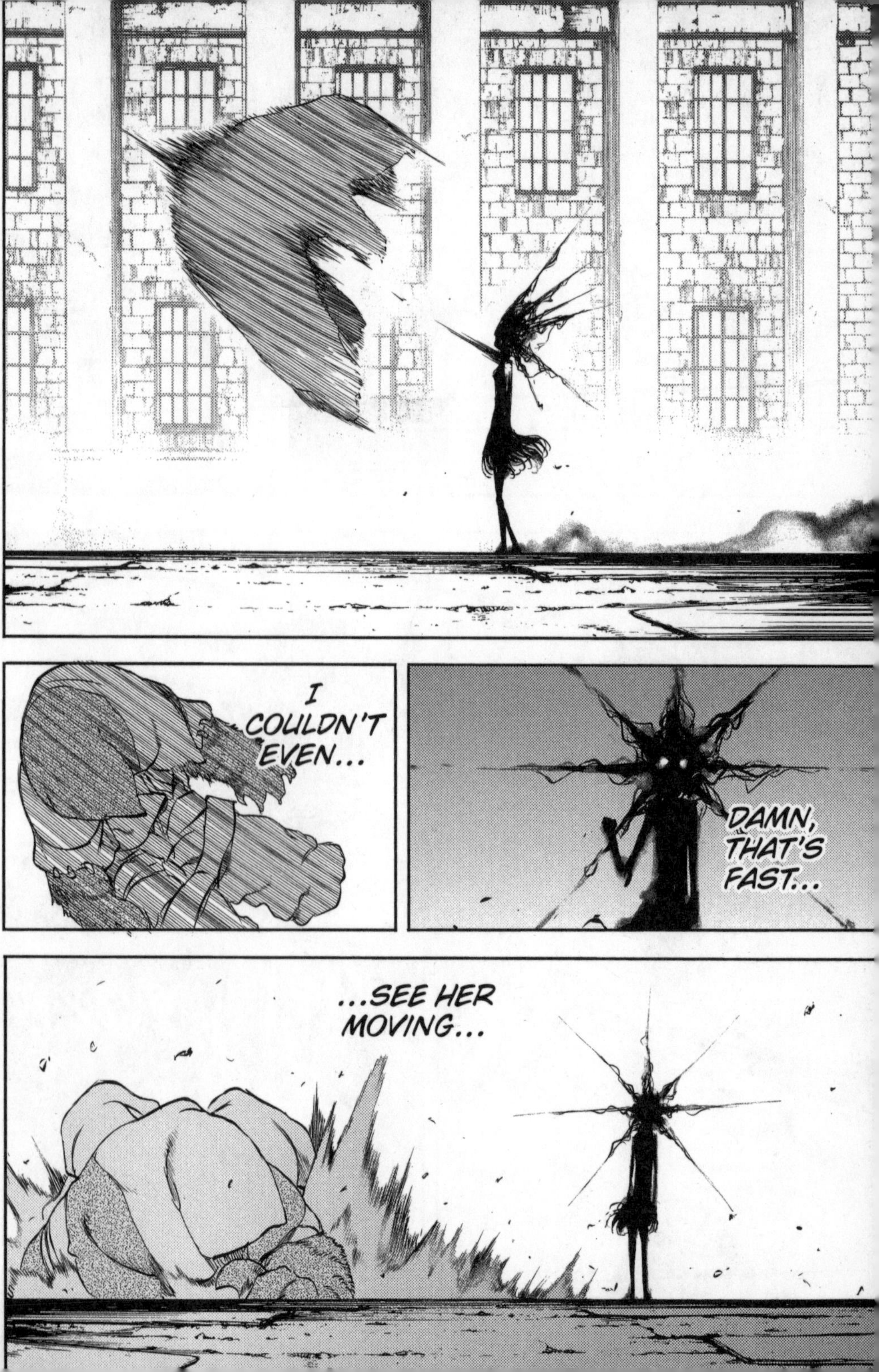
DAMN, THAT'S FAST...
I COULDN'T EVEN...
...SEE HER MOVING...

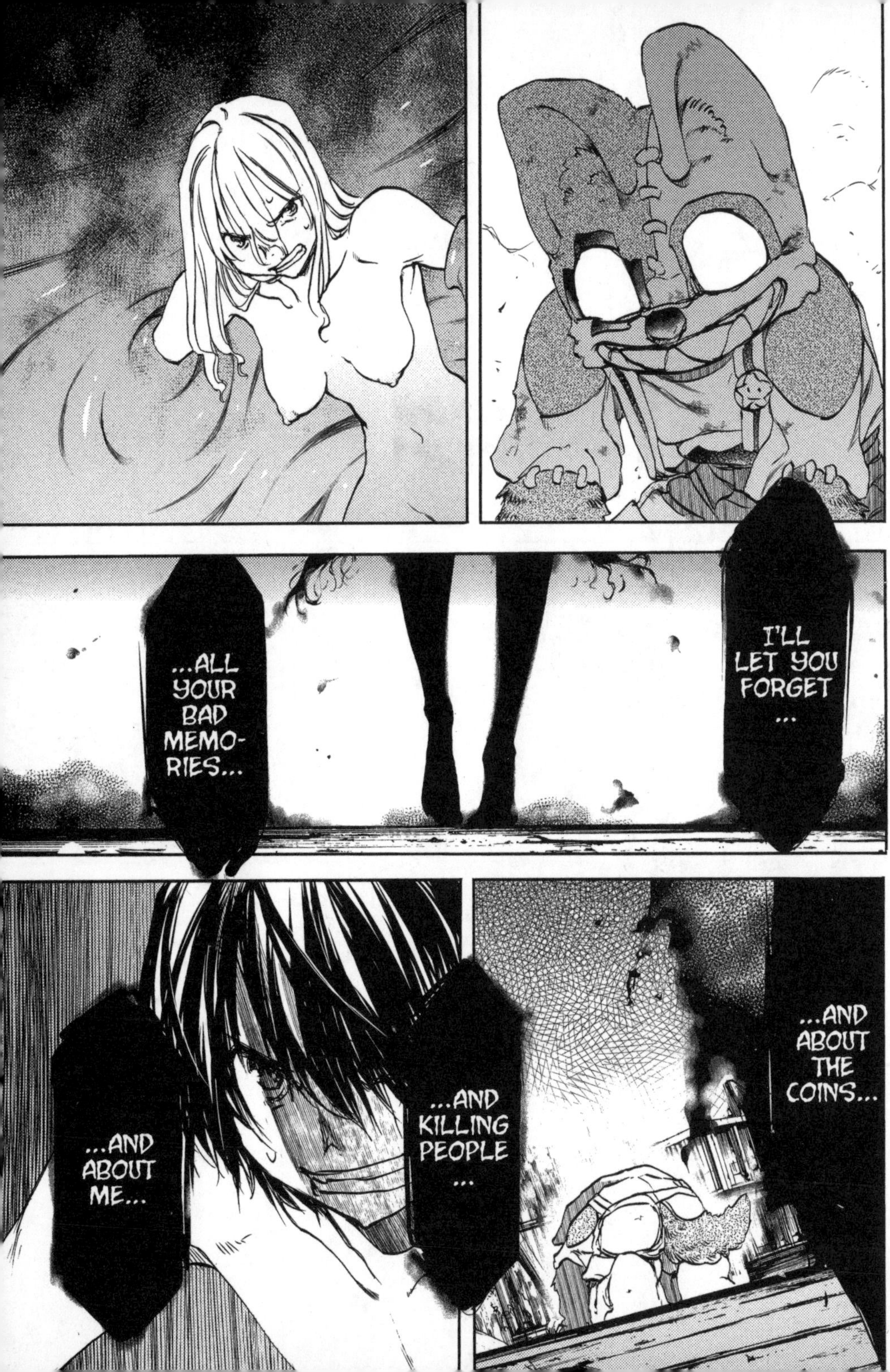
I'LL LET YOU FORGET ...
...ALL YOUR BAD MEMO- RIES...
...AND ABOUT THE COINS...
...AND KILLING PEOPLE ...
...AND ABOUT ME...

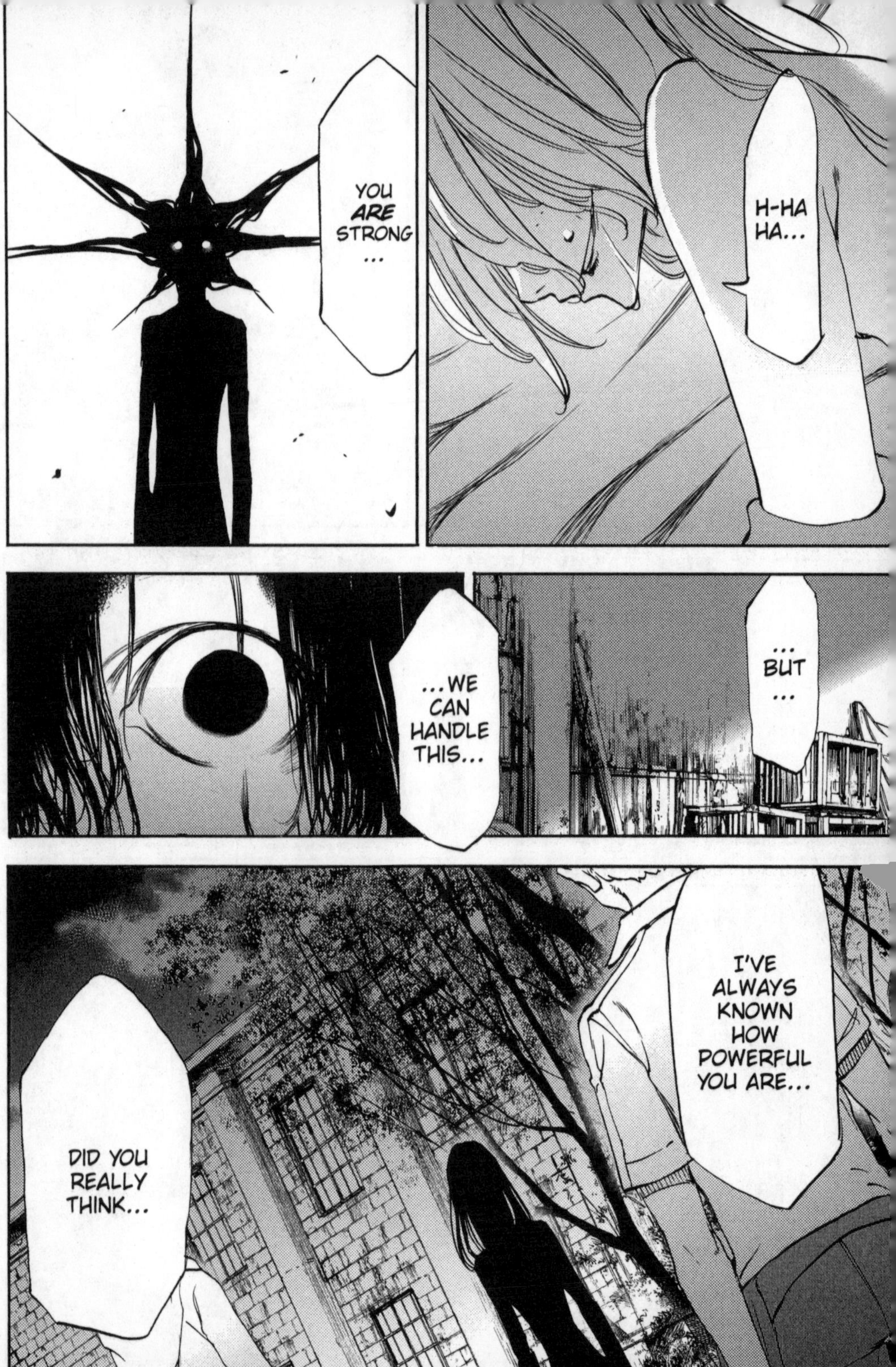
H-HA HA...
YOU **ARE** STRONG ...
... BUT ...
...WE CAN HANDLE THIS...
I'VE ALWAYS KNOWN HOW POWERFUL YOU ARE...
DID YOU REALLY THINK...

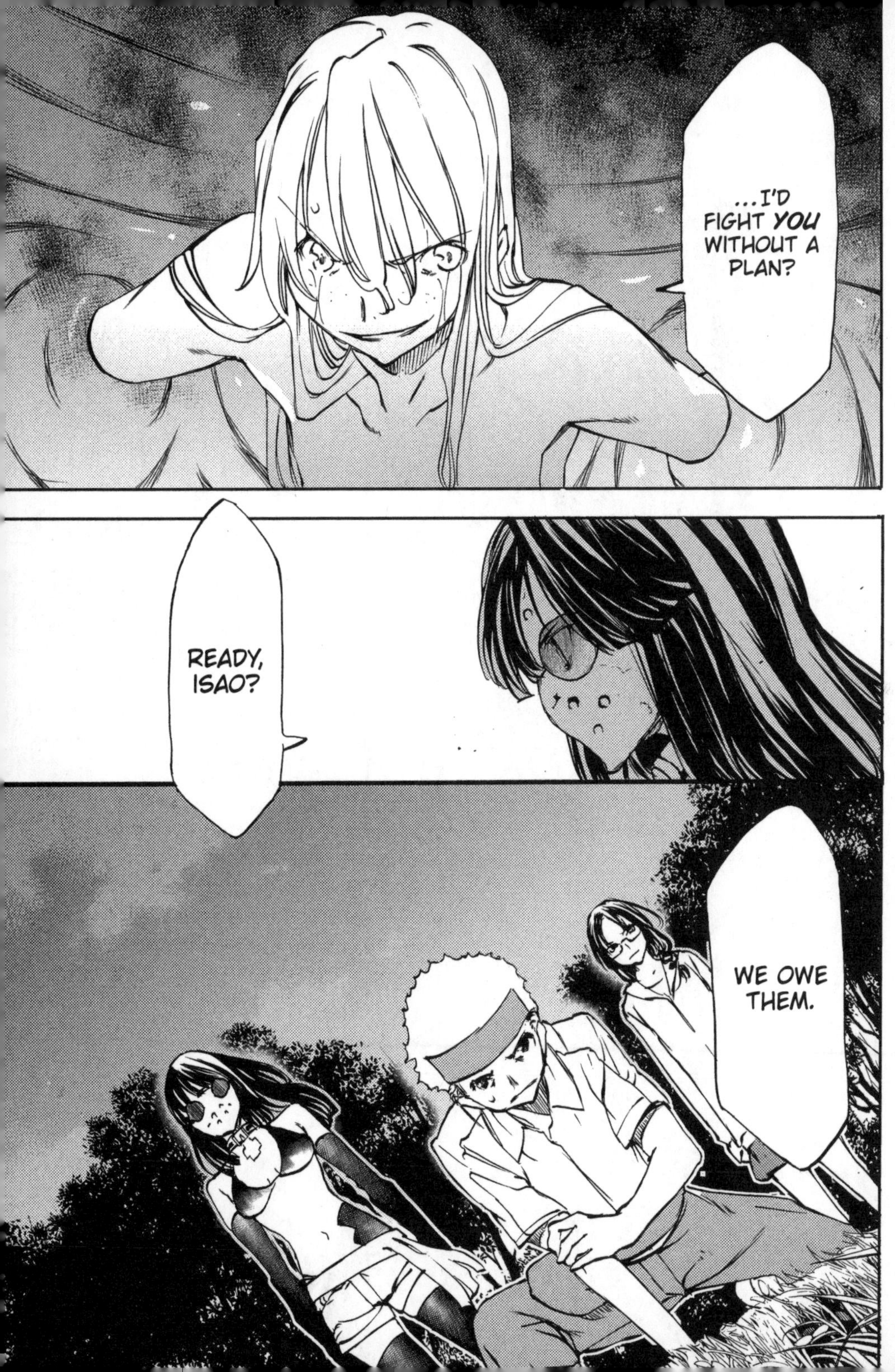
...I'D FIGHT *YOU* WITHOUT A PLAN?
READY, ISAO?
WE OWE THEM.

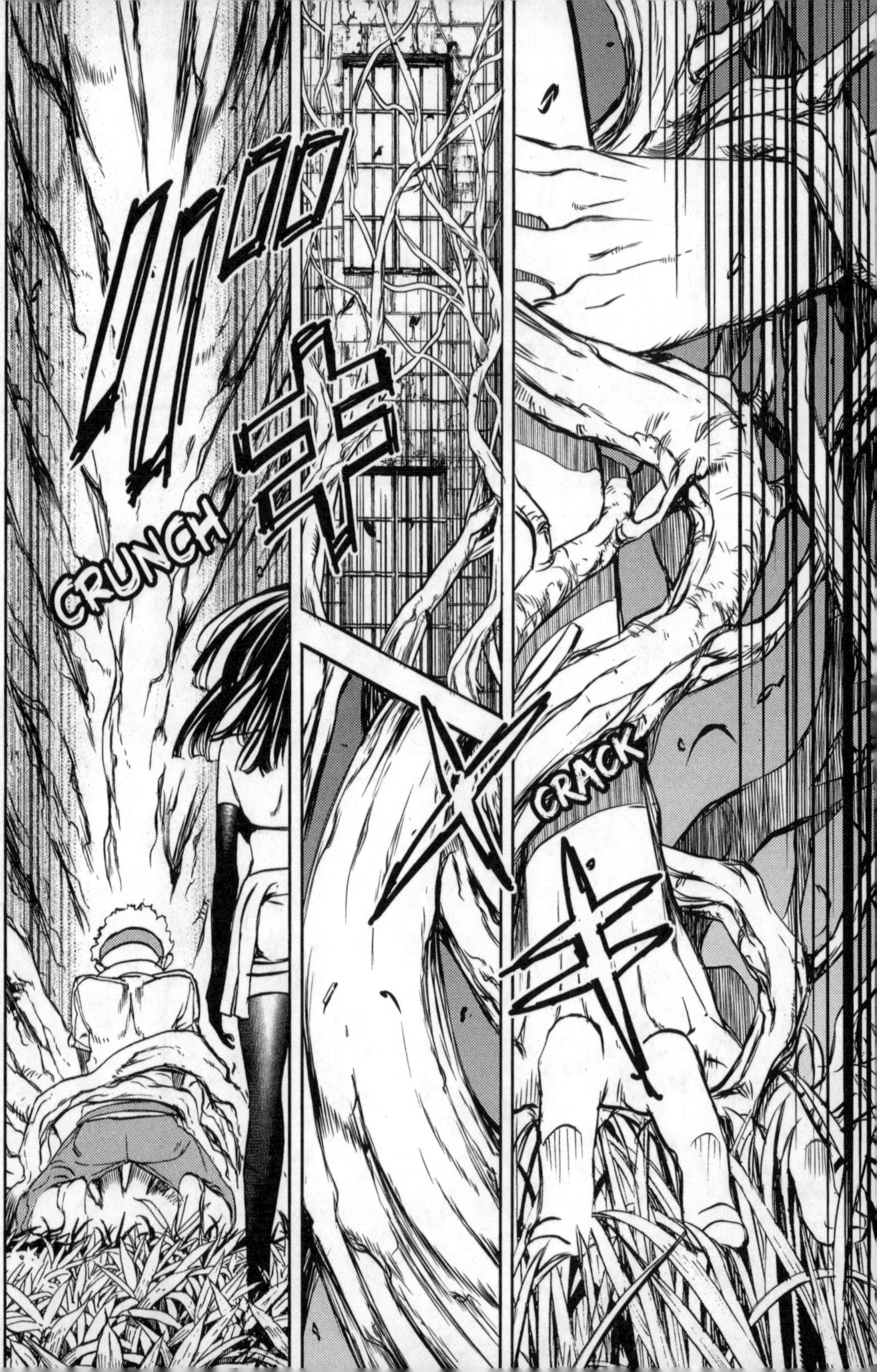
CRACK
CRUNCH

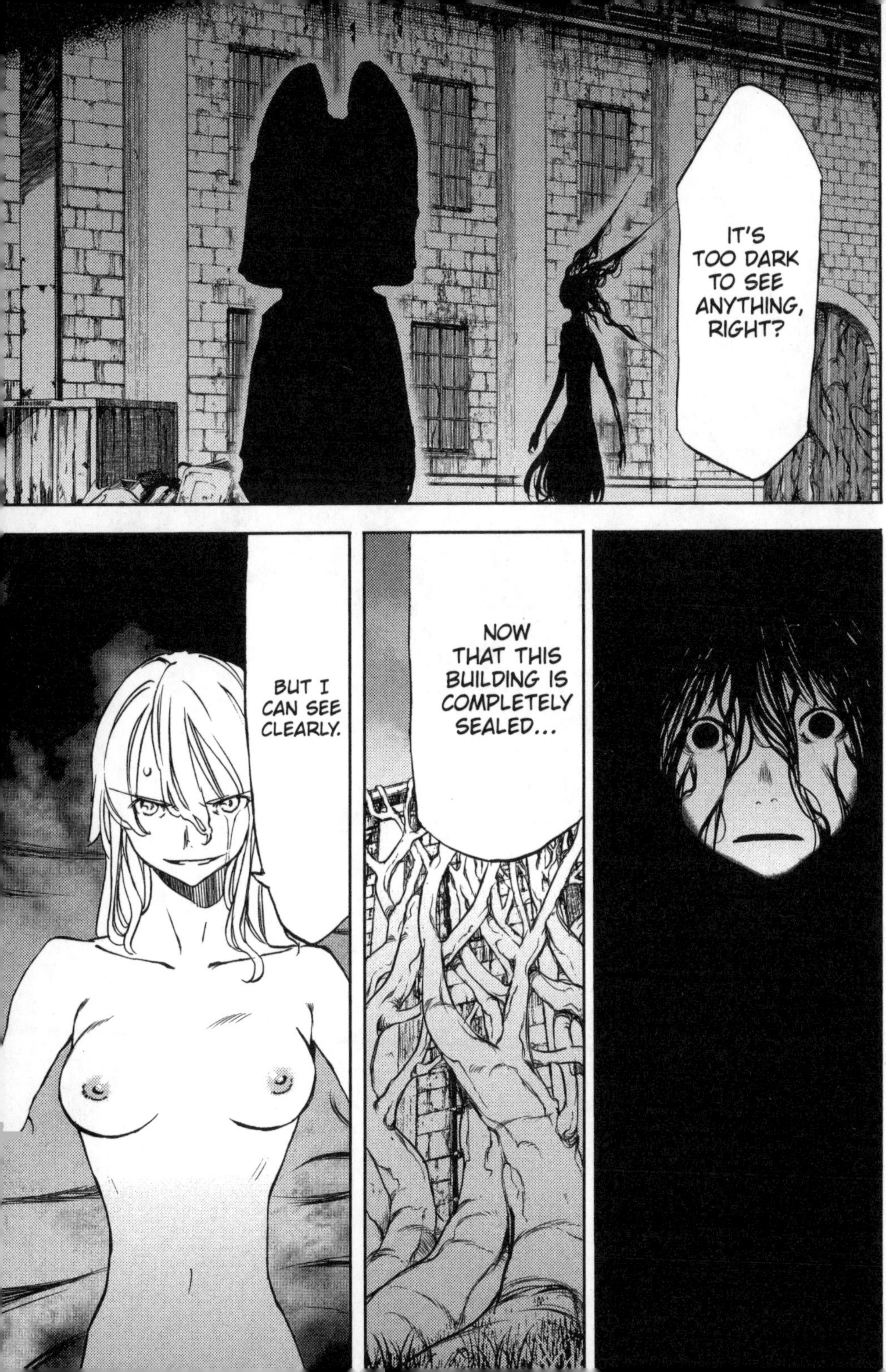
IT'S TOO DARK TO SEE ANYTHING, RIGHT?
NOW THAT THIS BUILDING IS COMPLETELY SEALED...
BUT I CAN SEE CLEARLY.

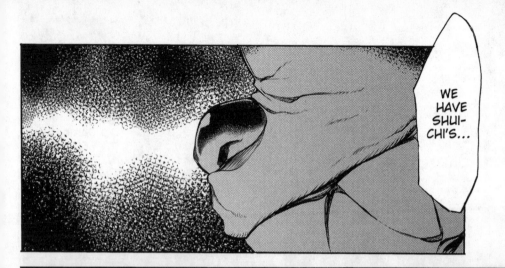

WE HAVE SHUI-CHI'S...

...SENSE OF SMELL.

CHAPTER 49

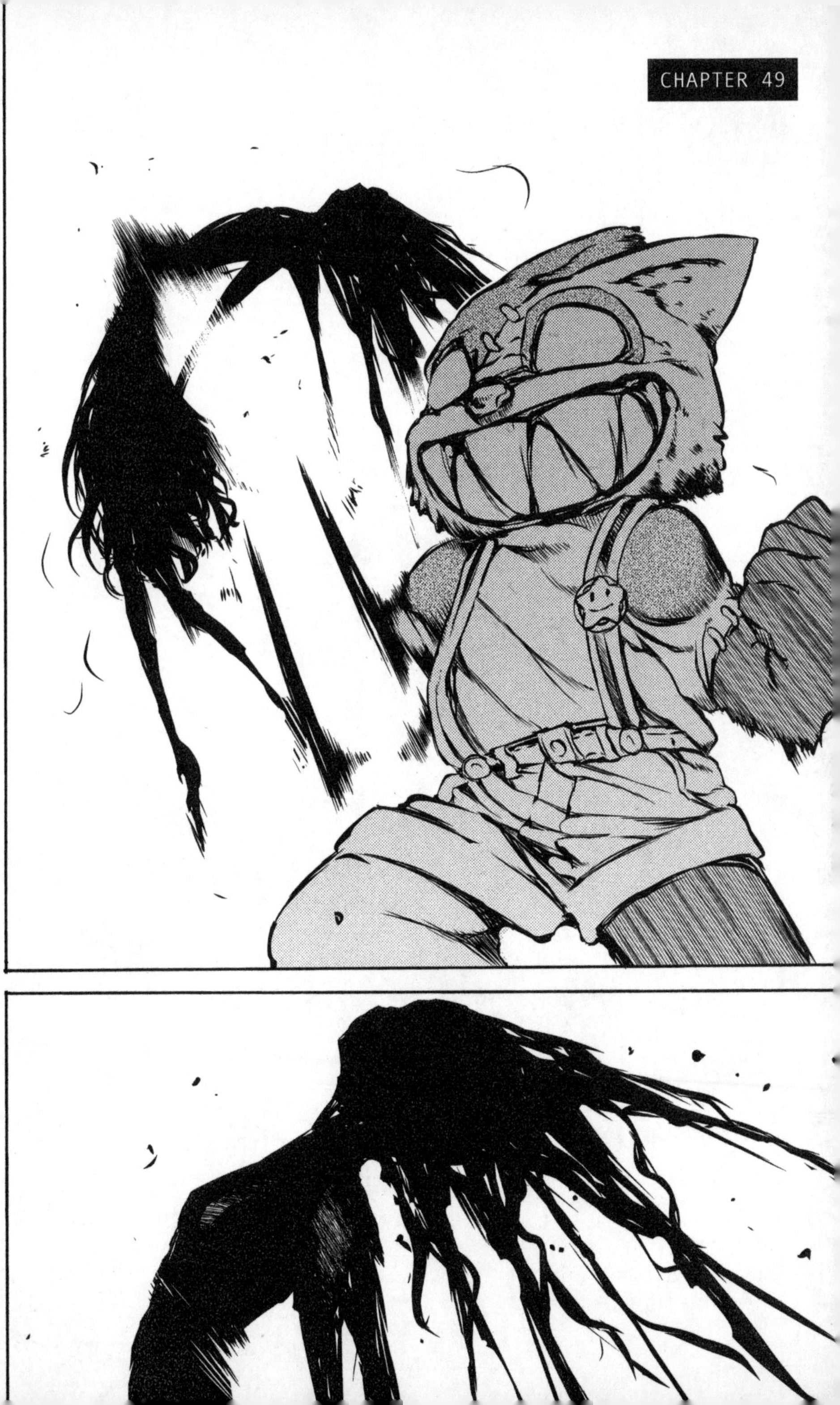

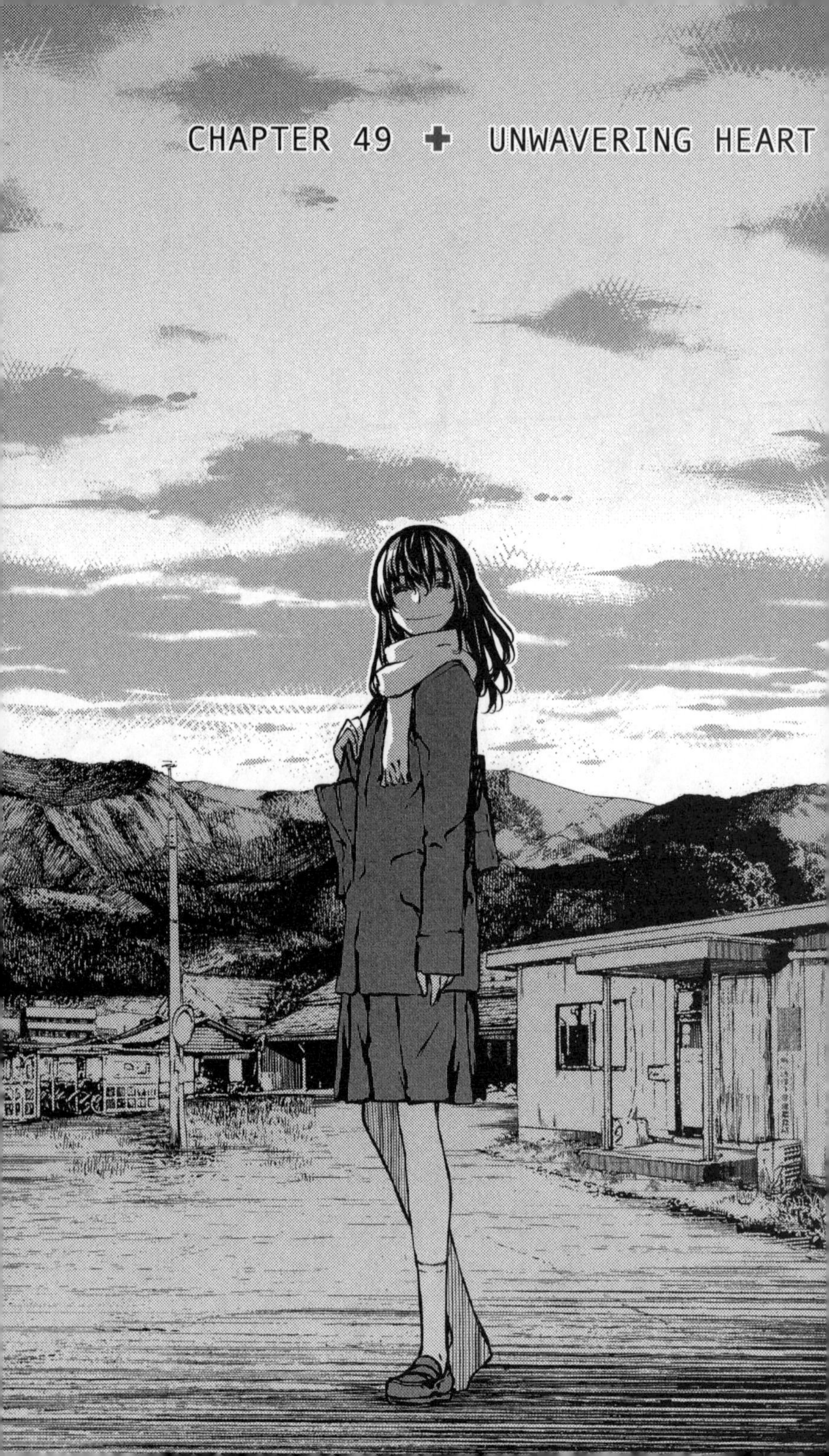
CHAPTER 49 ✚ UNWAVERING HEART

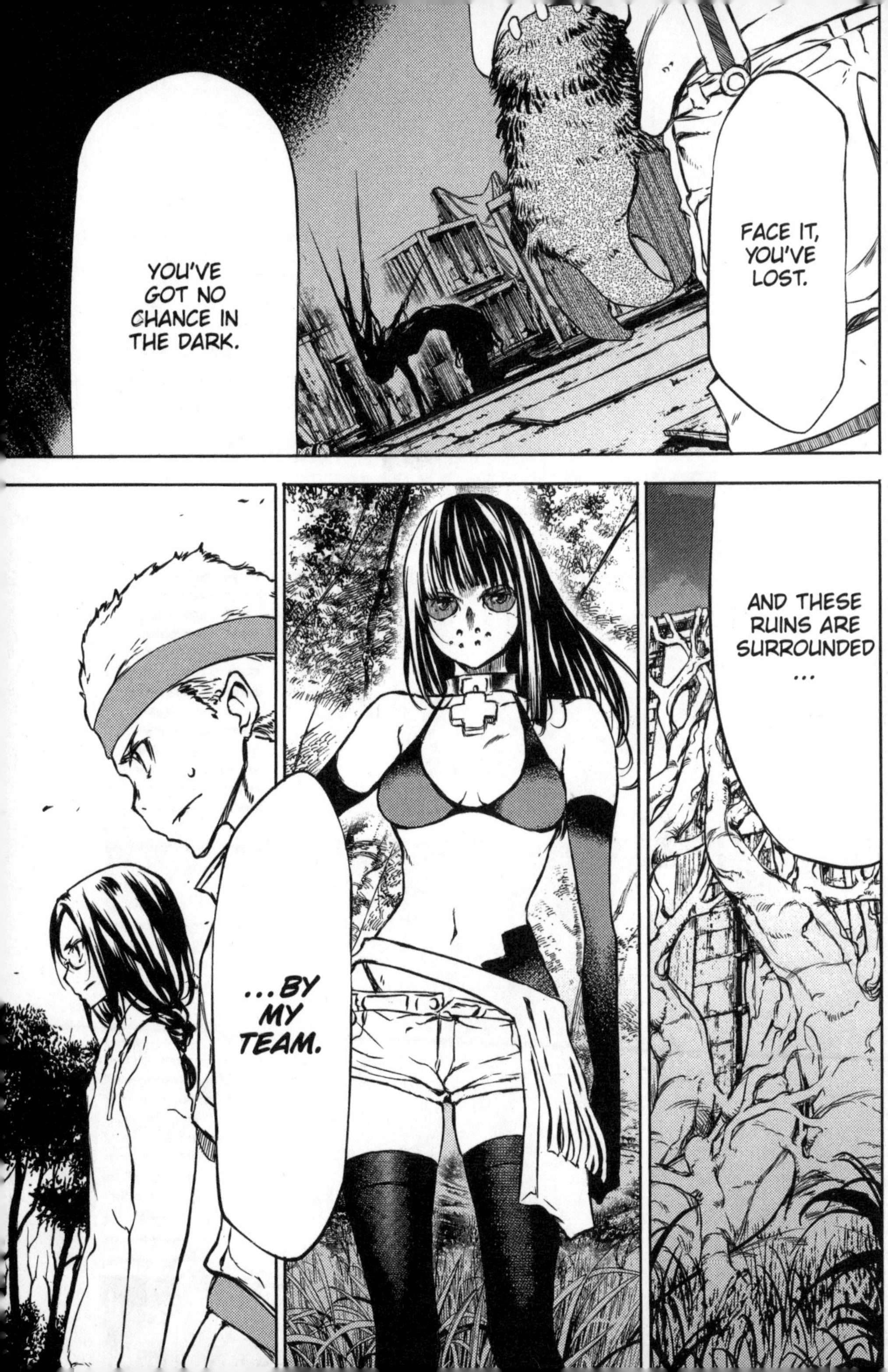
FACE IT, YOU'VE LOST.
YOU'VE GOT NO CHANCE IN THE DARK.
AND THESE RUINS ARE SURROUNDED ...
...BY MY TEAM.

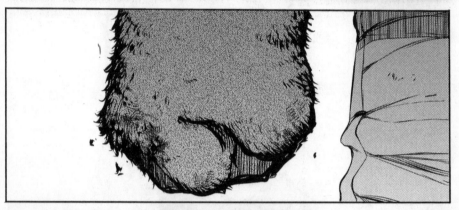

I MET THAT KAITO GUY.

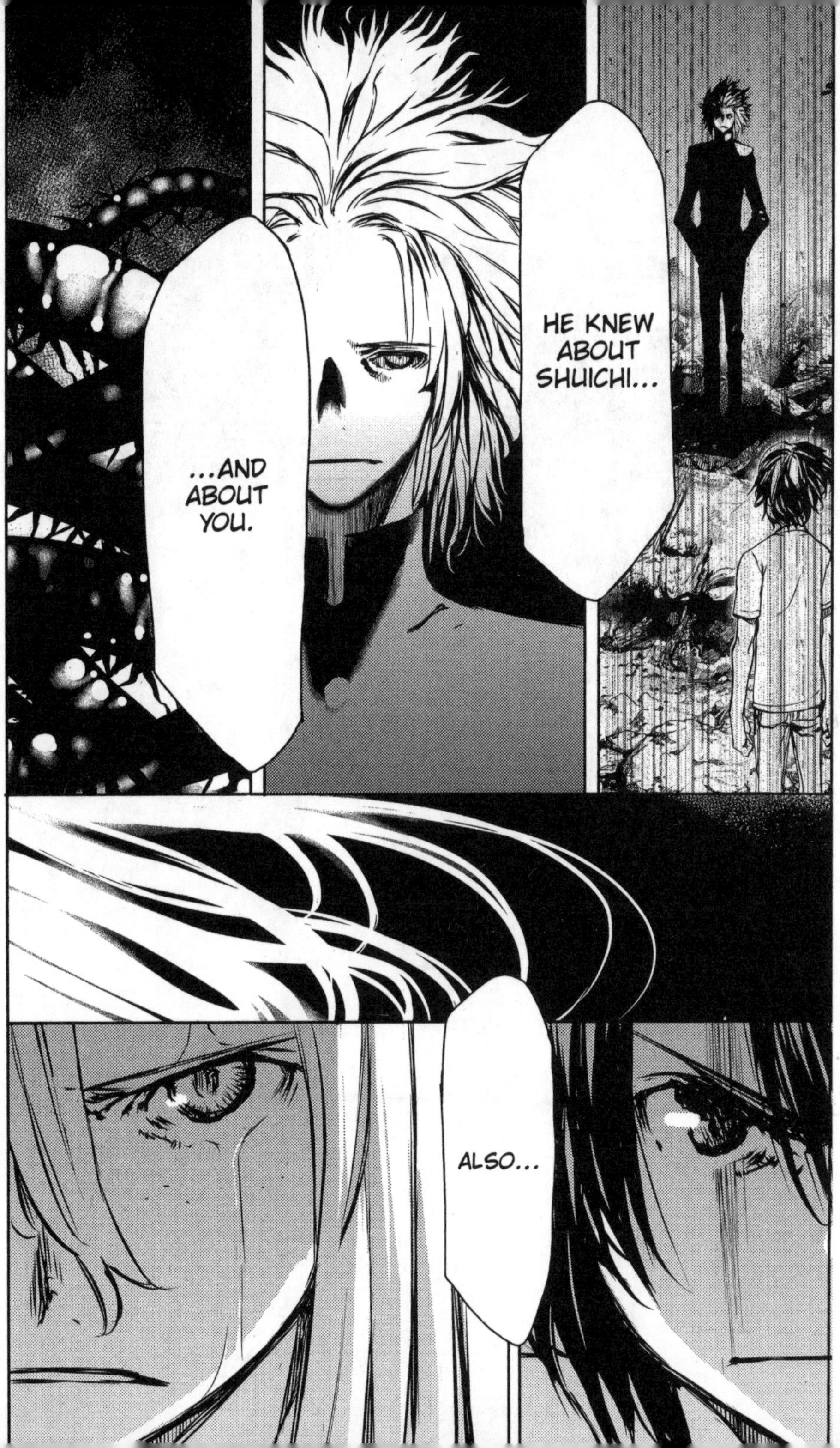
HE KNEW ABOUT SHUICHI...
...AND ABOUT YOU.
ALSO...

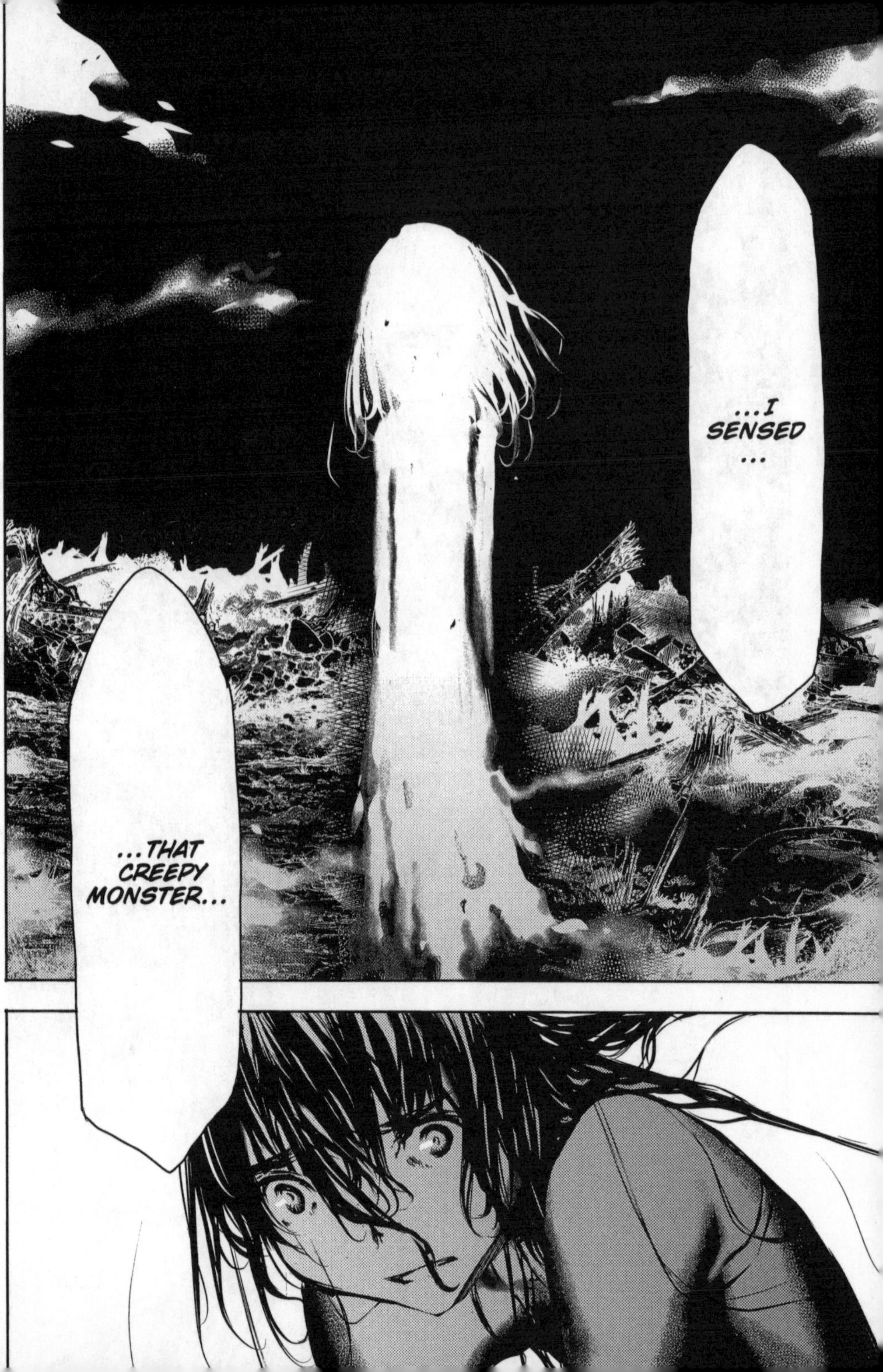
...I SENSED ...
...THAT CREEPY MONSTER...

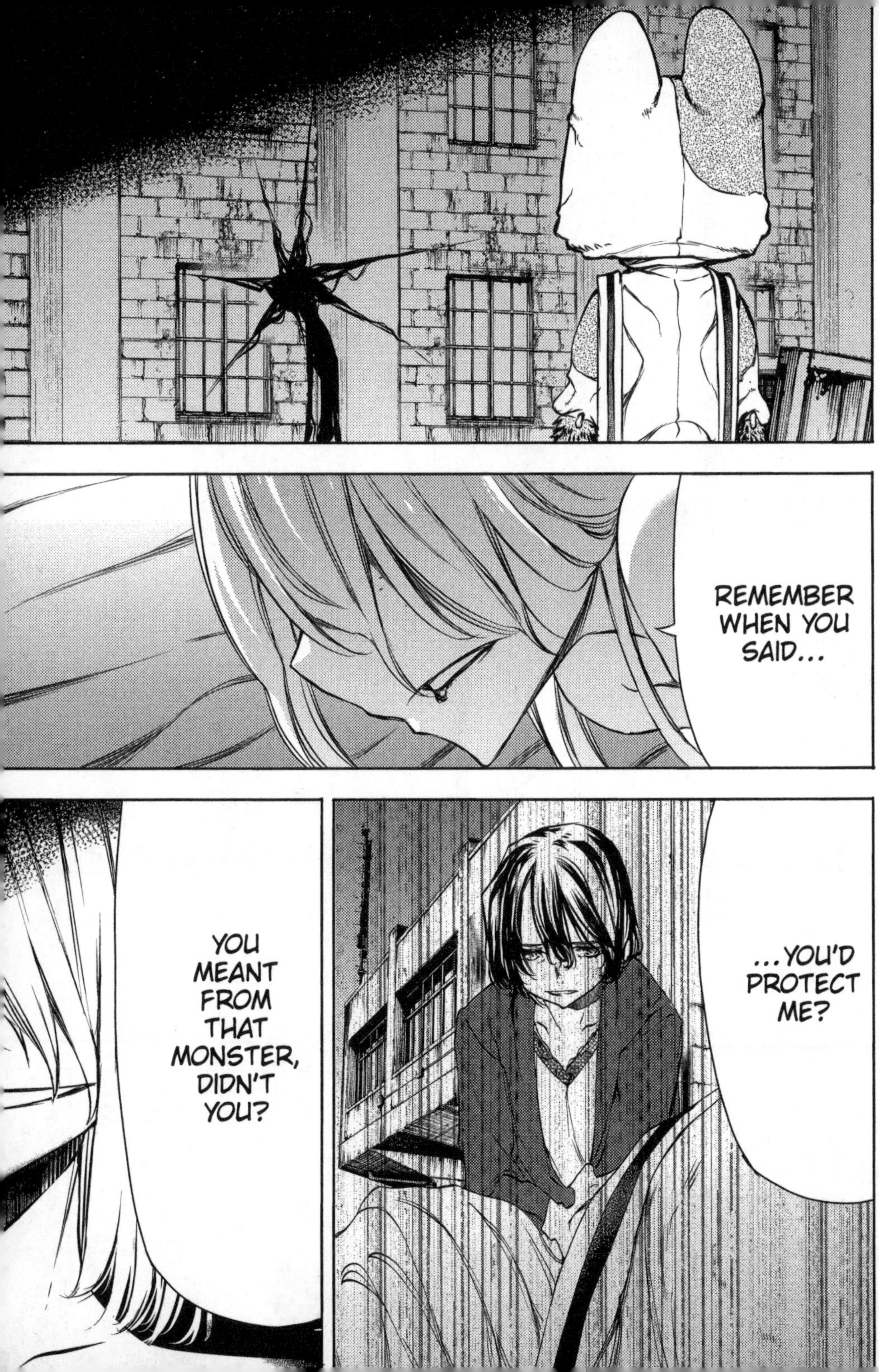
REMEMBER WHEN YOU SAID...
...YOU'D PROTECT ME?
YOU MEANT FROM THAT MONSTER, DIDN'T YOU?

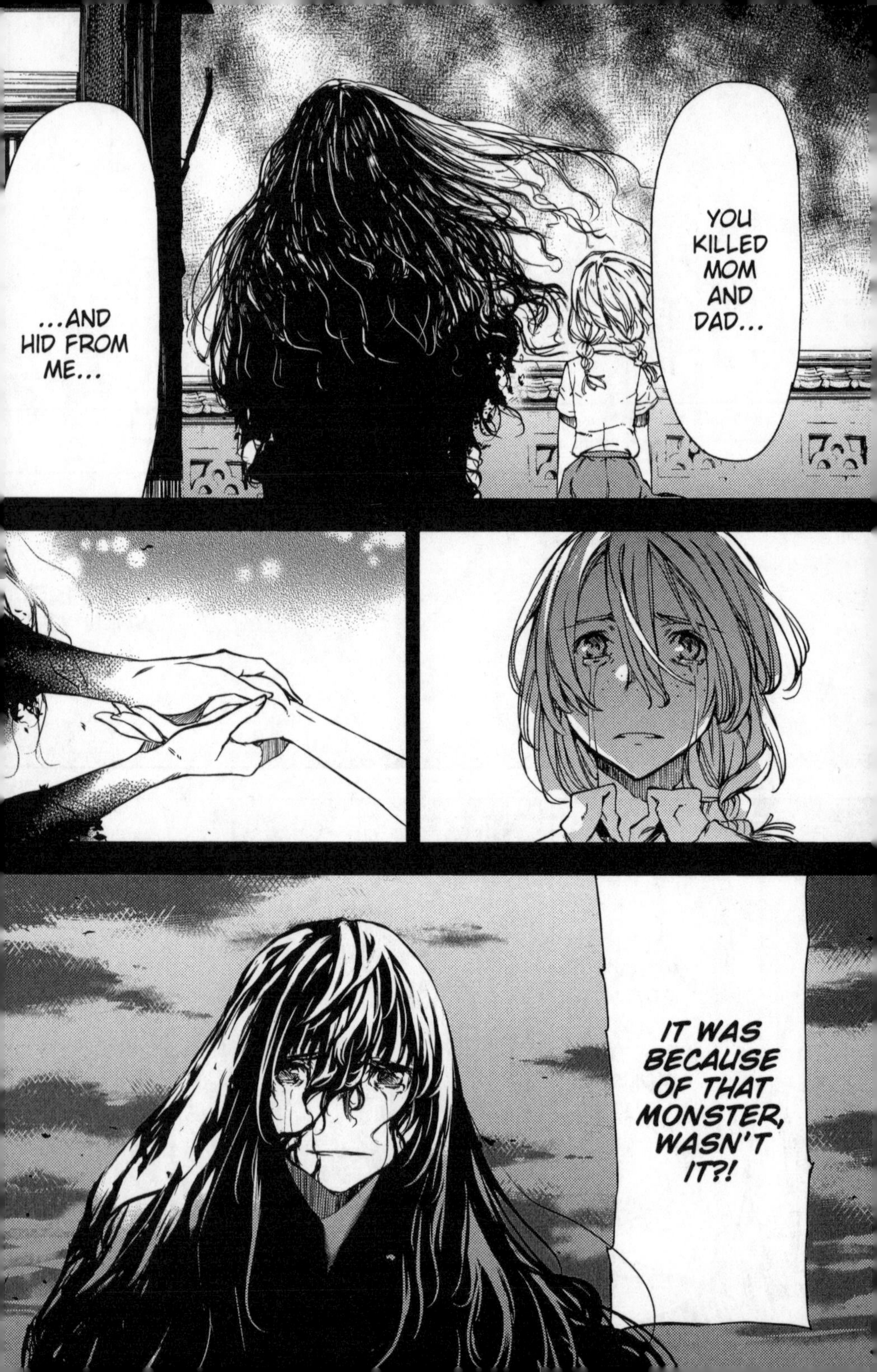
YOU KILLED MOM AND DAD...
...AND HID FROM ME...
IT WAS BECAUSE OF THAT MONSTER, WASN'T IT?!

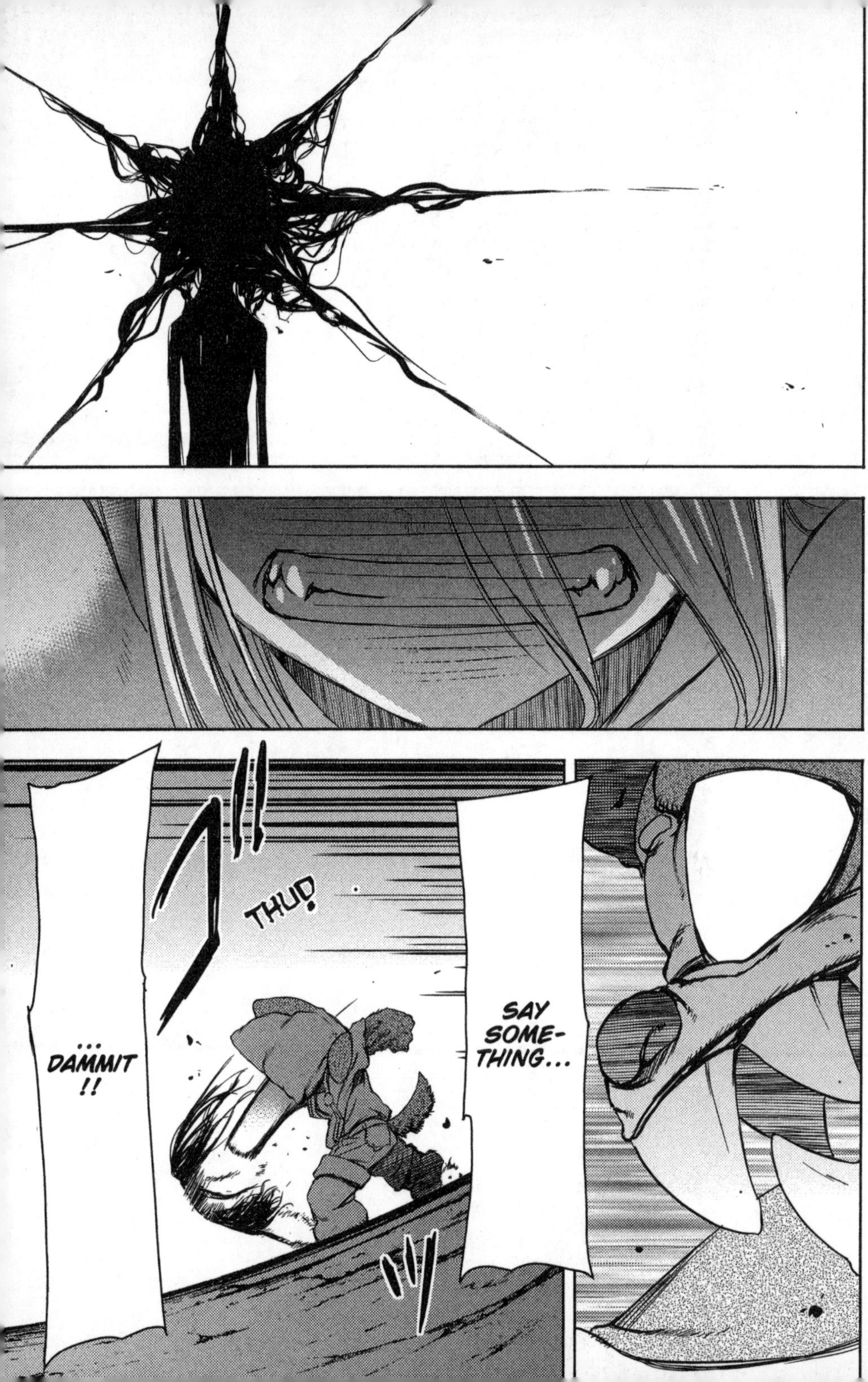
SAY SOMETHING...
THUD
...DAMMIT!!

WHY DID YOU ERASE OUR MEMORY?!

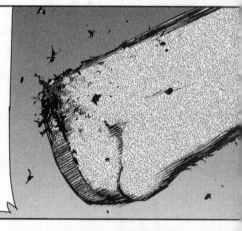

I KNOW THAT'S NOT SOMETHING YOU'D JUST DO BECAUSE YOU WANTED TO!

YOU WERE TRYING TO PROTECT SOMEONE...

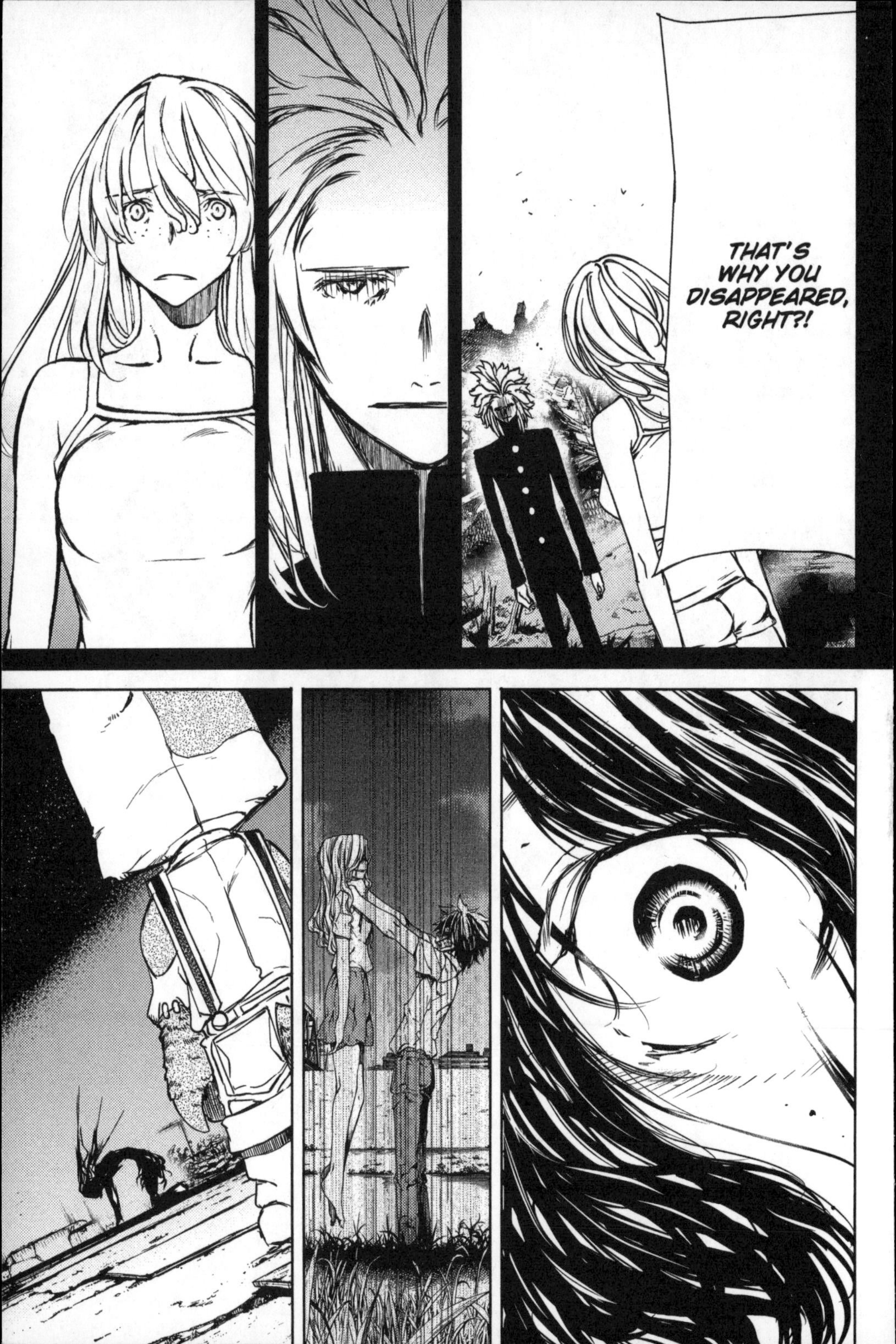
THAT'S WHY YOU DISAPPEARED, RIGHT?!

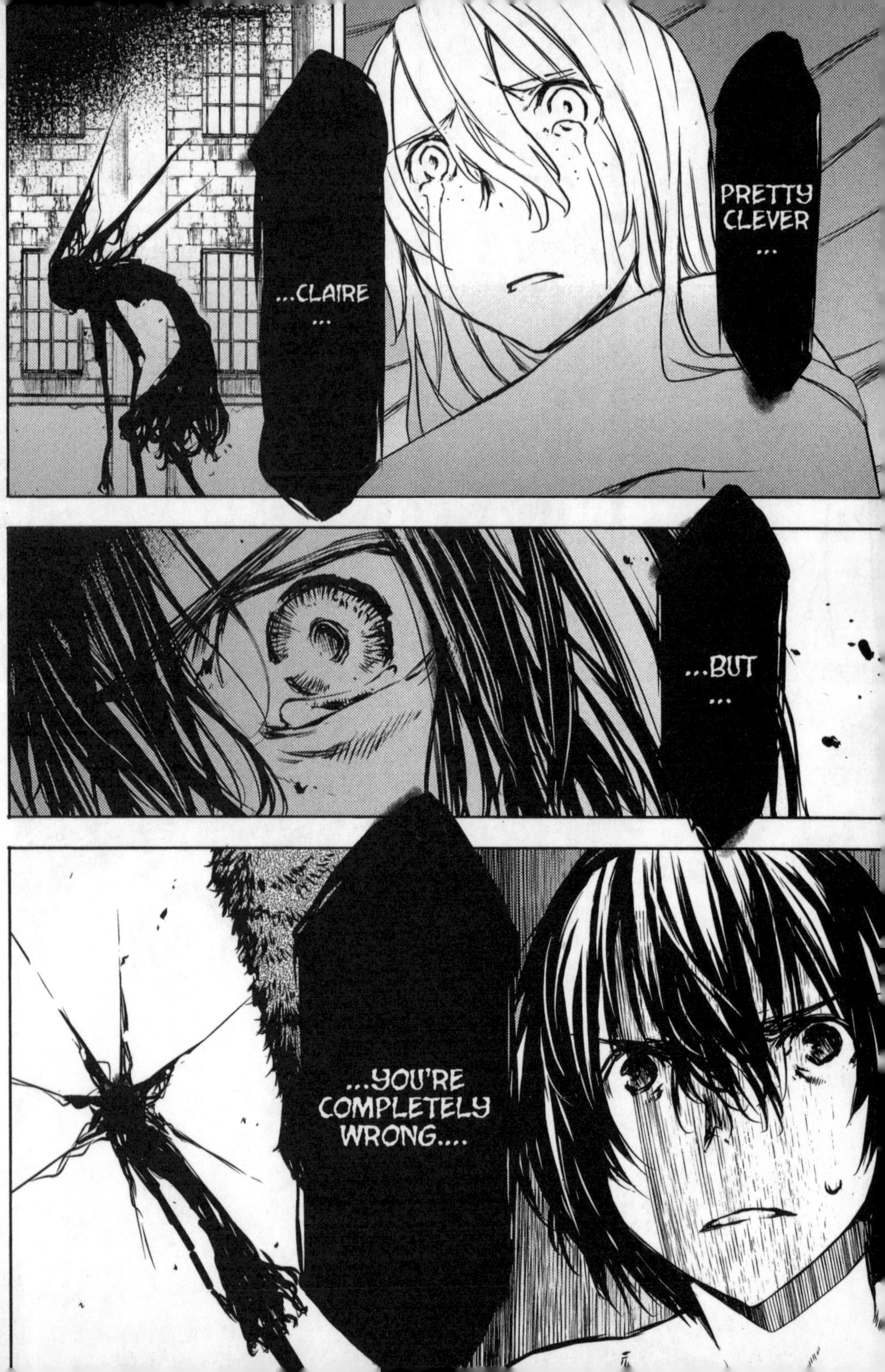
PRETTY CLEVER ...
...CLAIRE ...
...BUT ...
...YOU'RE COMPLETELY WRONG....

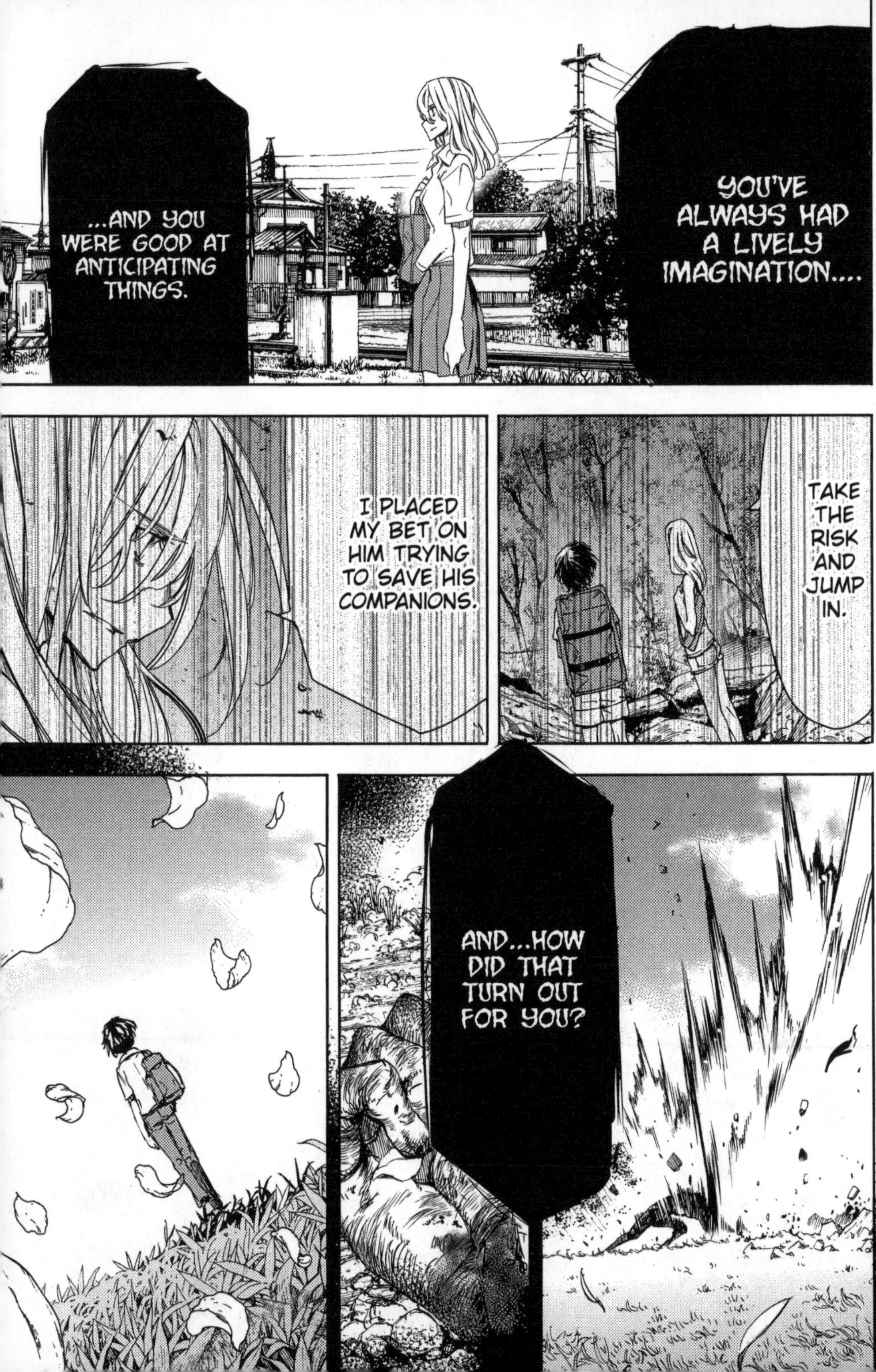
YOU'VE ALWAYS HAD A LIVELY IMAGINATION....
...AND YOU WERE GOOD AT ANTICIPATING THINGS.
TAKE THE RISK AND JUMP IN.
I PLACED MY BET ON HIM TRYING TO SAVE HIS COMPANIONS.
AND...HOW DID THAT TURN OUT FOR YOU?

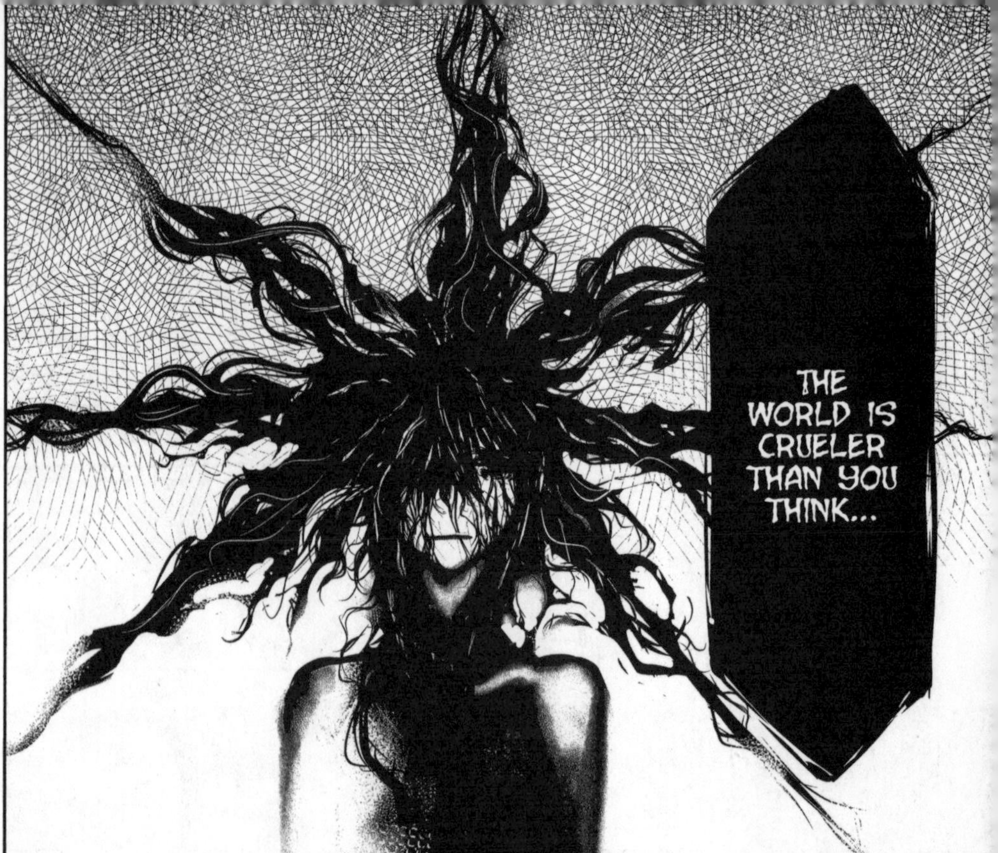
THE WORLD IS CRUELER THAN YOU THINK...
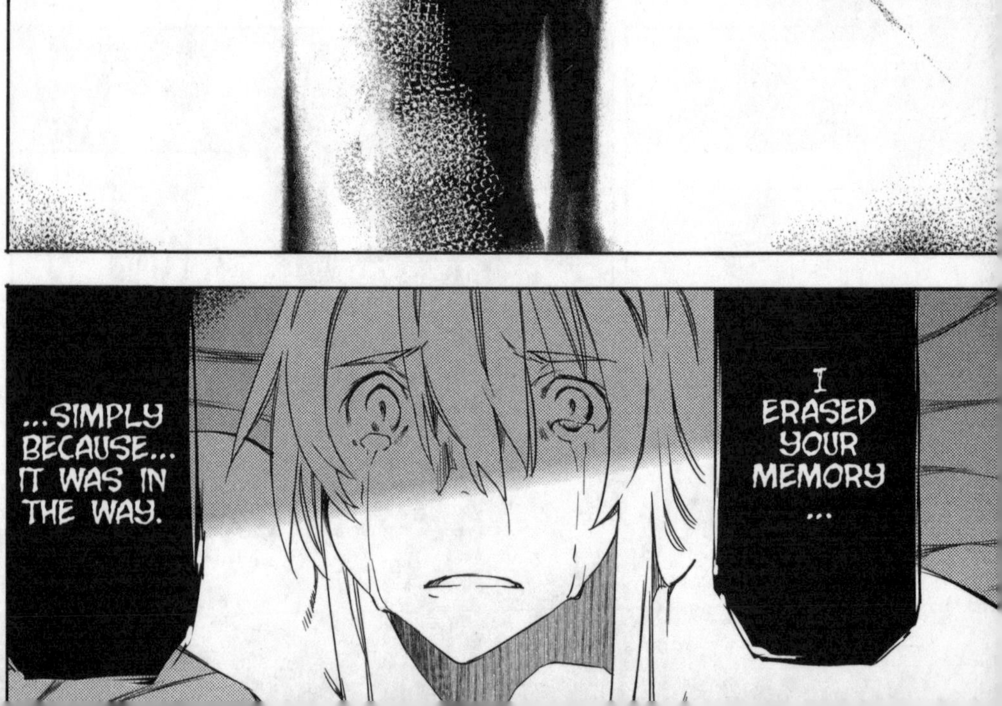
I ERASED YOUR MEMORY ...
...SIMPLY BECAUSE... IT WAS IN THE WAY.

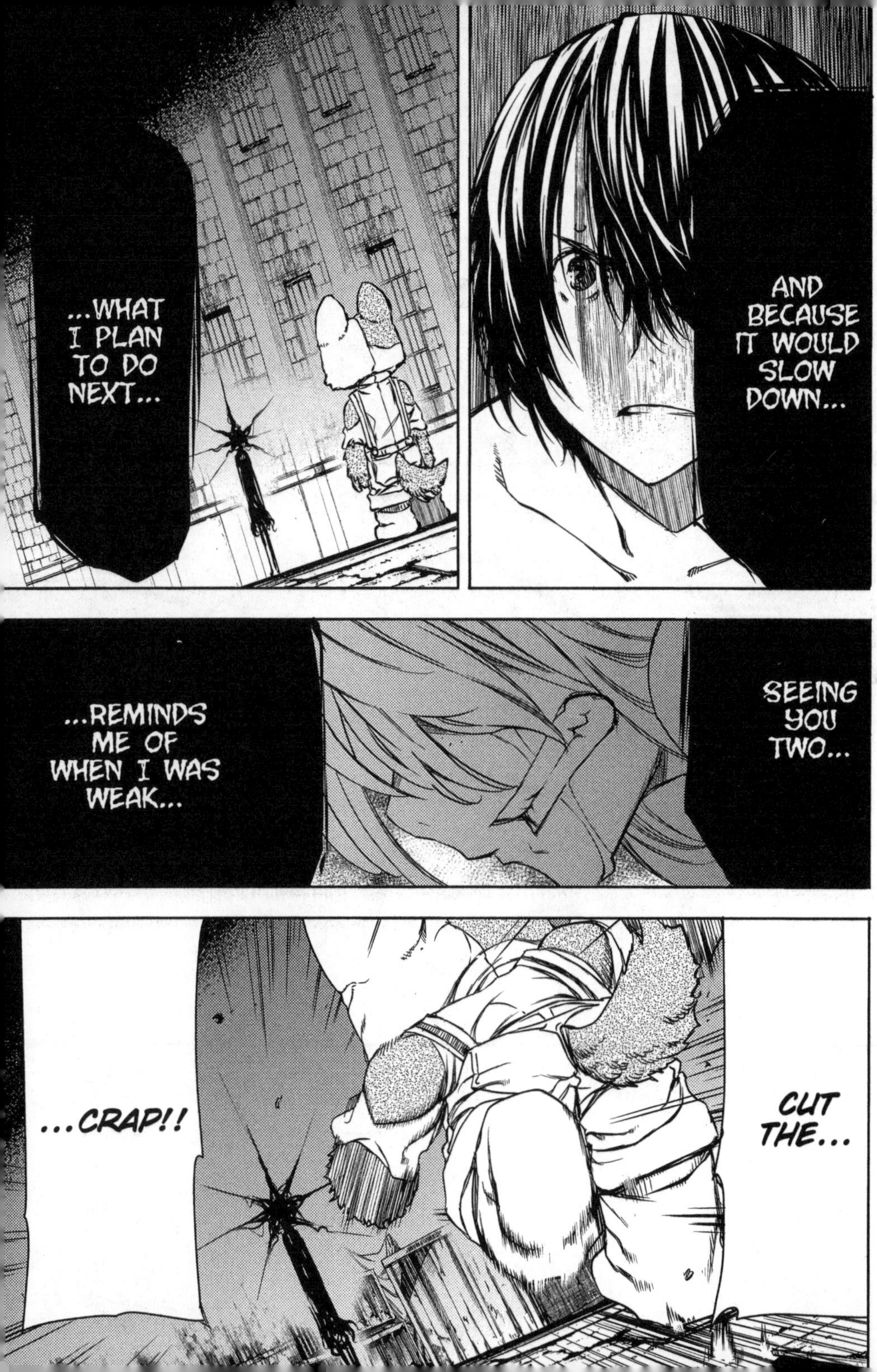
AND BECAUSE IT WOULD SLOW DOWN...
...WHAT I PLAN TO DO NEXT...
SEEING YOU TWO...
...REMINDS ME OF WHEN I WAS WEAK...
CUT THE...
...CRAP!!

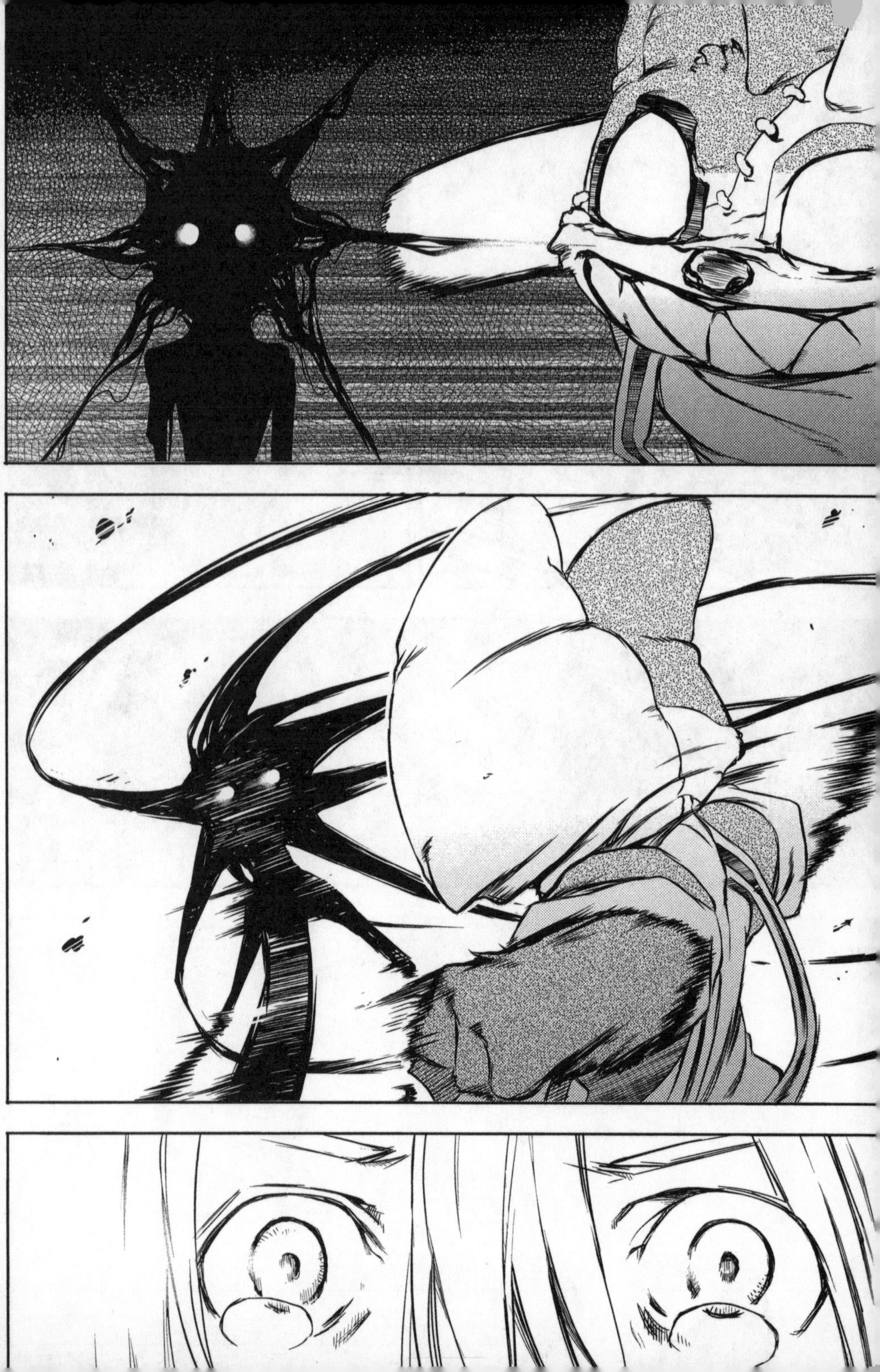

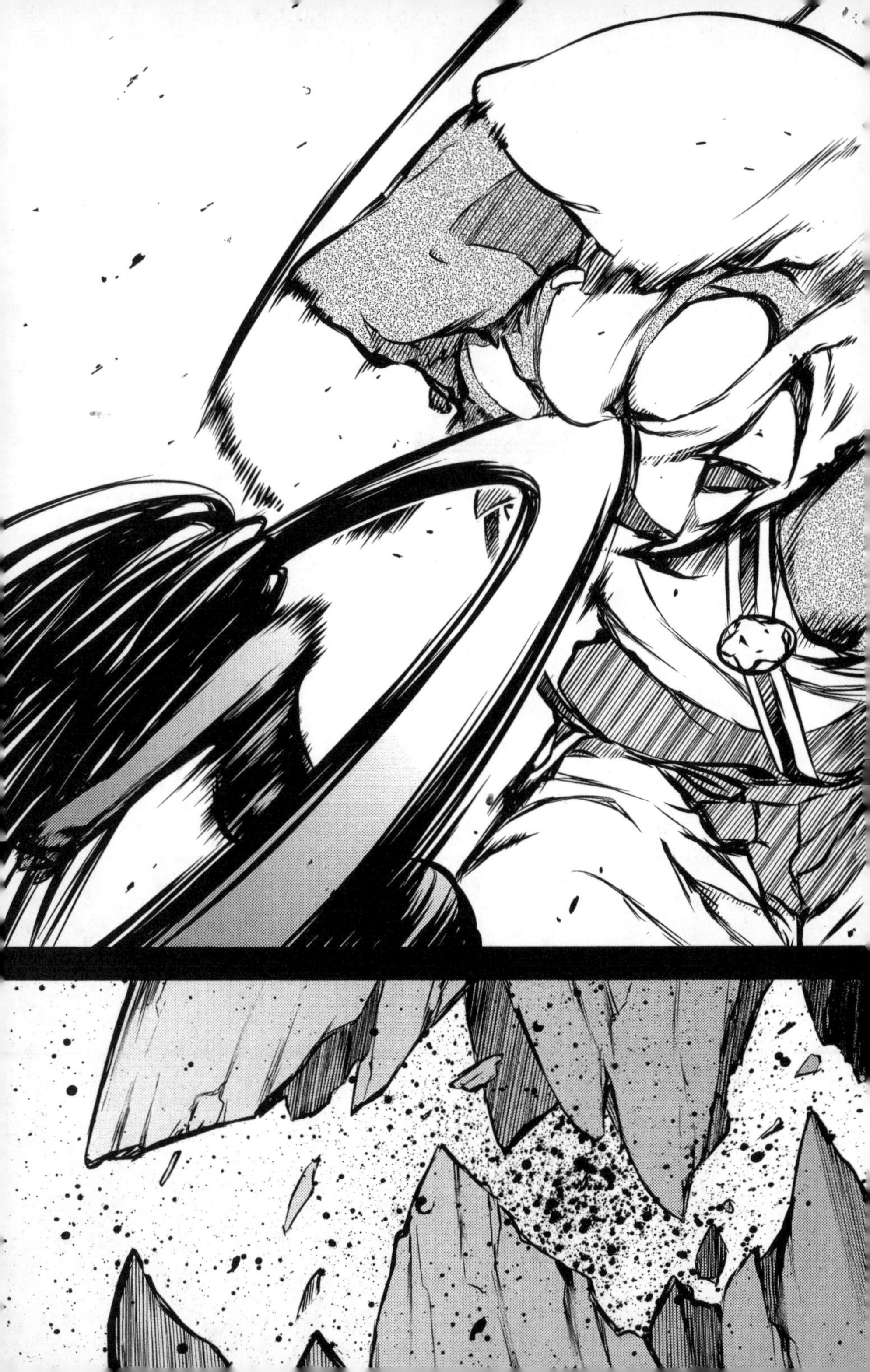

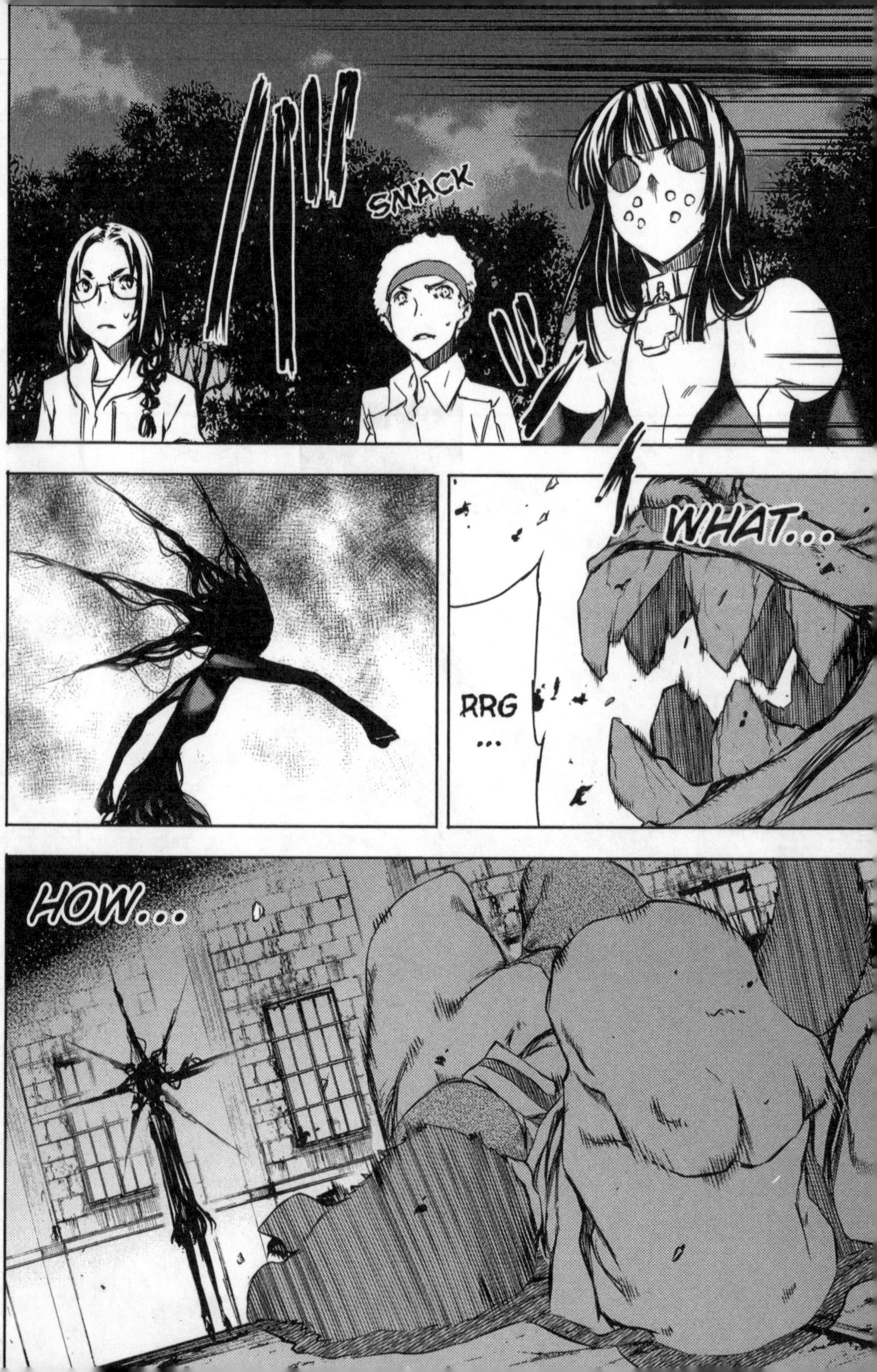
SMACK
WHAT...
RRG...
HOW...

I THOUGHT SHE COULDN'T SEE...?

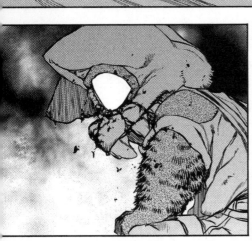

HOW DID SHE KNOW...WHERE WE WERE...

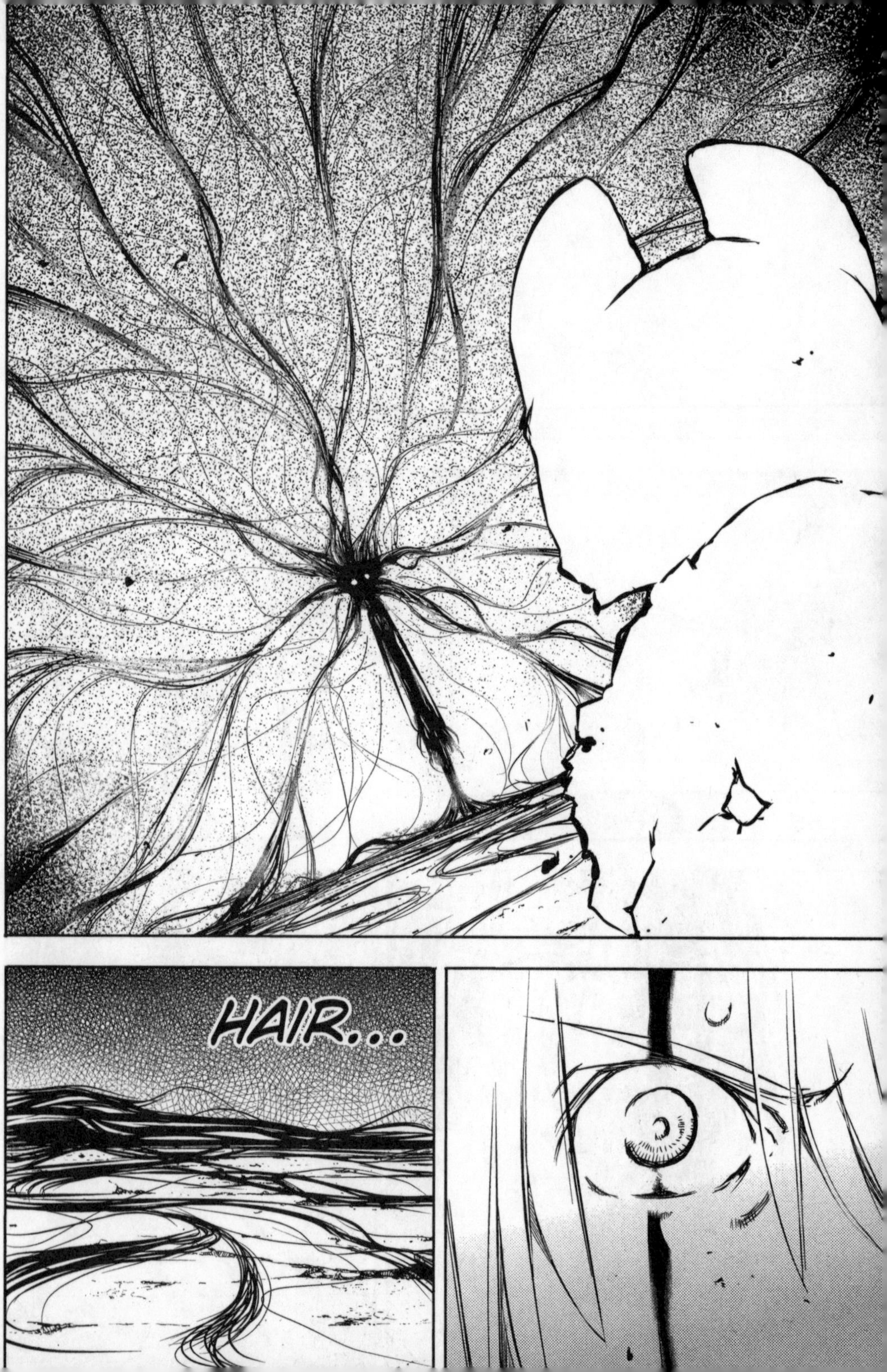
HAIR...

IS SHE USING IT AS SOME KIND OF RADAR...?

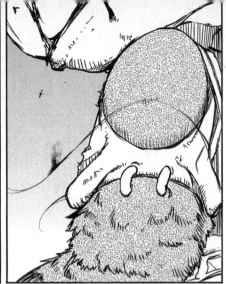

HONOKA...

...THAT'S THE NAME OF THE MONSTER YOU MET.

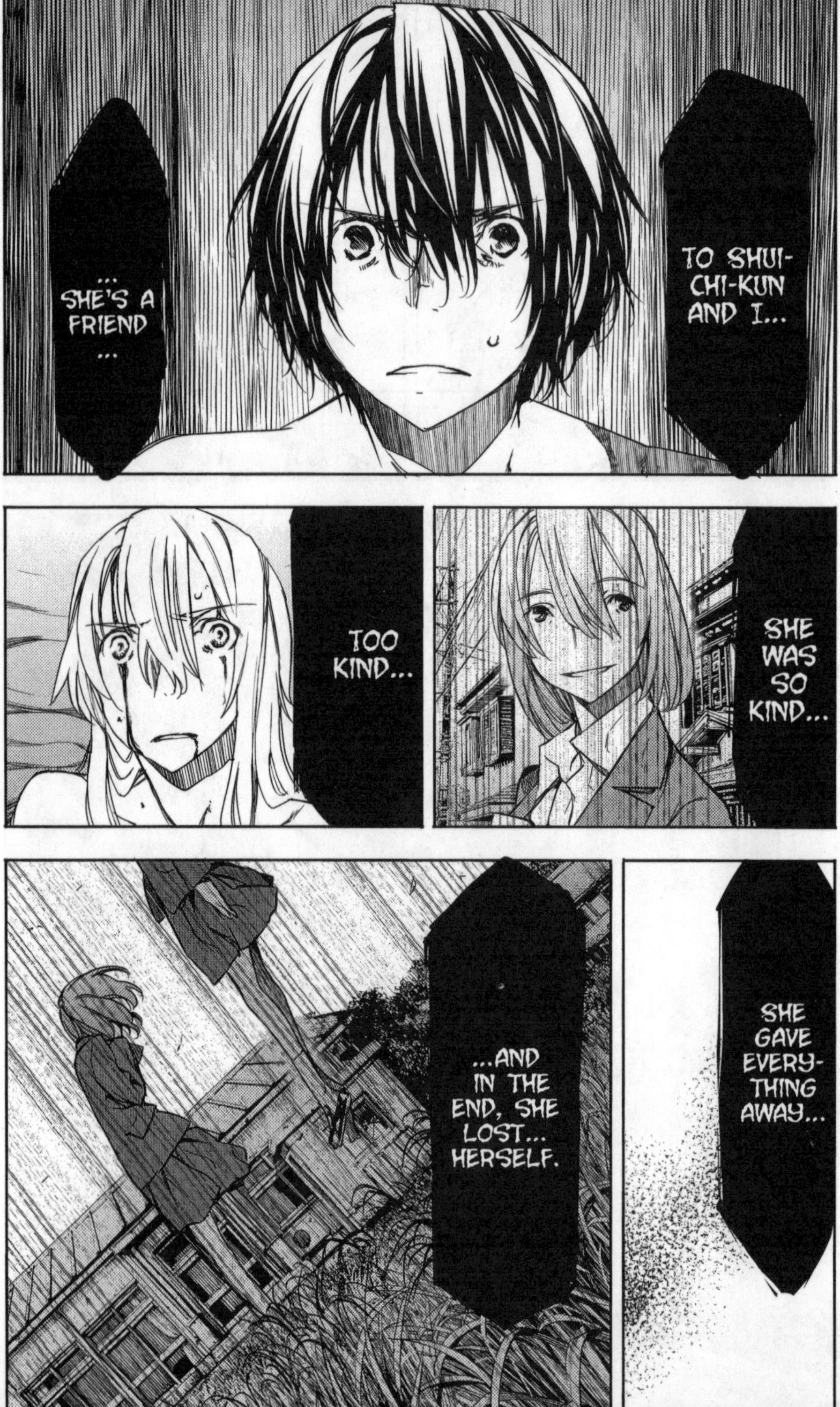
TO SHUI-CHI-KUN AND I...
...SHE'S A FRIEND ...
SHE WAS SO KIND...
TOO KIND...
SHE GAVE EVERY-THING AWAY...
...AND IN THE END, SHE LOST... HERSELF.

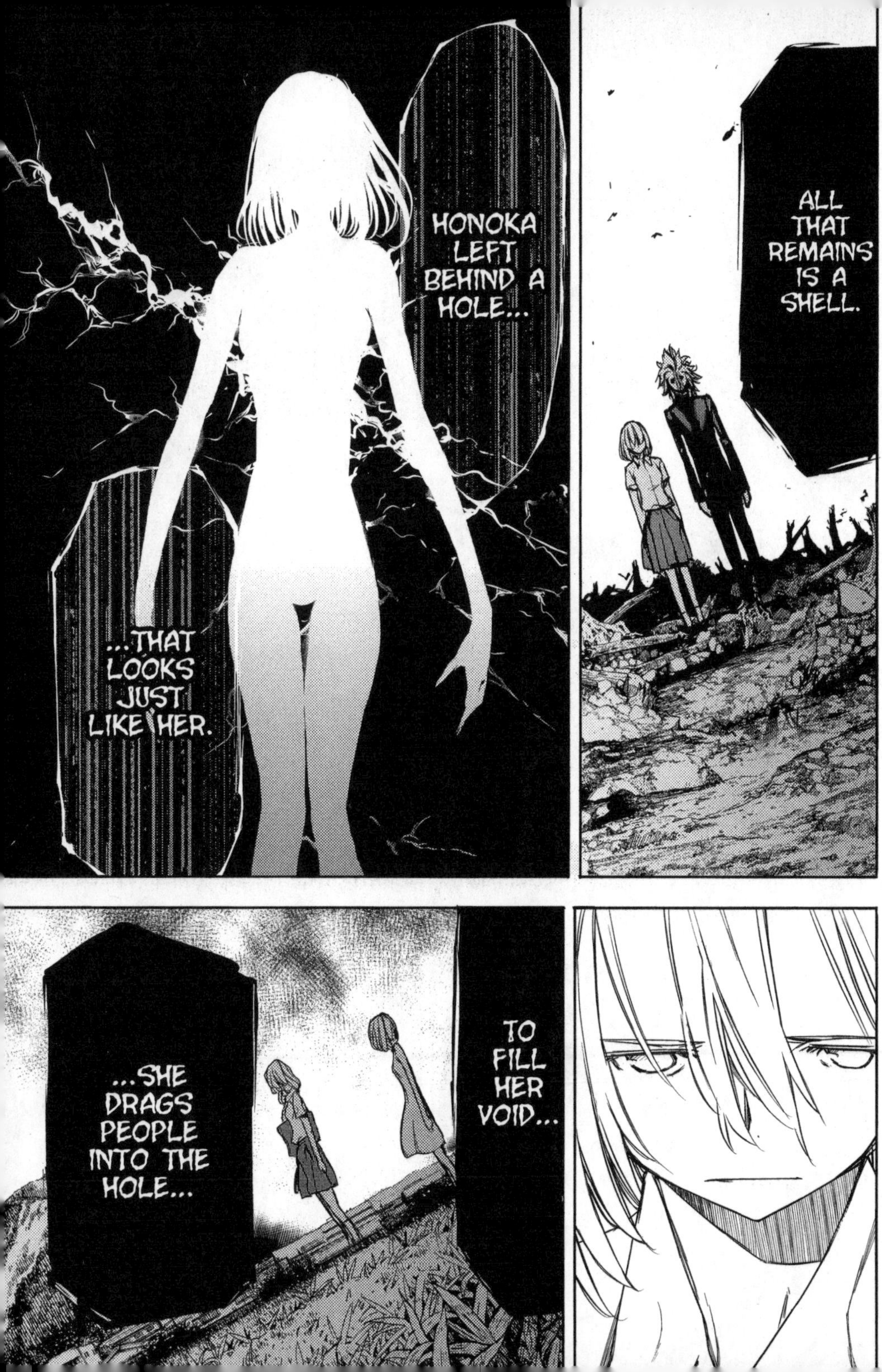
ALL THAT REMAINS IS A SHELL.
HONOKA LEFT BEHIND A HOLE...
...THAT LOOKS JUST LIKE HER.
TO FILL HER VOID...
...SHE DRAGS PEOPLE INTO THE HOLE...

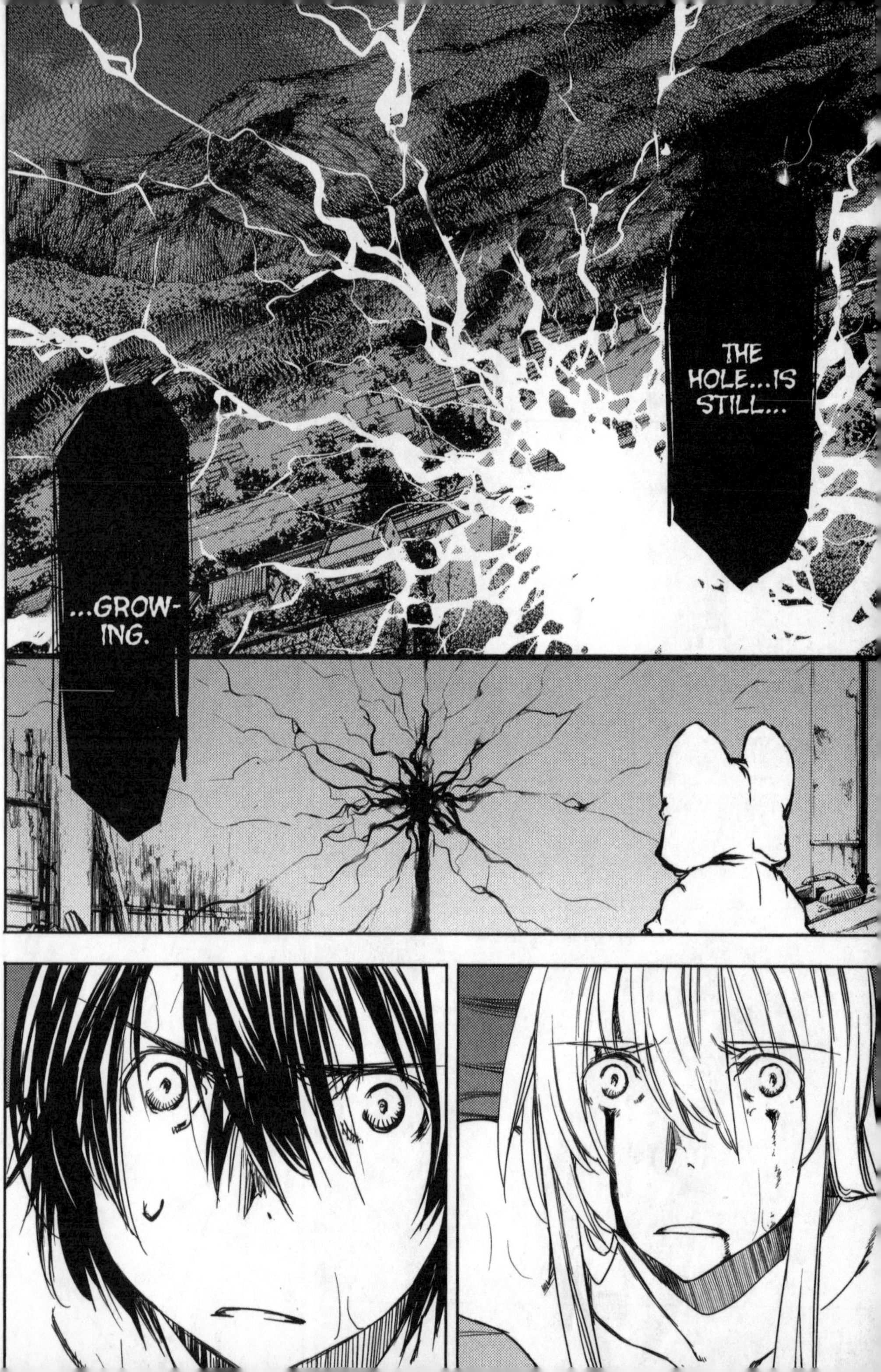
THE HOLE...IS STILL...
...GROW-ING.

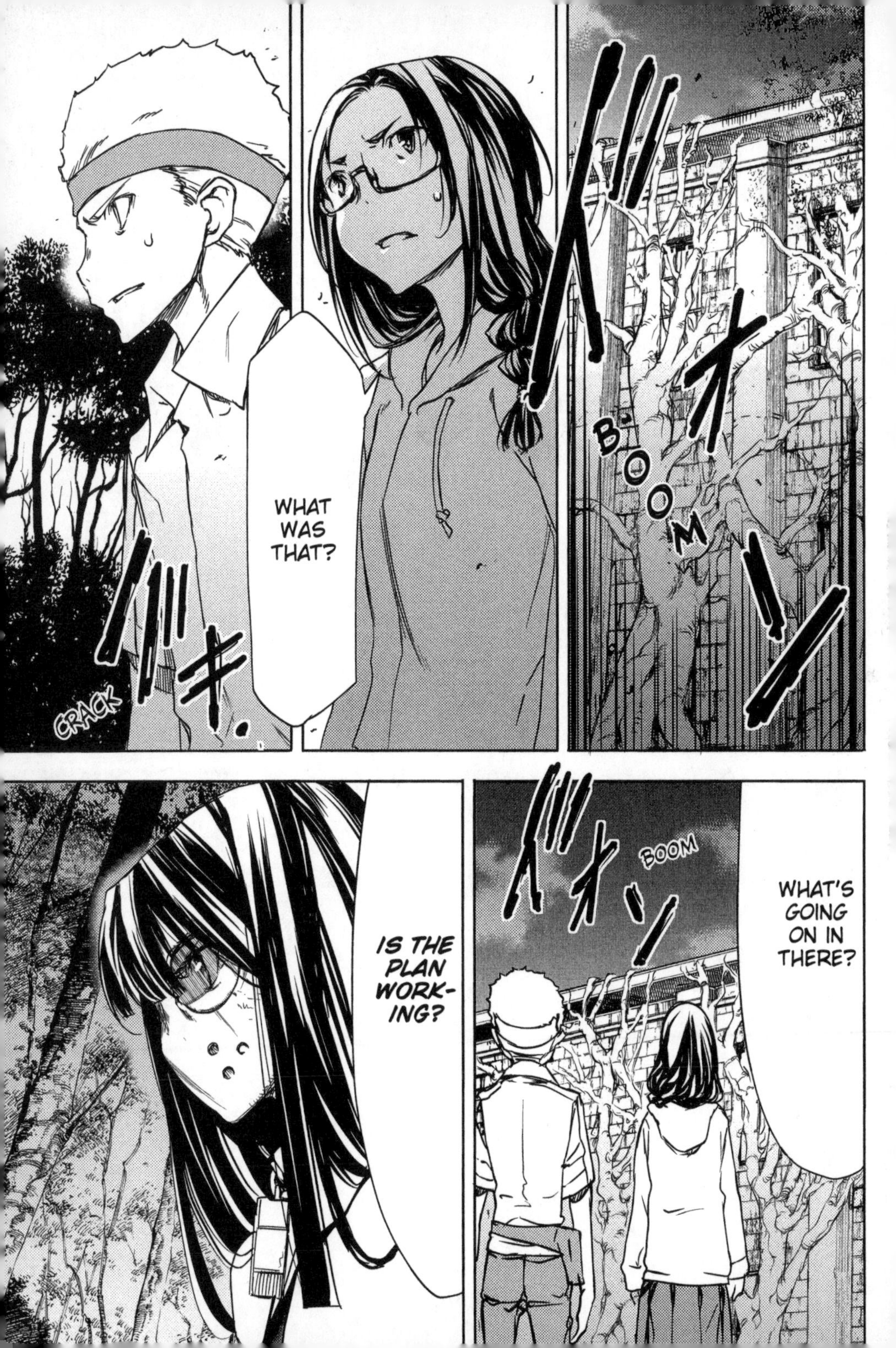
B-O-O-M
WHAT WAS THAT?
CRACK
BOOM
WHAT'S GOING ON IN THERE?
IS THE PLAN WORKING?

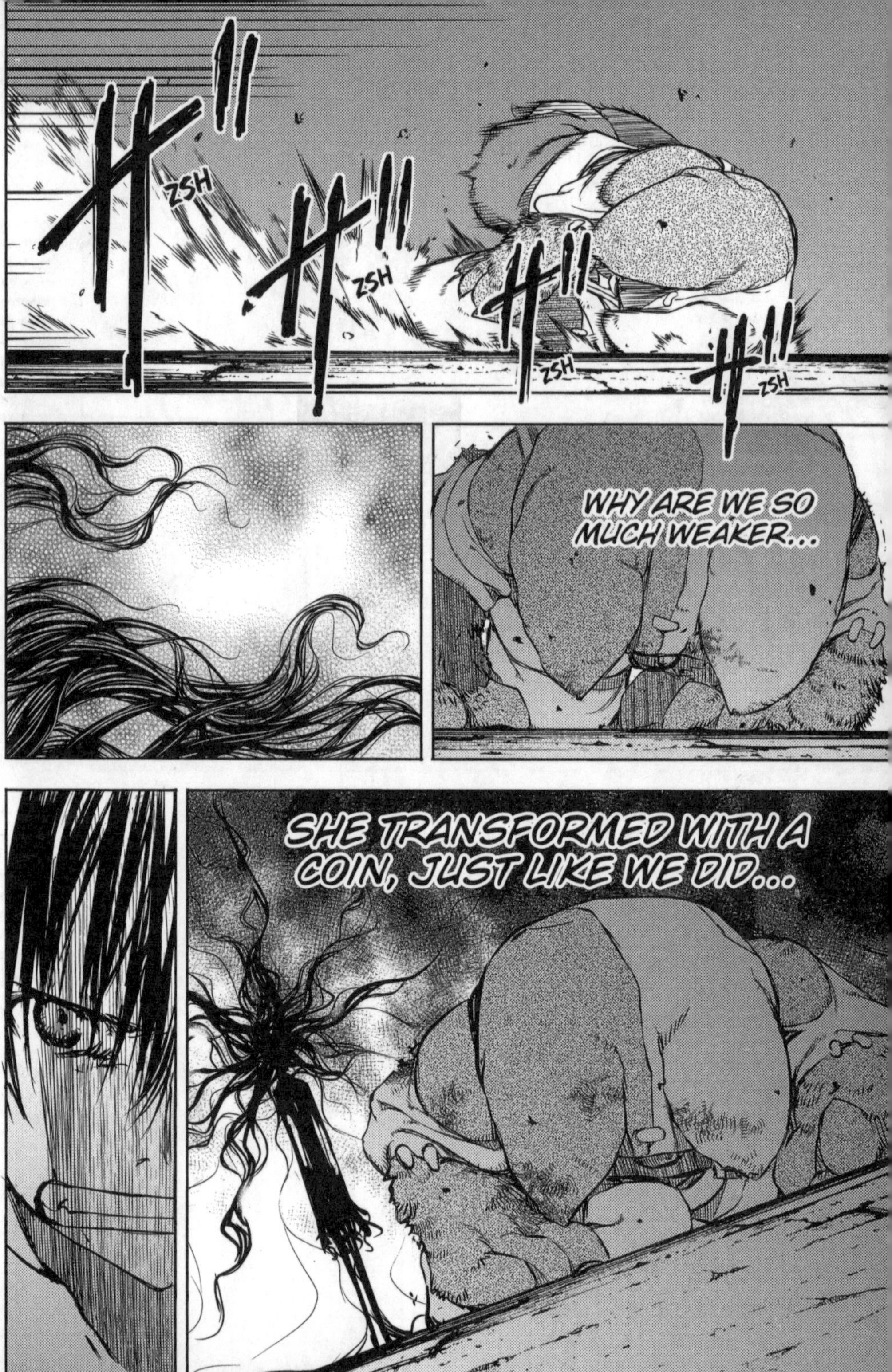
ZSH
ZSH
ZSH
ZSH
WHY ARE WE SO MUCH WEAKER...
SHE TRANSFORMED WITH A COIN, JUST LIKE WE DID...

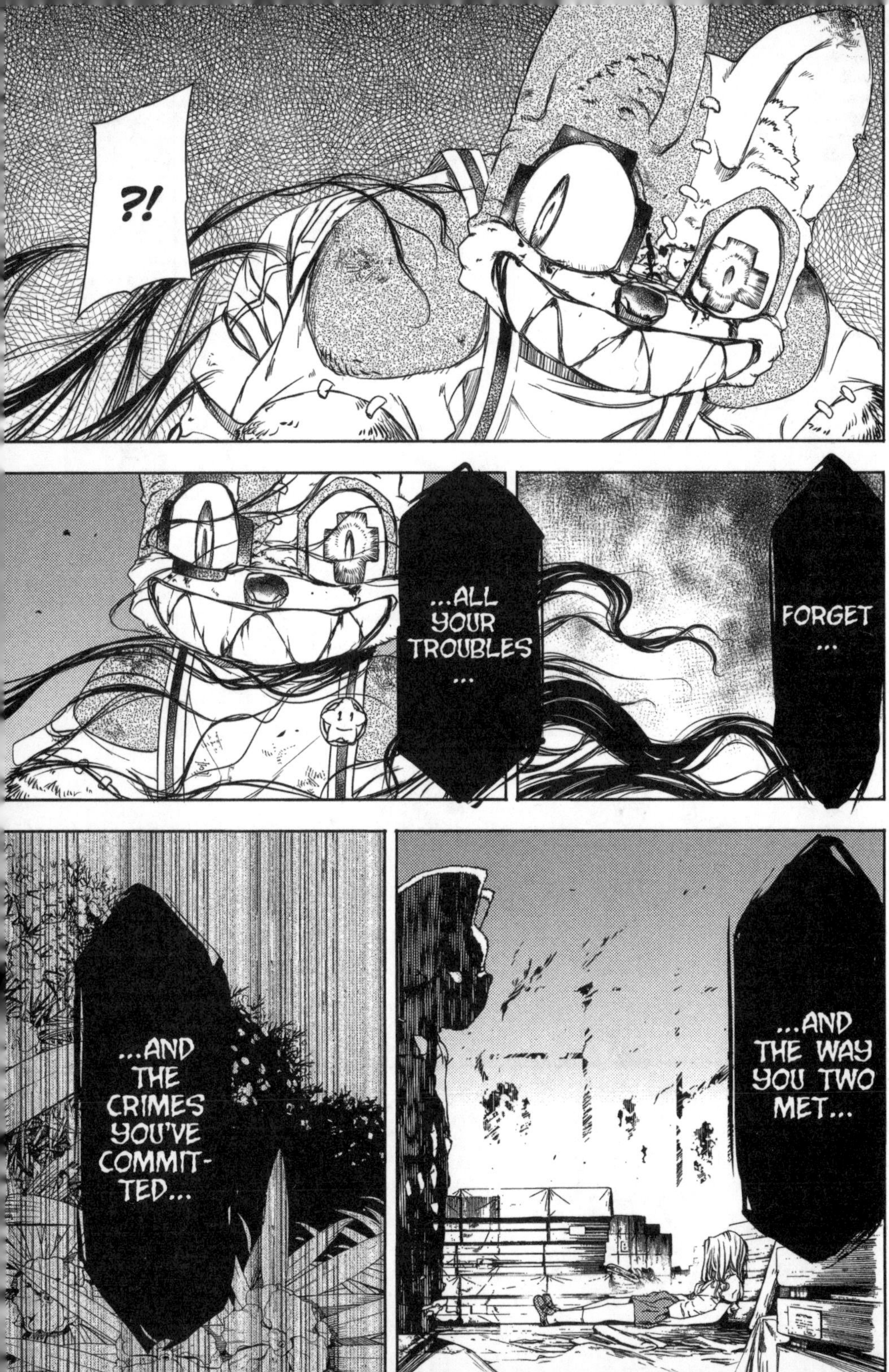
?!
FORGET ...
...ALL YOUR TROUBLES ...
...AND THE WAY YOU TWO MET...
...AND THE CRIMES YOU'VE COMMIT-TED...

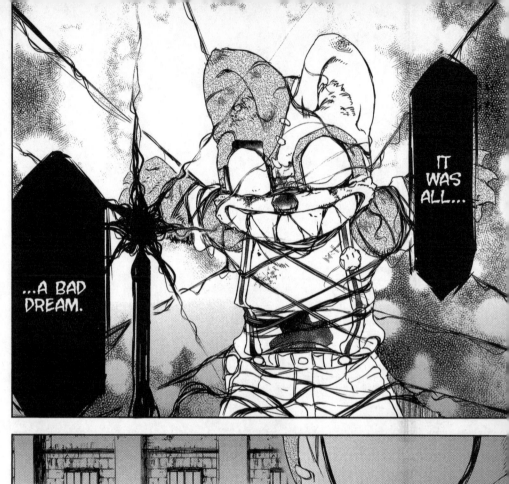

IT WAS ALL...

...A BAD DREAM.

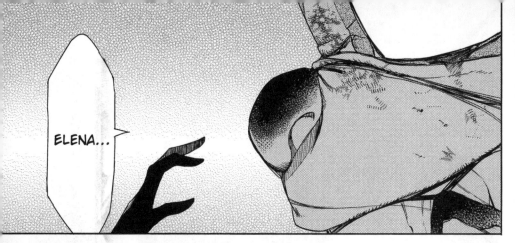

ELENA...

LET ME SEE YOUR FACE ONE LAST TIME...BEFORE YOU ERASE MY MEMORY...

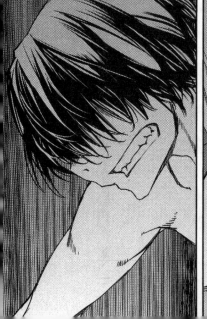

PLEASE ...

IT'S TOO DARK FOR YOU TO SEE ANYTHING.

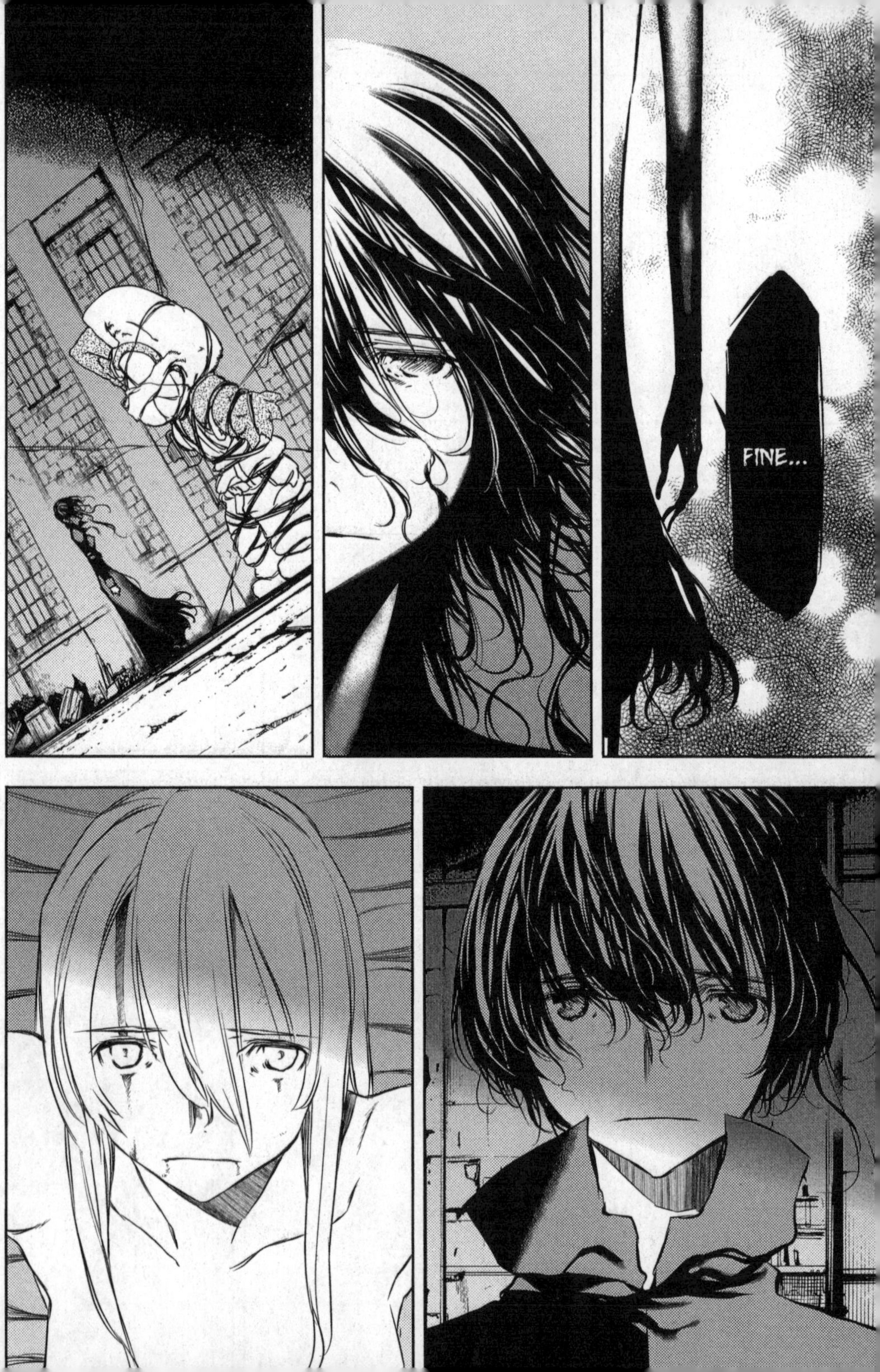
FINE...

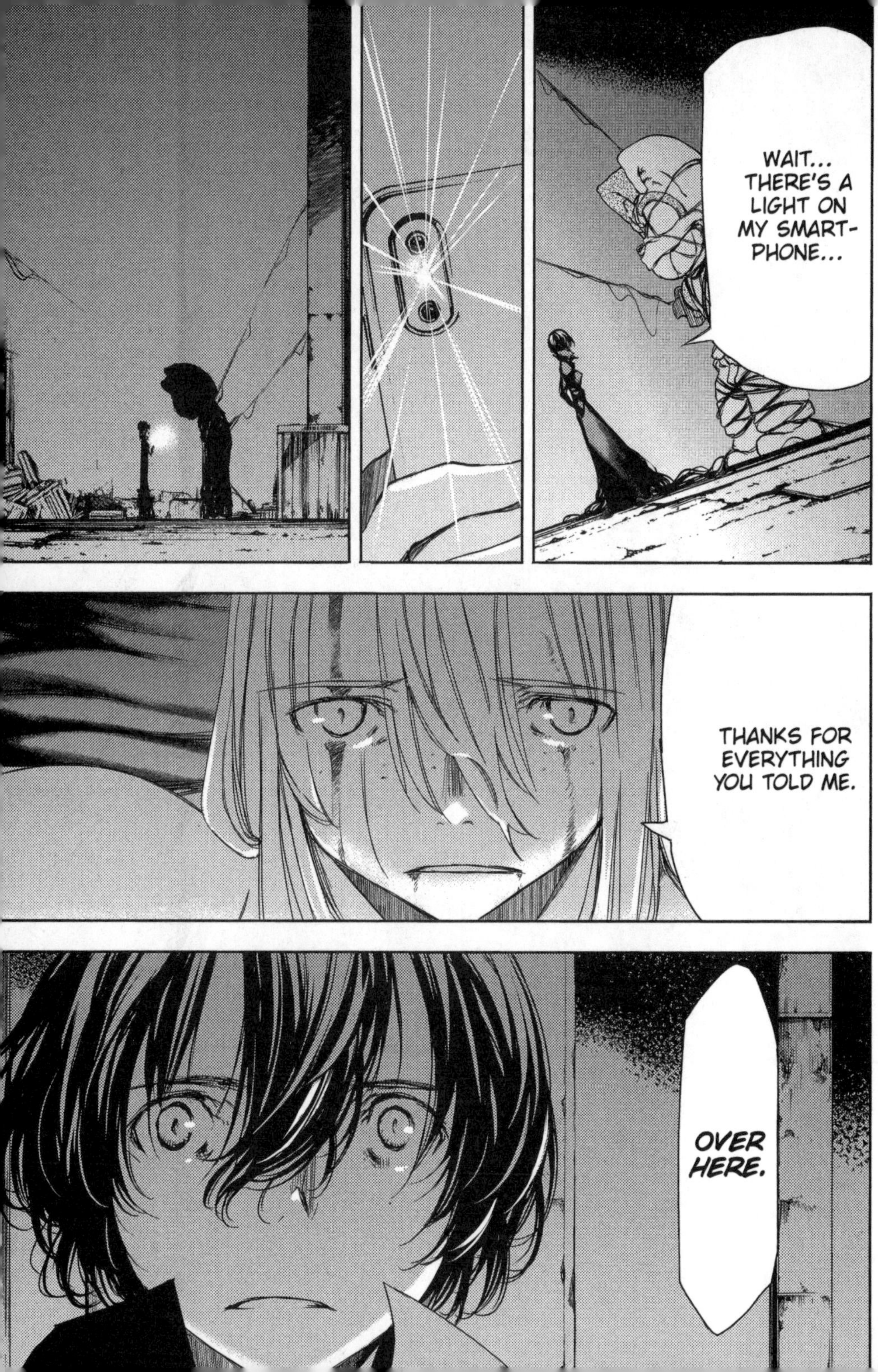
WAIT... THERE'S A LIGHT ON MY SMART-PHONE...
THANKS FOR EVERYTHING YOU TOLD ME.
OVER HERE.

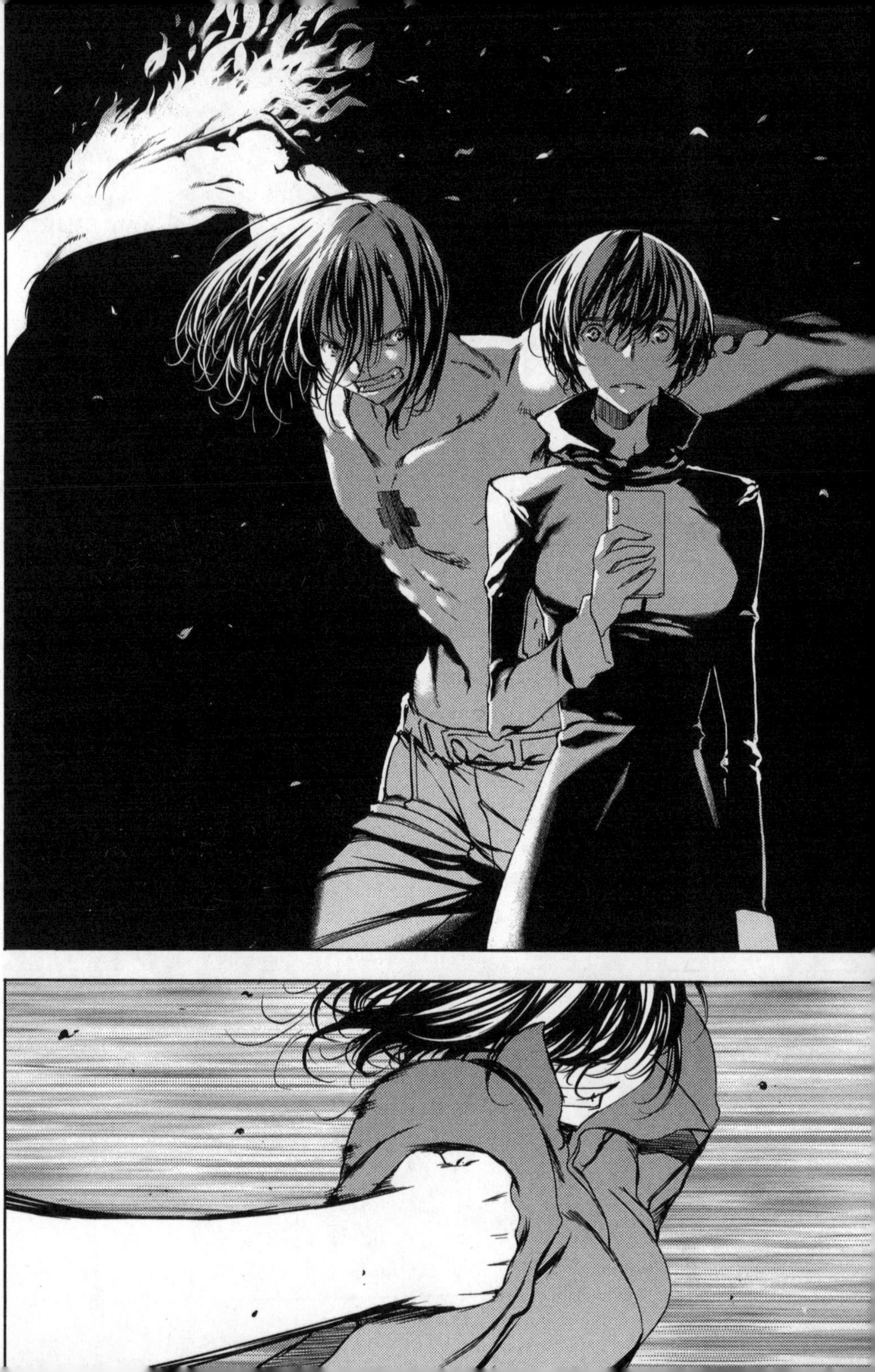

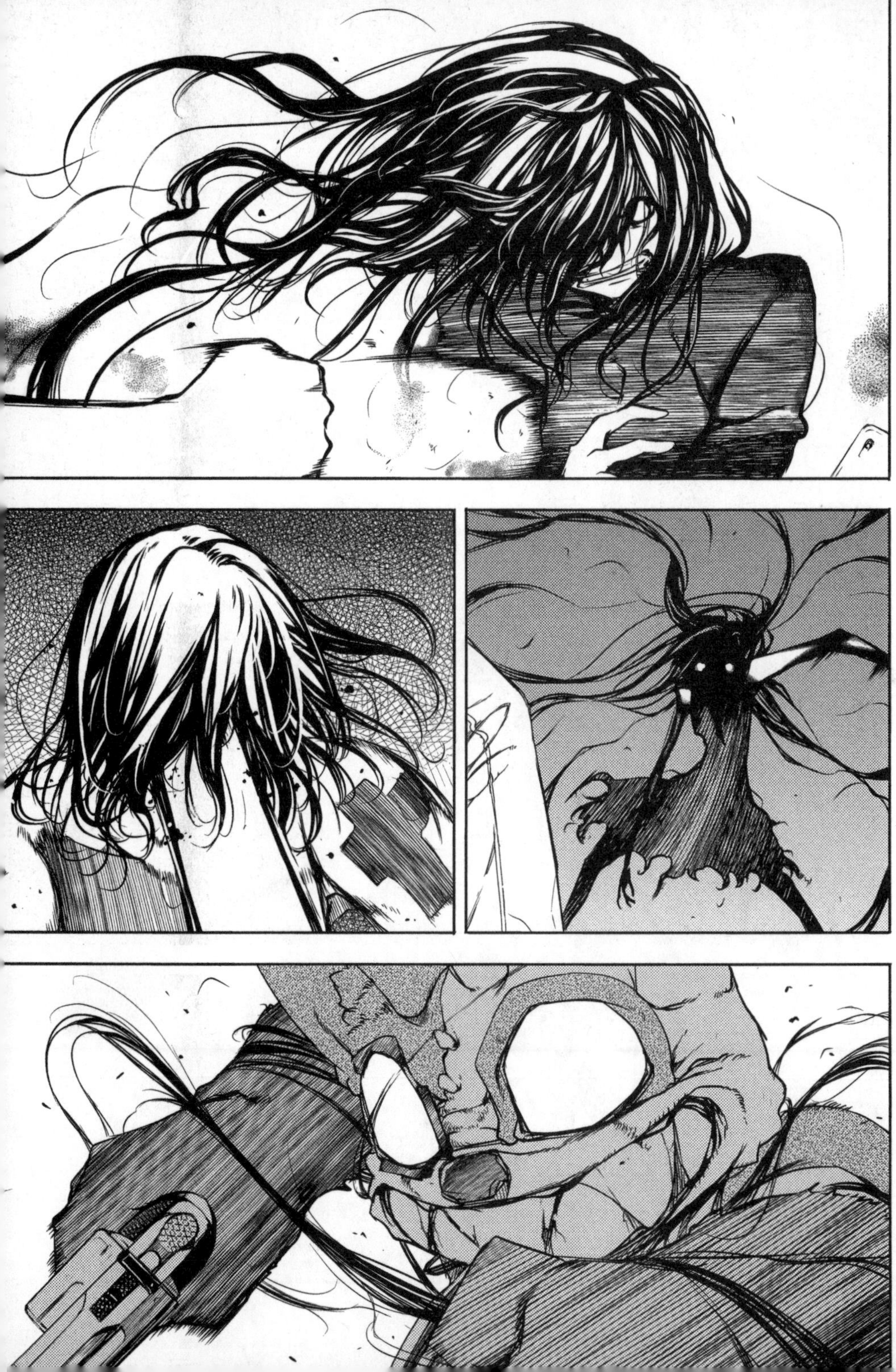

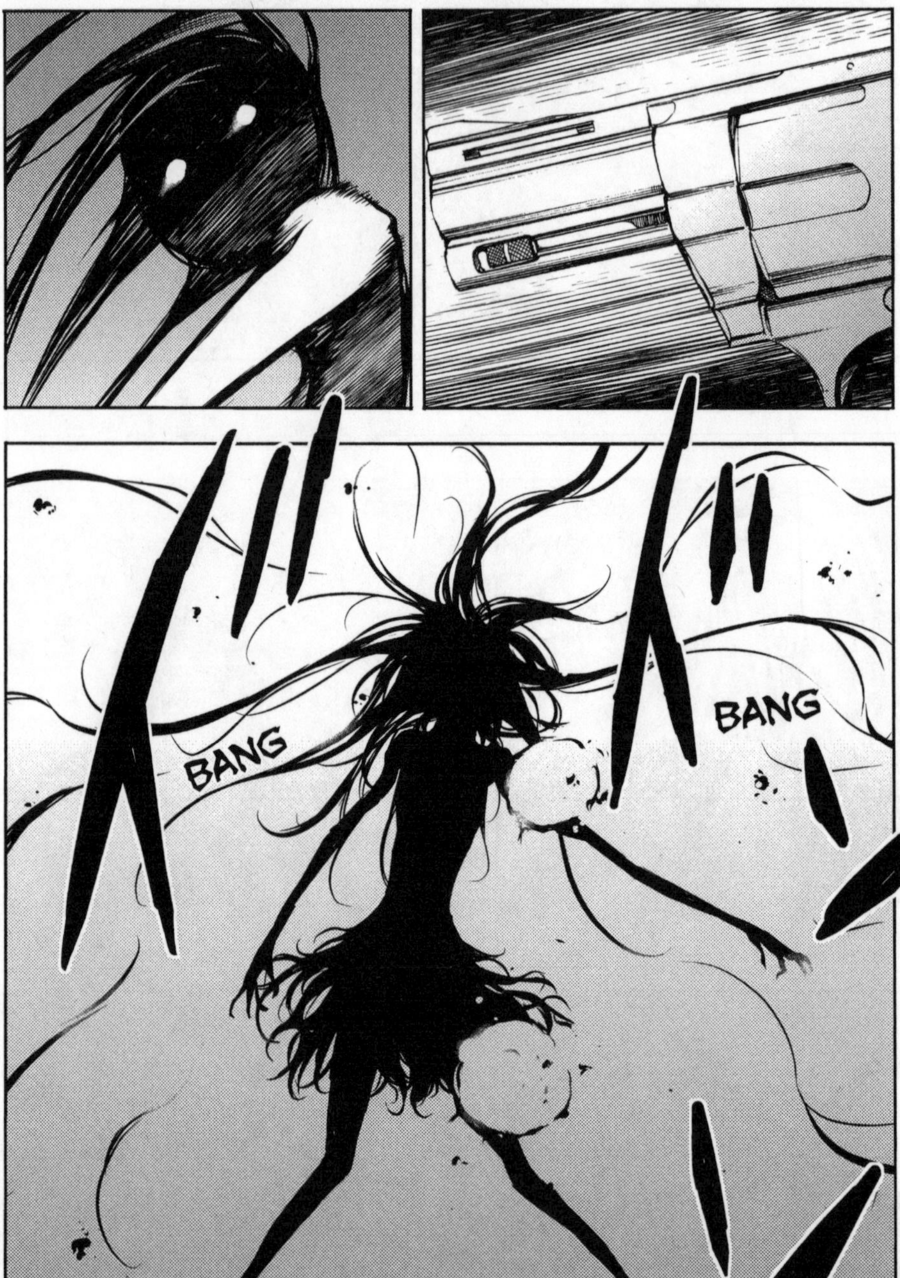
BANG
BANG

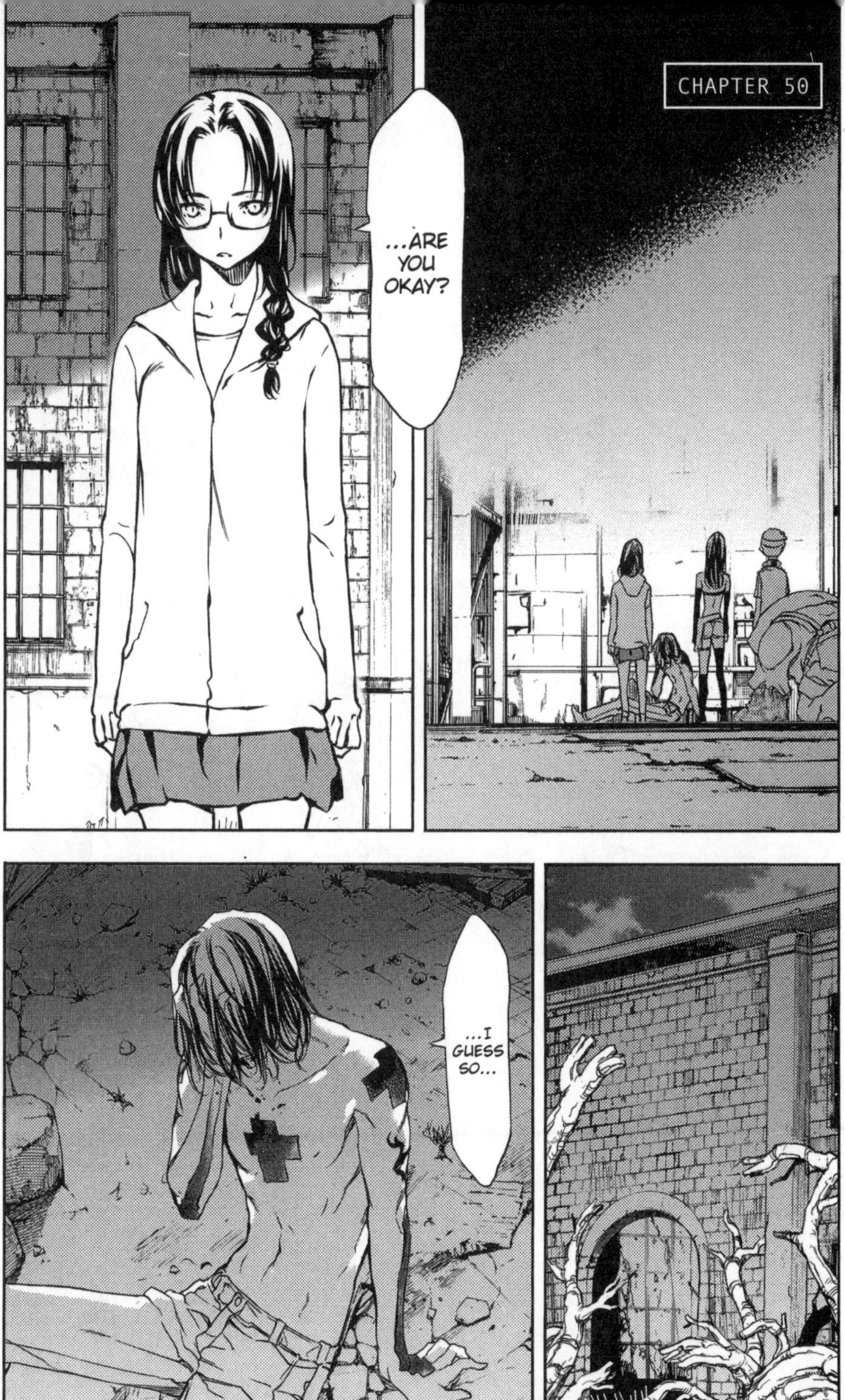
CHAPTER 50
...ARE YOU OKAY?
...I GUESS SO...

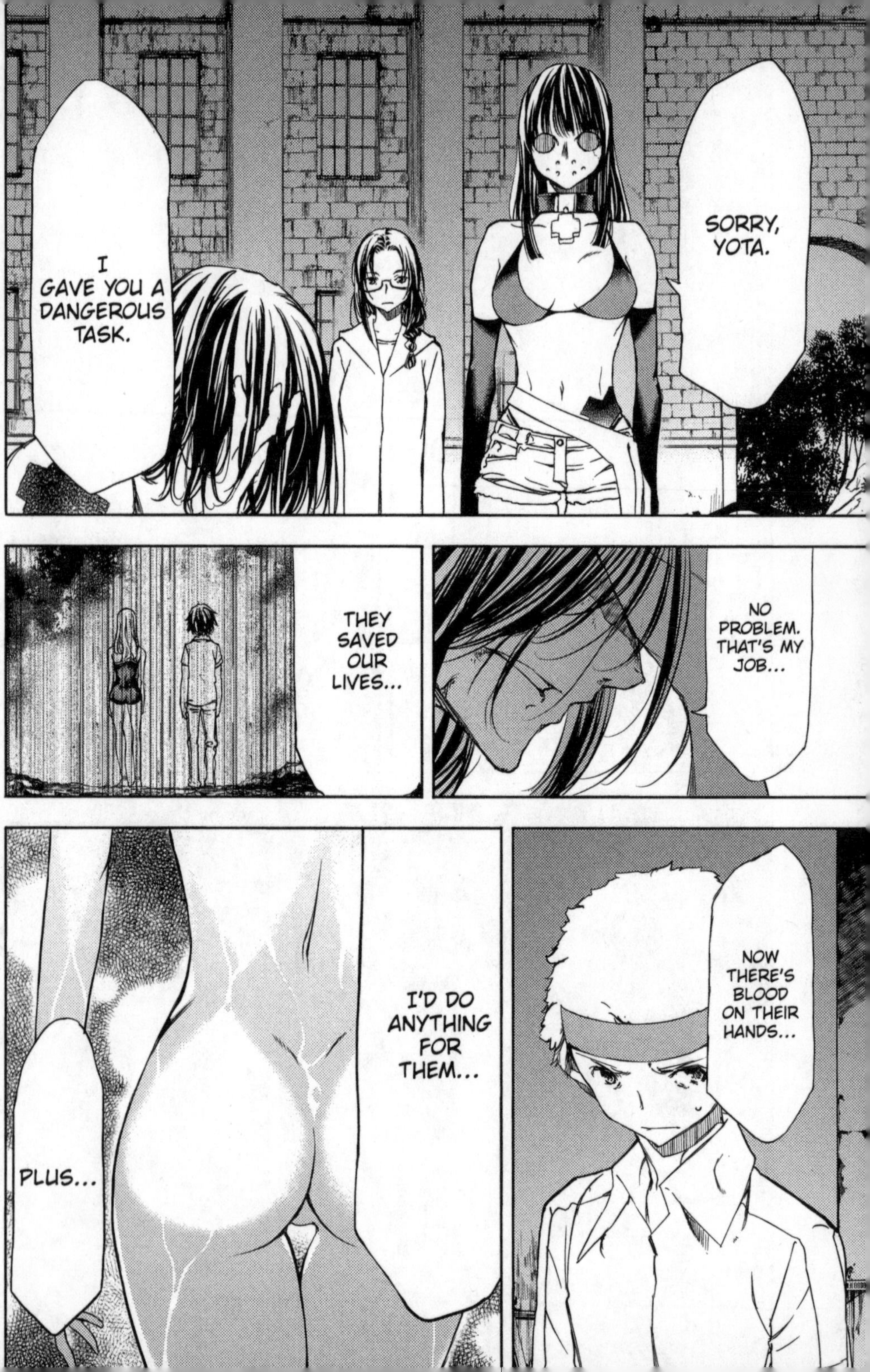
SORRY, YOTA.
I GAVE YOU A DANGEROUS TASK.
NO PROBLEM. THAT'S MY JOB...
THEY SAVED OUR LIVES...
NOW THERE'S BLOOD ON THEIR HANDS...
I'D DO ANYTHING FOR THEM...
PLUS...

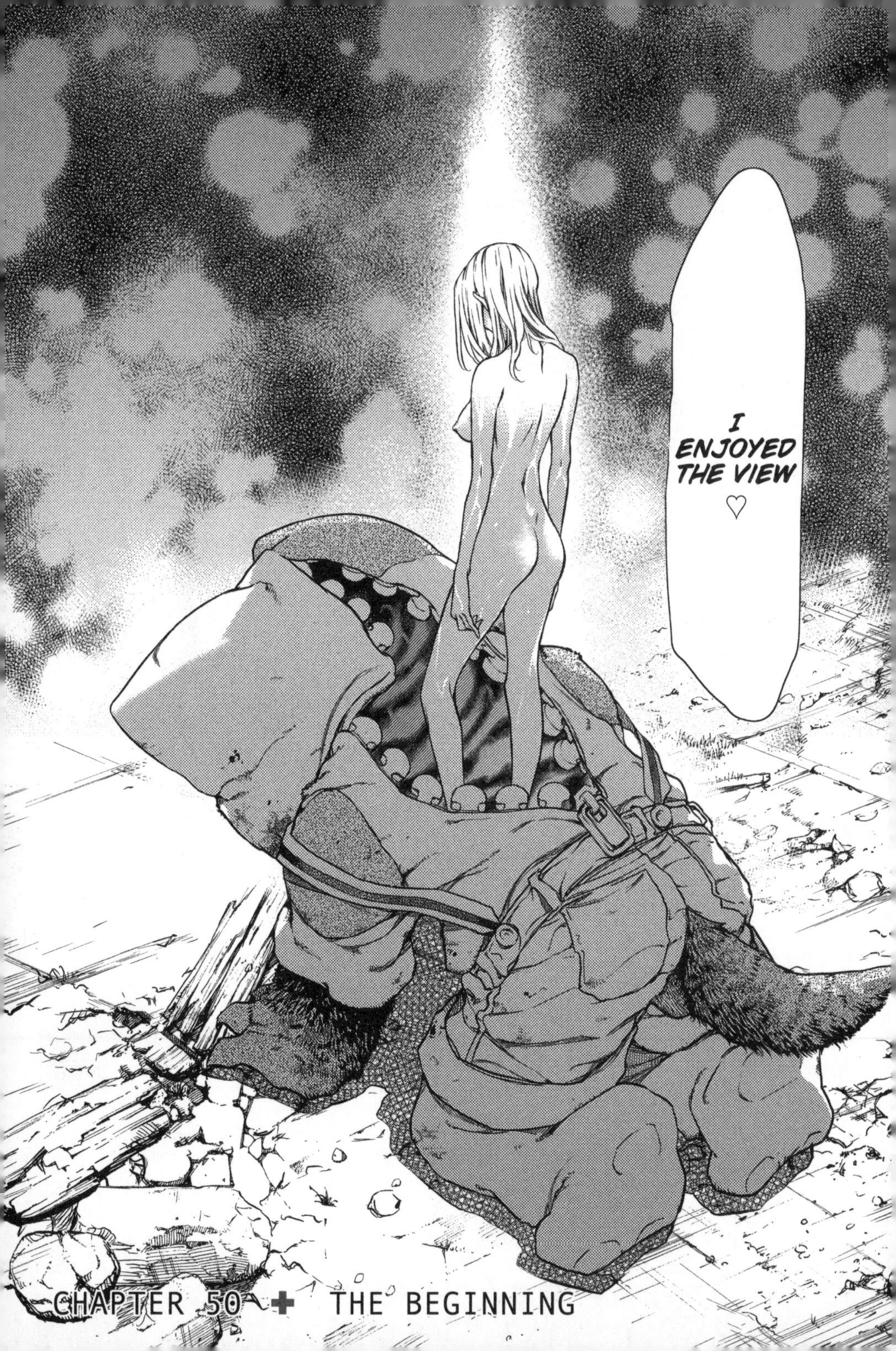
I ENJOYED THE VIEW ♡

CHAPTER 50 ✚ THE BEGINNING

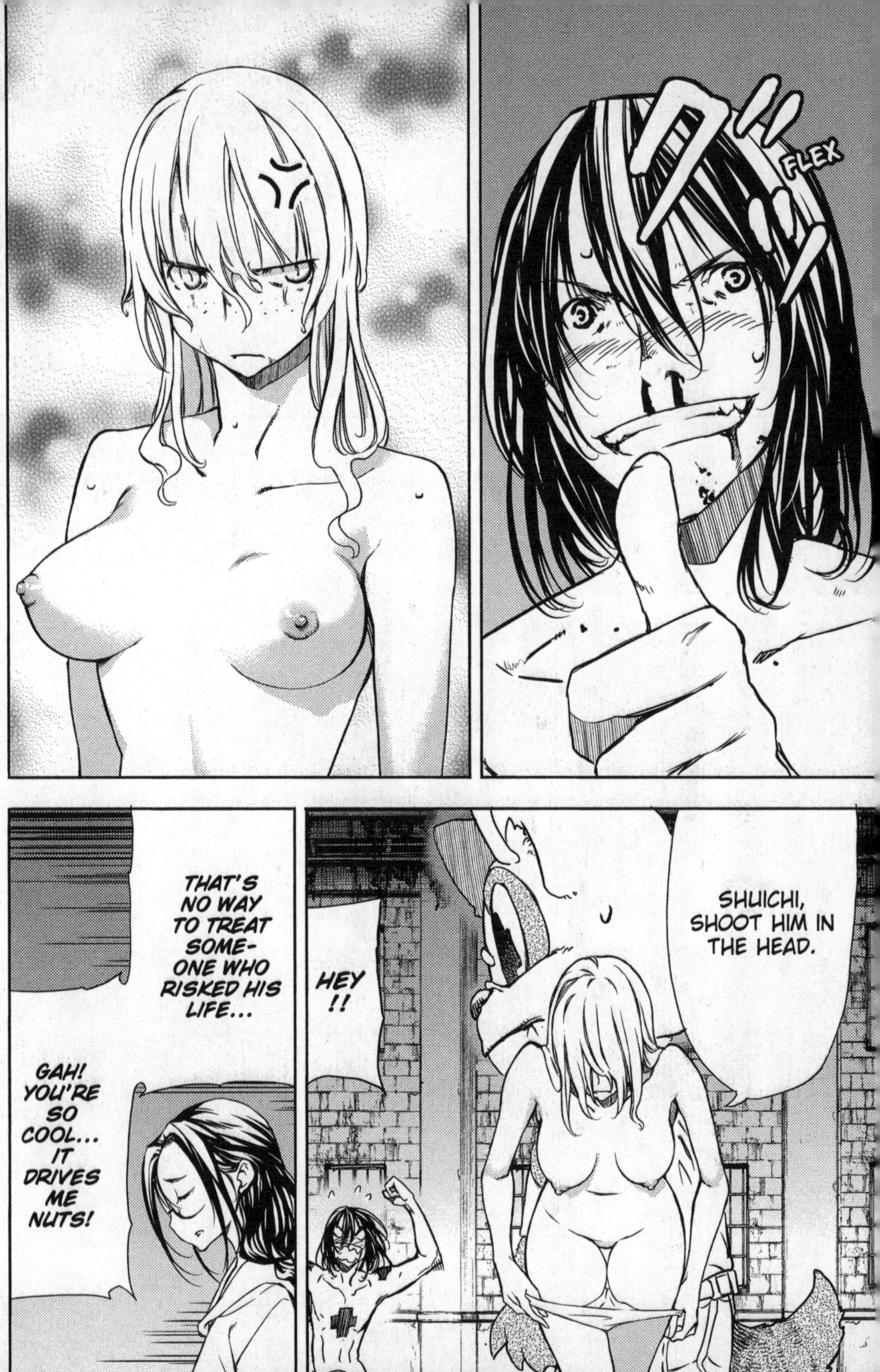
FLEX
SHUICHI, SHOOT HIM IN THE HEAD.
HEY !!
THAT'S NO WAY TO TREAT SOME-ONE WHO RISKED HIS LIFE...
GAH! YOU'RE SO COOL... IT DRIVES ME NUTS!

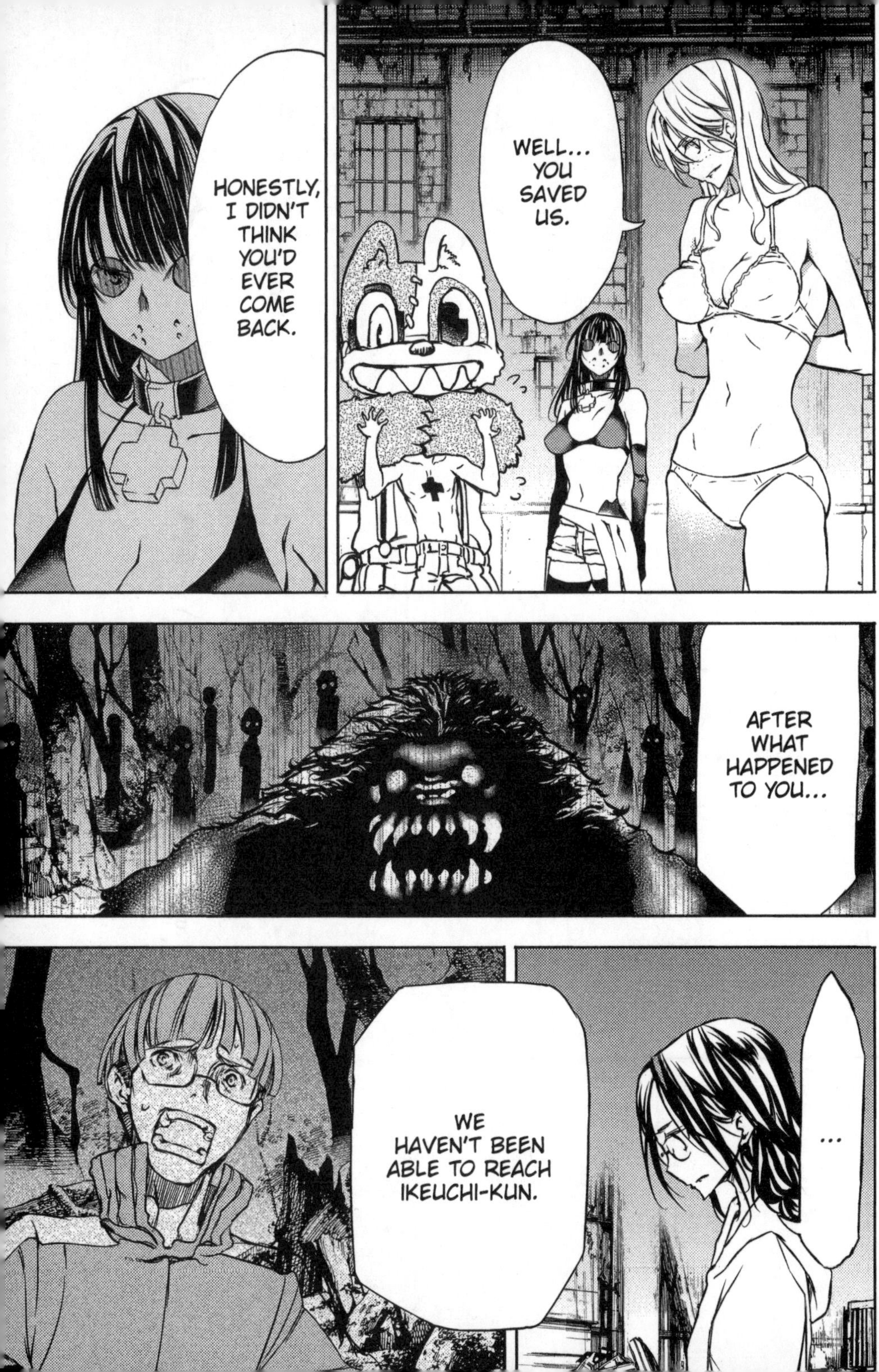
WELL... YOU SAVED US.
HONESTLY, I DIDN'T THINK YOU'D EVER COME BACK.
AFTER WHAT HAPPENED TO YOU...
...
WE HAVEN'T BEEN ABLE TO REACH IKEUCHI-KUN.

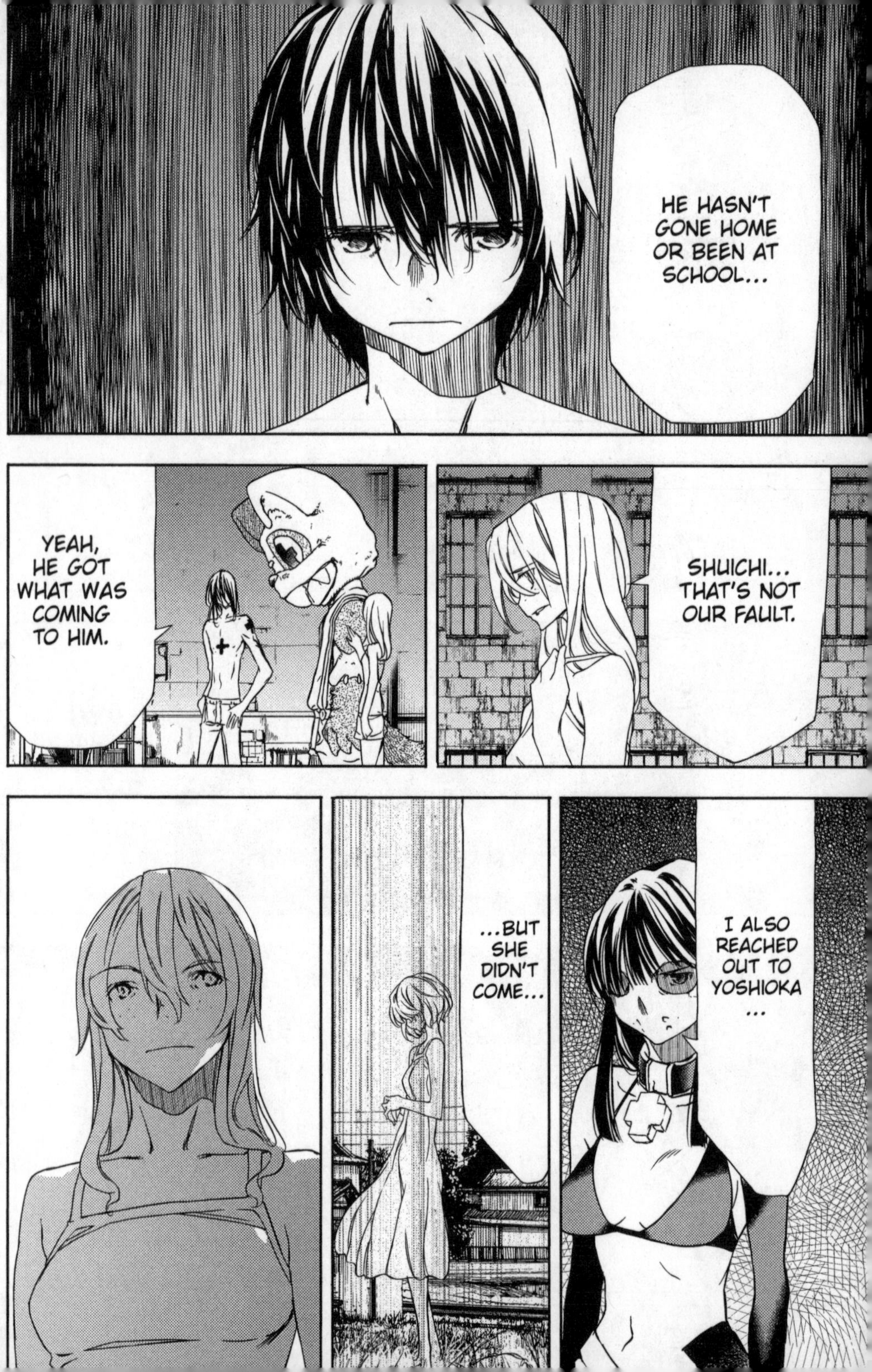
HE HASN'T GONE HOME OR BEEN AT SCHOOL...
SHUICHI... THAT'S NOT OUR FAULT.
YEAH, HE GOT WHAT WAS COMING TO HIM.
I ALSO REACHED OUT TO YOSHIOKA ...
...BUT SHE DIDN'T COME...

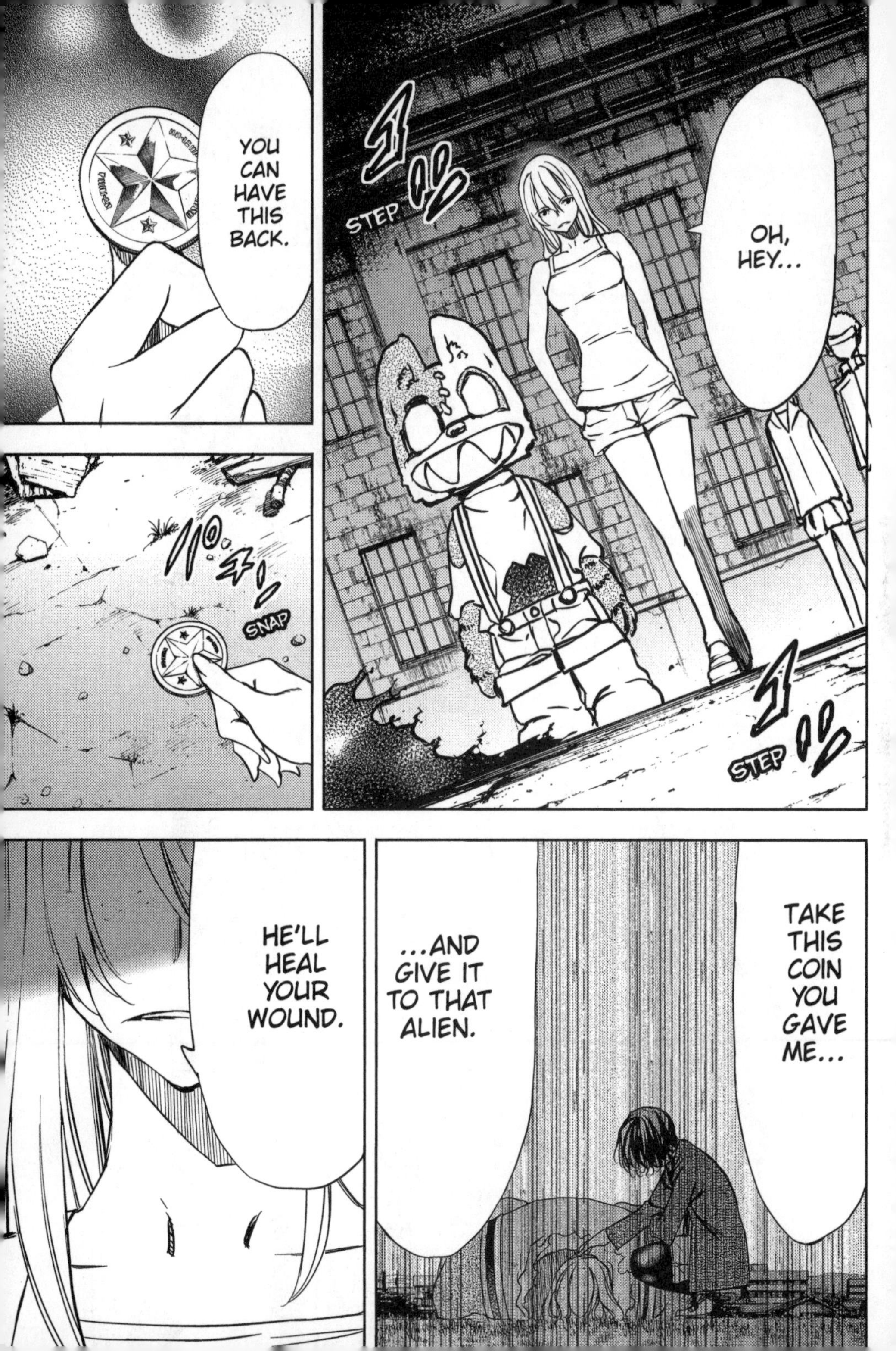
STEP
OH, HEY...
STEP
YOU CAN HAVE THIS BACK.
SNAP
TAKE THIS COIN YOU GAVE ME...
...AND GIVE IT TO THAT ALIEN.
HE'LL HEAL YOUR WOUND.

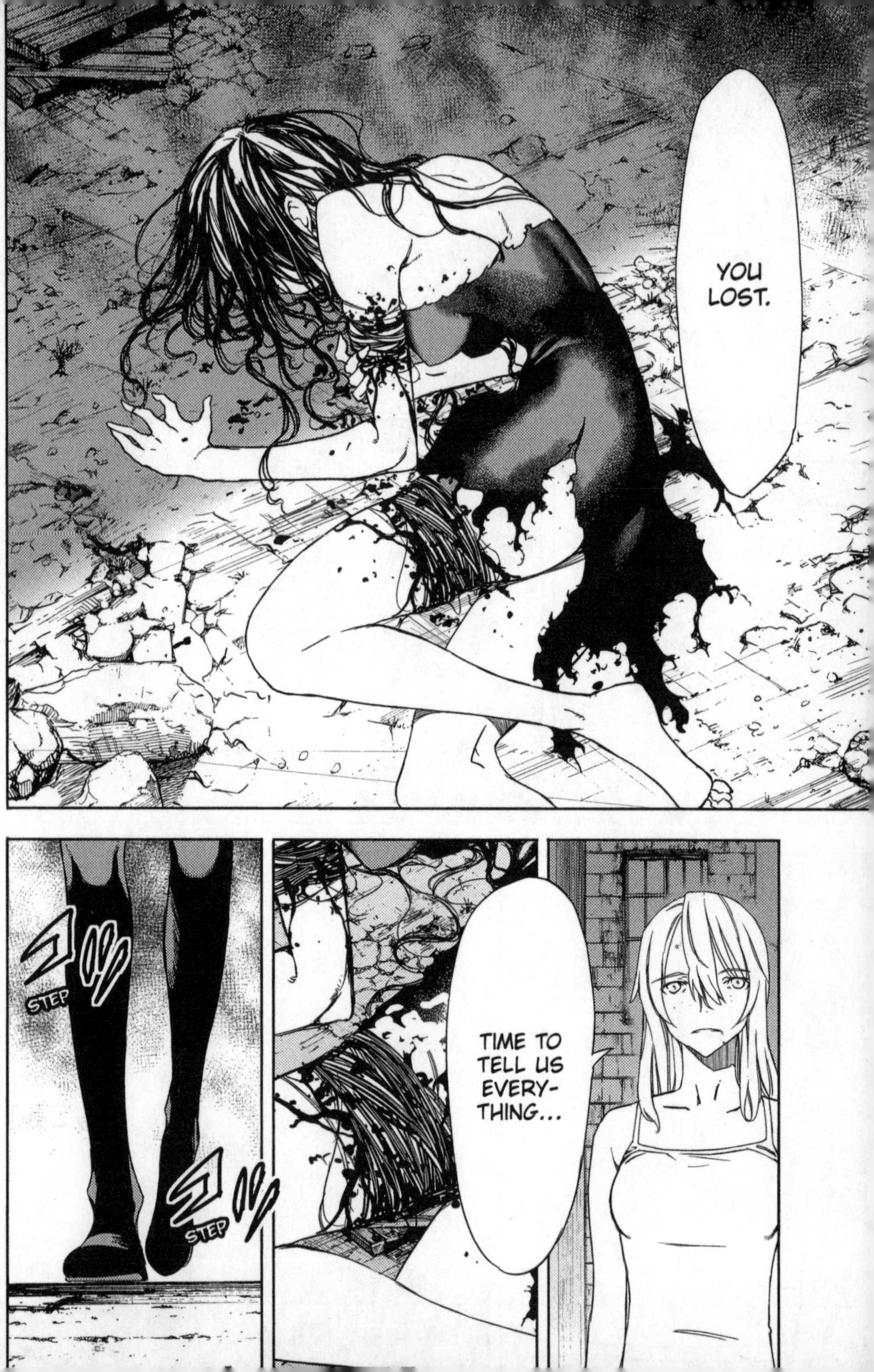
YOU LOST.
TIME TO TELL US EVERY-THING…
STEP
STEP

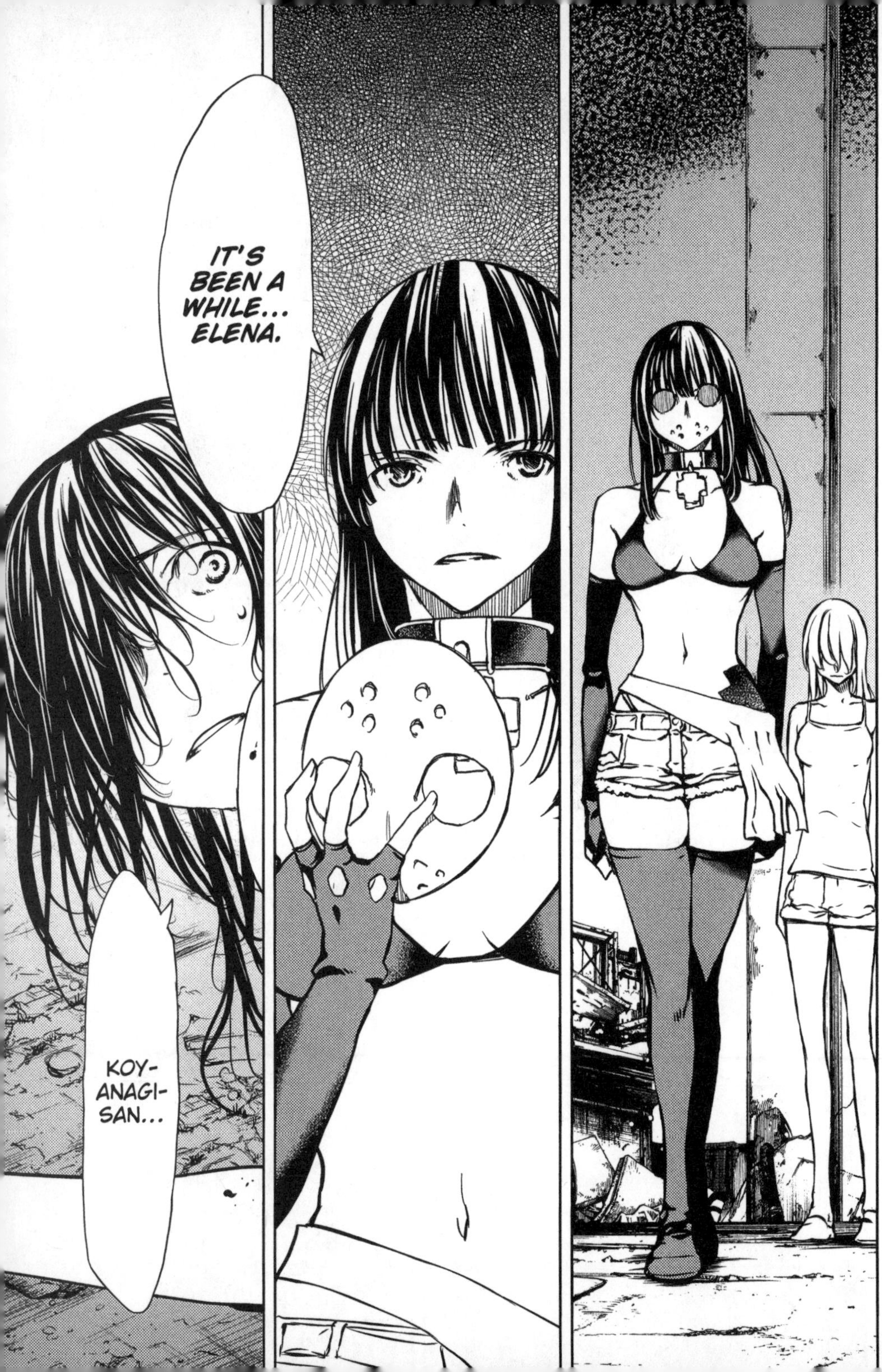
IT'S BEEN A WHILE... ELENA.
KOY-ANAGI-SAN...

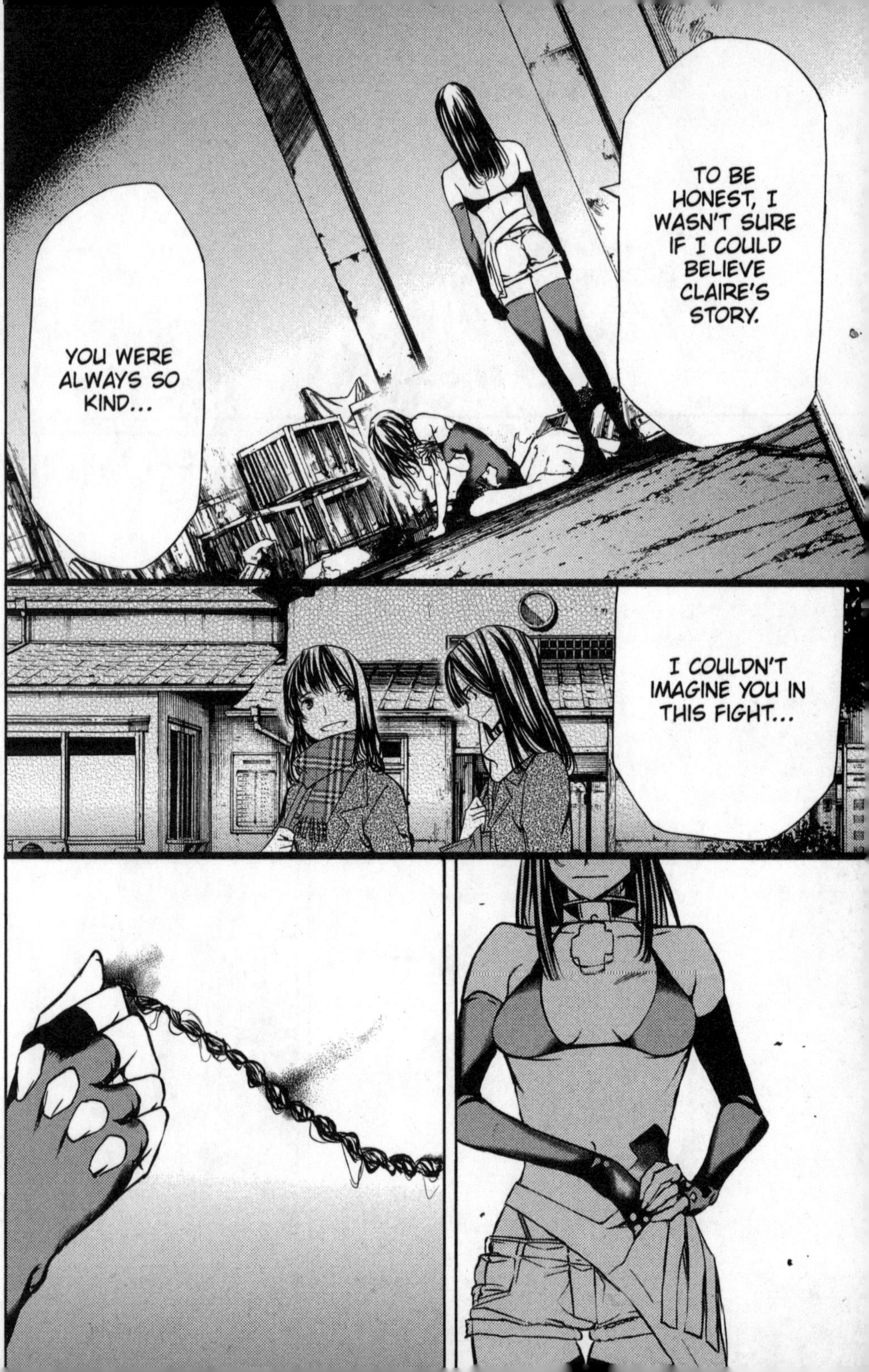
TO BE HONEST, I WASN'T SURE IF I COULD BELIEVE CLAIRE'S STORY.
YOU WERE ALWAYS SO KIND...
I COULDN'T IMAGINE YOU IN THIS FIGHT...

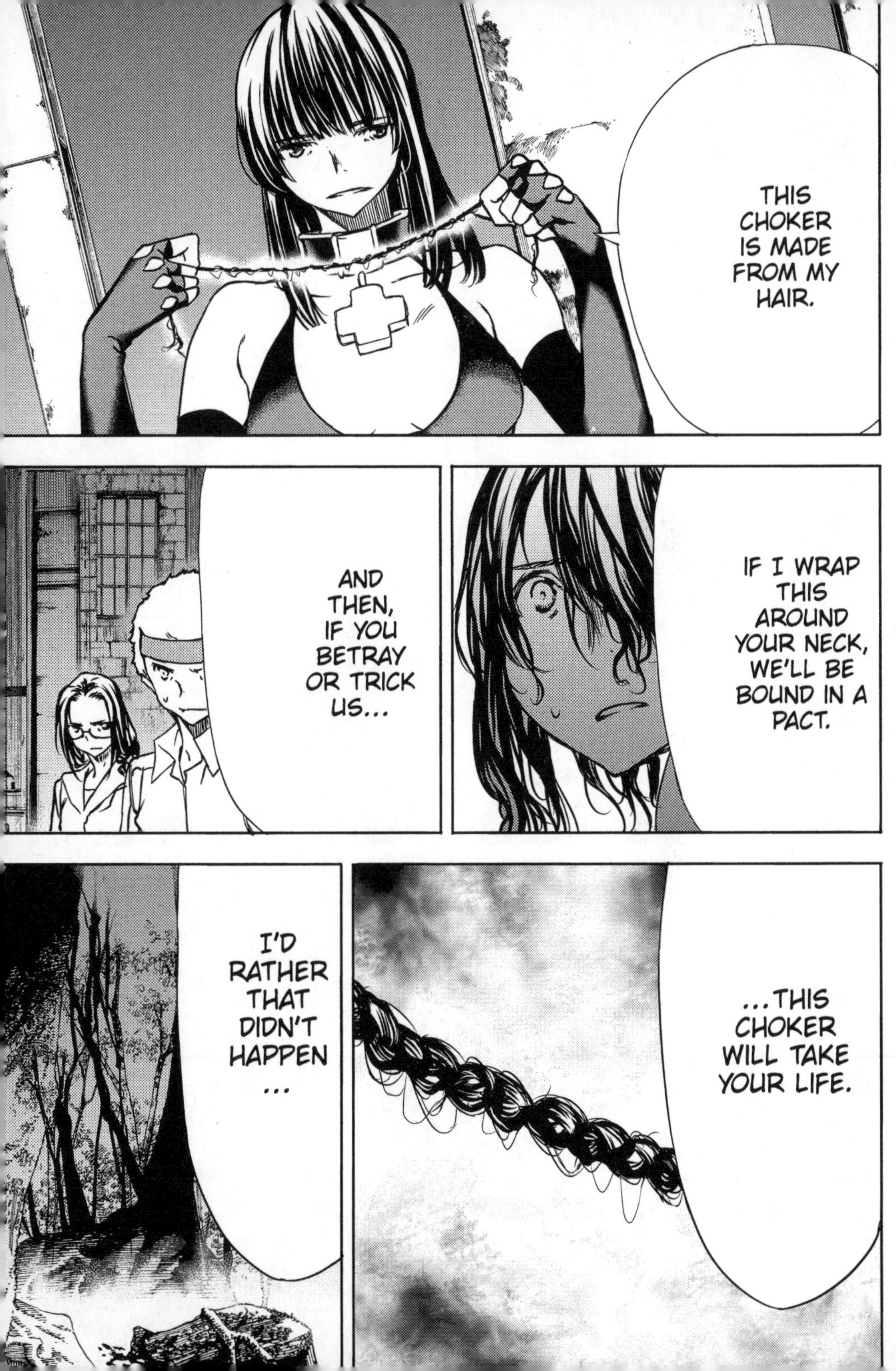
THIS CHOKER IS MADE FROM MY HAIR.
IF I WRAP THIS AROUND YOUR NECK, WE'LL BE BOUND IN A PACT.
AND THEN, IF YOU BETRAY OR TRICK US...
...THIS CHOKER WILL TAKE YOUR LIFE.
I'D RATHER THAT DIDN'T HAPPEN...

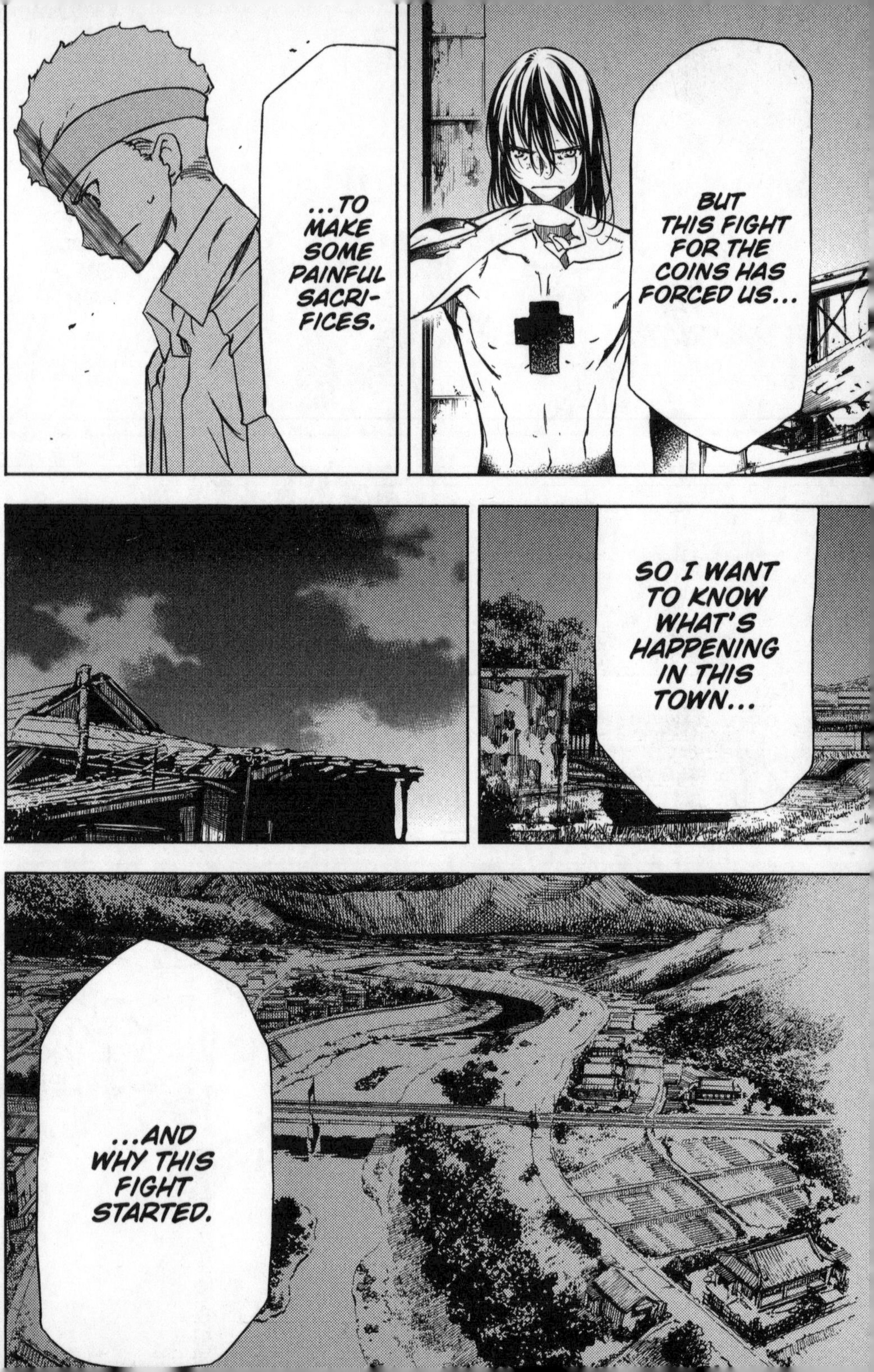
BUT THIS FIGHT FOR THE COINS HAS FORCED US...
...TO MAKE SOME PAINFUL SACRI- FICES.
SO I WANT TO KNOW WHAT'S HAPPENING IN THIS TOWN...
...AND WHY THIS FIGHT STARTED.

I WANT THE TRUTH.

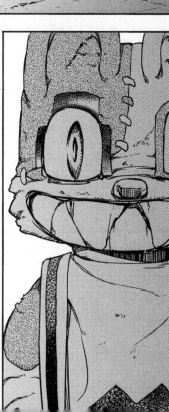

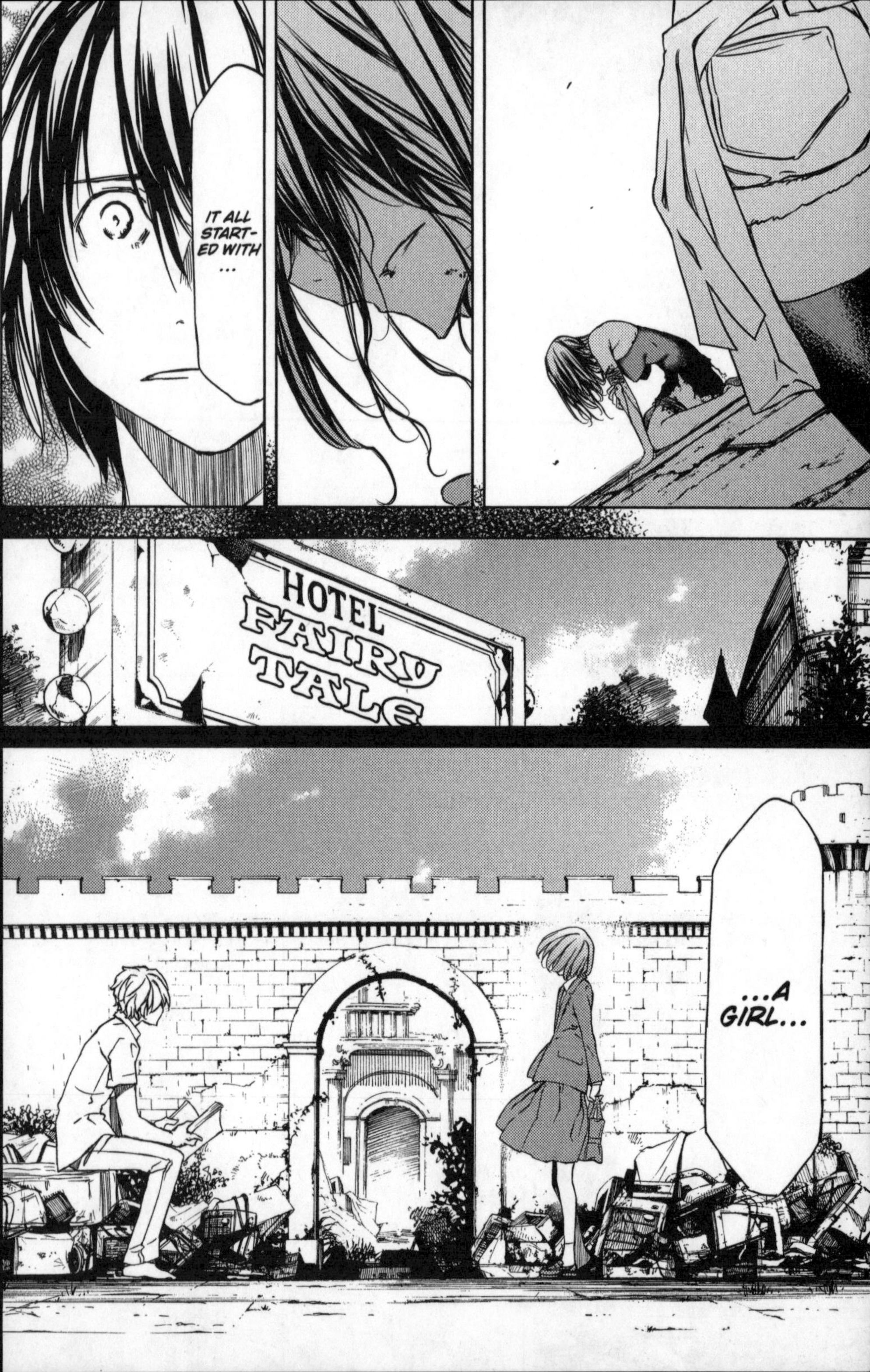
IT ALL STARTED WITH ...
HOTEL FAIRY TALE
...A GIRL...

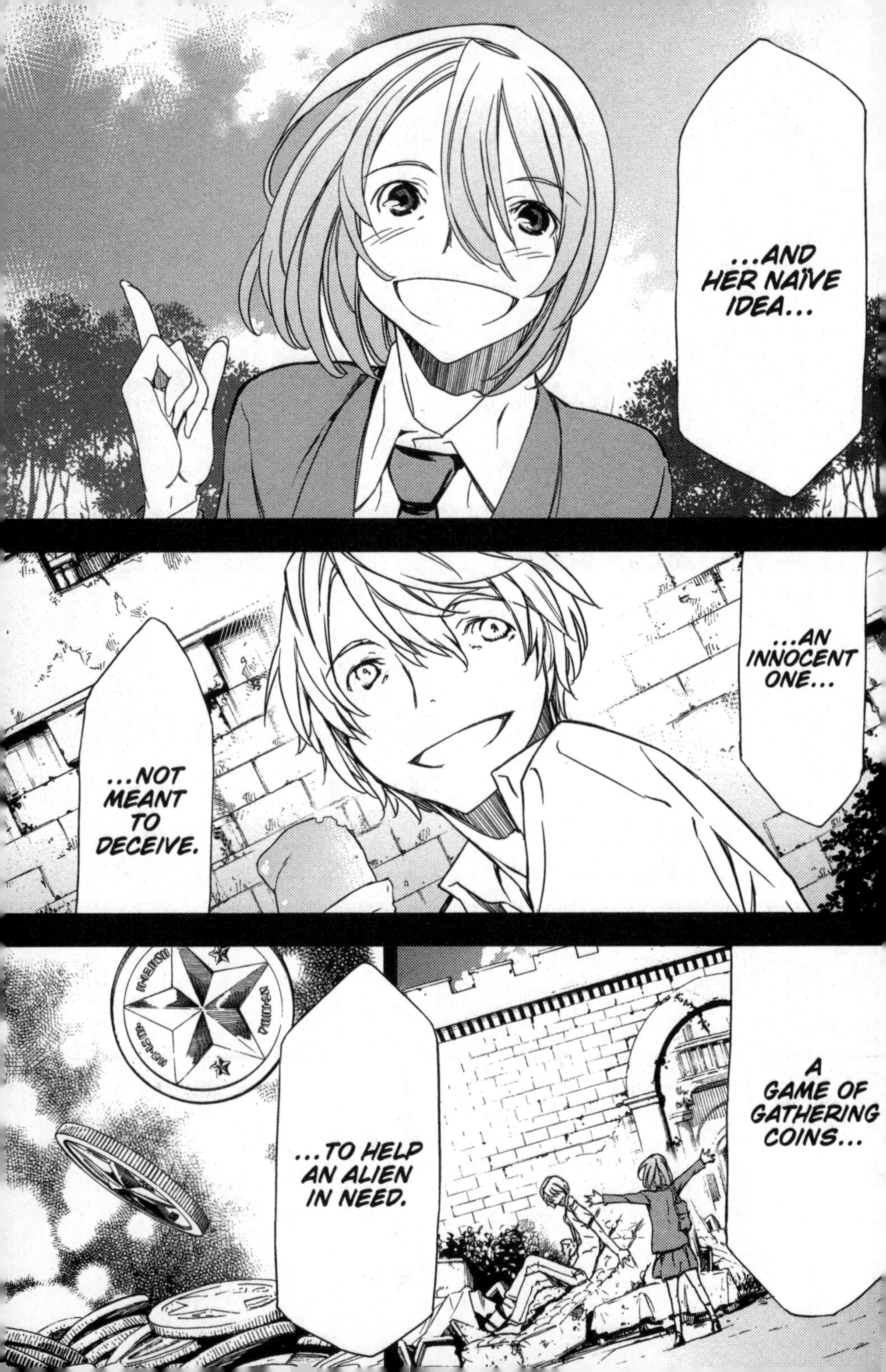
...AND HER NAÏVE IDEA...
...AN INNOCENT ONE...
...NOT MEANT TO DECEIVE.
A GAME OF GATHERING COINS...
...TO HELP AN ALIEN IN NEED.

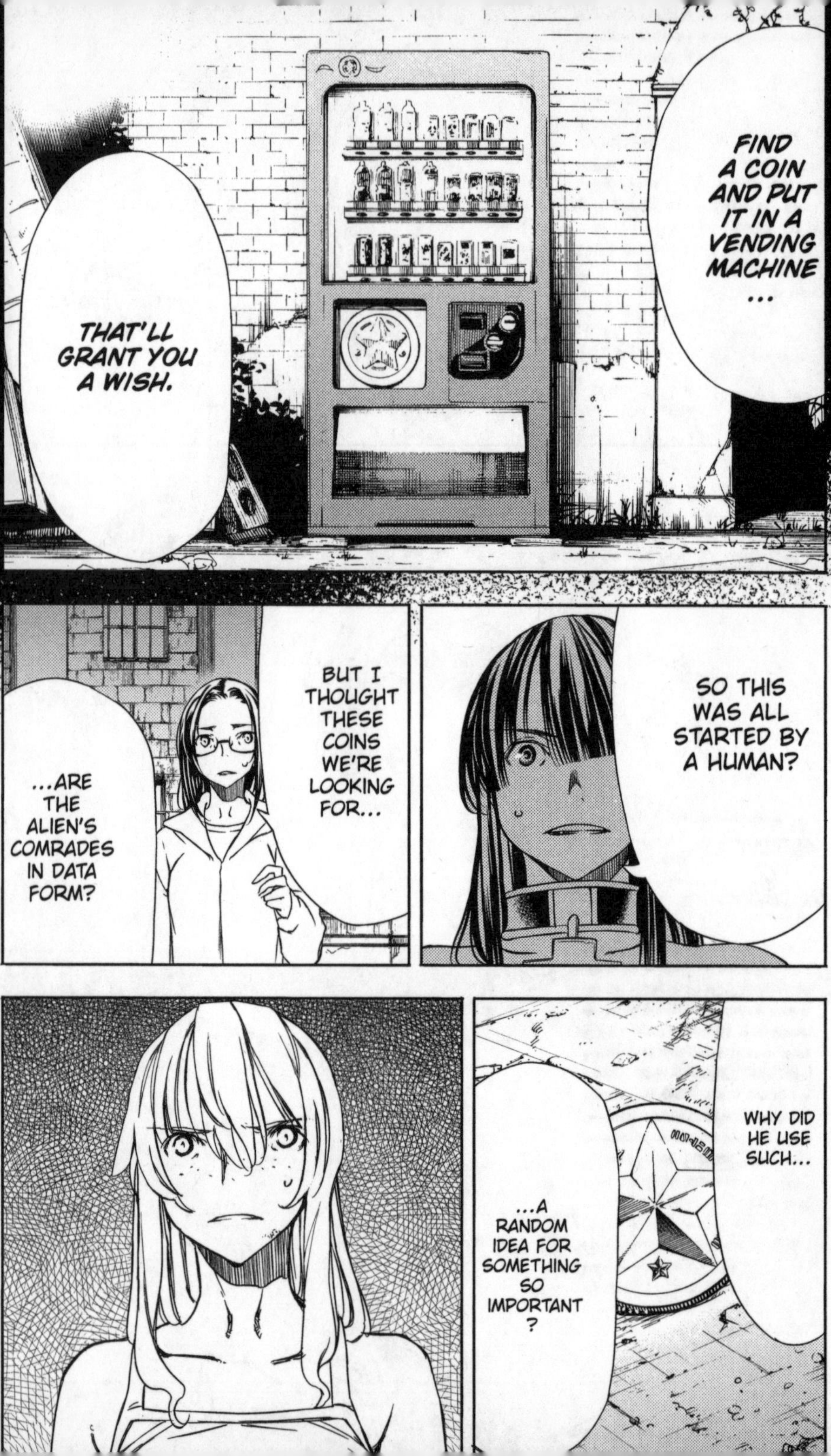
FIND A COIN AND PUT IT IN A VENDING MACHINE...
THAT'LL GRANT YOU A WISH.
SO THIS WAS ALL STARTED BY A HUMAN?
BUT I THOUGHT THESE COINS WE'RE LOOKING FOR...
...ARE THE ALIEN'S COMRADES IN DATA FORM?
WHY DID HE USE SUCH...
...A RANDOM IDEA FOR SOMETHING SO IMPORTANT?

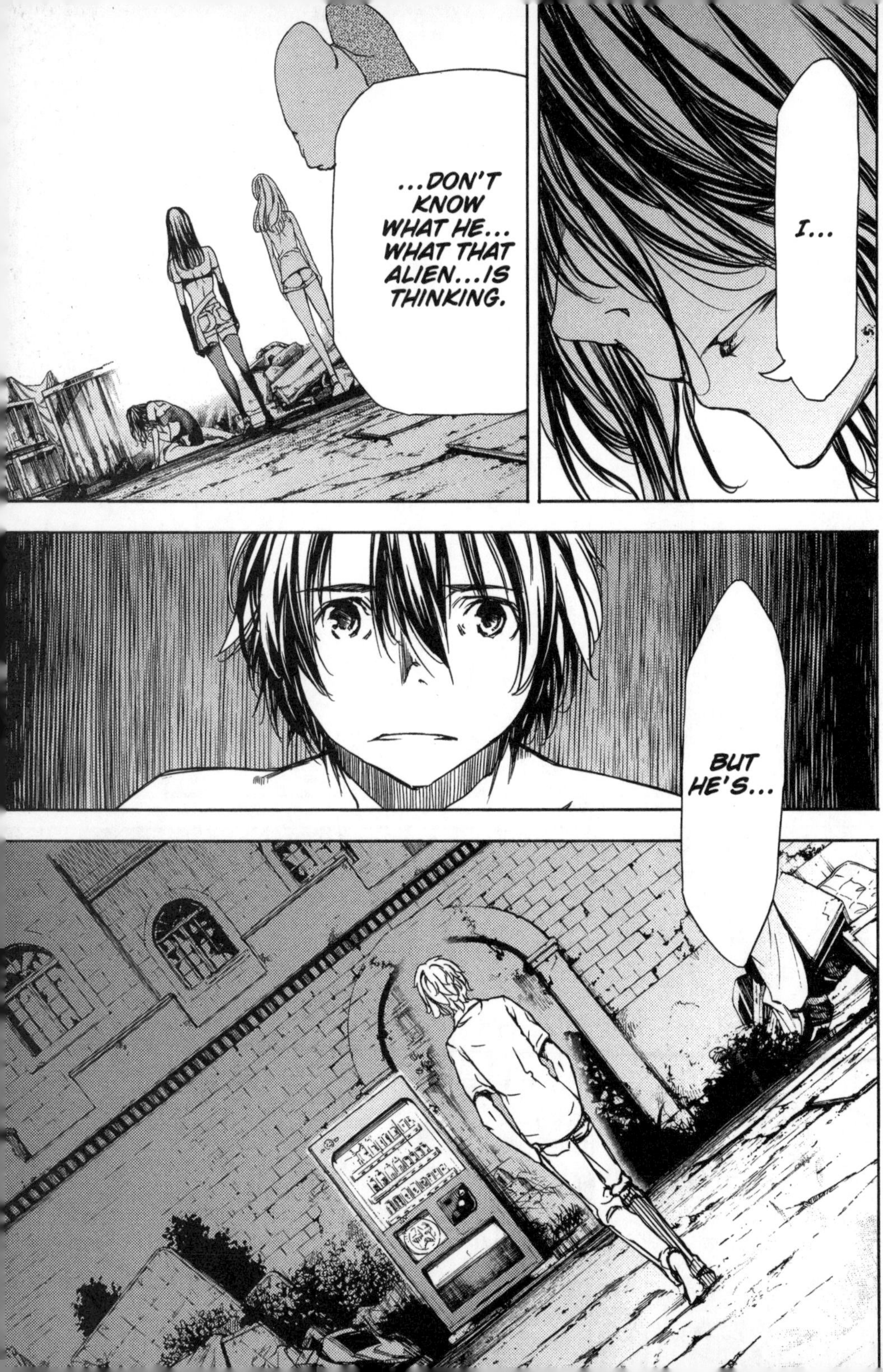
I...
...DON'T KNOW WHAT HE... WHAT THAT ALIEN...IS THINKING.
BUT HE'S...

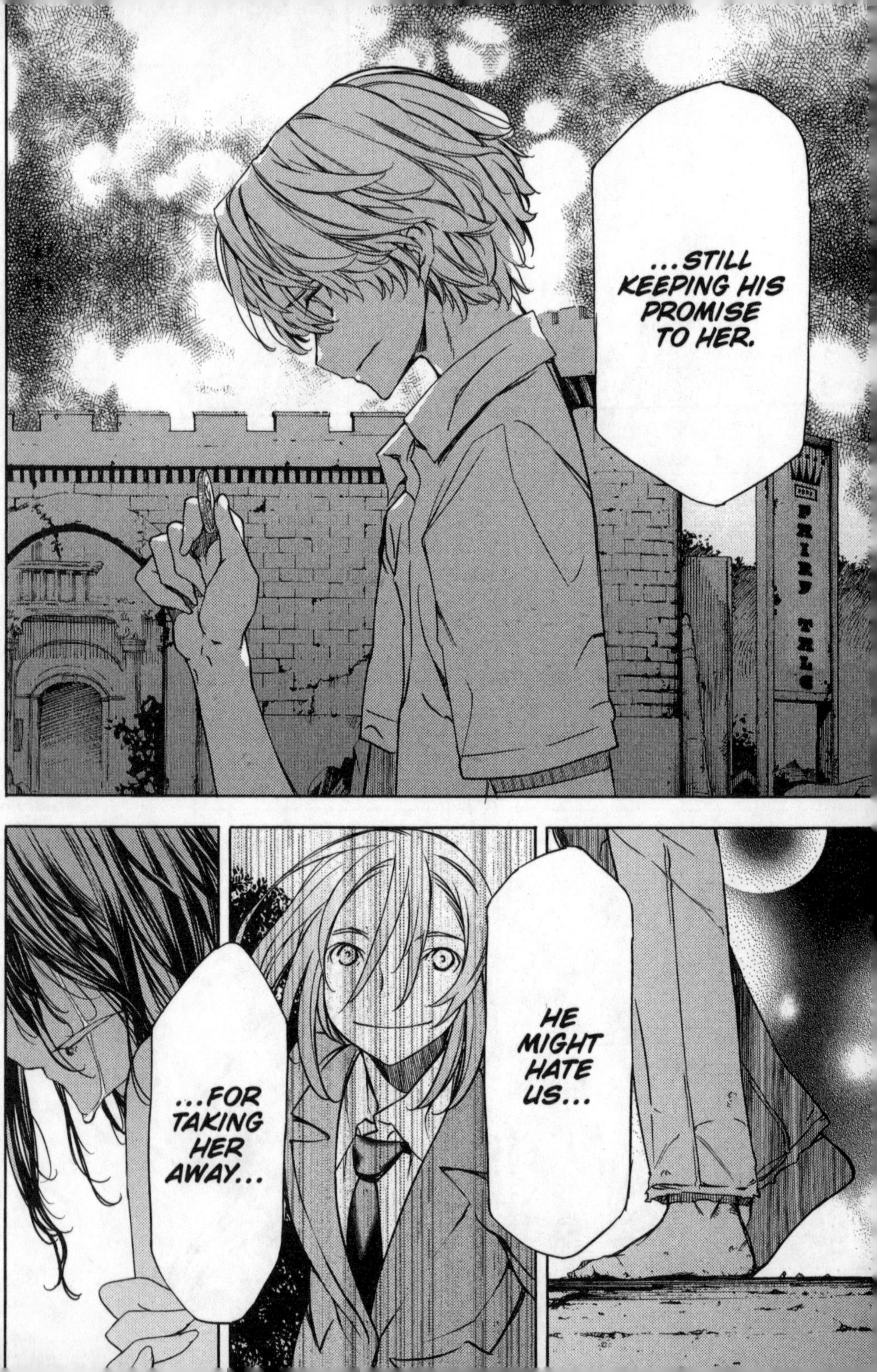
...STILL KEEPING HIS PROMISE TO HER.
FAIRY TALE
HE MIGHT HATE US...
...FOR TAKING HER AWAY...

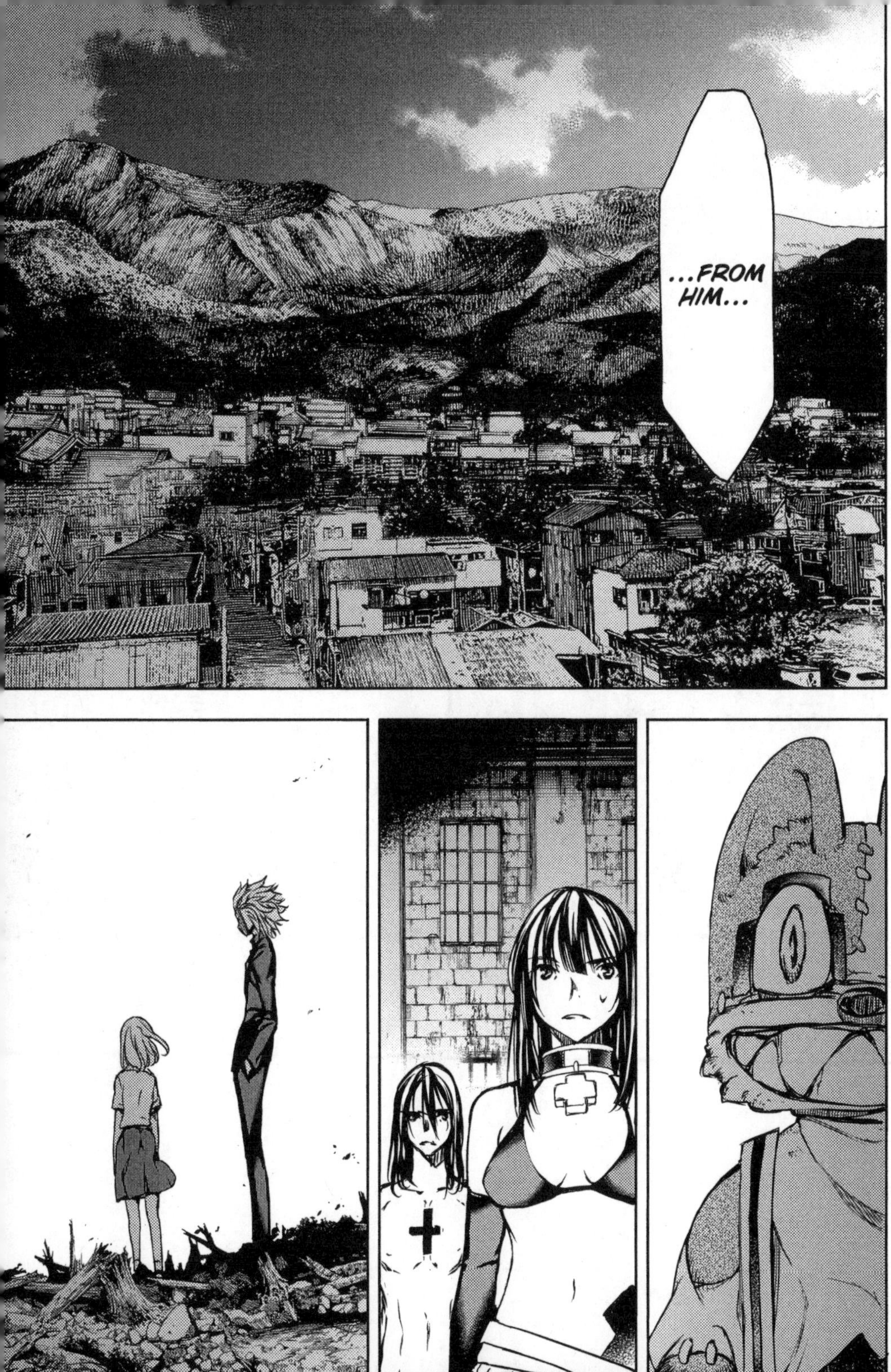
...FROM HIM...

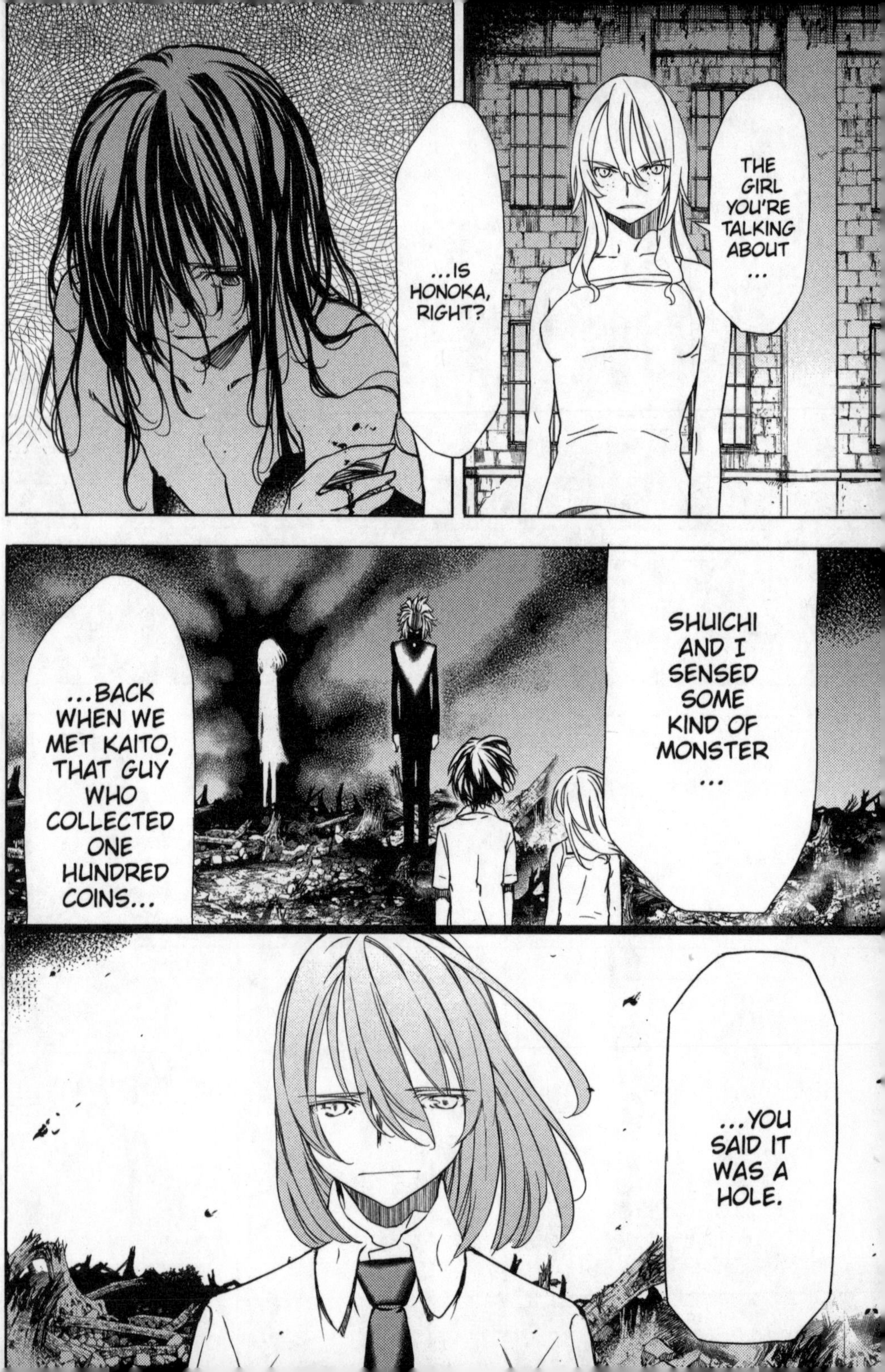
THE GIRL YOU'RE TALKING ABOUT ...
...IS HONOKA, RIGHT?
SHUICHI AND I SENSED SOME KIND OF MONSTER ...
...BACK WHEN WE MET KAITO, THAT GUY WHO COLLECTED ONE HUNDRED COINS...
...YOU SAID IT WAS A HOLE.

YOU AND SHUICHI... THAT THING WAS YOUR...

...FRIEND.

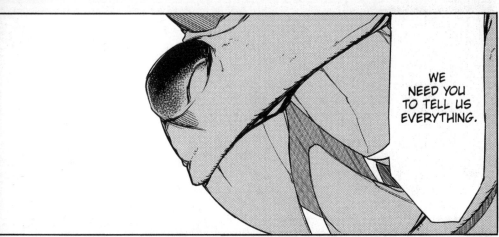

WE NEED YOU TO TELL US EVERYTHING.

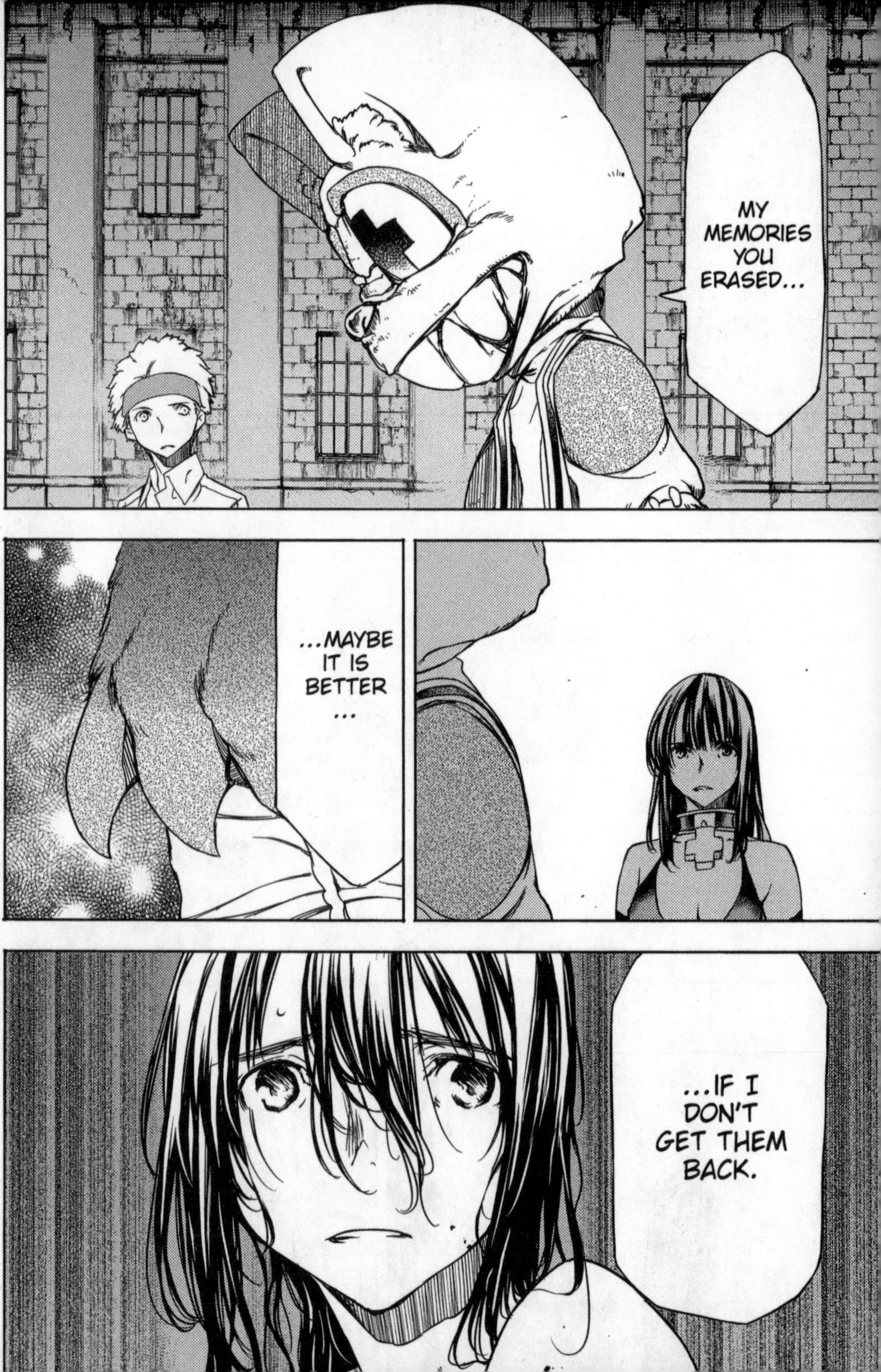
MY MEMORIES YOU ERASED...
...MAYBE IT IS BETTER ...
...IF I DON'T GET THEM BACK.

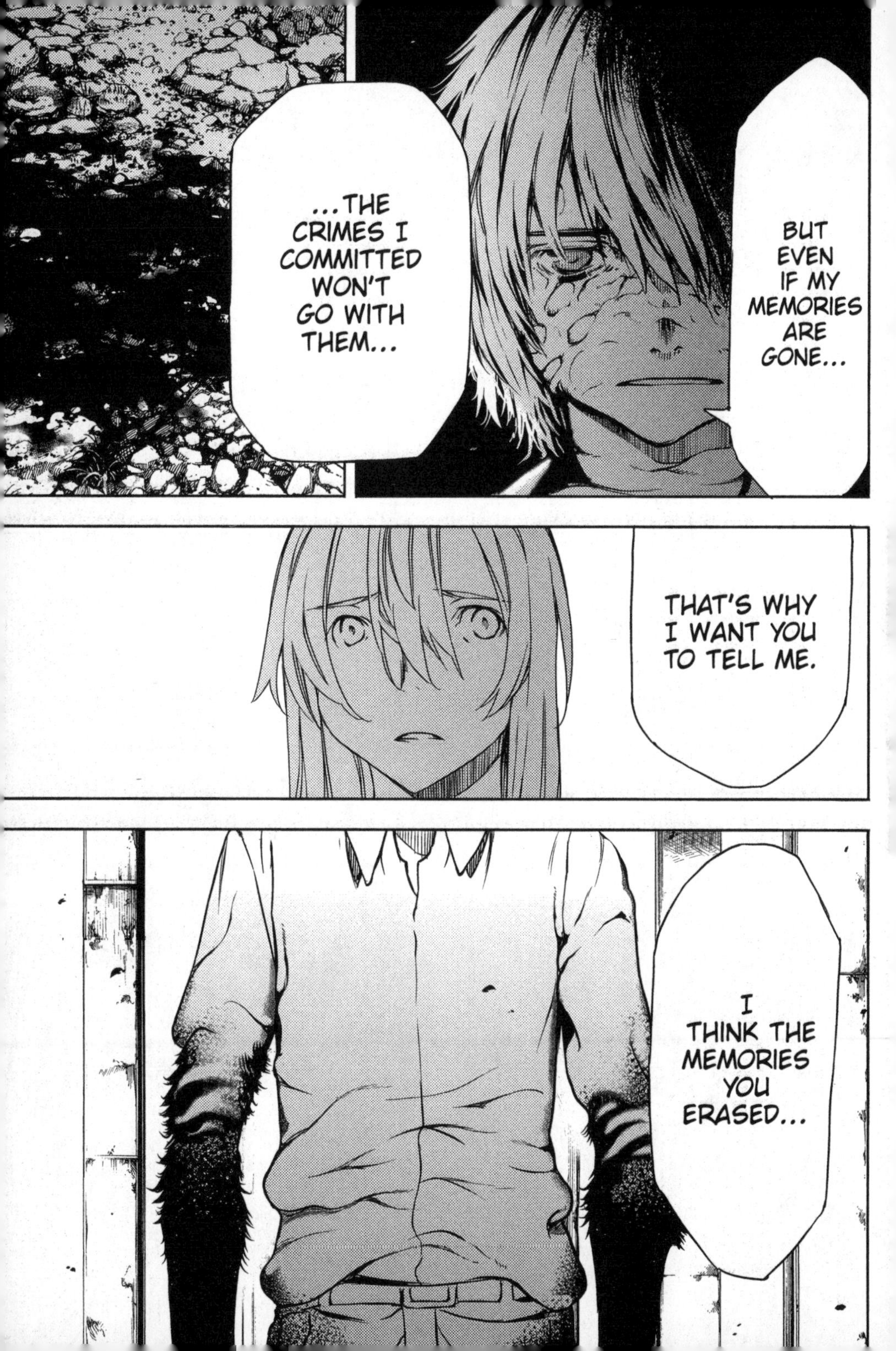
BUT EVEN IF MY MEMORIES ARE GONE...
...THE CRIMES I COMMITTED WON'T GO WITH THEM...
THAT'S WHY I WANT YOU TO TELL ME.
I THINK THE MEMORIES YOU ERASED...

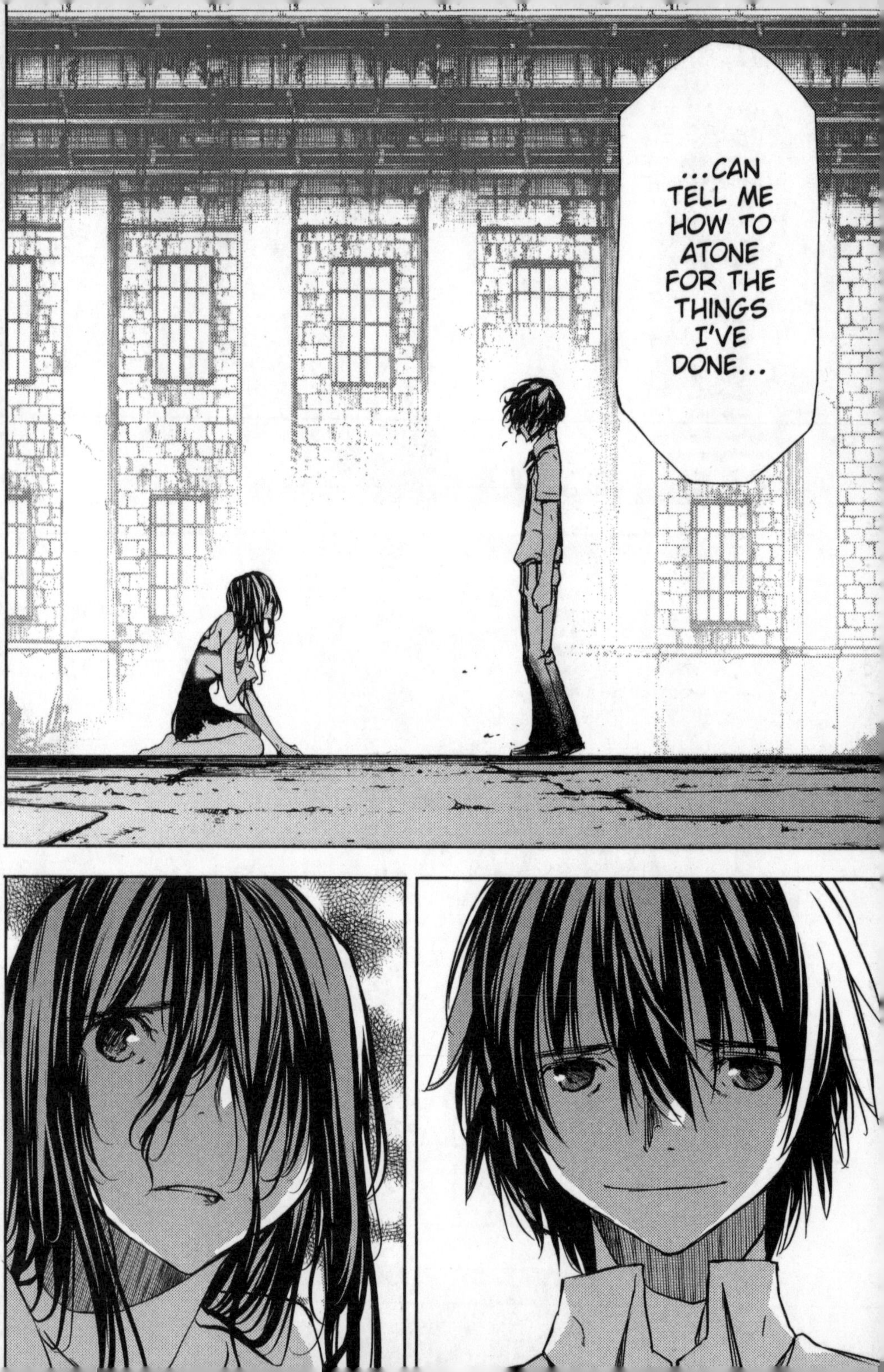
...CAN TELL ME HOW TO ATONE FOR THE THINGS I'VE DONE...

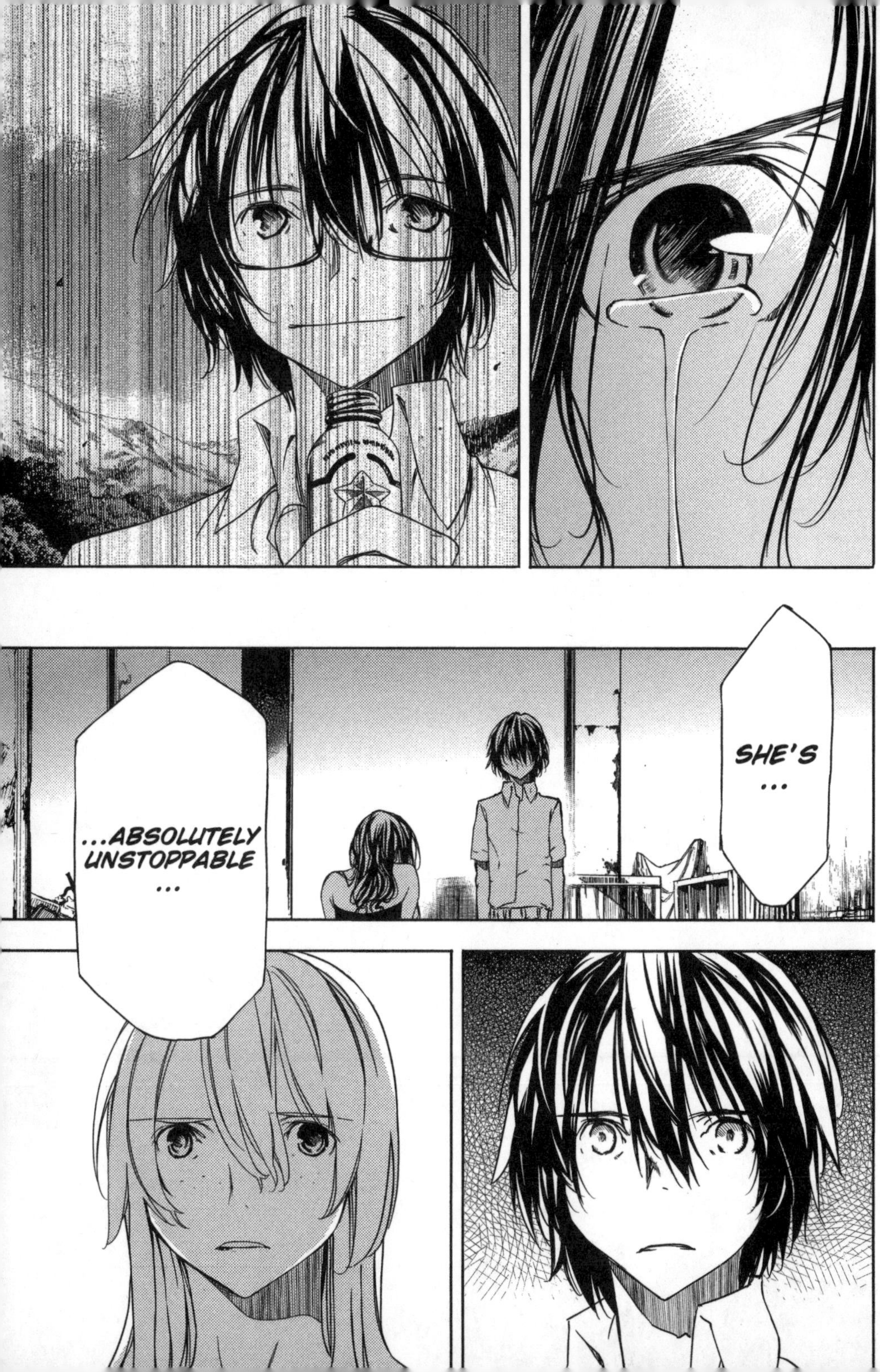
SHE'S ...
...ABSOLUTELY UNSTOPPABLE ...

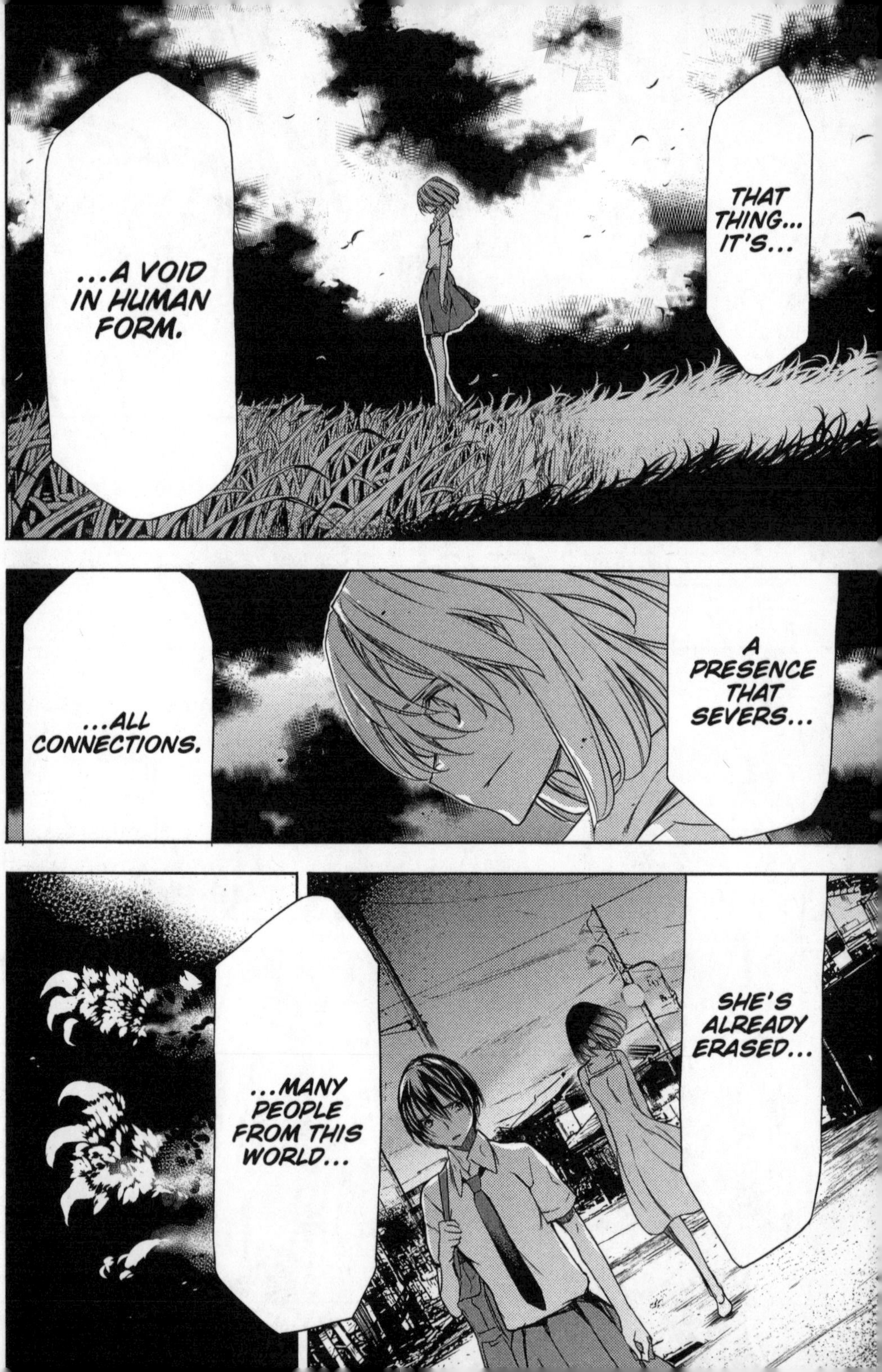
THAT THING... IT'S...
...A VOID IN HUMAN FORM.
A PRESENCE THAT SEVERS...
...ALL CONNECTIONS.
SHE'S ALREADY ERASED...
...MANY PEOPLE FROM THIS WORLD...

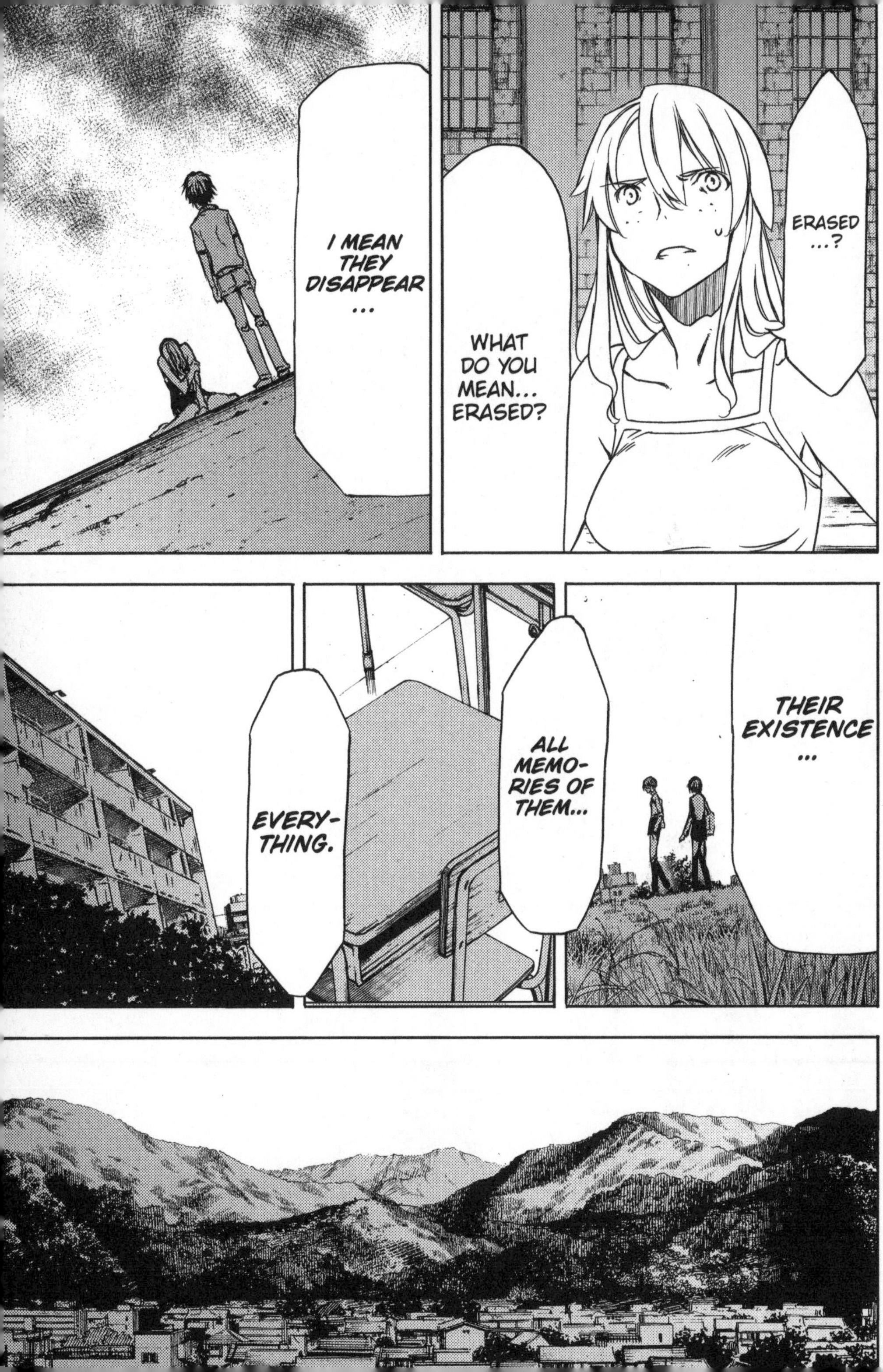
ERASED...?
WHAT DO YOU MEAN... ERASED?
I MEAN THEY DISAPPEAR...
THEIR EXISTENCE...
ALL MEMO-RIES OF THEM...
EVERY-THING.

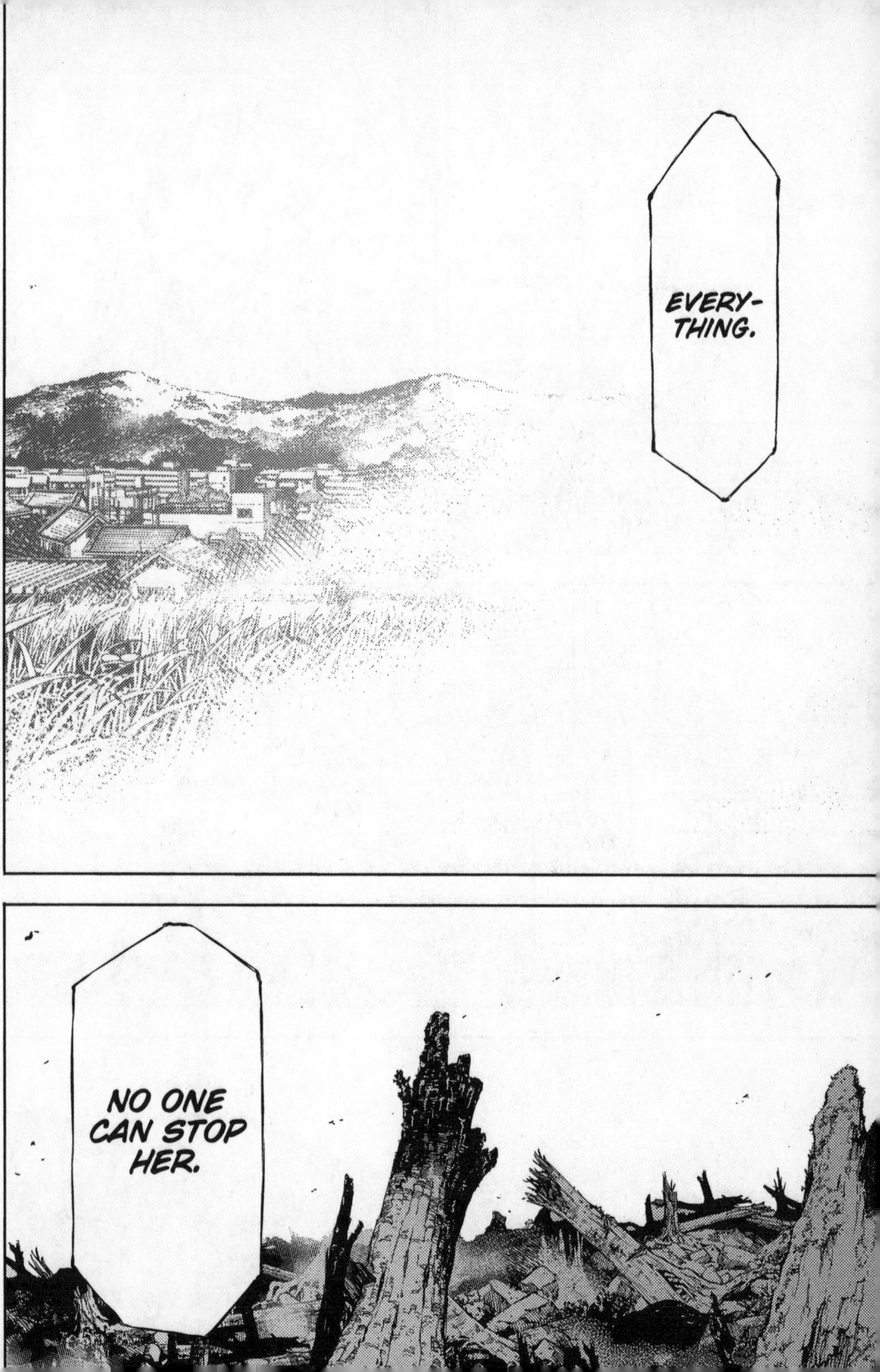
EVERY-THING.
NO ONE CAN STOP HER.

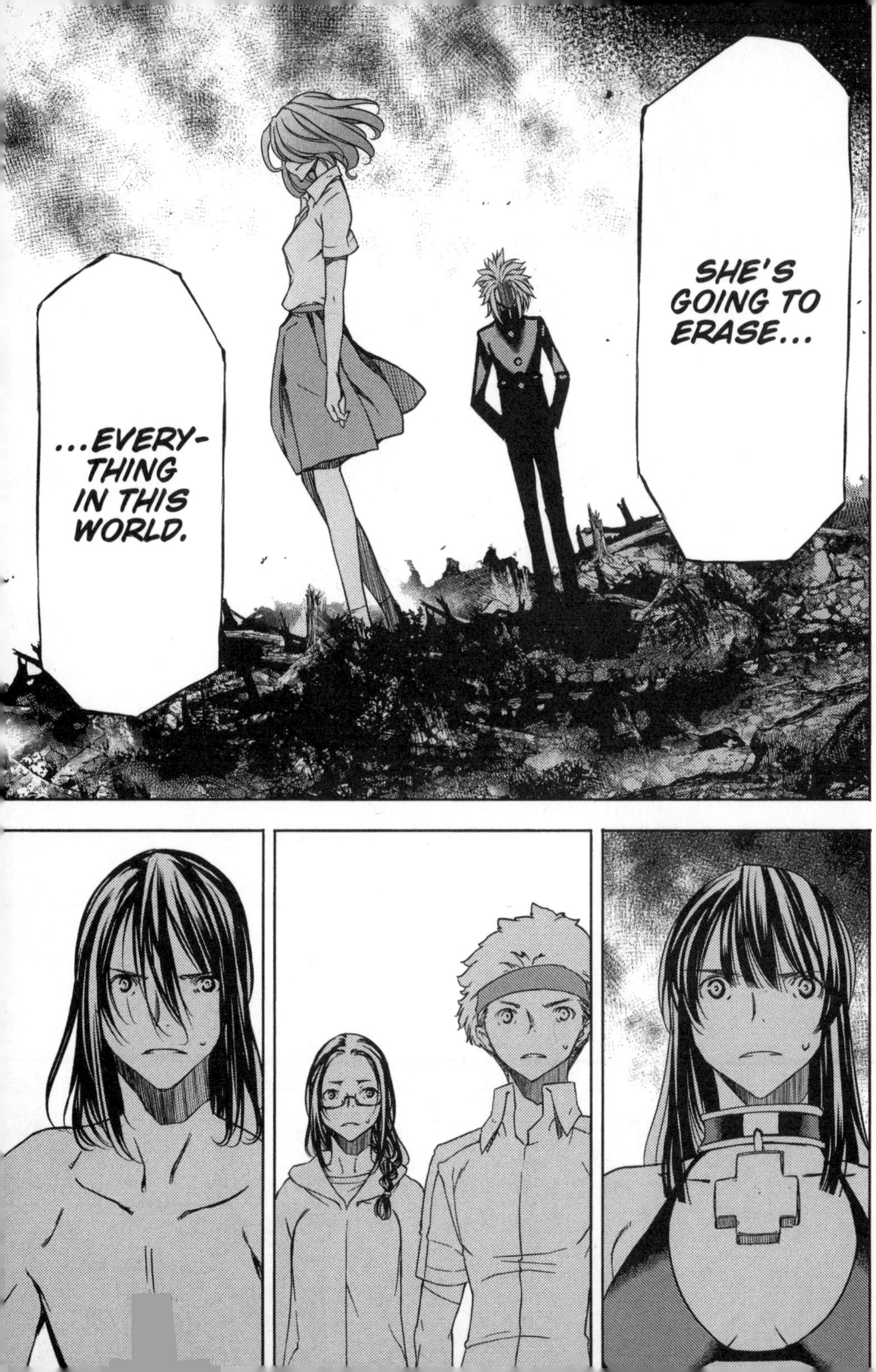
SHE'S GOING TO ERASE...
...EVERYTHING IN THIS WORLD.

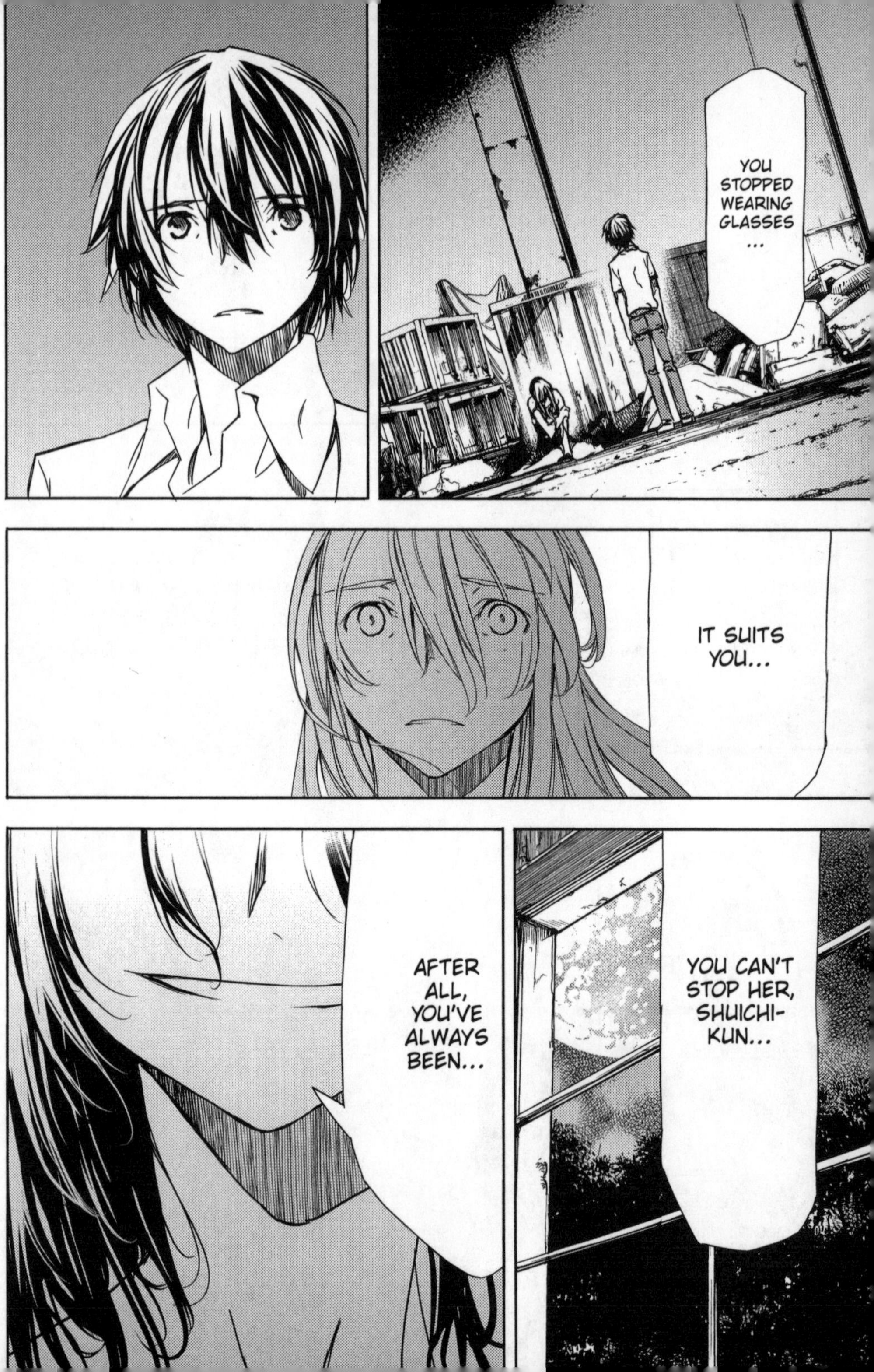
YOU STOPPED WEARING GLASSES...
IT SUITS YOU...
YOU CAN'T STOP HER, SHUICHI-KUN...
AFTER ALL, YOU'VE ALWAYS BEEN...

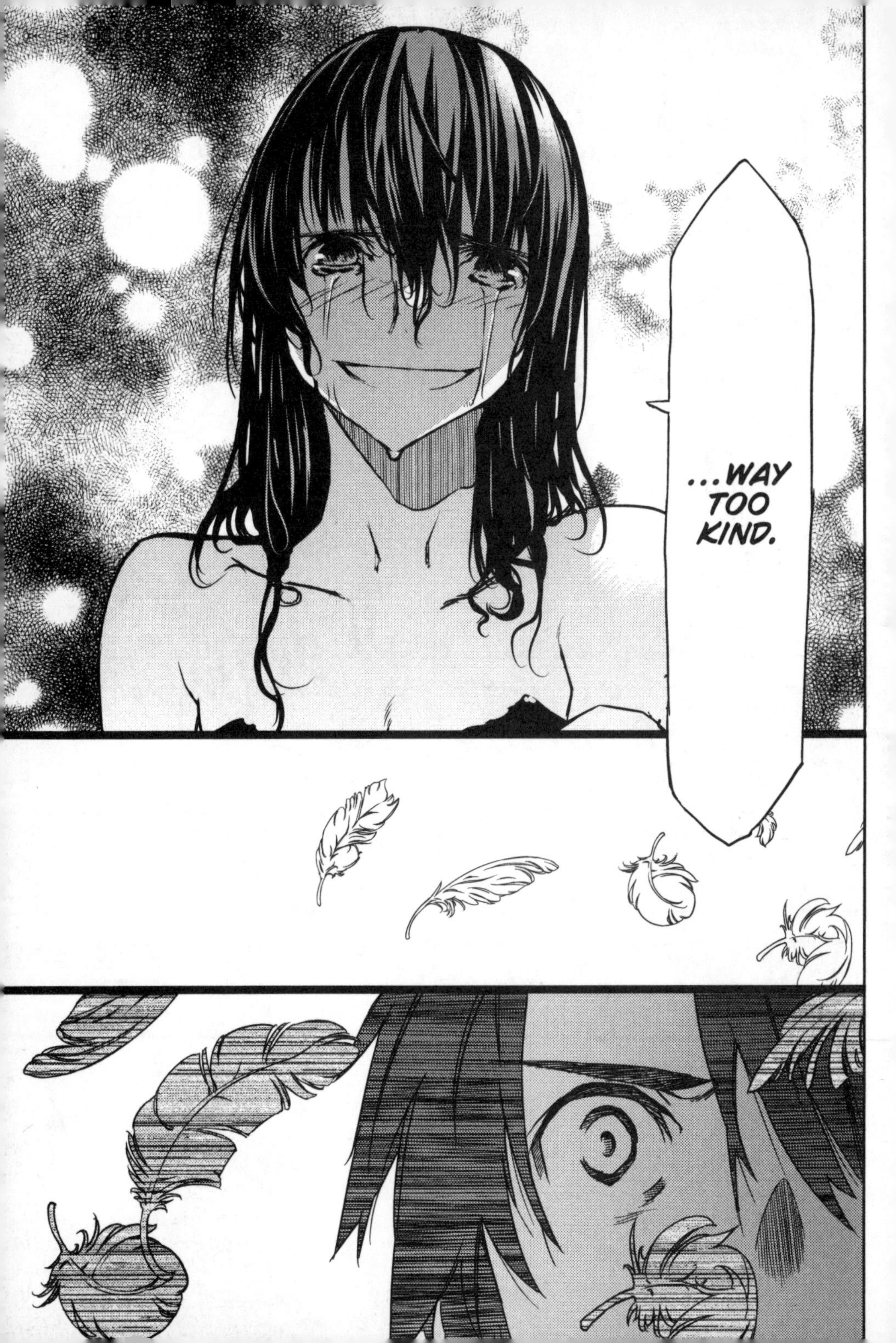
...WAY TOO KIND.

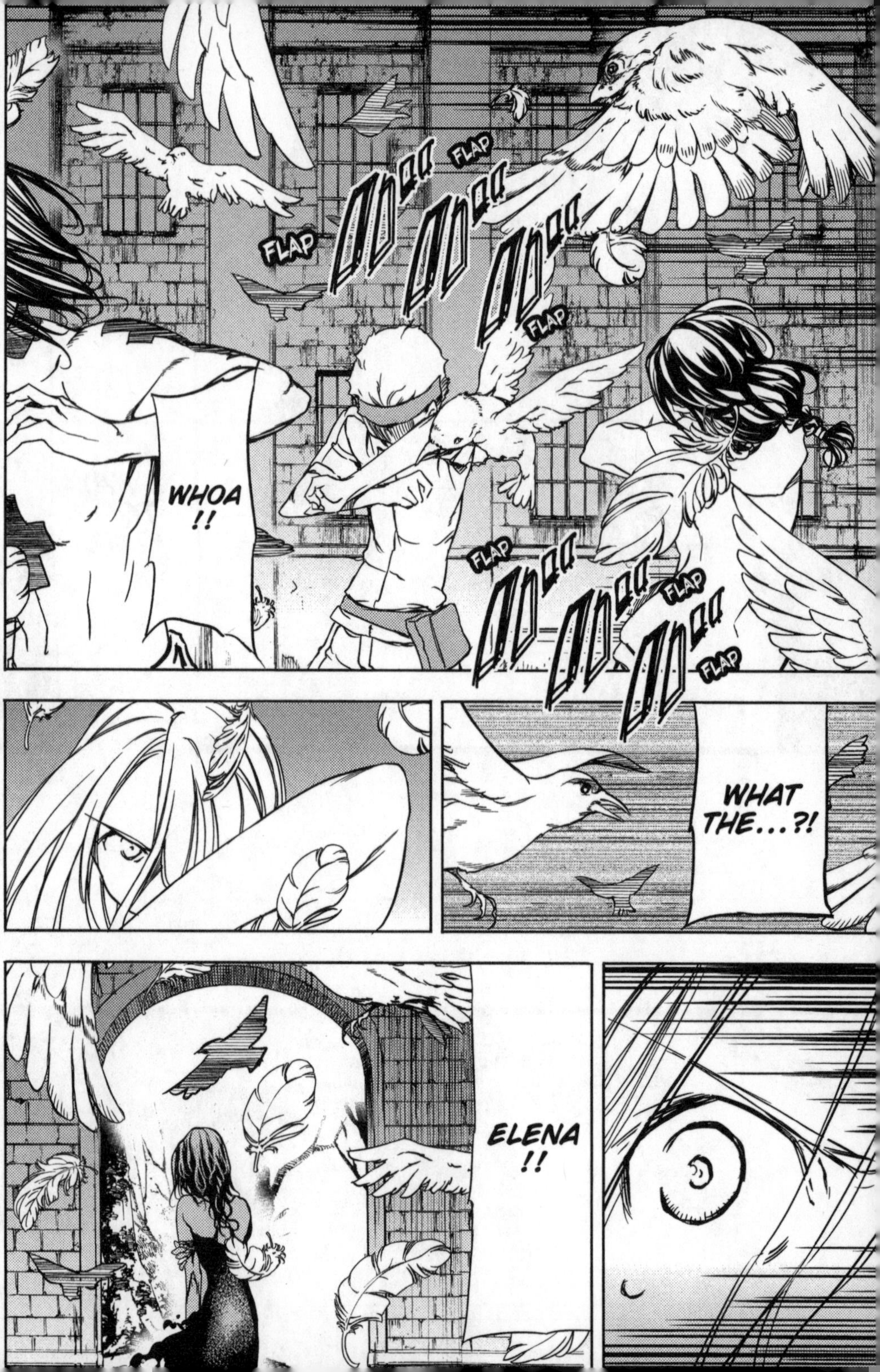
FLAP
FLAP
FLAP
FLAP
FLAP
FLAP
FLAP
WHOA !!
WHAT THE...?!
ELENA !!

WHAT'S WITH ALL THE BIRDS...

DAMN IT!

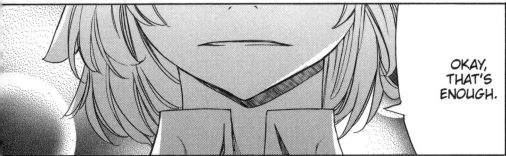

OKAY, THAT'S ENOUGH.

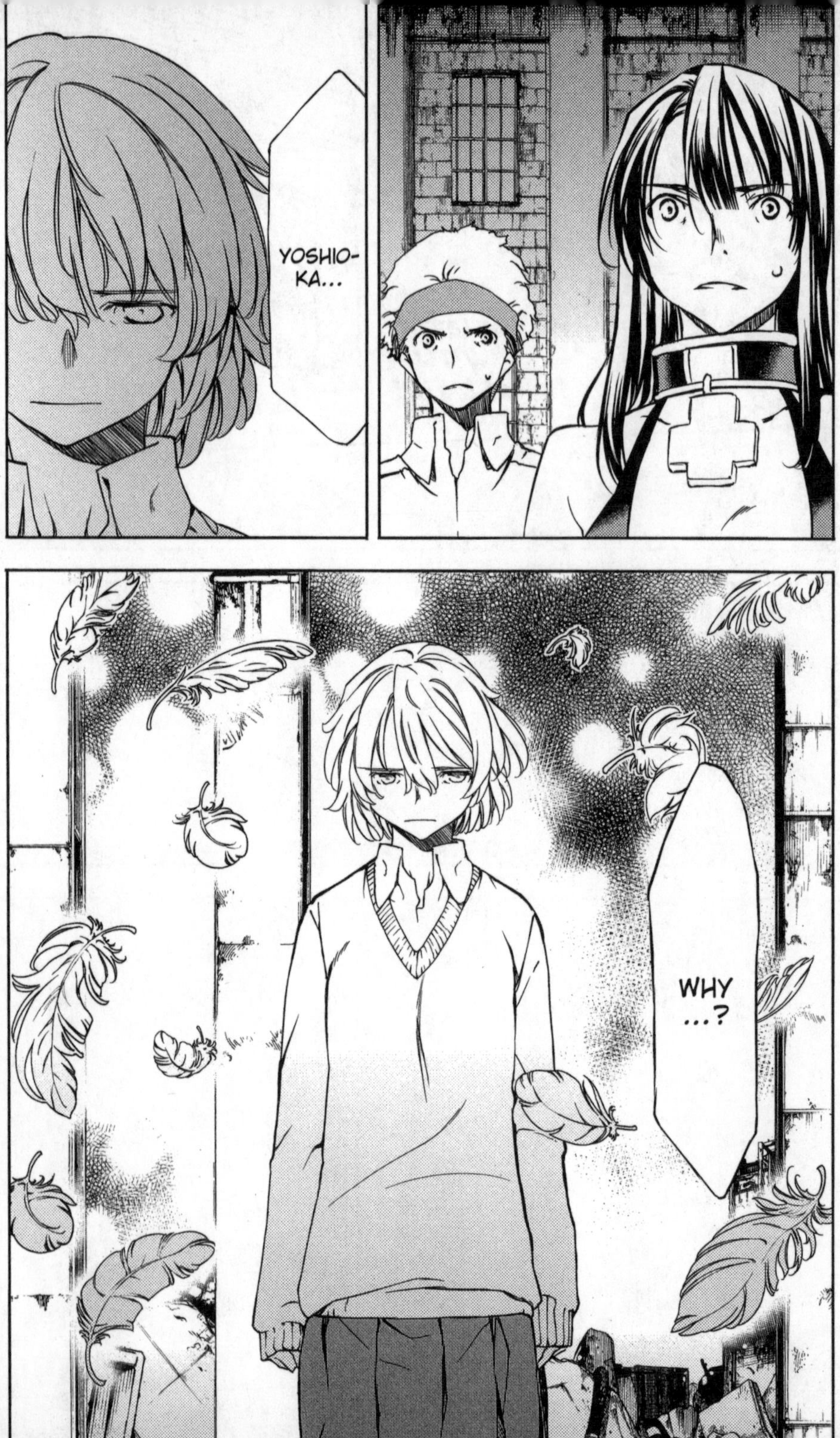
YOSHIO-
KA...
WHY
...?

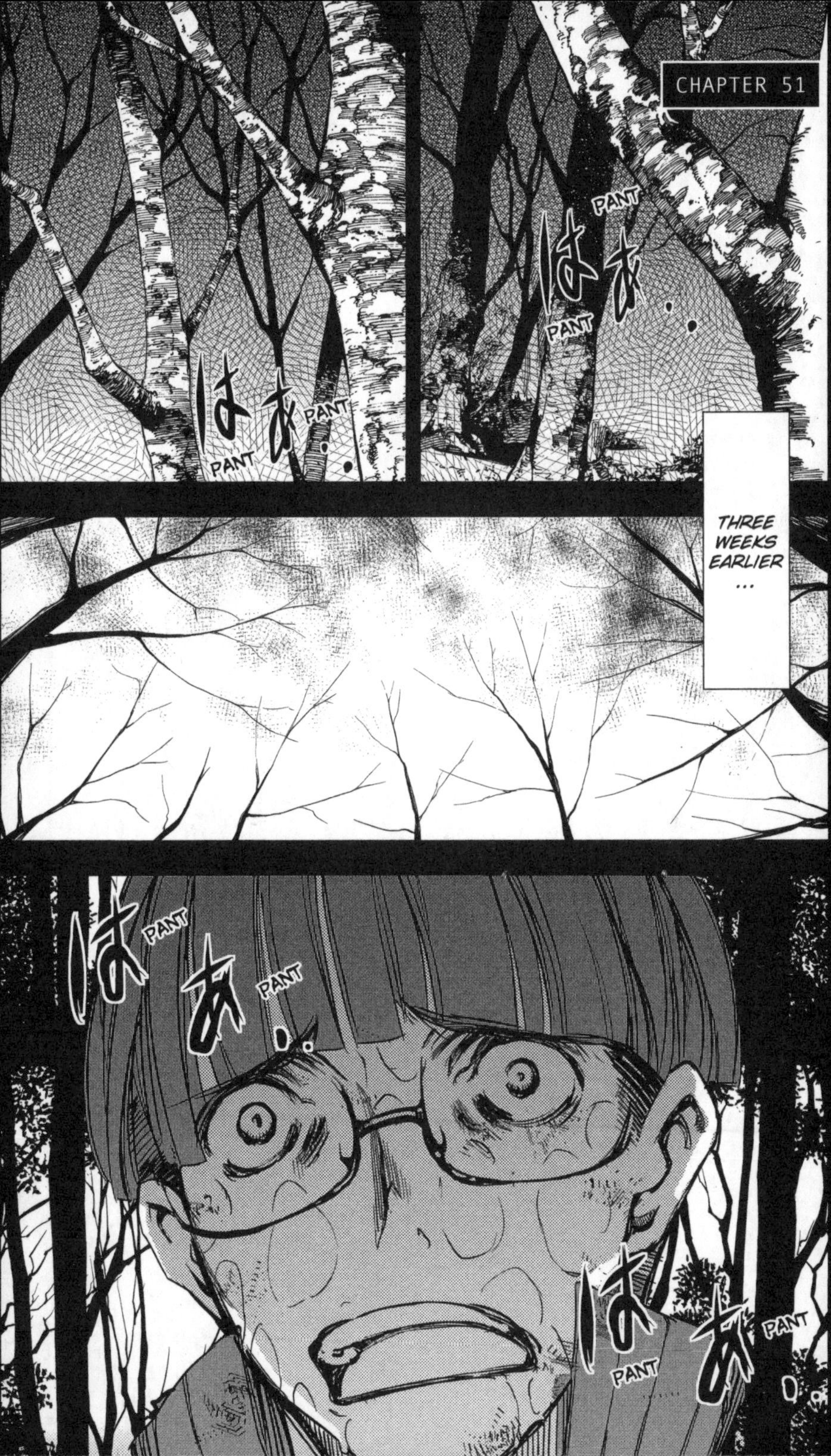
CHAPTER 51
はぁ..
PANT
PANT
はぁ.
PANT
PANT
THREE WEEKS EARLIER ...
はぁ..
PANT
PANT
はぁ..
PANT
PANT

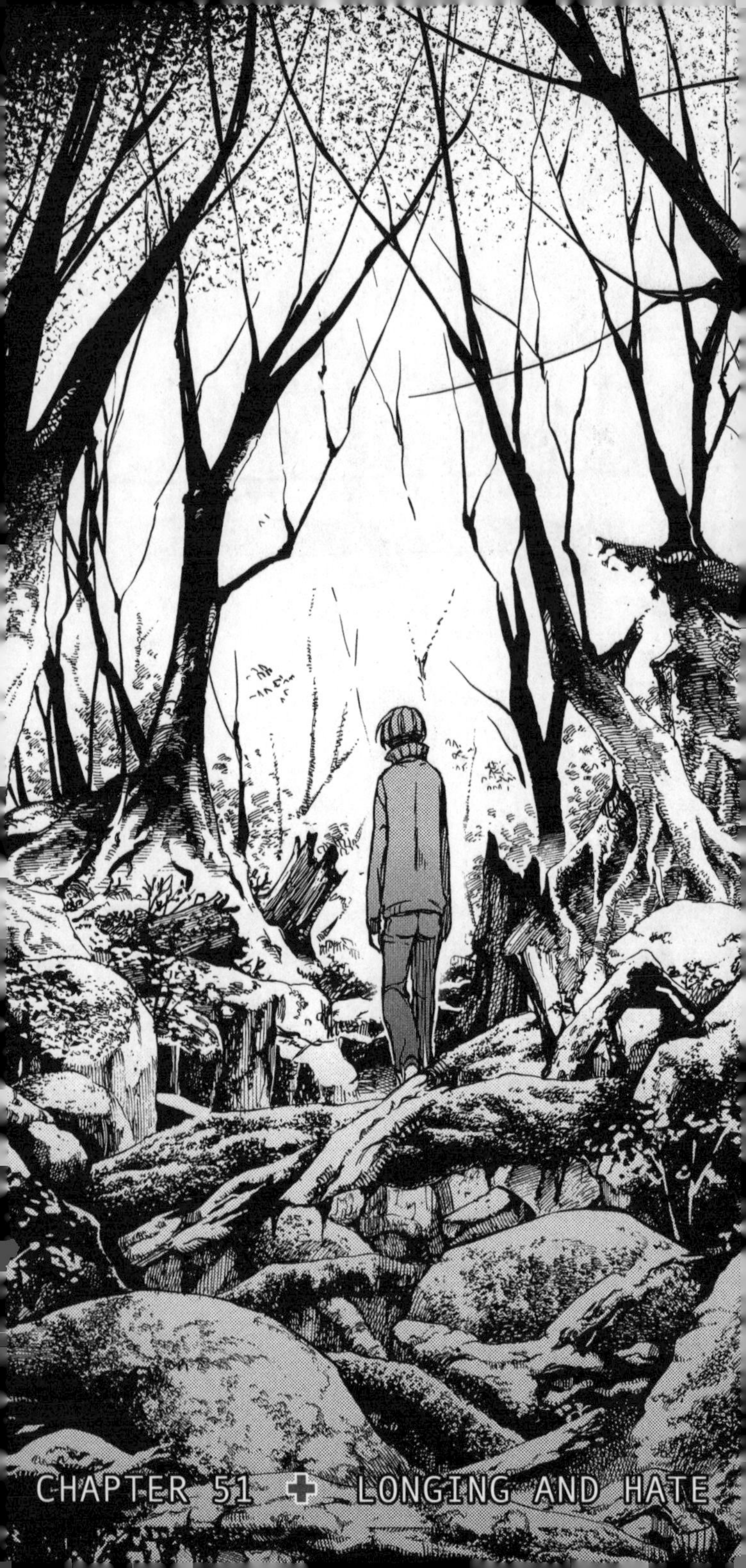
CHAPTER 51 ✚ LONGING AND HATE

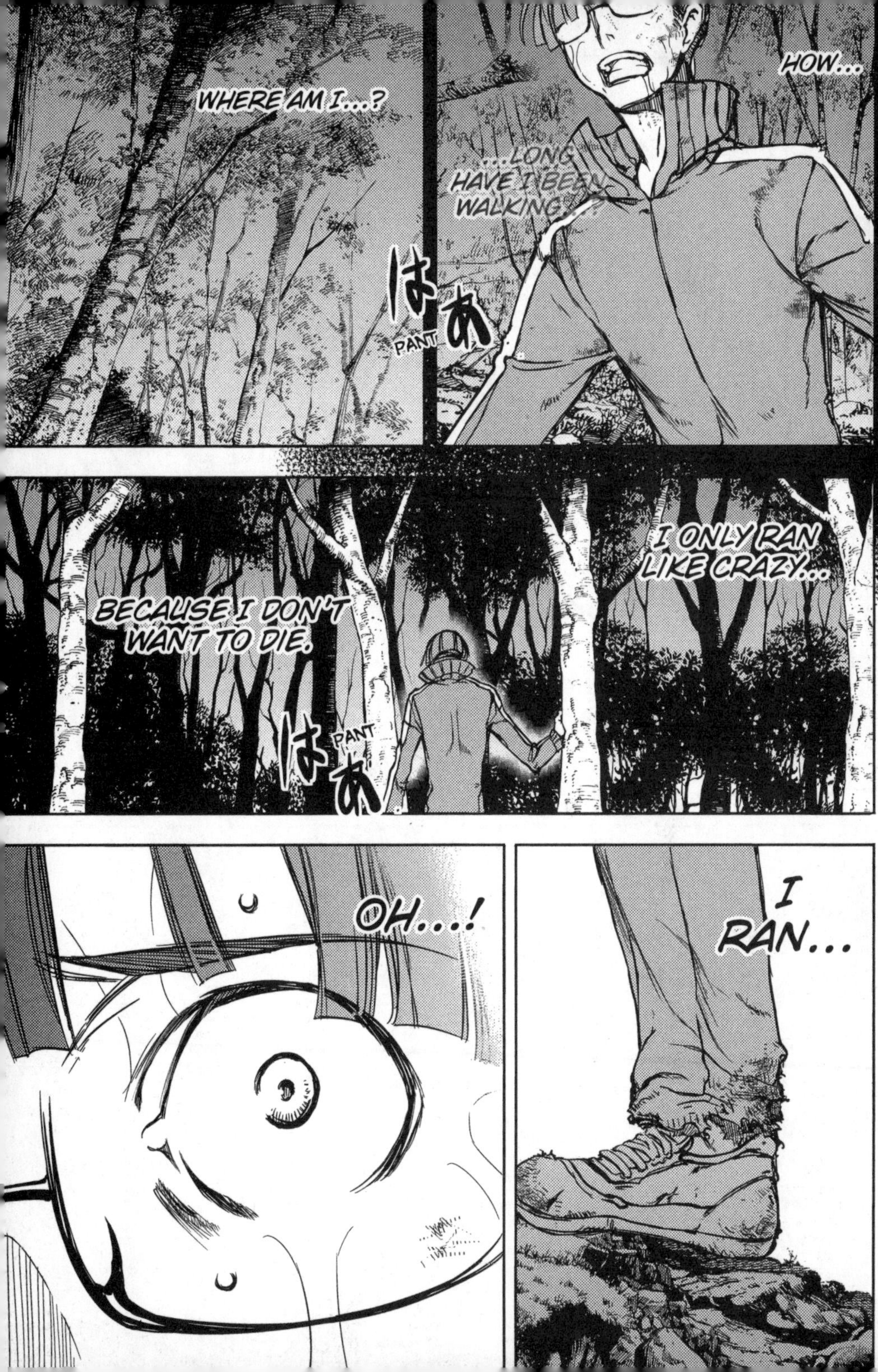
HOW...
...LONG HAVE I BEEN WALKING...?
はあ
PANT
WHERE AM I...?
I ONLY RAN LIKE CRAZY...
BECAUSE I DON'T WANT TO DIE.
はあ
PANT
I RAN...
OH...!

...ABANDONING THEM...

I RAN AWAY...

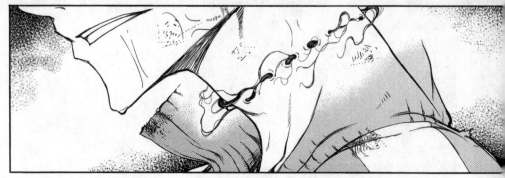

NO!!

I DIDN'T BE-TRAY YOU!!

?!

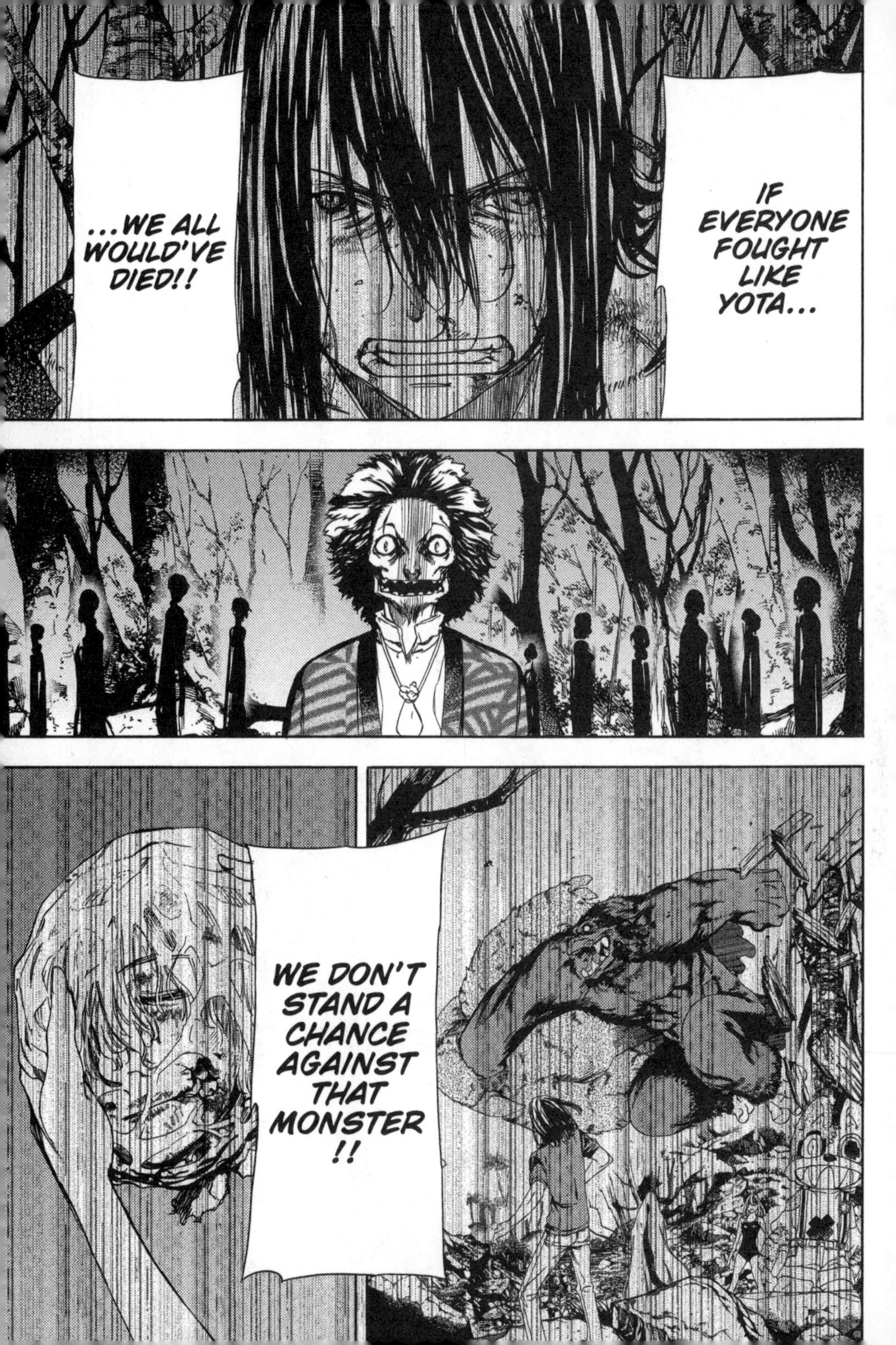
IF EVERYONE FOUGHT LIKE YOTA...
...WE ALL WOULD'VE DIED!!
WE DON'T STAND A CHANCE AGAINST THAT MONSTER!!

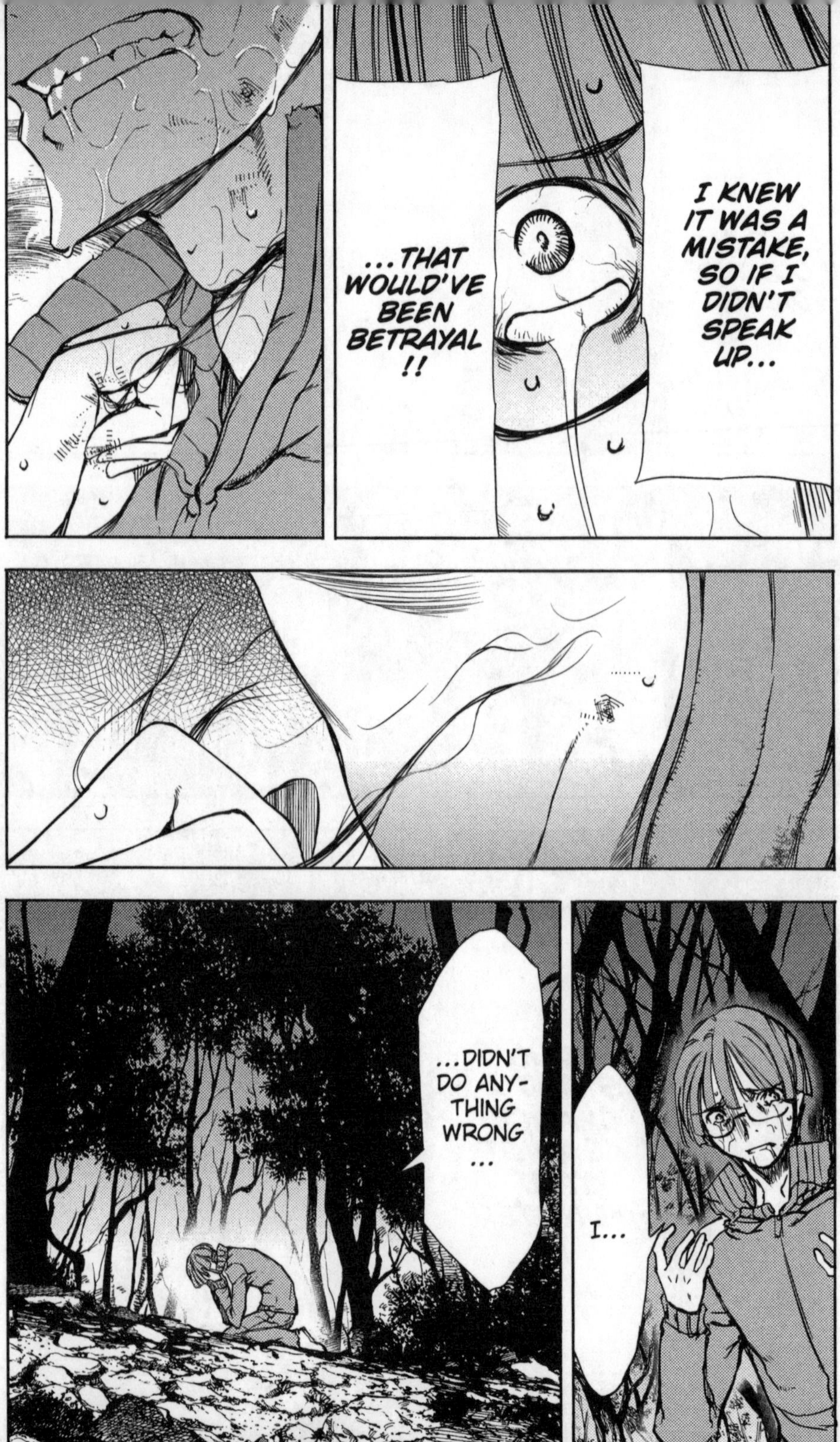
I KNEW IT WAS A MISTAKE, SO IF I DIDN'T SPEAK UP...
...THAT WOULD'VE BEEN BETRAYAL!!
......
I...
...DIDN'T DO ANYTHING WRONG ...

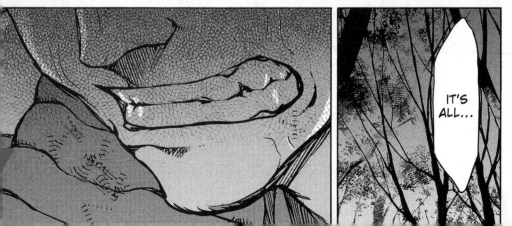

IT'S
ALL...

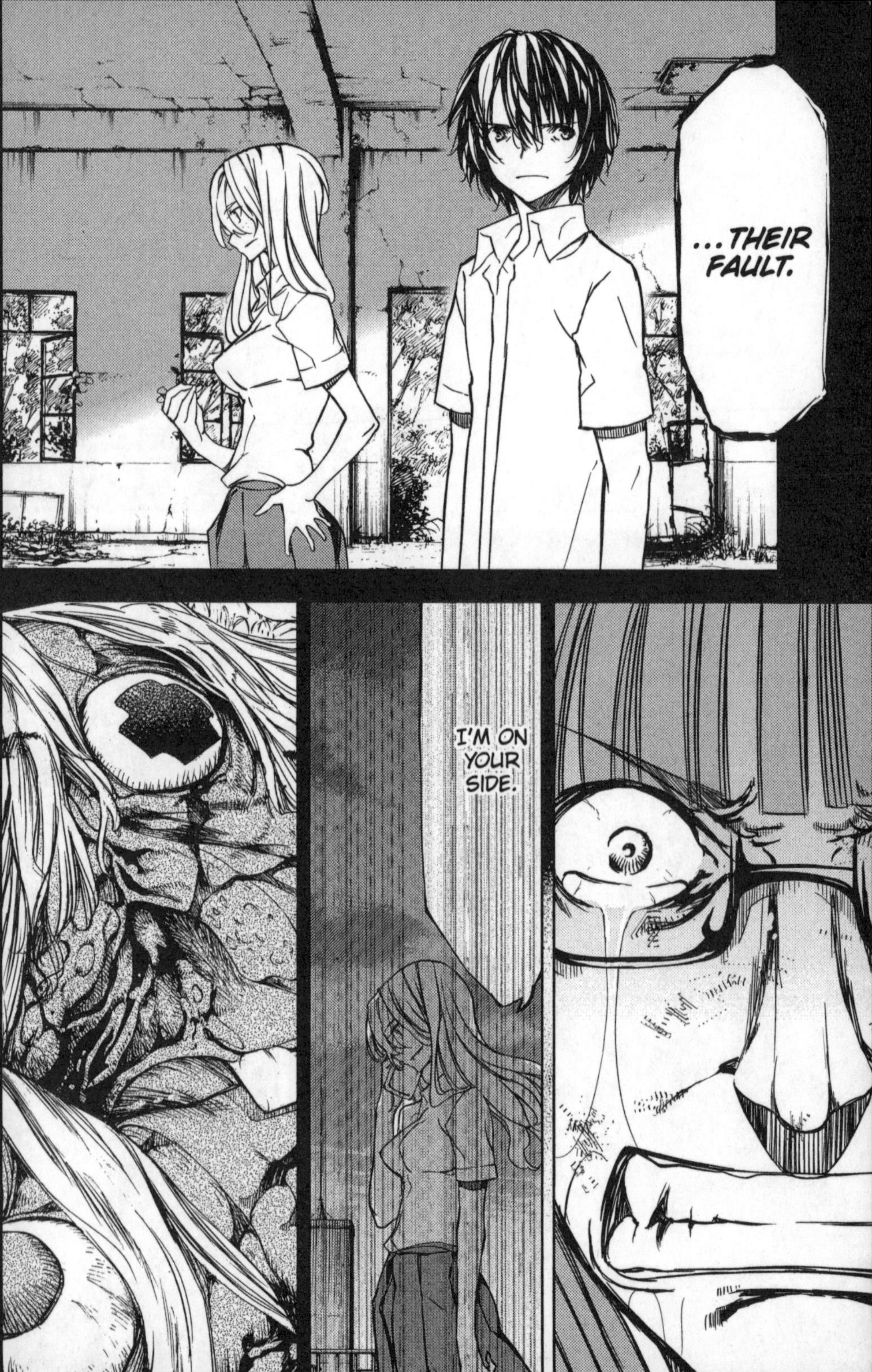
...THEIR FAULT.
I'M ON YOUR SIDE.

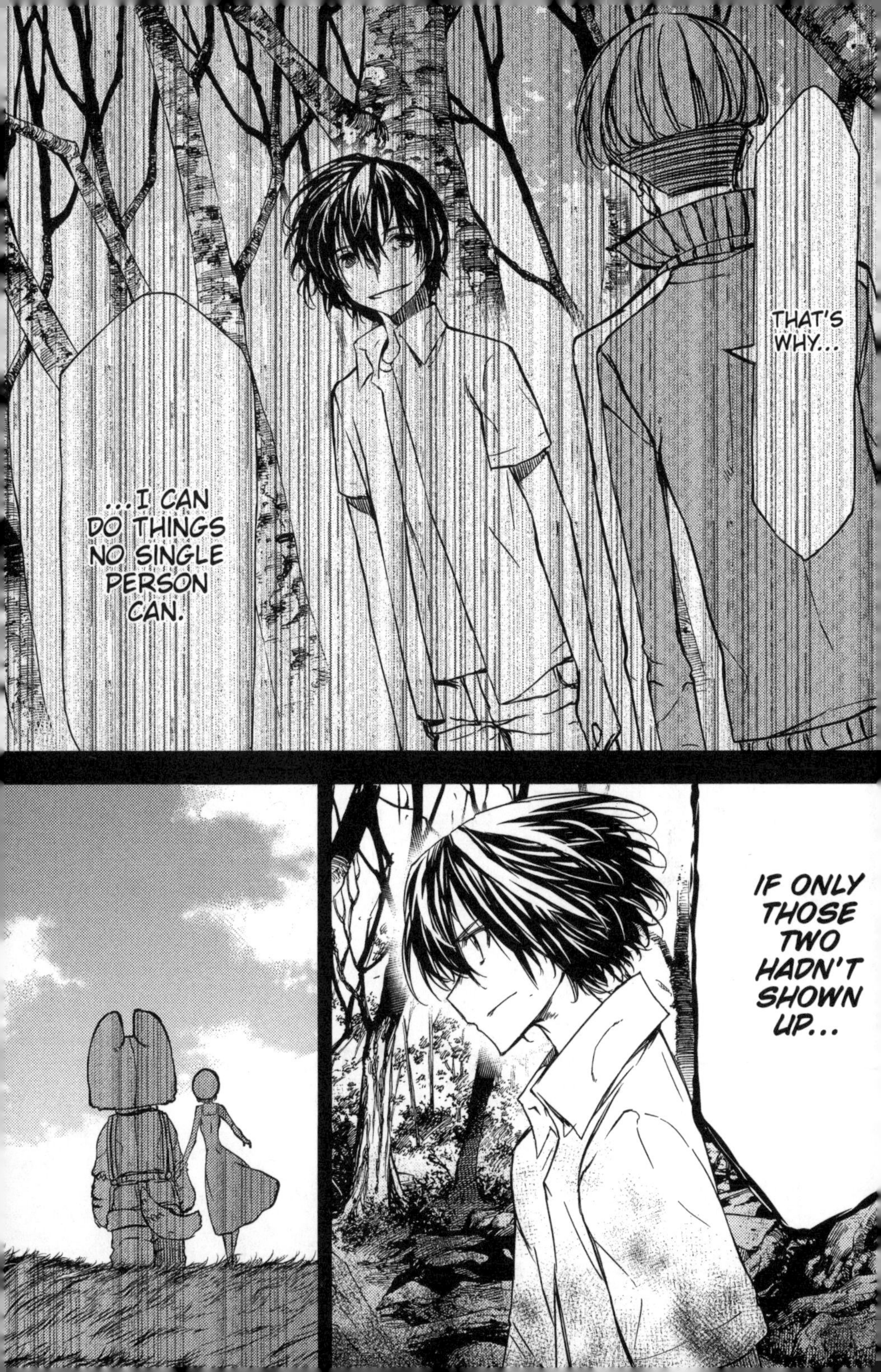
THAT'S WHY...
...I CAN DO THINGS NO SINGLE PERSON CAN.
IF ONLY THOSE TWO HADN'T SHOWN UP...

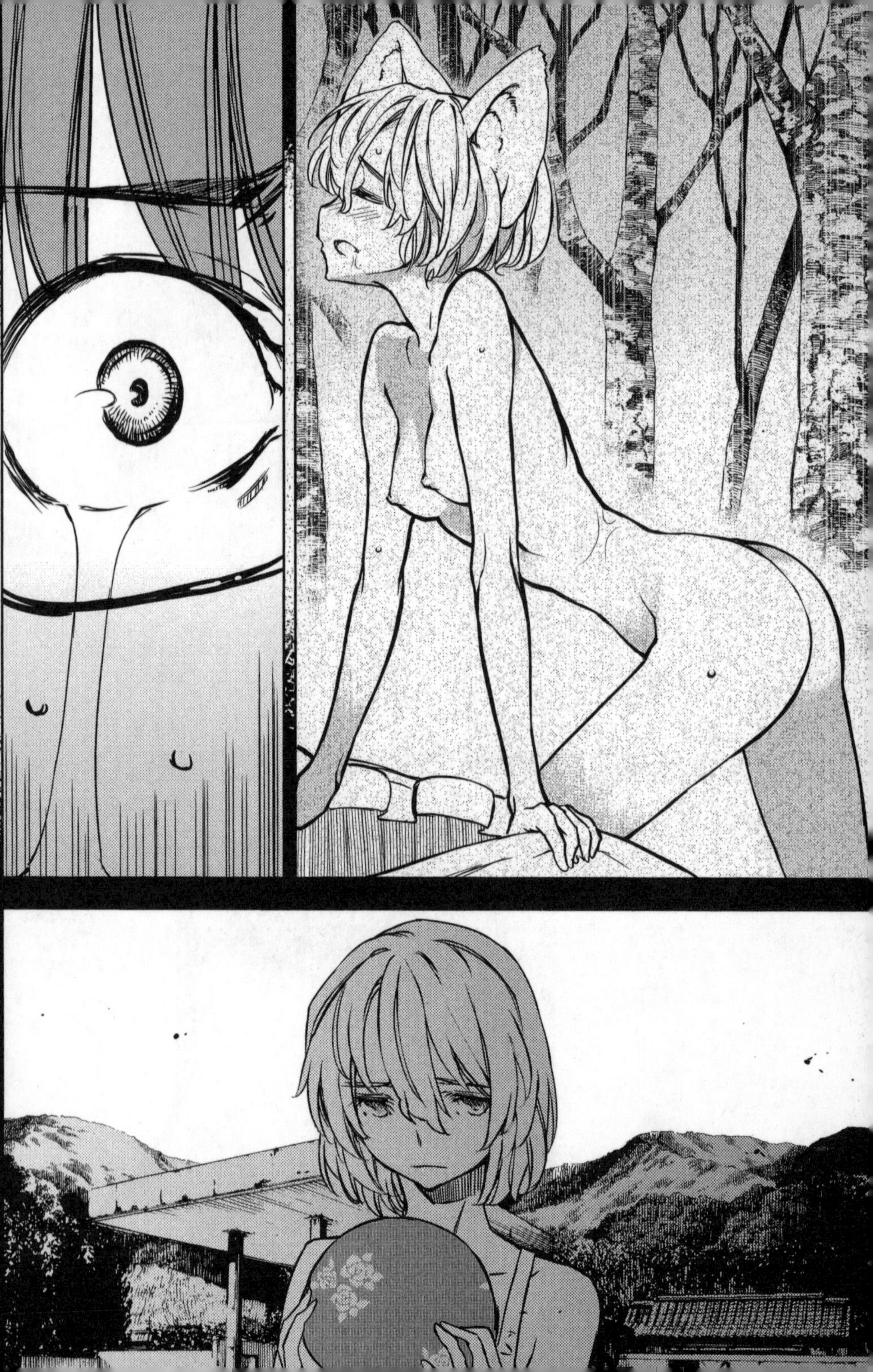

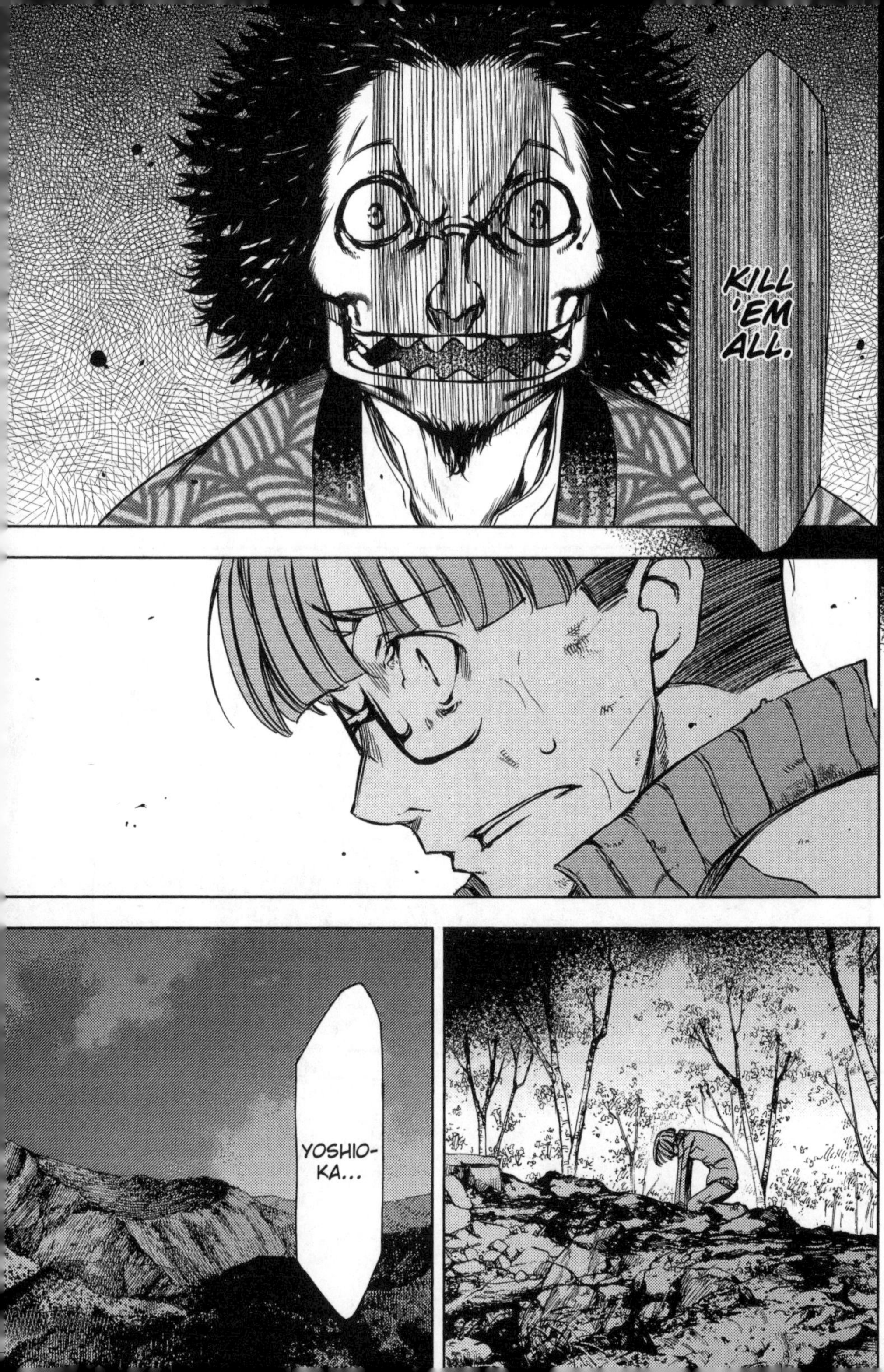
KILL 'EM ALL.
YOSHIO-KA...

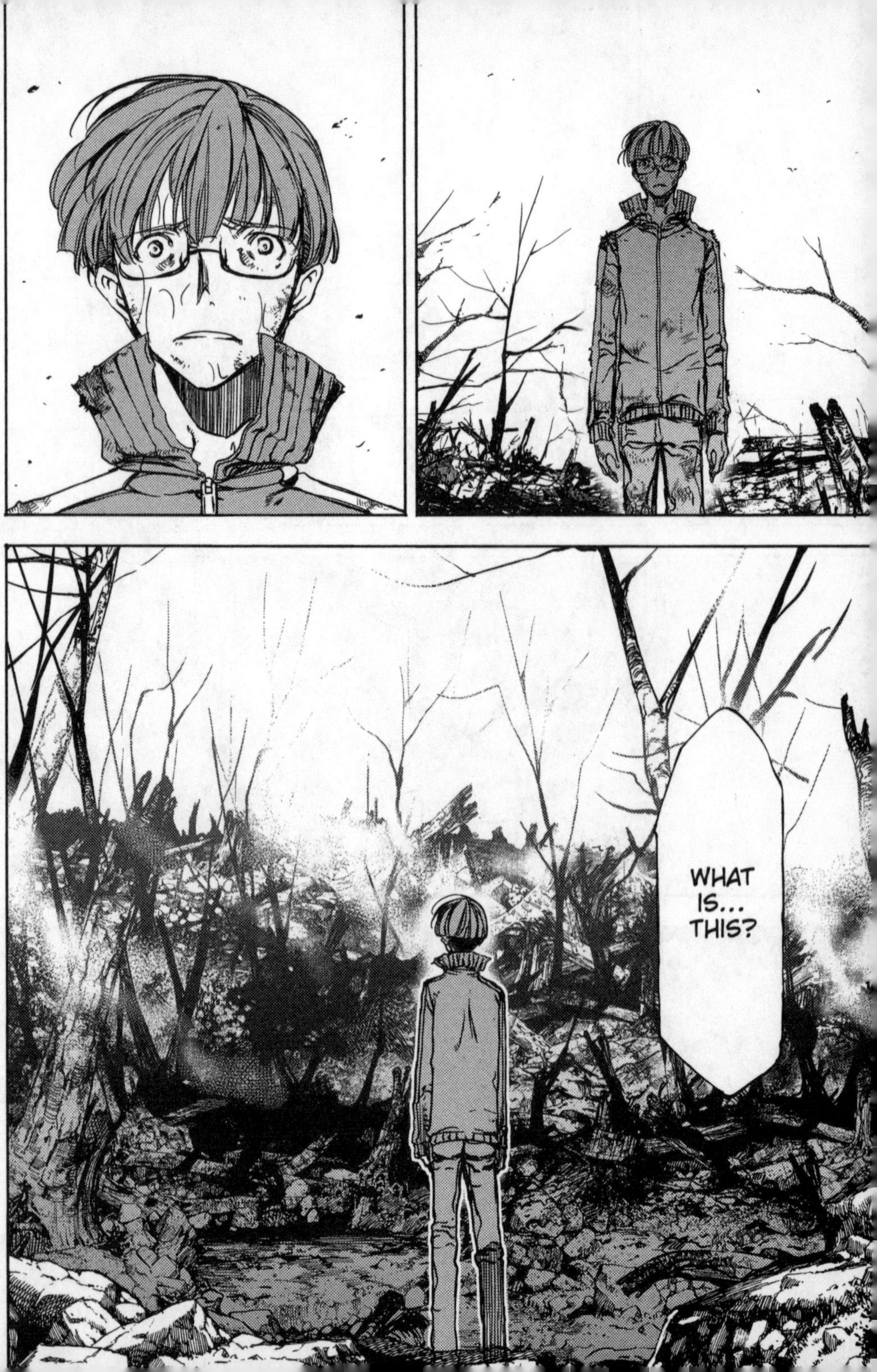
WHAT IS... THIS?

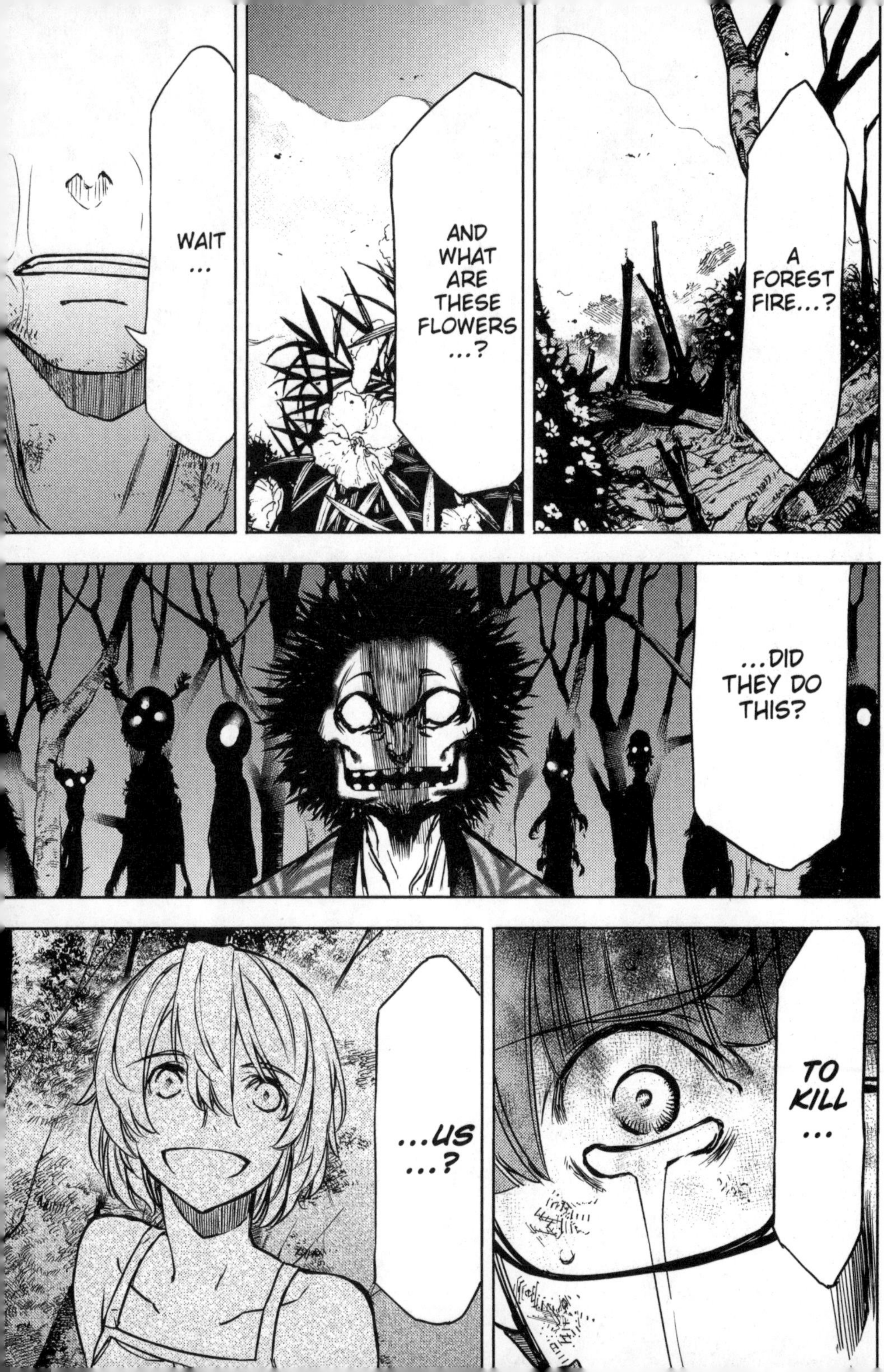

A FOREST FIRE...?
AND WHAT ARE THESE FLOWERS...?
WAIT...
...DID THEY DO THIS?
TO KILL...
...US...?

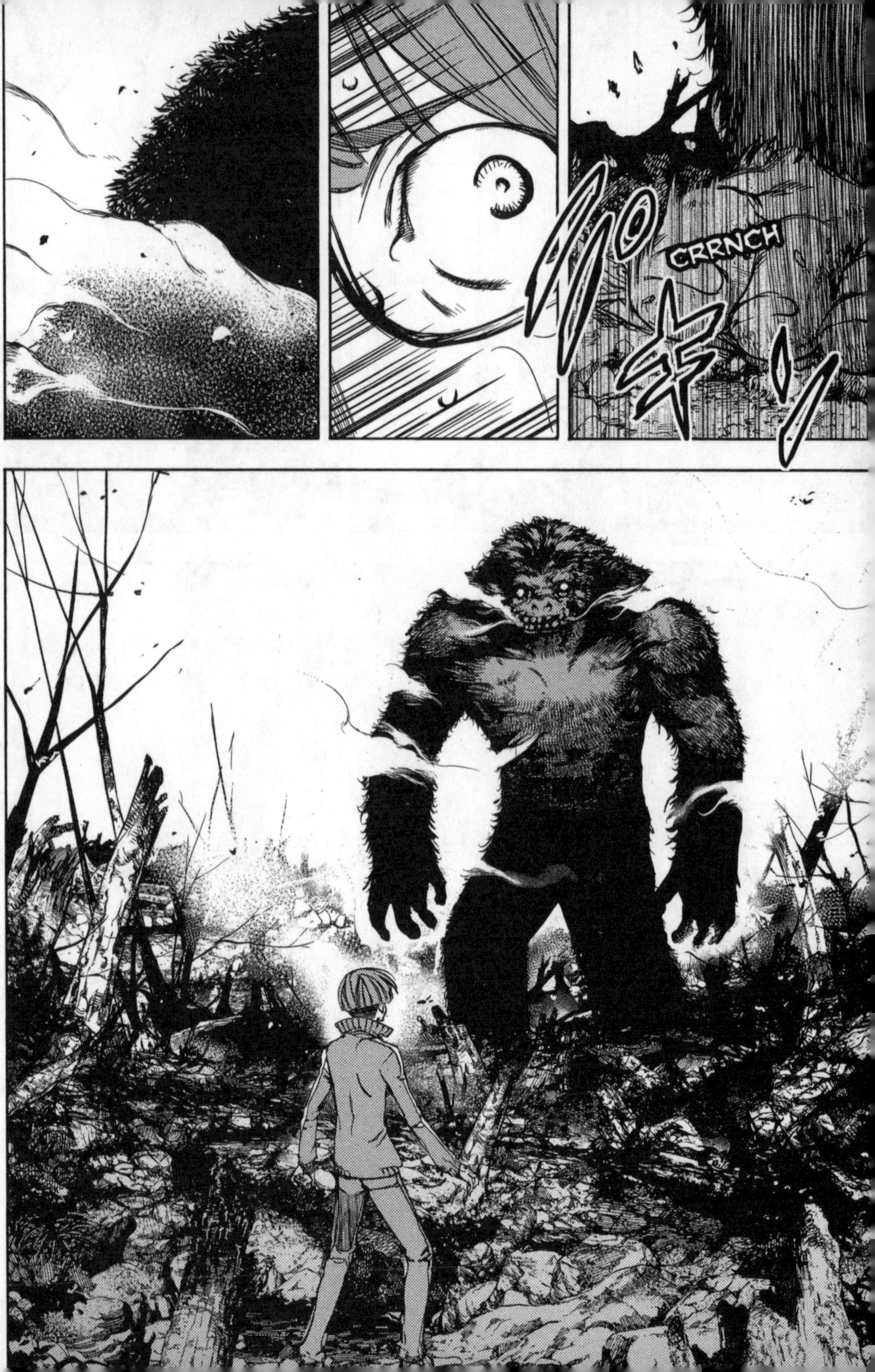
CRRNCH

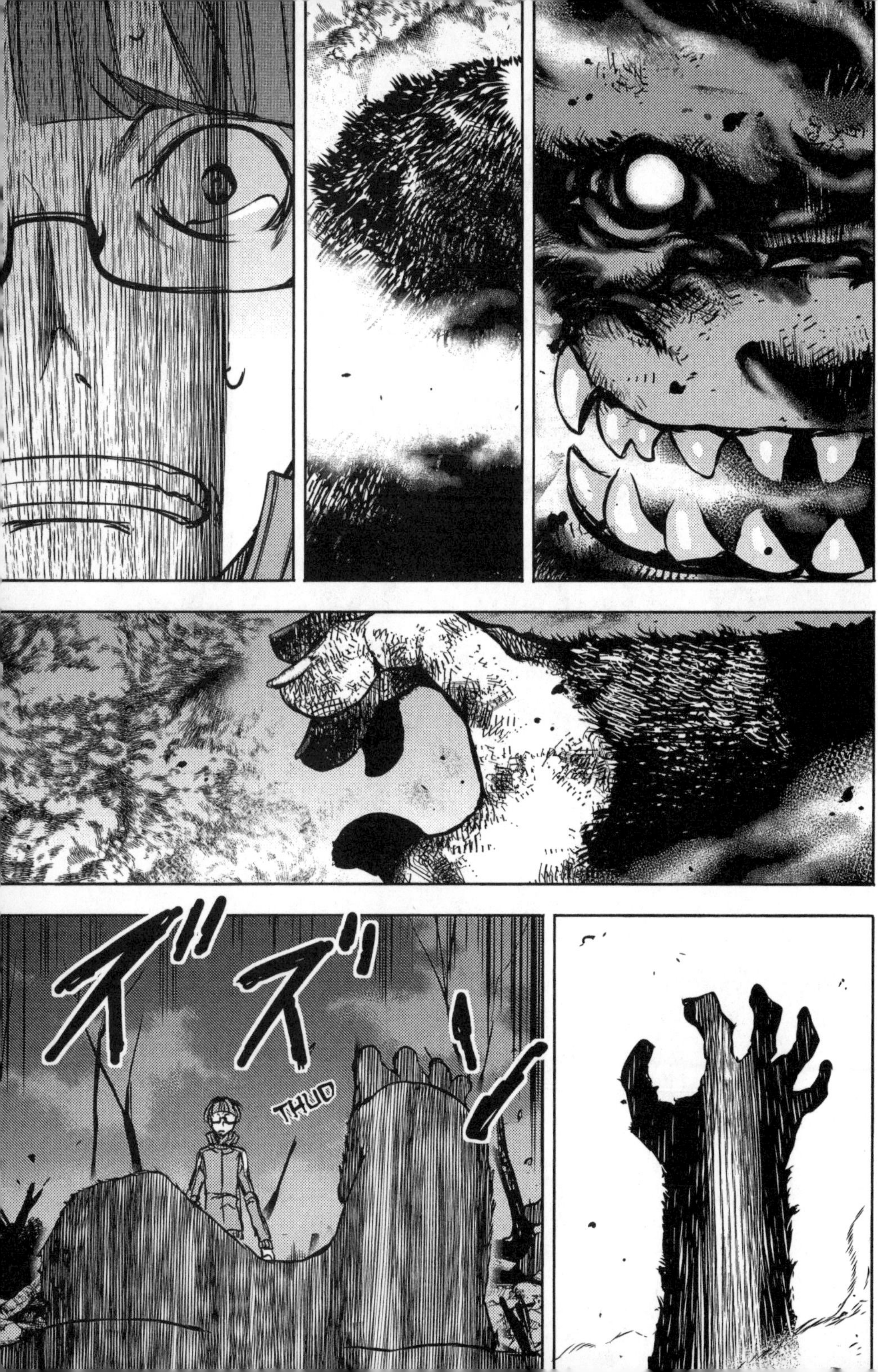
ズズ
THUD

WHAT'S GOING ON...?

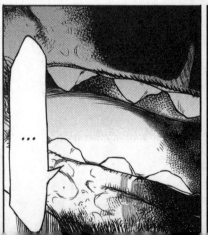

...

WHY IS THIS GUY...

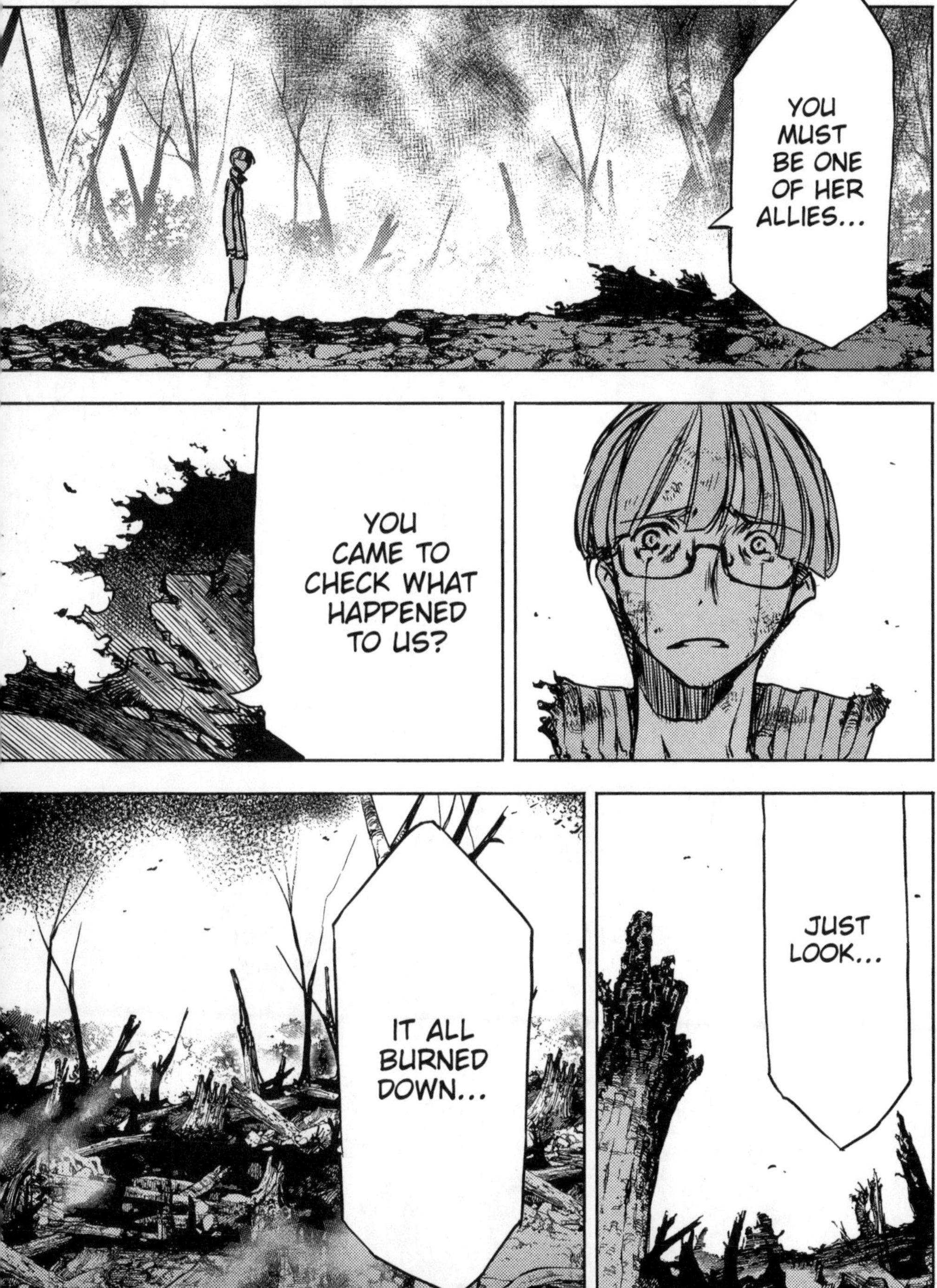
YOU MUST BE ONE OF HER ALLIES...
YOU CAME TO CHECK WHAT HAPPENED TO US?
JUST LOOK...
IT ALL BURNED DOWN...

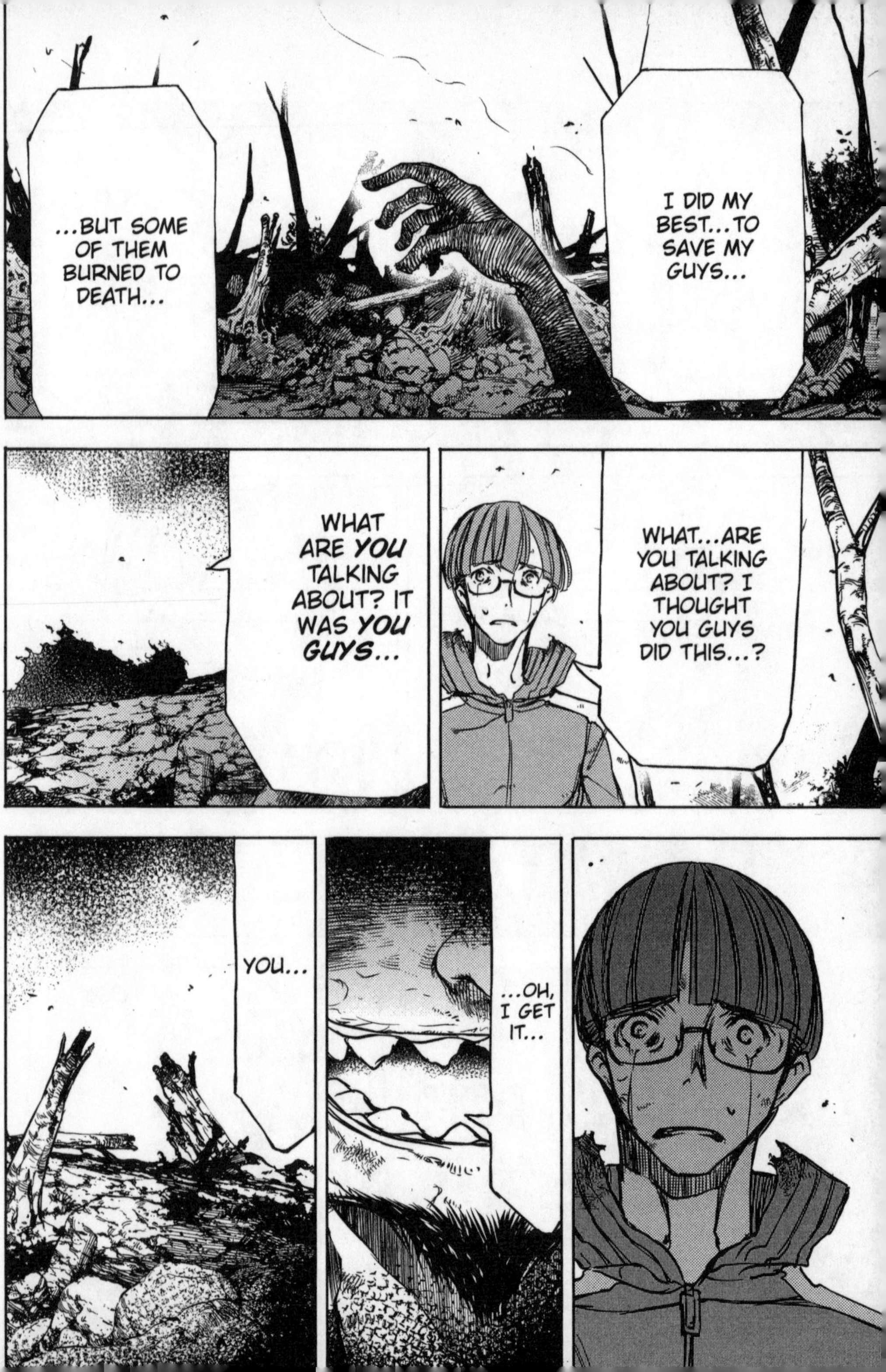
I DID MY BEST...TO SAVE MY GUYS...
...BUT SOME OF THEM BURNED TO DEATH...
WHAT...ARE YOU TALKING ABOUT? I THOUGHT YOU GUYS DID THIS...?
WHAT ARE *YOU* TALKING ABOUT? IT WAS *YOU GUYS*...
...OH, I GET IT...
YOU...

...ABAN-DONED THEM...

YOU RAN AWAY, HUH?

RELAX.

NO! I...

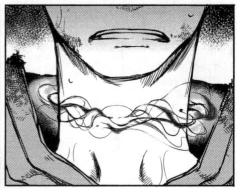

YOUR FRIENDS ARE ALIVE.

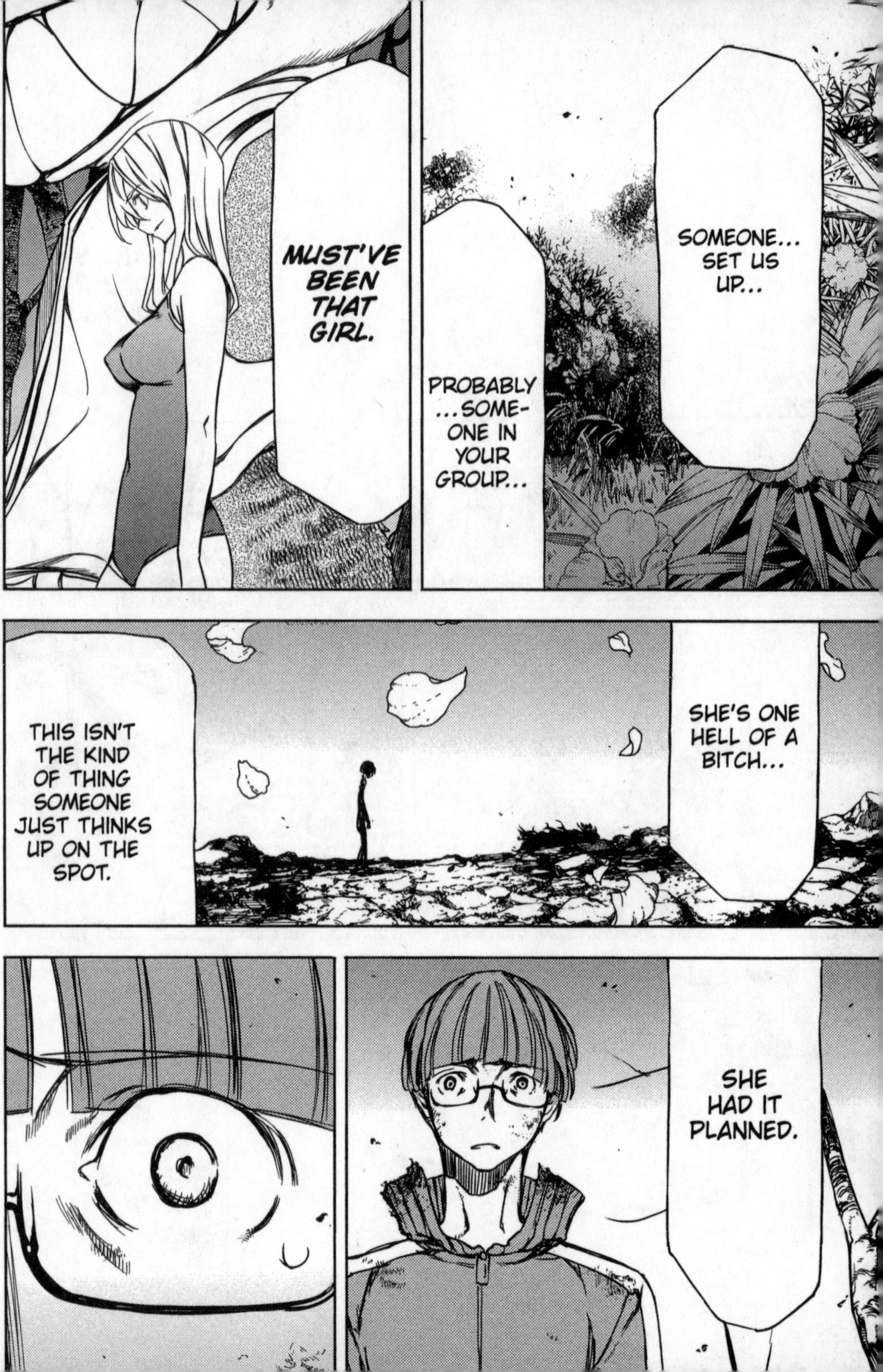
SOMEONE... SET US UP...
PROBABLY ...SOME-ONE IN YOUR GROUP...
MUST'VE BEEN THAT GIRL.
SHE'S ONE HELL OF A BITCH...
THIS ISN'T THE KIND OF THING SOMEONE JUST THINKS UP ON THE SPOT.
SHE HAD IT PLANNED.

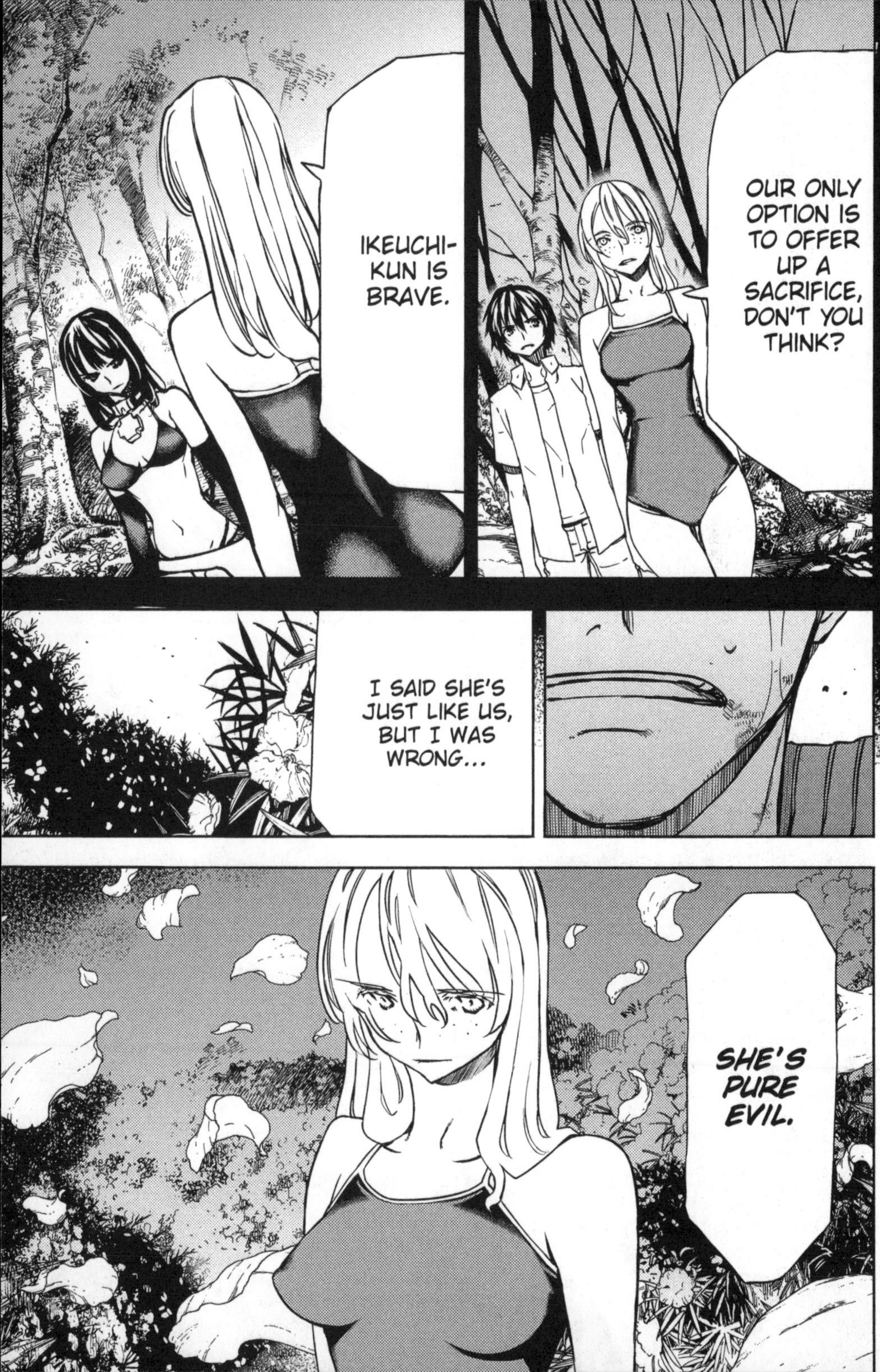
OUR ONLY OPTION IS TO OFFER UP A SACRIFICE, DON'T YOU THINK?
IKEUCHI-KUN IS BRAVE.
I SAID SHE'S JUST LIKE US, BUT I WAS WRONG...
SHE'S PURE EVIL.

...DID I...

THEN WHY...

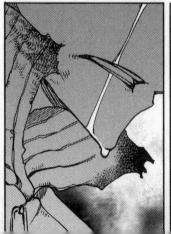

...ABANDON MY FRIENDS...

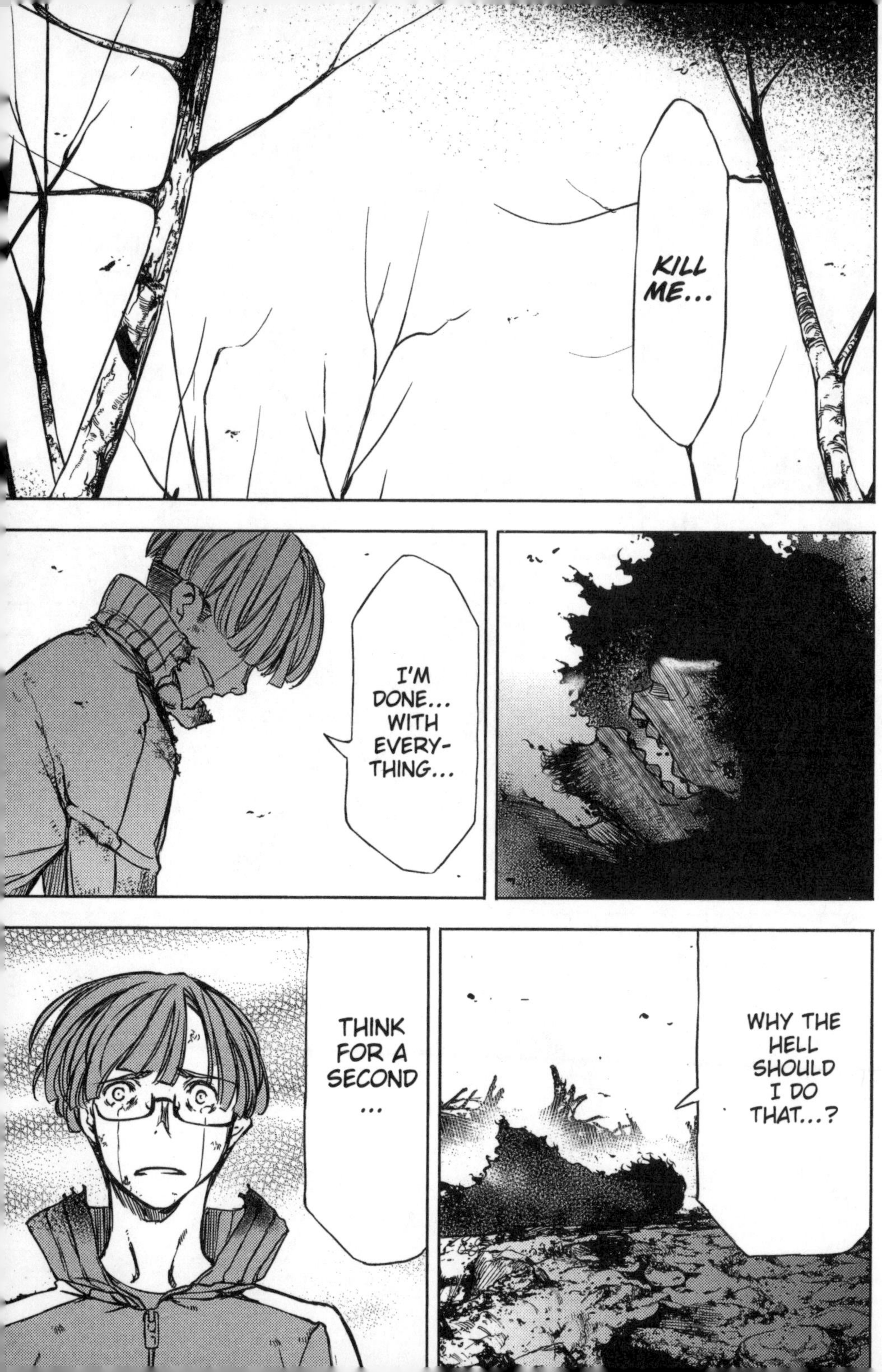
KILL ME…
I'M DONE… WITH EVERY-THING…
WHY THE HELL SHOULD I DO THAT…?
THINK FOR A SECOND …

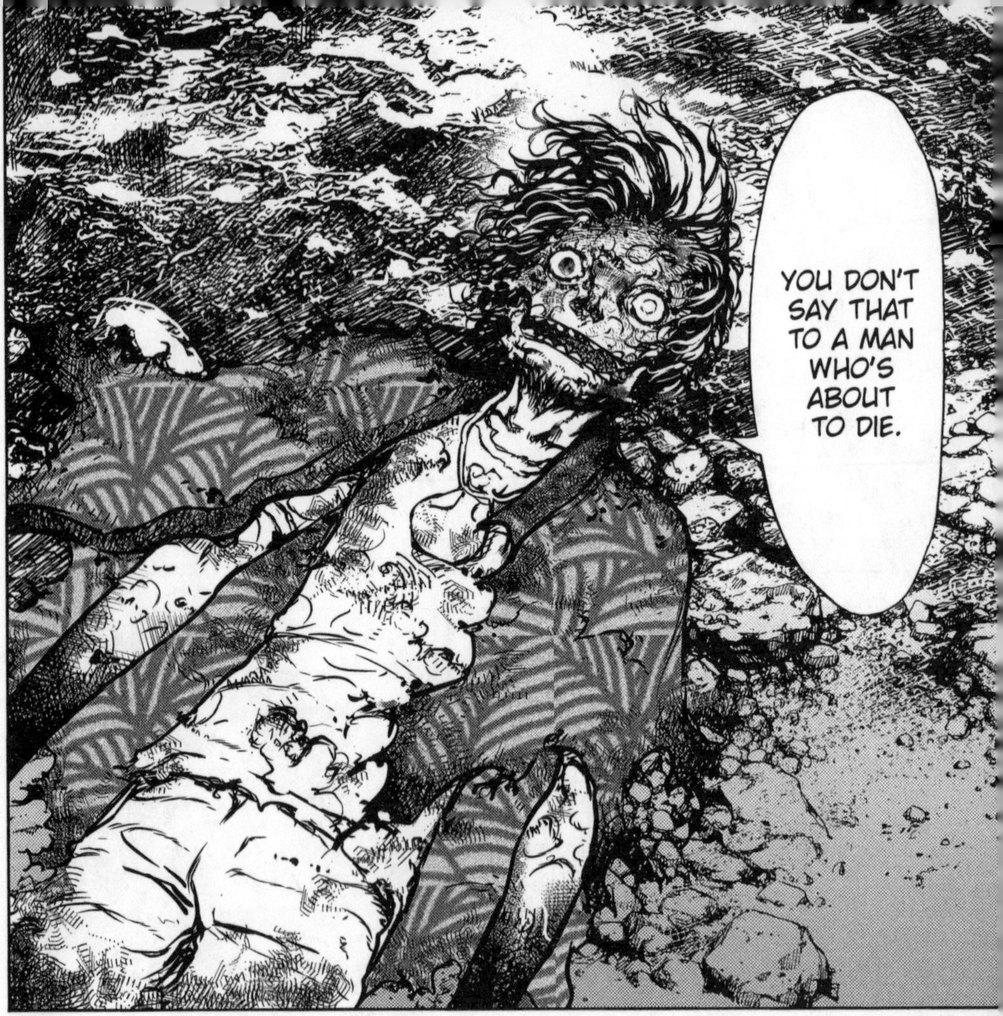
YOU DON'T SAY THAT TO A MAN WHO'S ABOUT TO DIE.
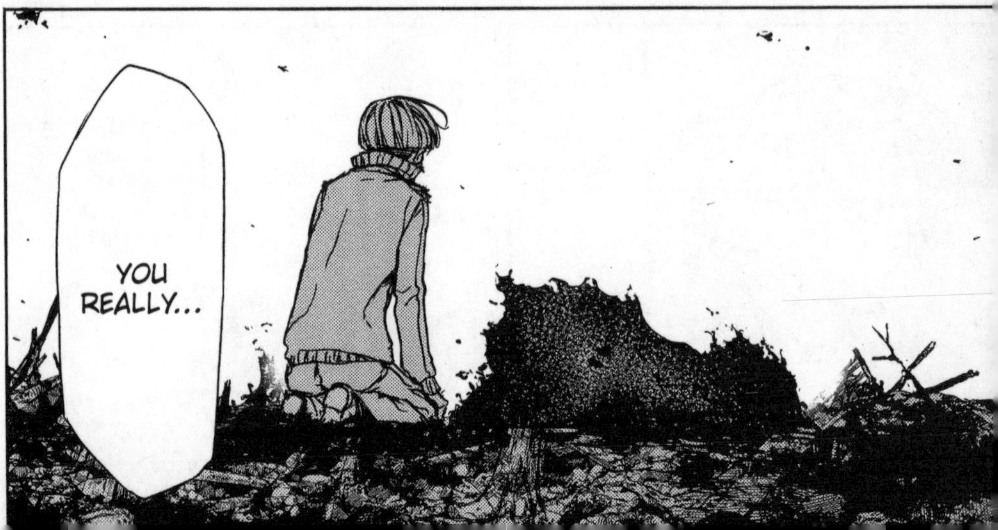
YOU REALLY...

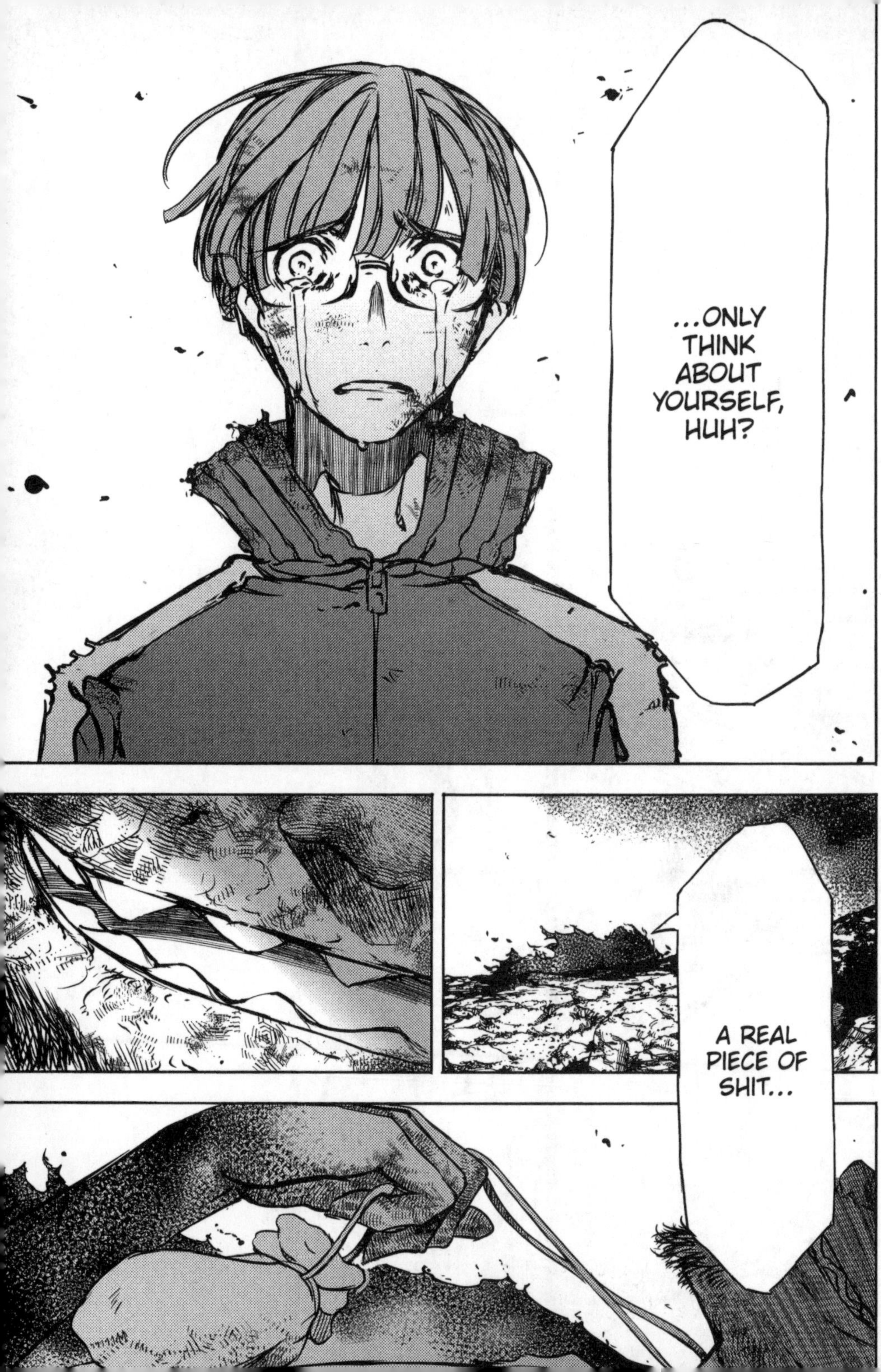
...ONLY THINK ABOUT YOURSELF, HUH?
A REAL PIECE OF SHIT...

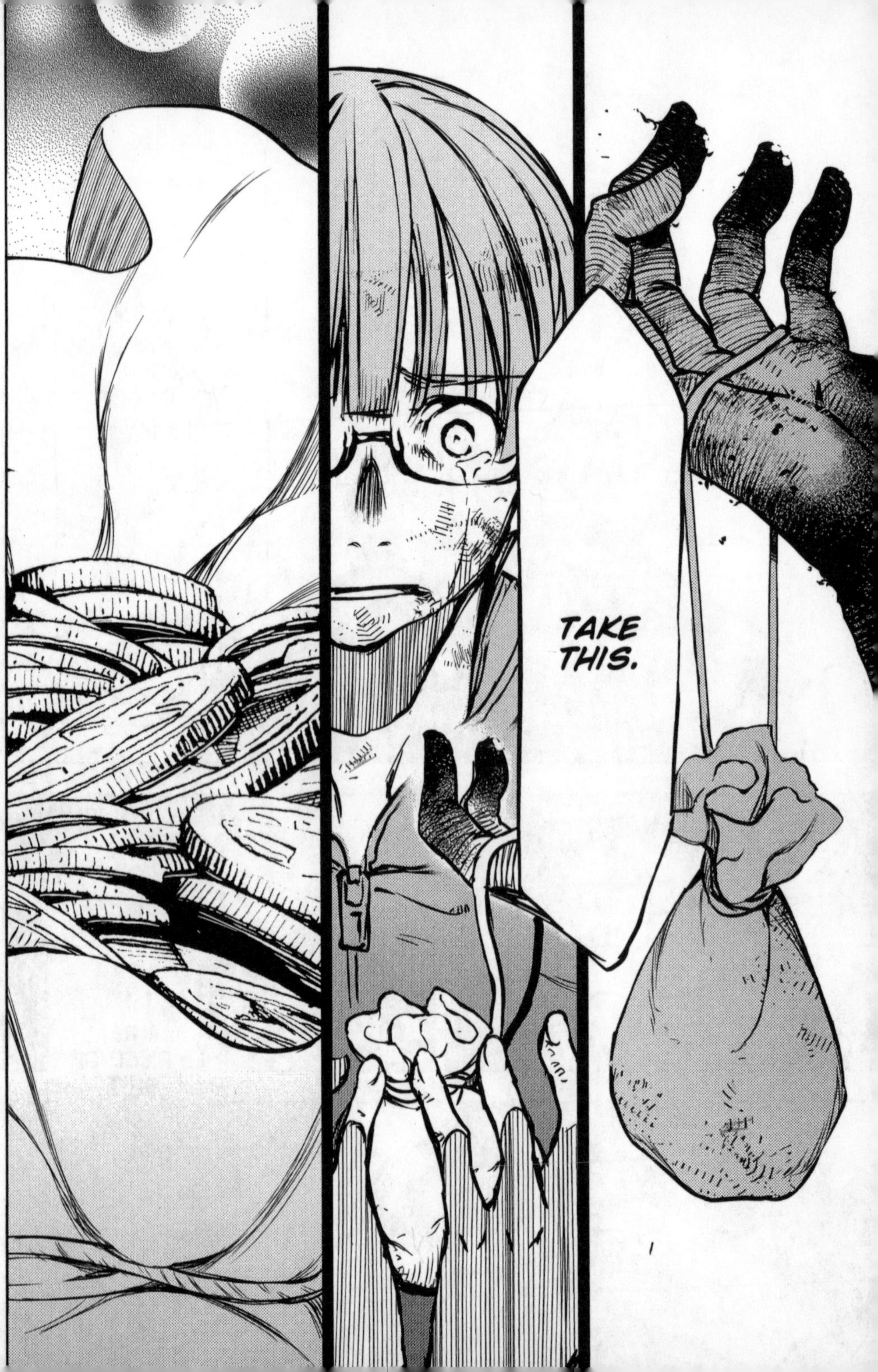
TAKE THIS.

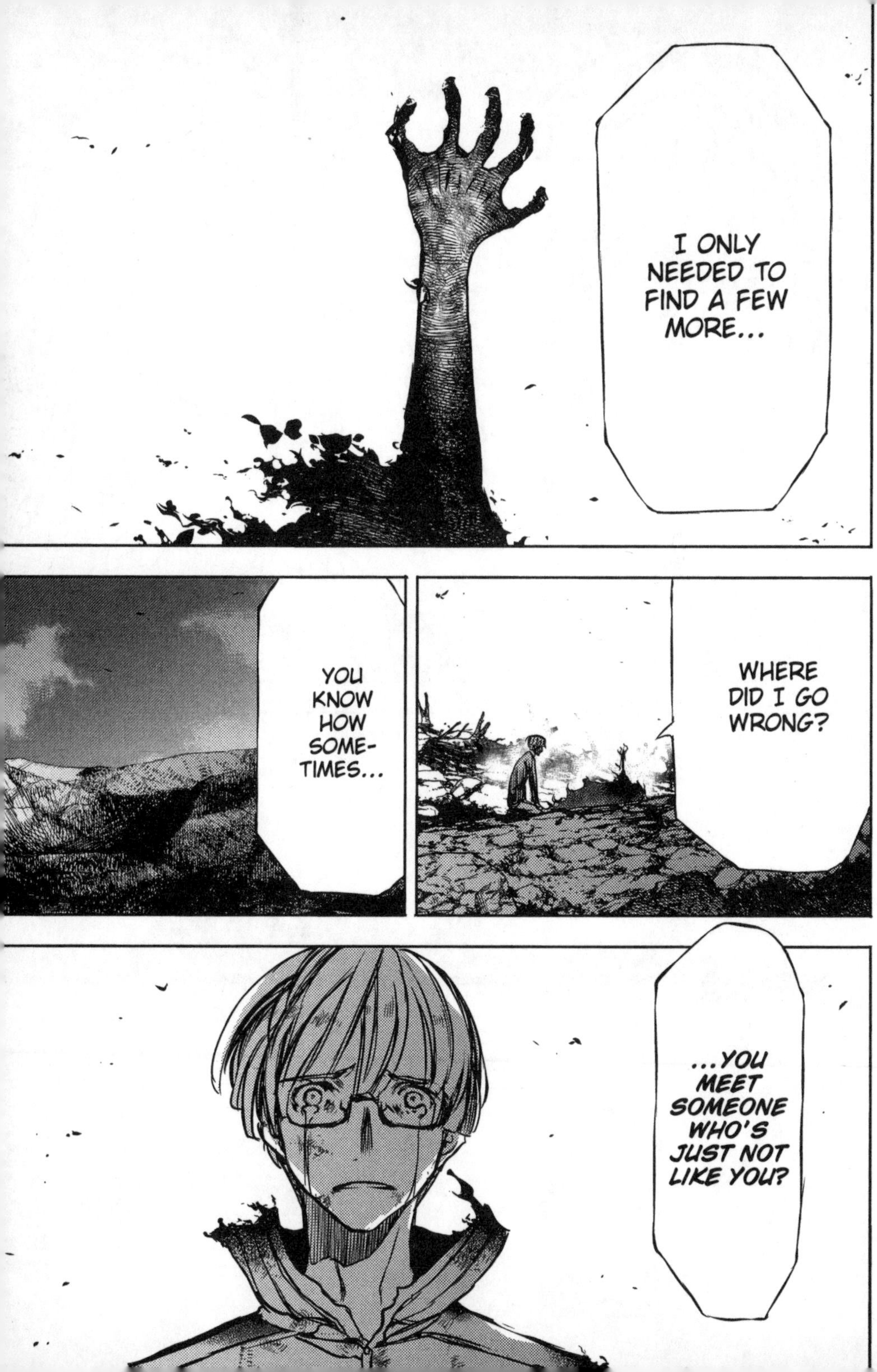
I ONLY NEEDED TO FIND A FEW MORE...
WHERE DID I GO WRONG?
YOU KNOW HOW SOME-TIMES...
...YOU MEET SOMEONE WHO'S JUST NOT LIKE YOU?

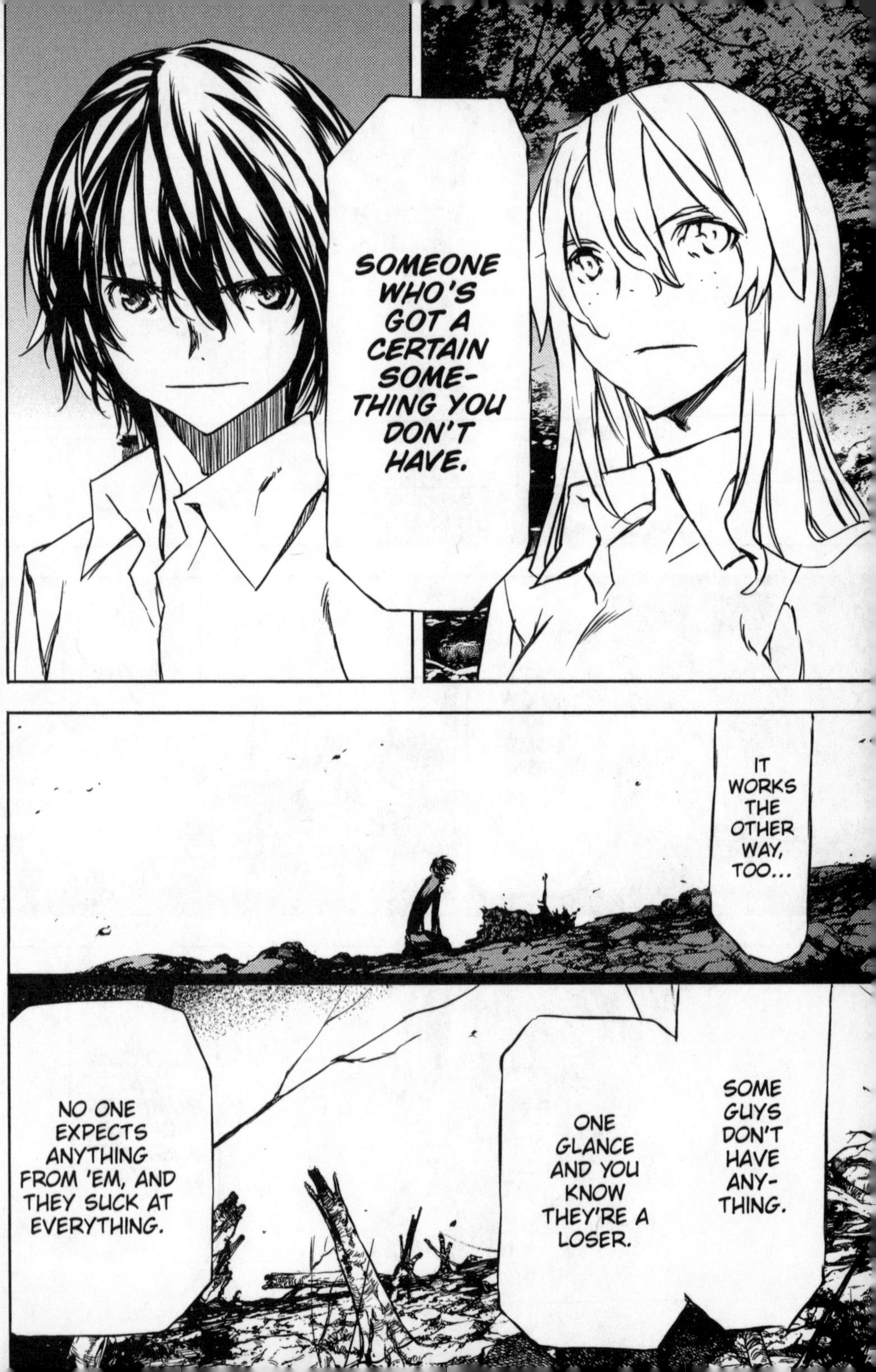
SOMEONE WHO'S GOT A CERTAIN SOME-THING YOU DON'T HAVE.
IT WORKS THE OTHER WAY, TOO...
SOME GUYS DON'T HAVE ANY-THING.
ONE GLANCE AND YOU KNOW THEY'RE A LOSER.
NO ONE EXPECTS ANYTHING FROM 'EM, AND THEY SUCK AT EVERYTHING.

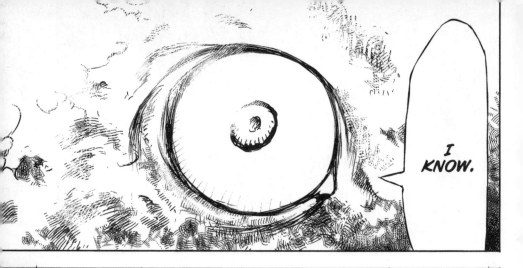

I KNOW.
BUT STILL... YOU LONG FOR THE LIGHT...
...AND WHEN YOU CAN'T REACH IT...
...YOU END UP HATING.

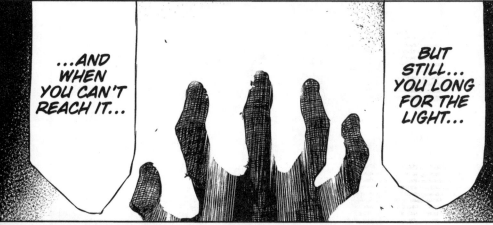

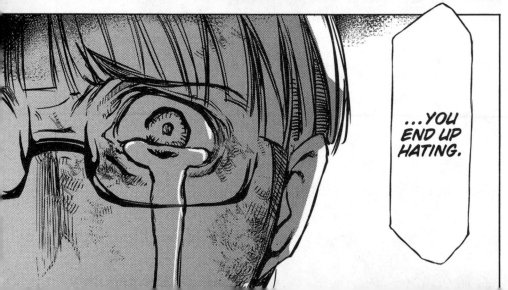

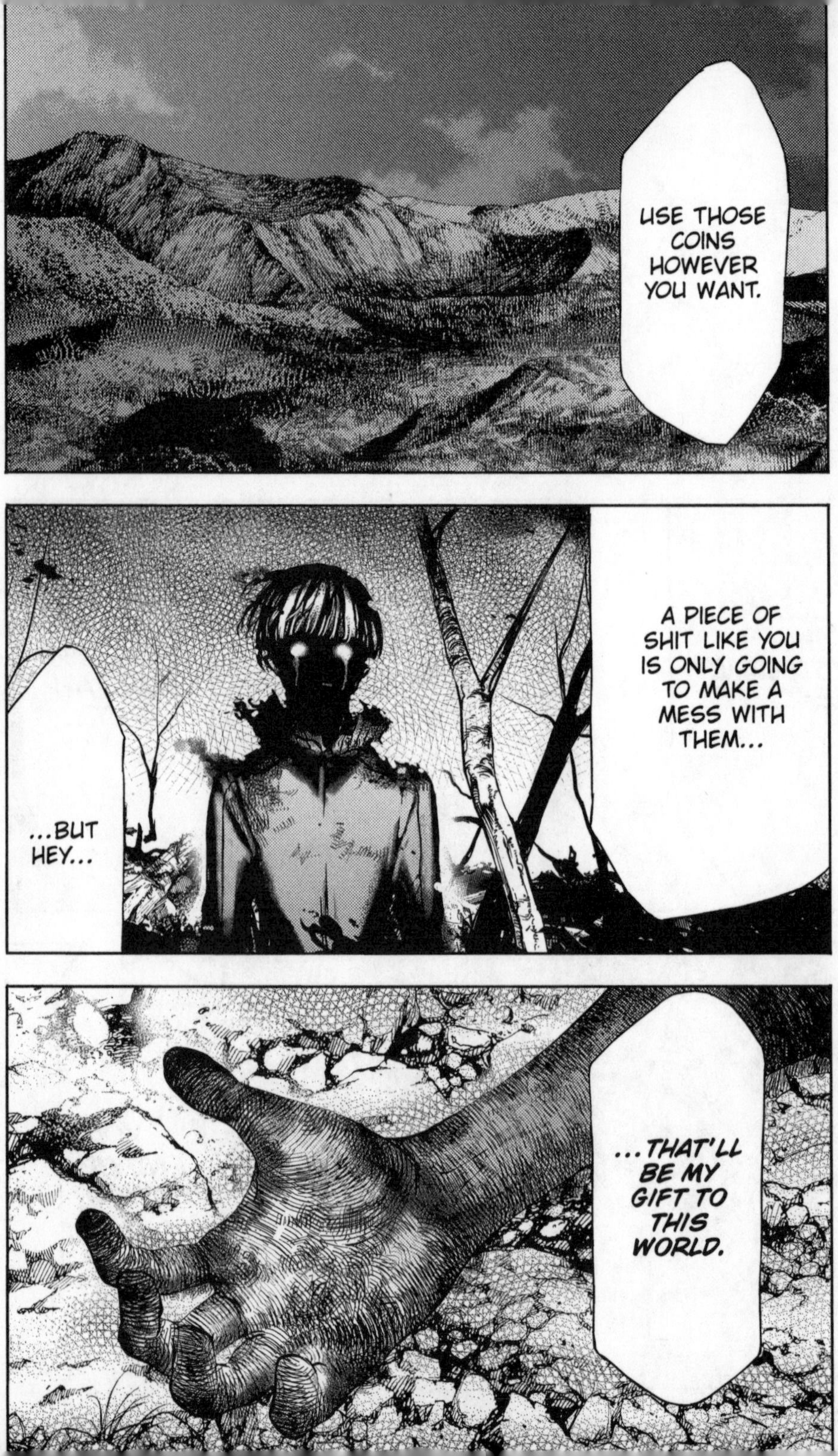
USE THOSE COINS HOWEVER YOU WANT.
A PIECE OF SHIT LIKE YOU IS ONLY GOING TO MAKE A MESS WITH THEM...
...BUT HEY...
...THAT'LL BE MY GIFT TO THIS WORLD.

CHAPTER 52 ✚ FATE

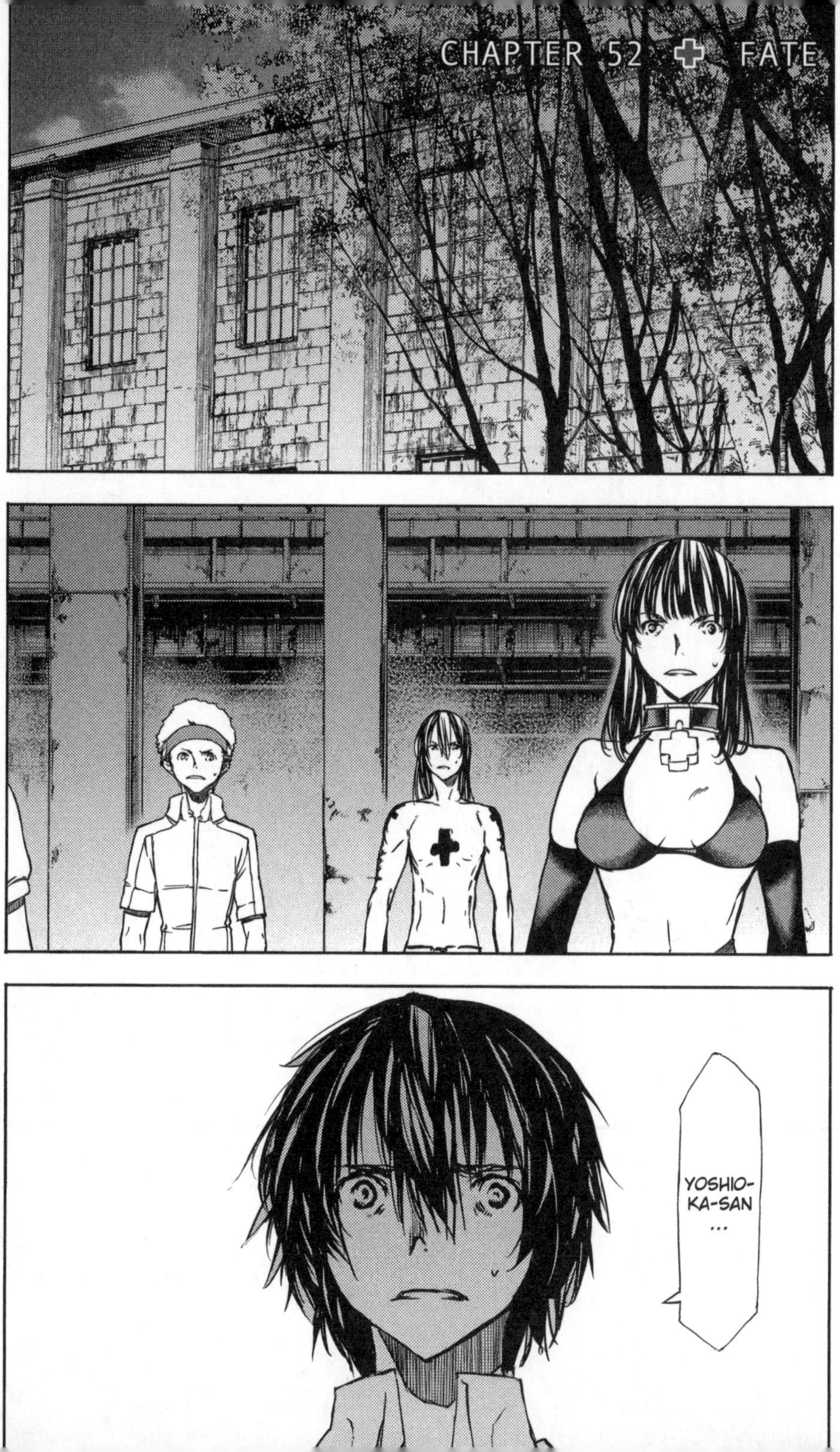
YOSHIOKA-SAN ...

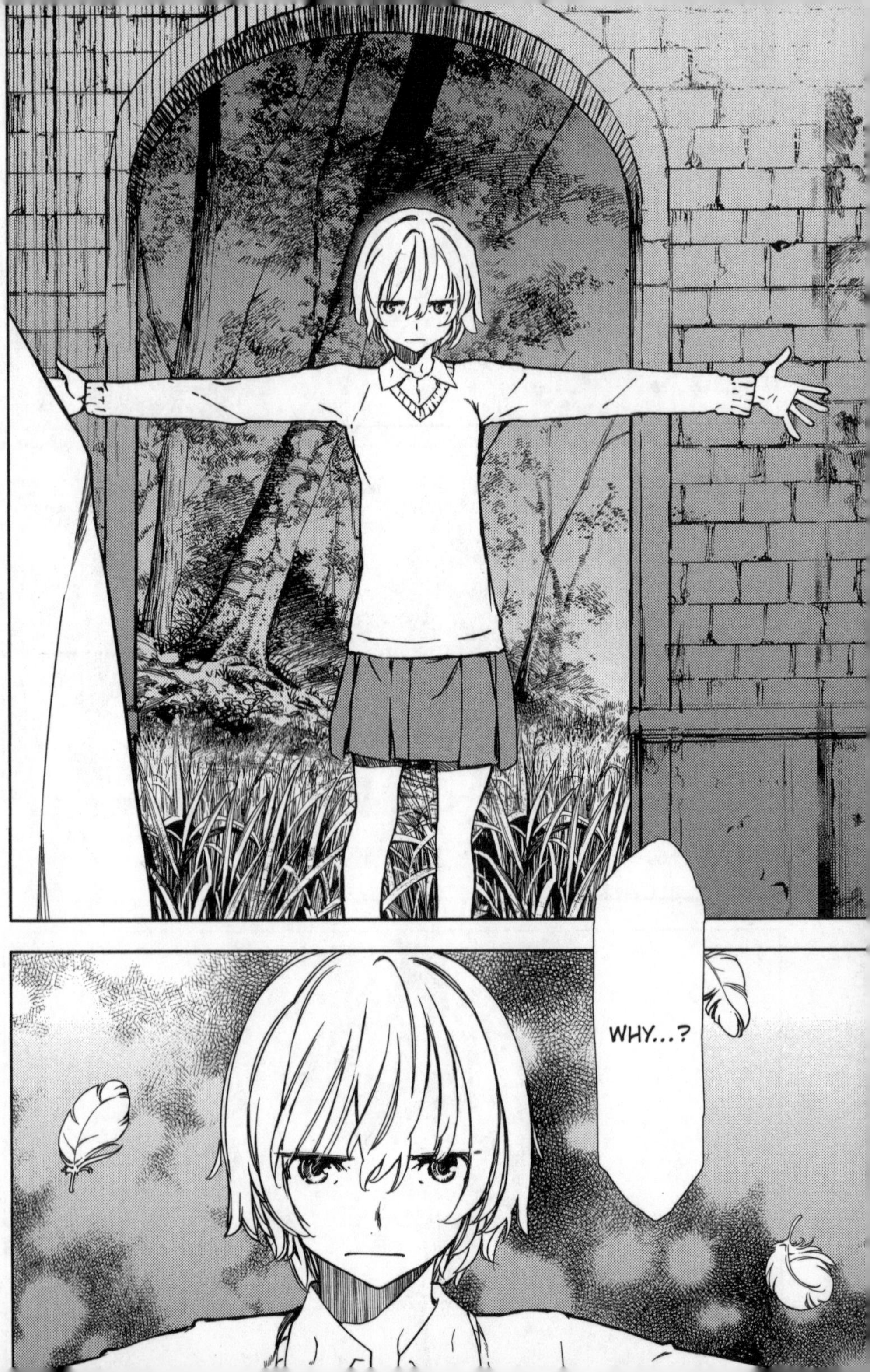
WHY...?

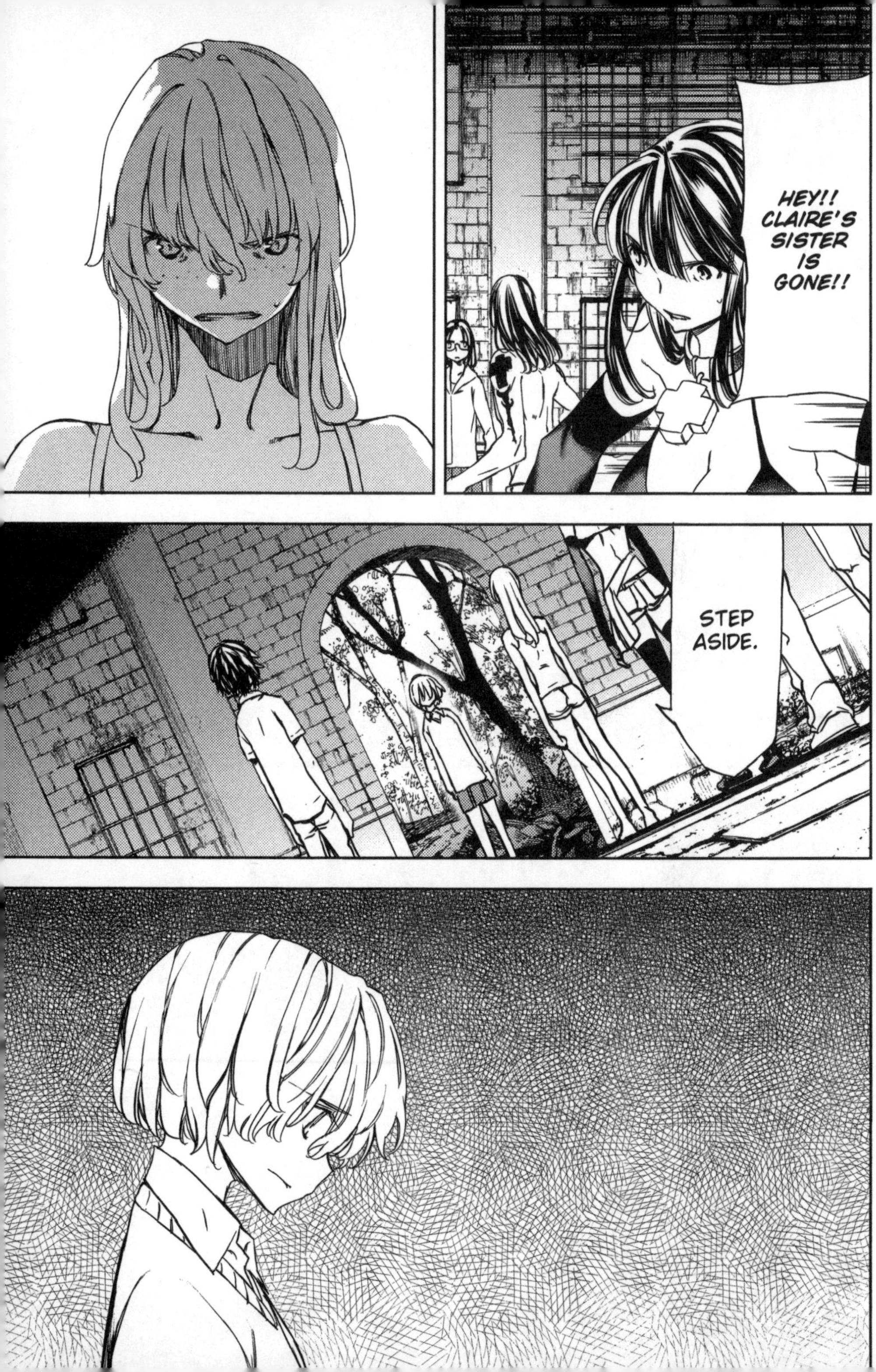
HEY!! CLAIRE'S SISTER IS GONE!!
STEP ASIDE.

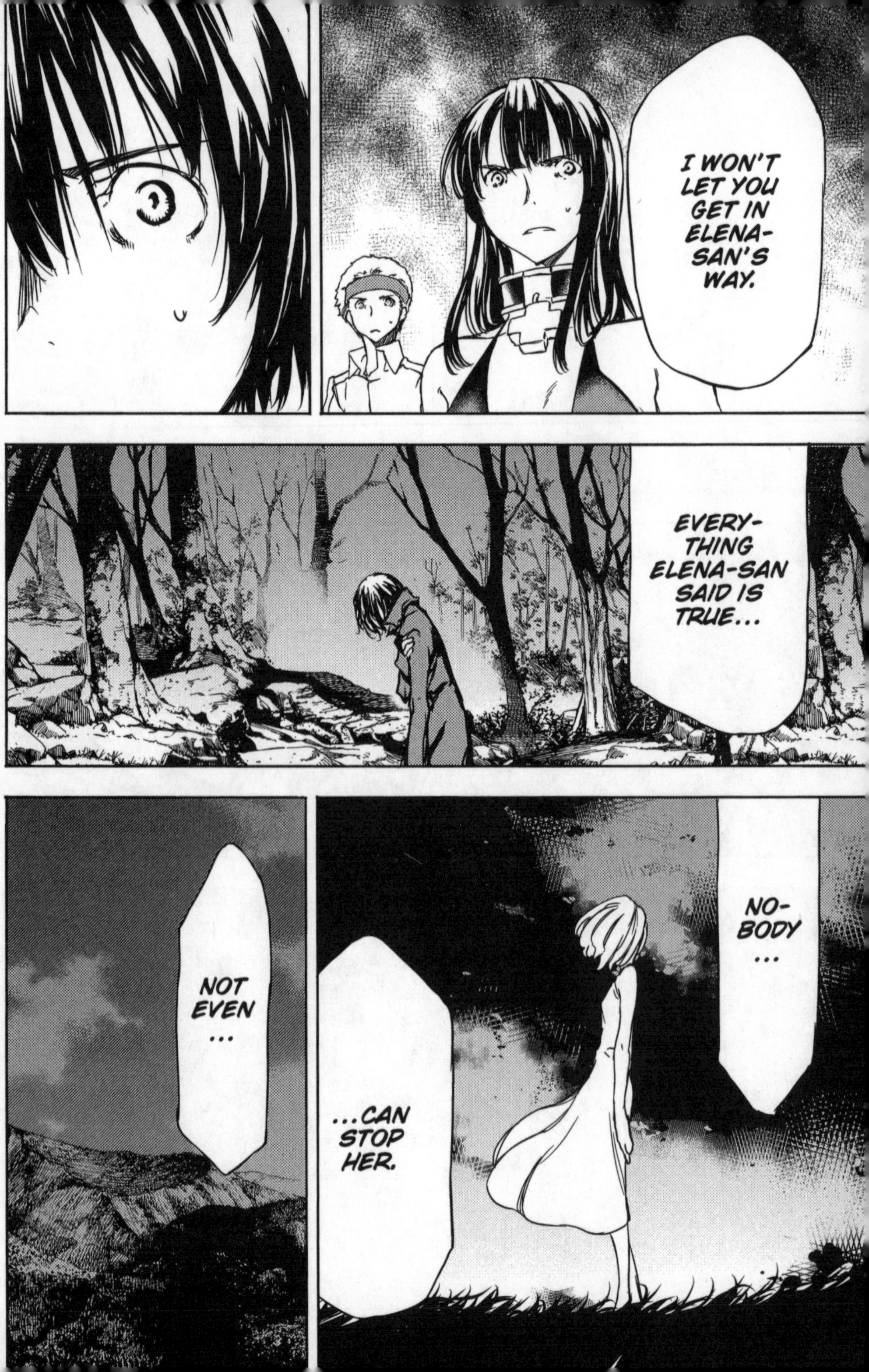
I WON'T LET YOU GET IN ELENA-SAN'S WAY.
EVERY-THING ELENA-SAN SAID IS TRUE...
NO-BODY...
...CAN STOP HER.
NOT EVEN...

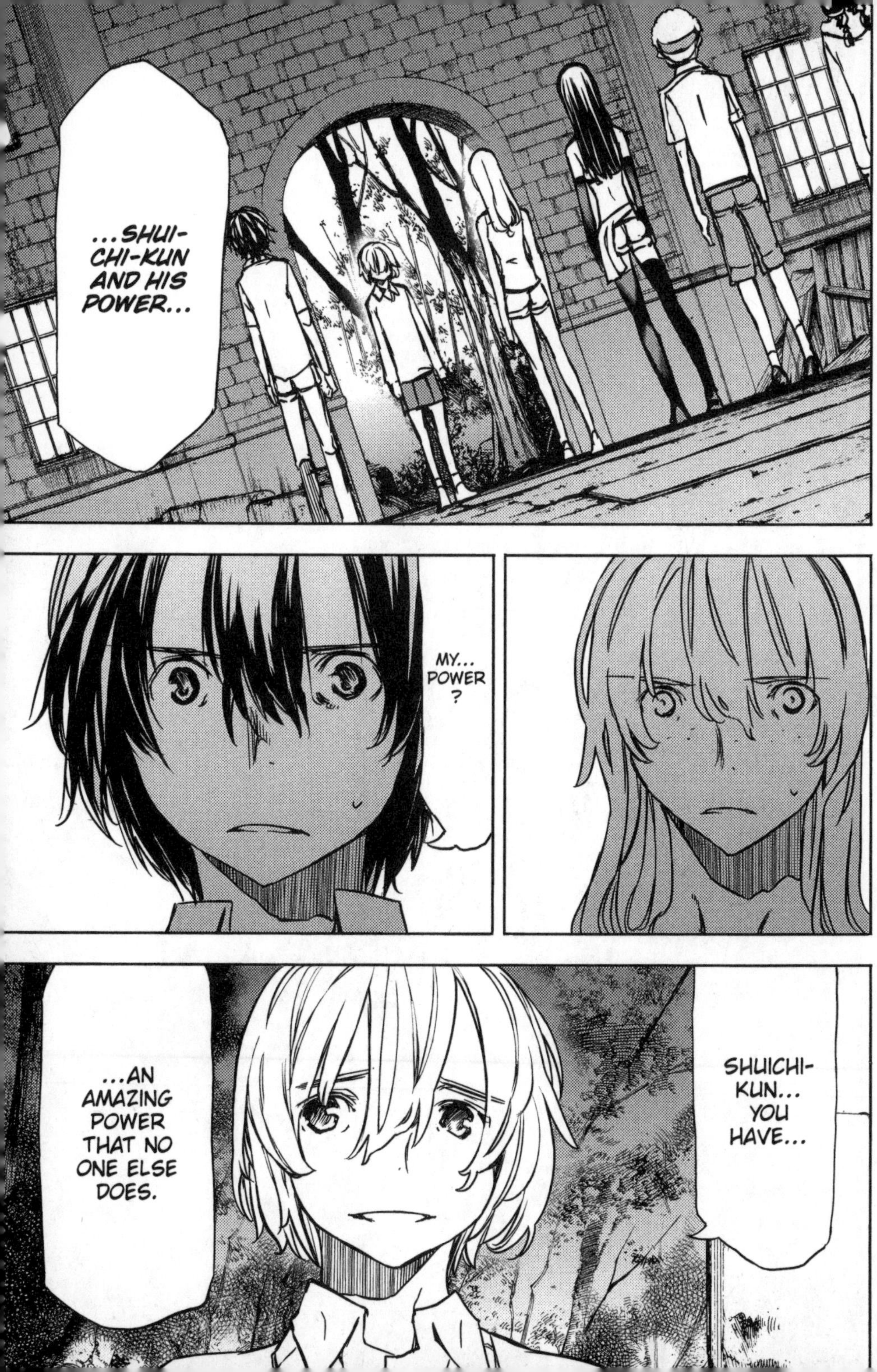
...SHUI-CHI-KUN AND HIS POWER...
MY... POWER?
SHUICHI-KUN... YOU HAVE...
...AN AMAZING POWER THAT NO ONE ELSE DOES.

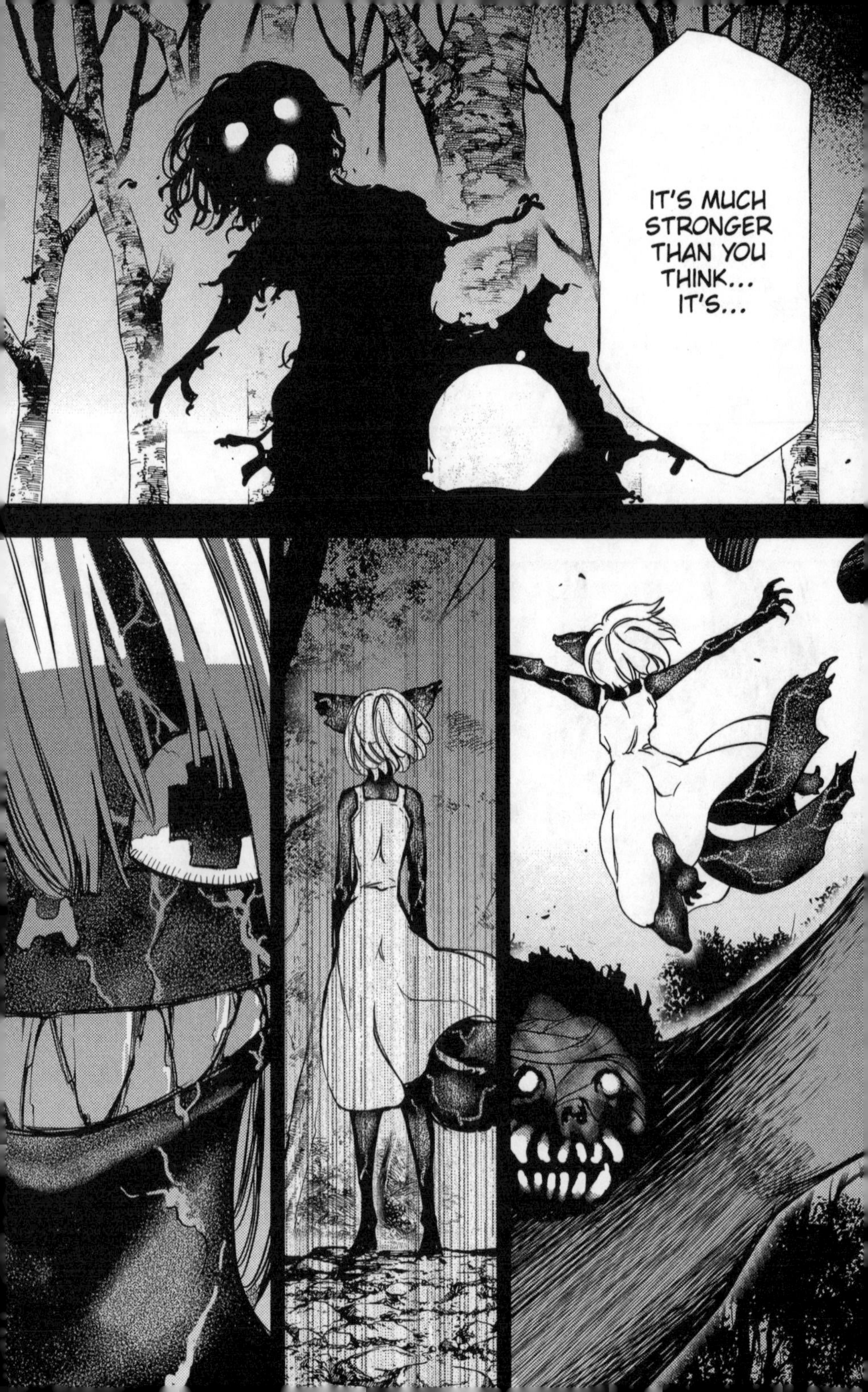
IT'S MUCH STRONGER THAN YOU THINK... IT'S...

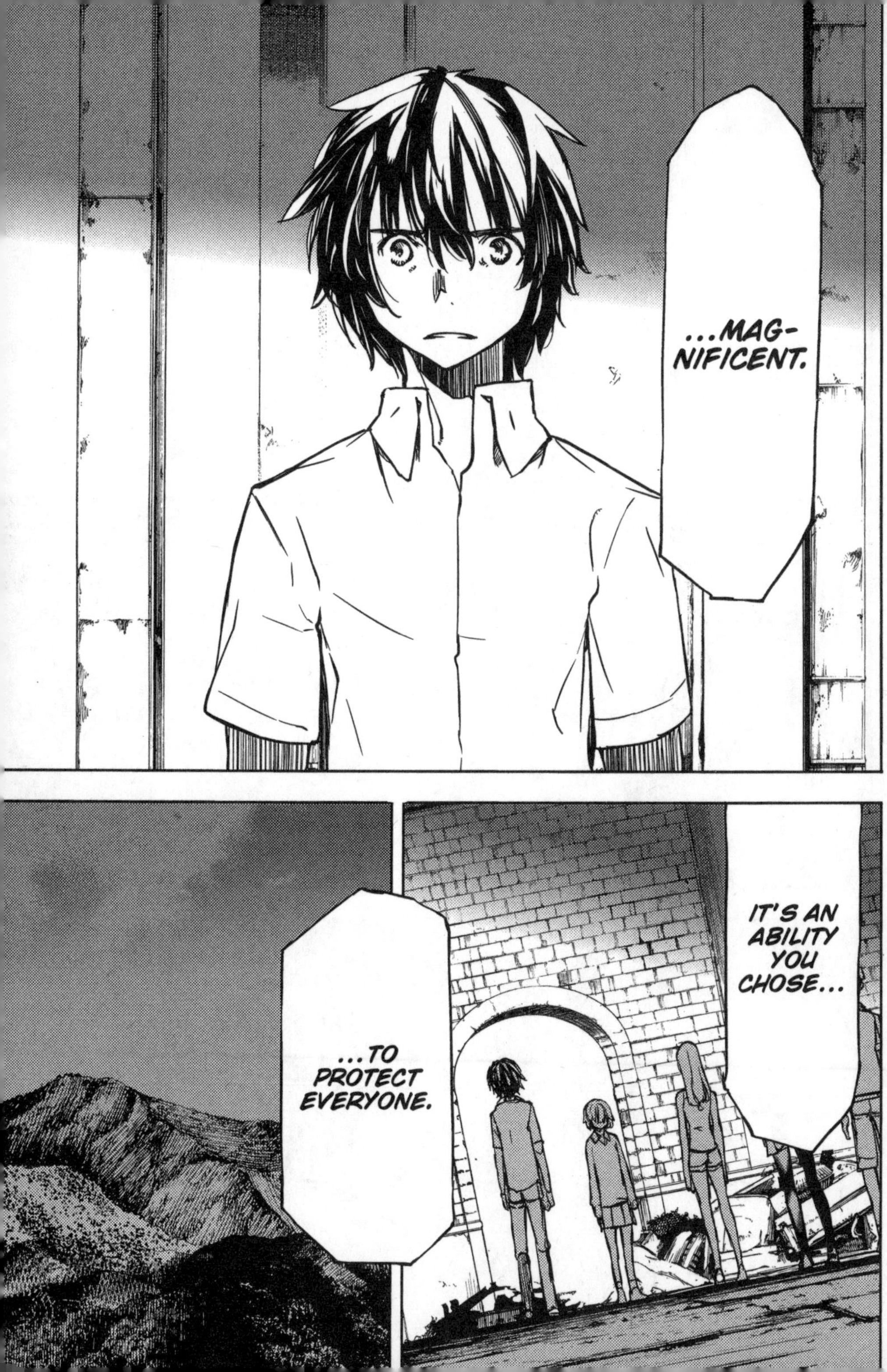
...MAG-
NIFICENT.
IT'S AN ABILITY YOU CHOSE...
...TO PROTECT EVERYONE.

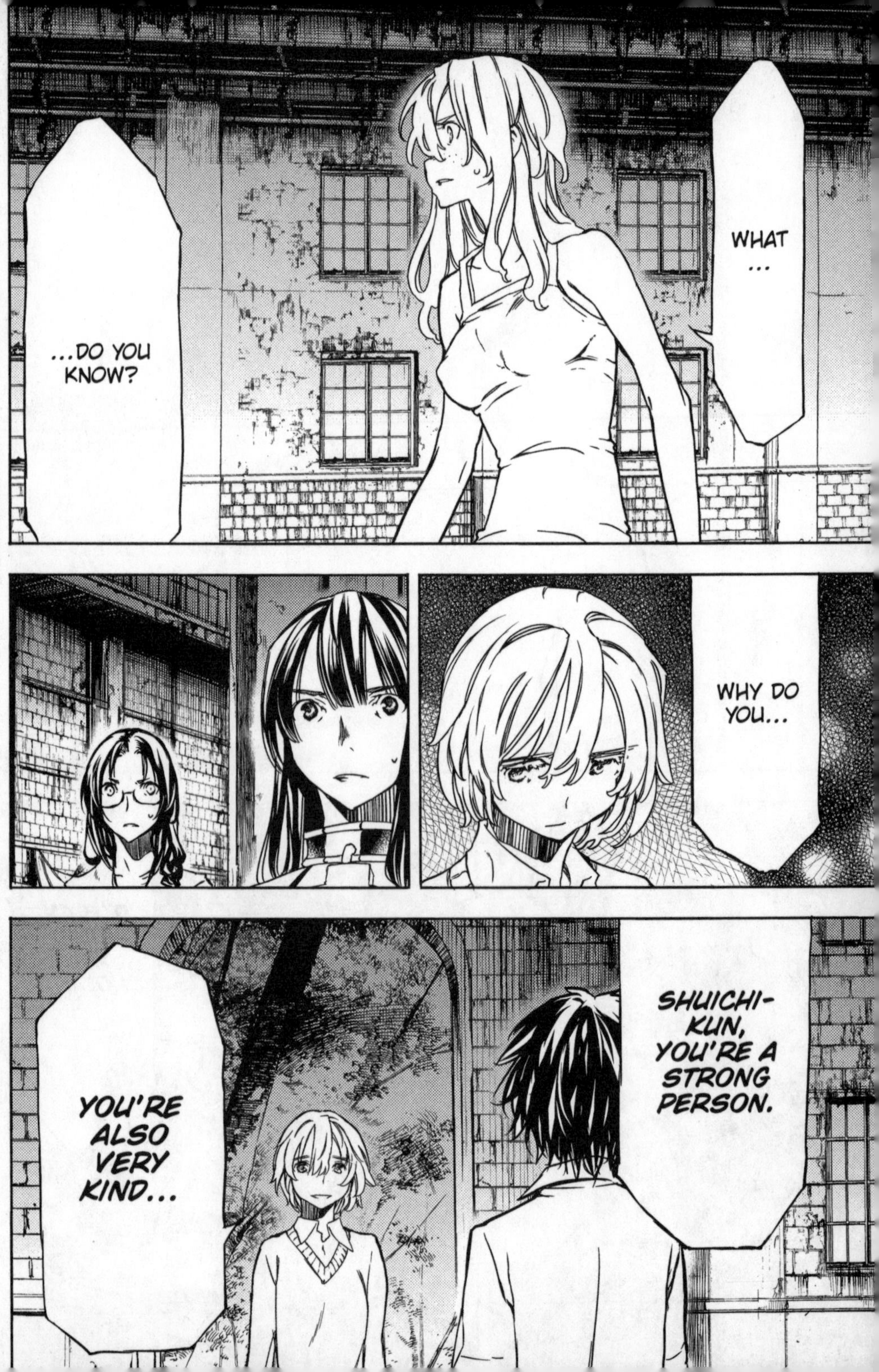
WHAT ...
...DO YOU KNOW?
WHY DO YOU...
SHUICHI-KUN, YOU'RE A STRONG PERSON.
YOU'RE ALSO VERY KIND...

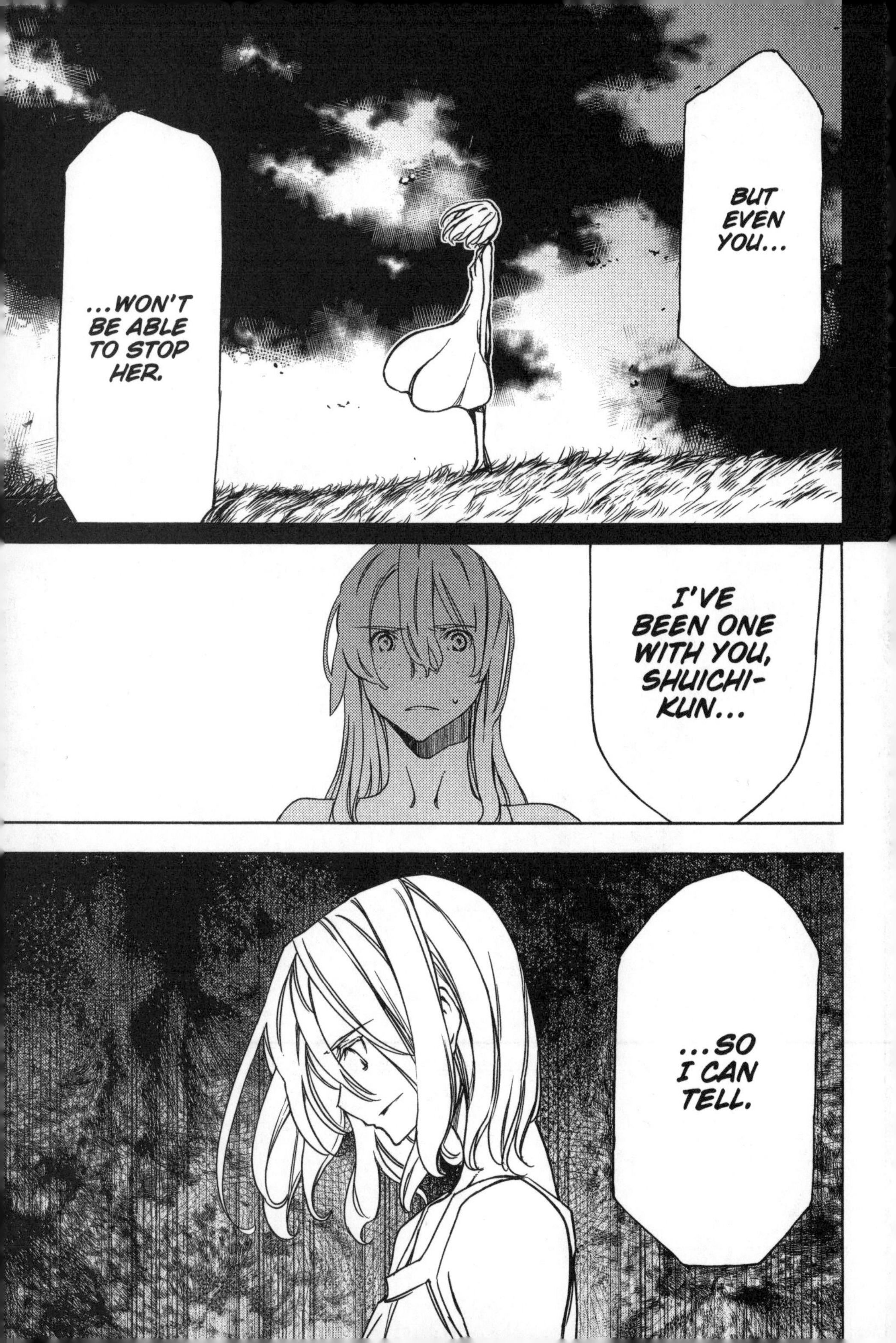
BUT EVEN YOU...
...WON'T BE ABLE TO STOP HER.
I'VE BEEN ONE WITH YOU, SHUICHI-KUN...
...SO I CAN TELL.

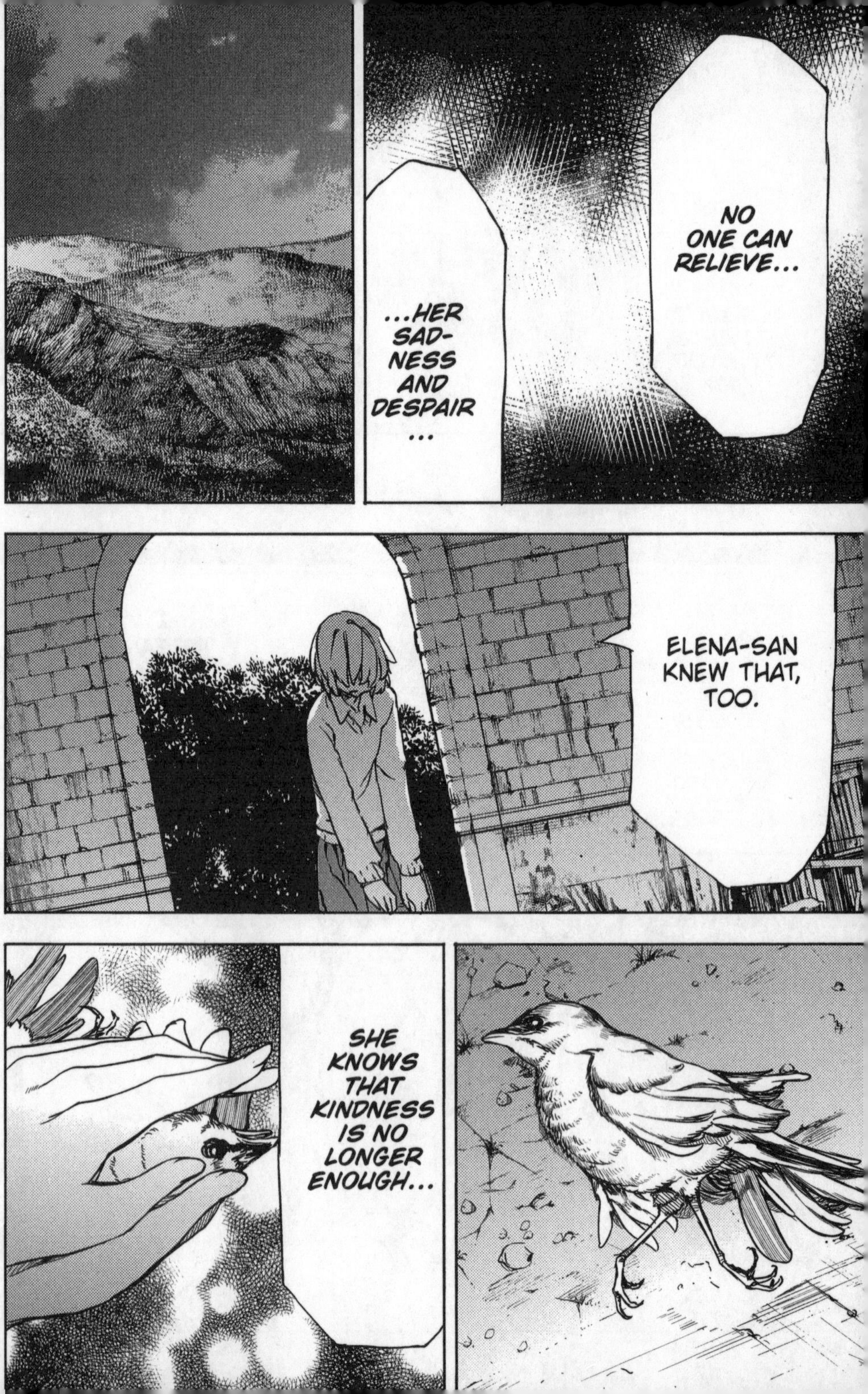
NO ONE CAN RELIEVE...
...HER SAD-NESS AND DESPAIR...
ELENA-SAN KNEW THAT, TOO.
SHE KNOWS THAT KINDNESS IS NO LONGER ENOUGH...

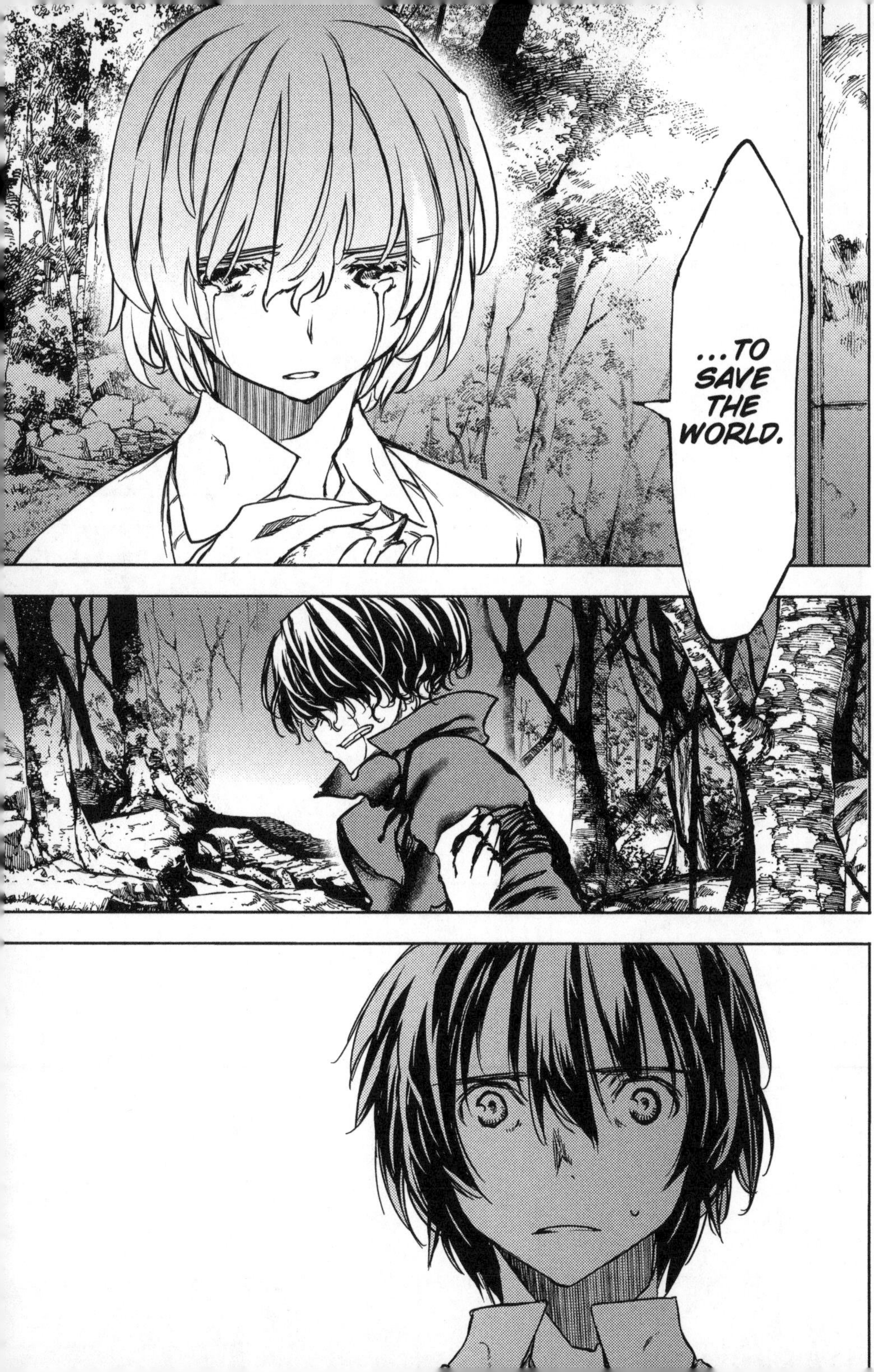
...TO SAVE THE WORLD.

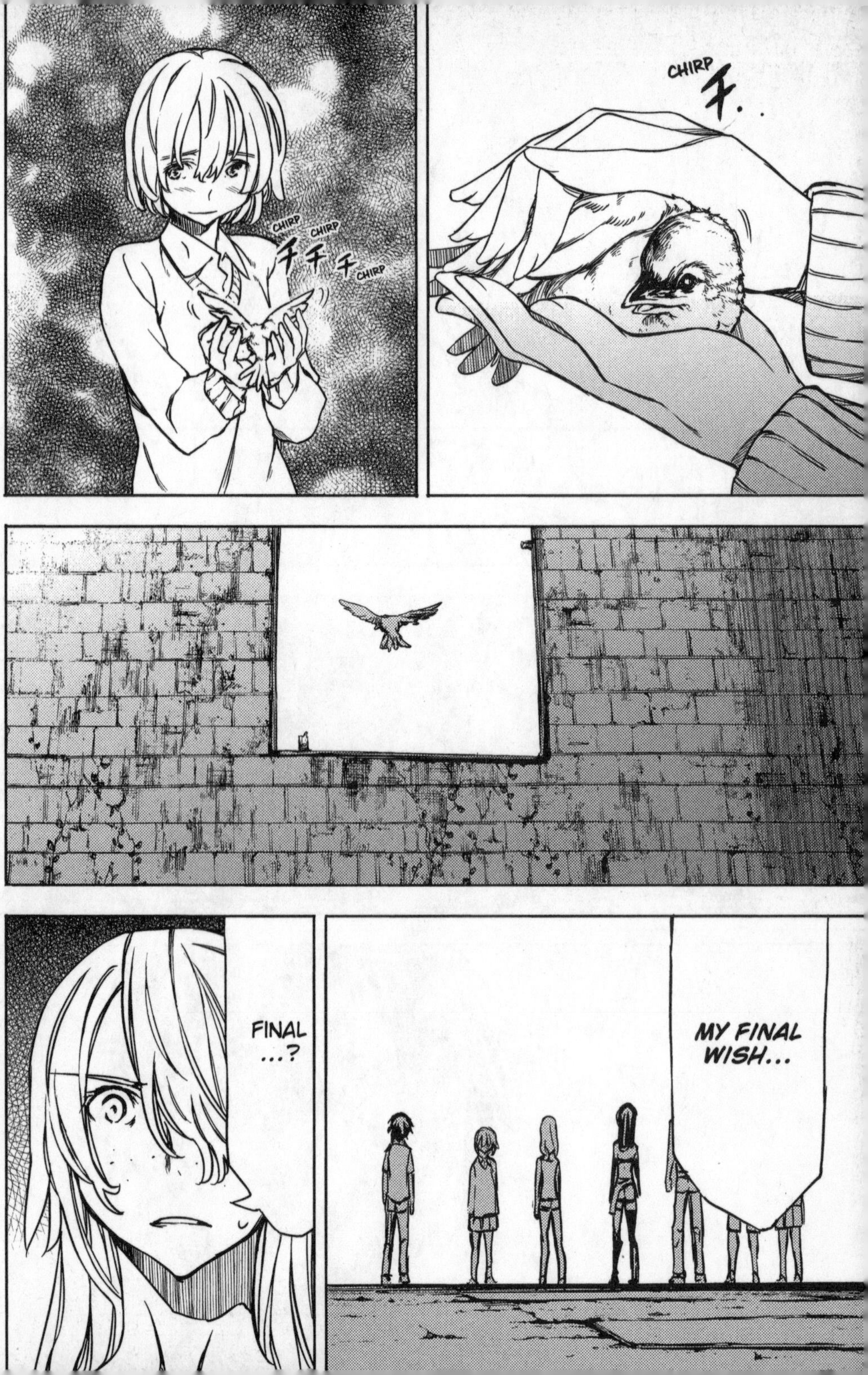
CHIRP
チ..
CHIRP CHIRP
チチチ
CHIRP
MY FINAL WISH...
FINAL ...?

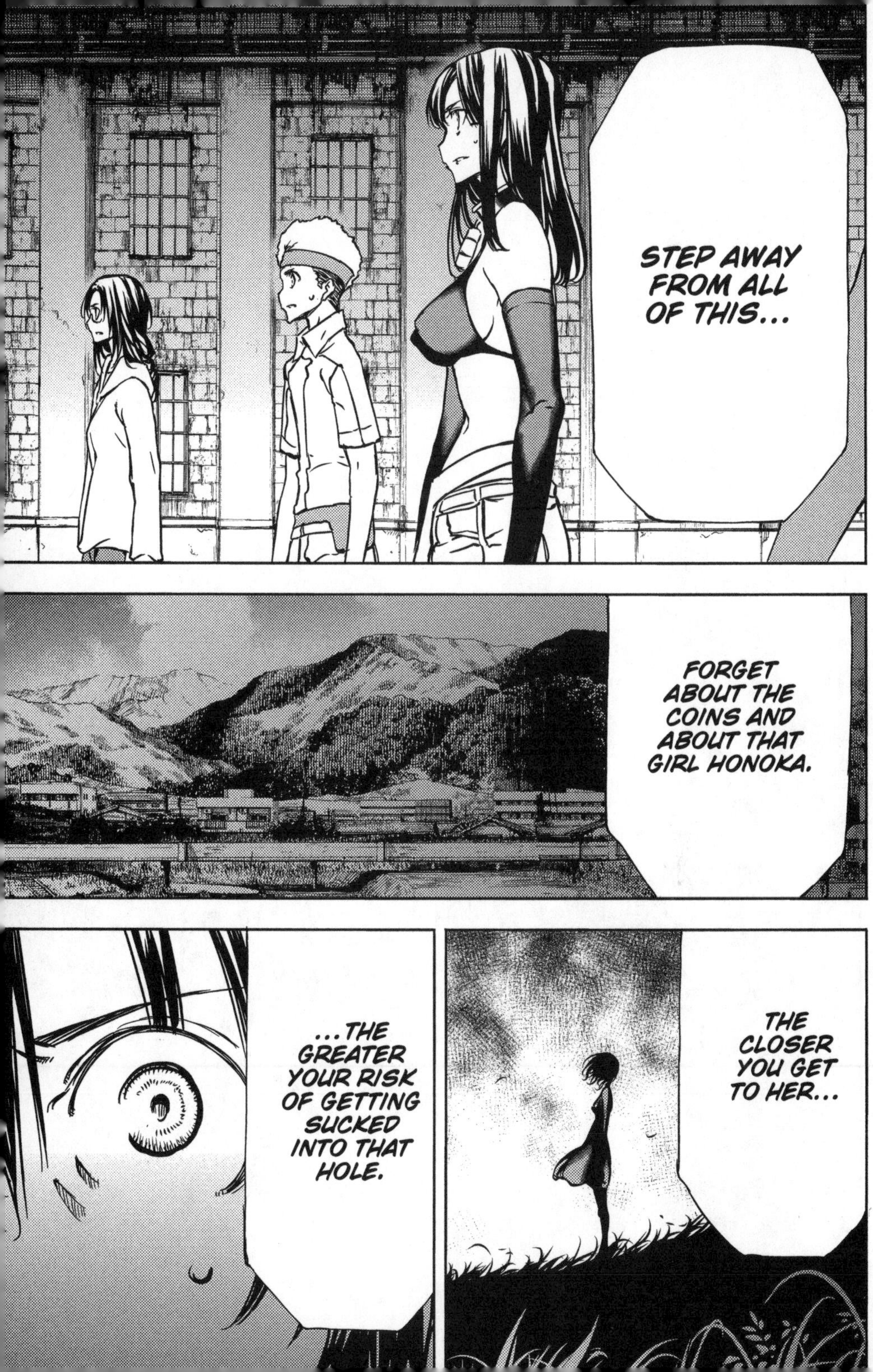
STEP AWAY FROM ALL OF THIS...
FORGET ABOUT THE COINS AND ABOUT THAT GIRL HONOKA.
THE CLOSER YOU GET TO HER...
...THE GREATER YOUR RISK OF GETTING SUCKED INTO THAT HOLE.

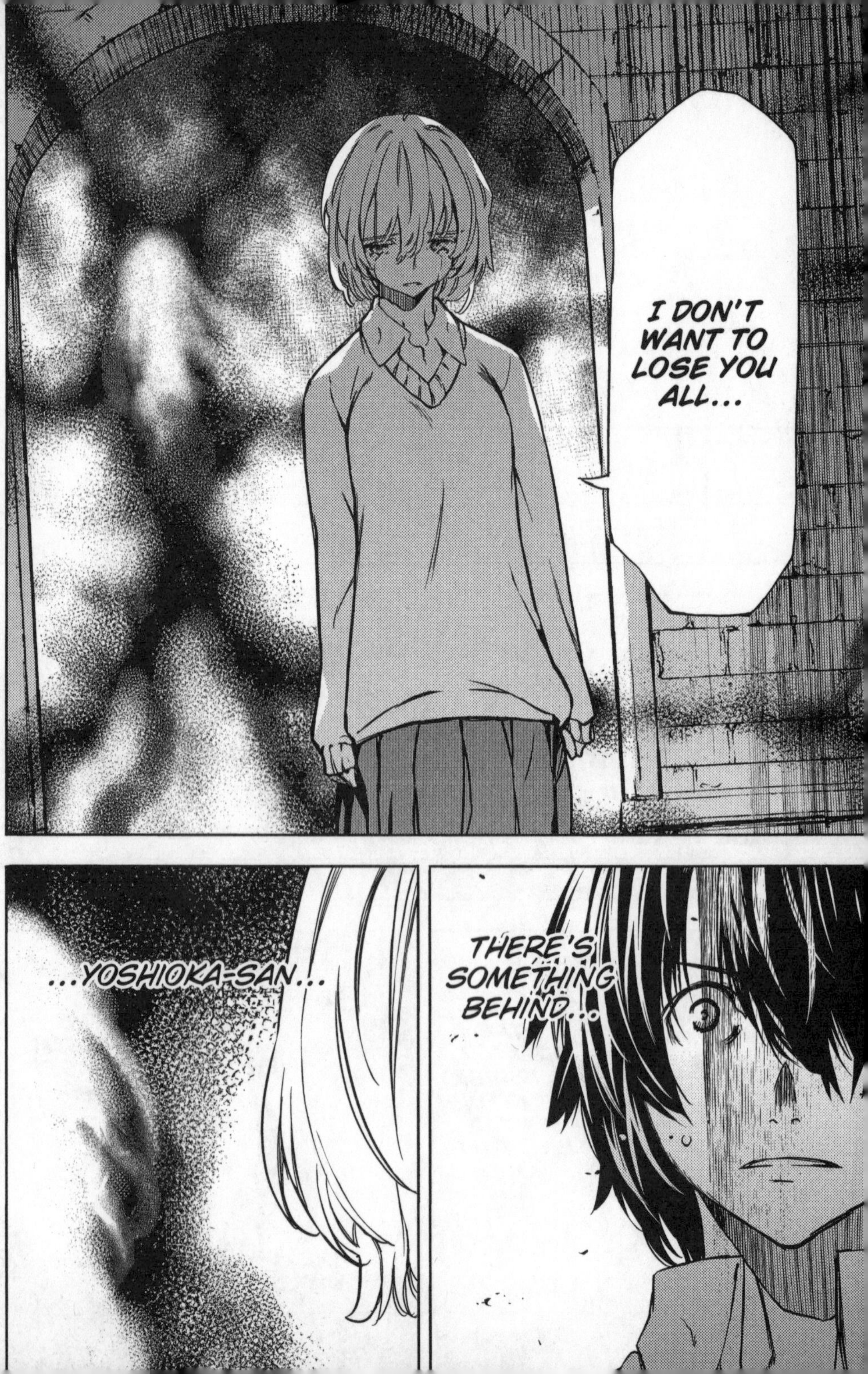
I DON'T WANT TO LOSE YOU ALL...
THERE'S SOMETHING BEHIND...
...YOSHIOKA-SAN...

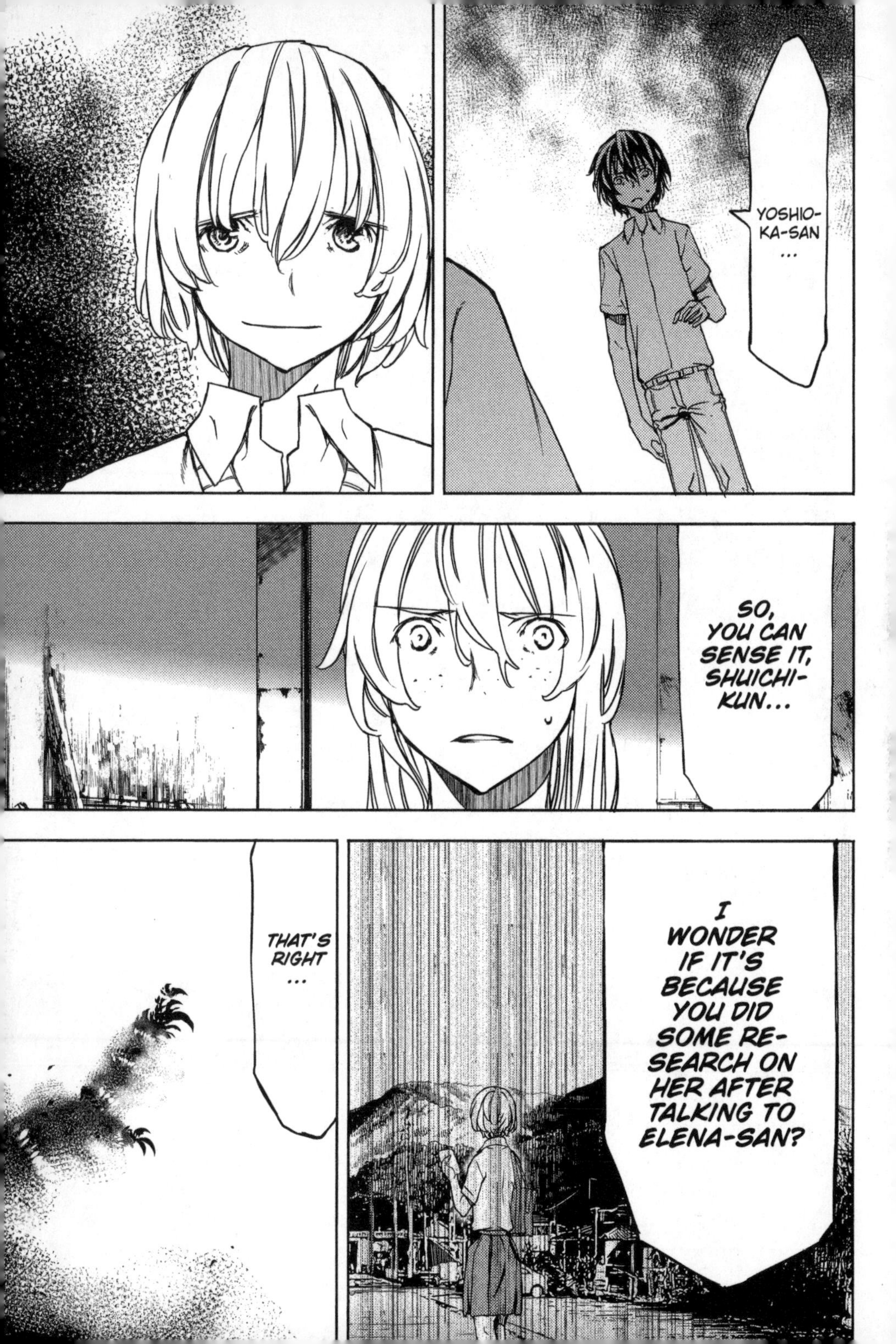
YOSHIOKA-SAN ...
SO, YOU CAN SENSE IT, SHUICHI-KUN...
I WONDER IF IT'S BECAUSE YOU DID SOME RESEARCH ON HER AFTER TALKING TO ELENA-SAN?
THAT'S RIGHT ...

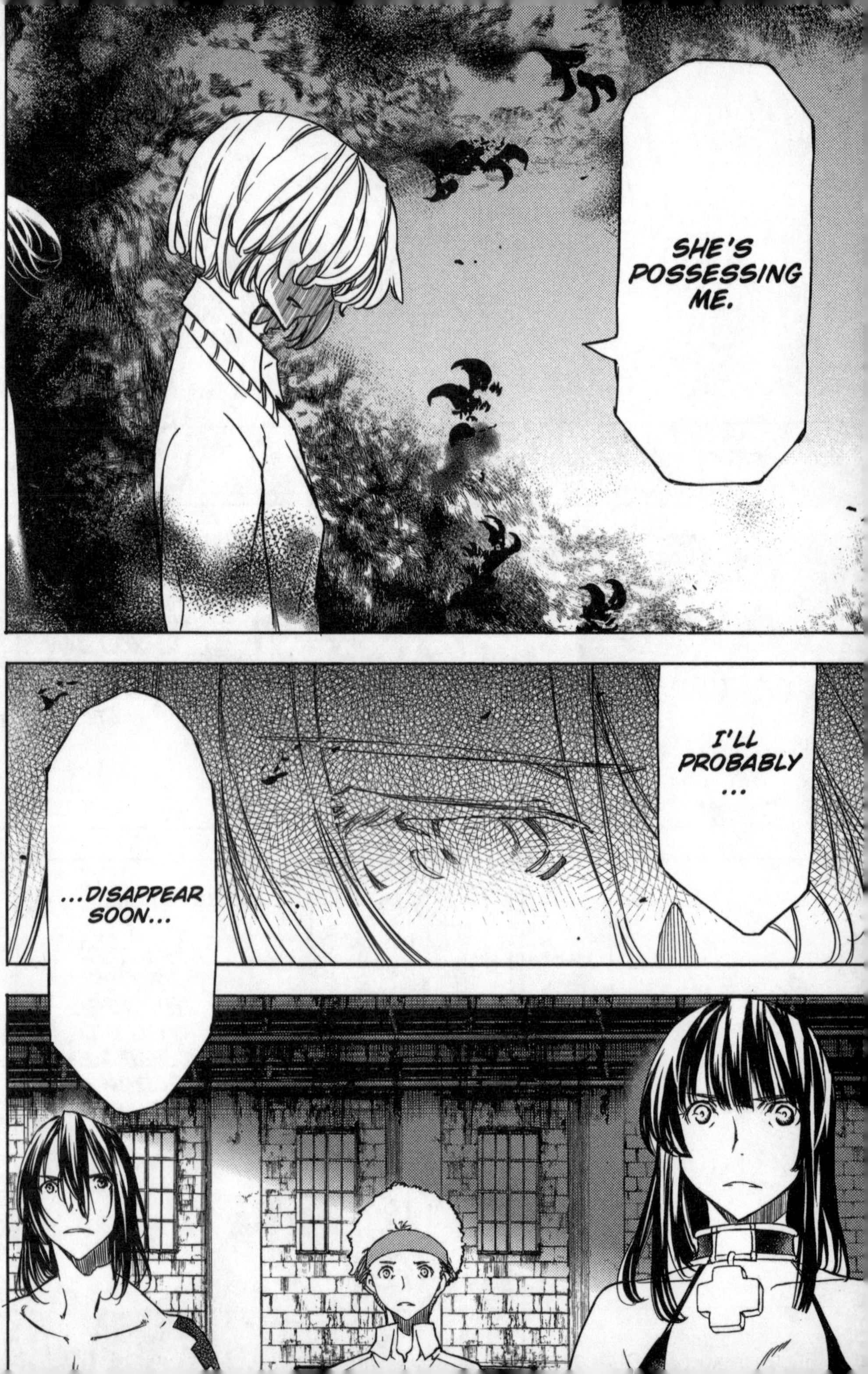
SHE'S POSSESSING ME.
I'LL PROBABLY ...
...DISAPPEAR SOON...

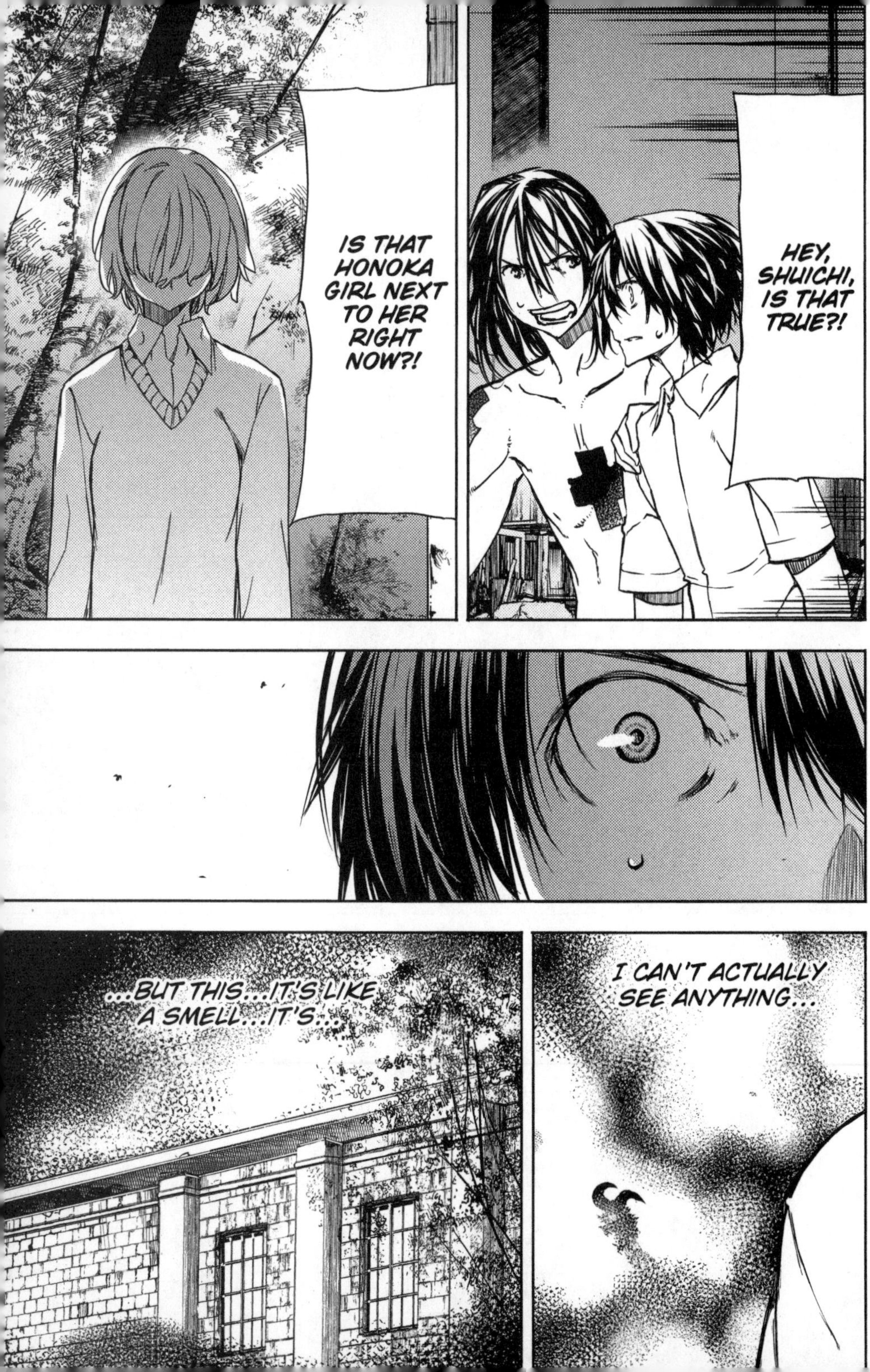
HEY, SHUICHI, IS THAT TRUE?!
IS THAT HONOKA GIRL NEXT TO HER RIGHT NOW?!
I CAN'T ACTUALLY SEE ANYTHING...
...BUT THIS...IT'S LIKE A SMELL...IT'S...

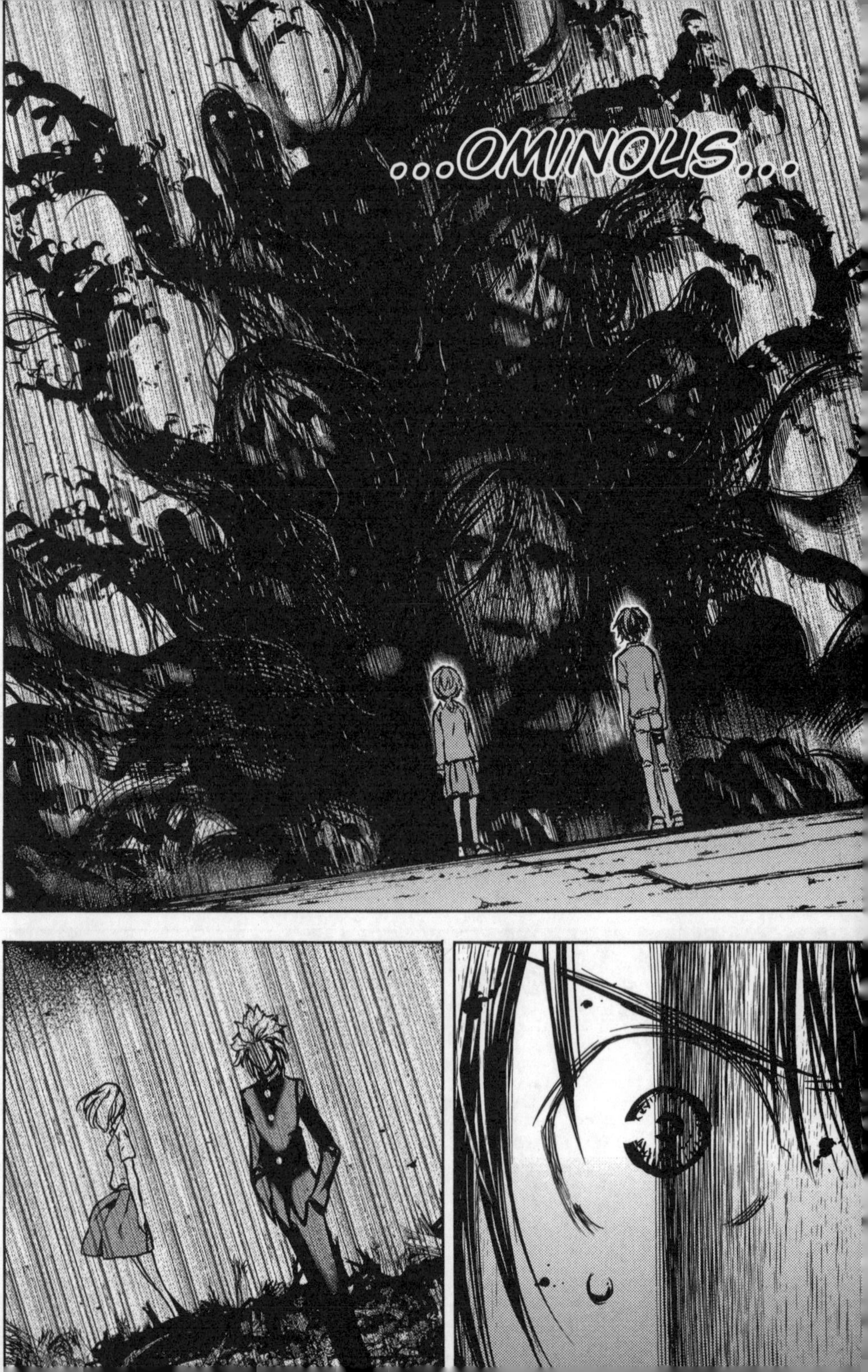
...OMINOUS...

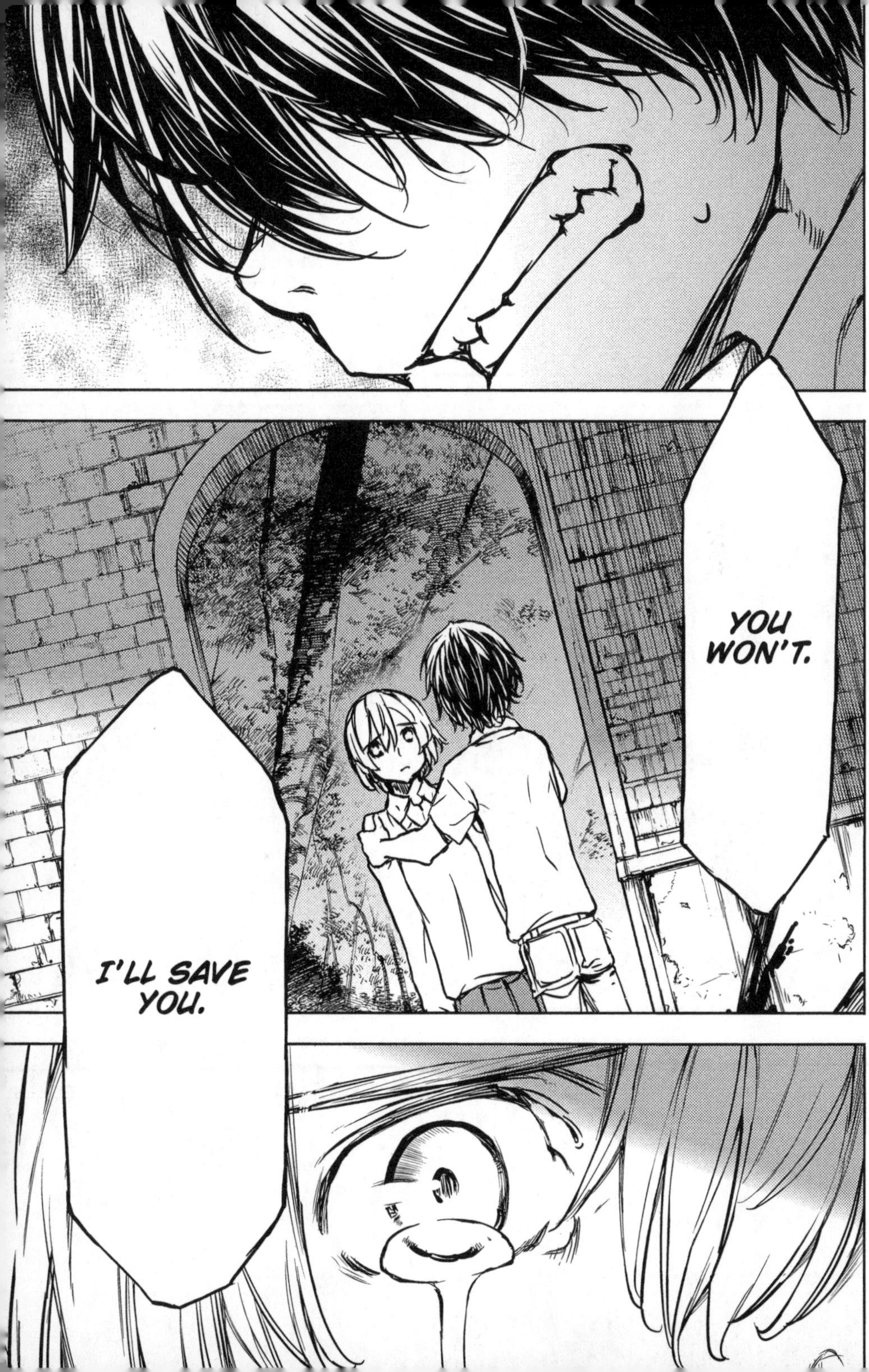
YOU WON'T.
I'LL SAVE YOU.

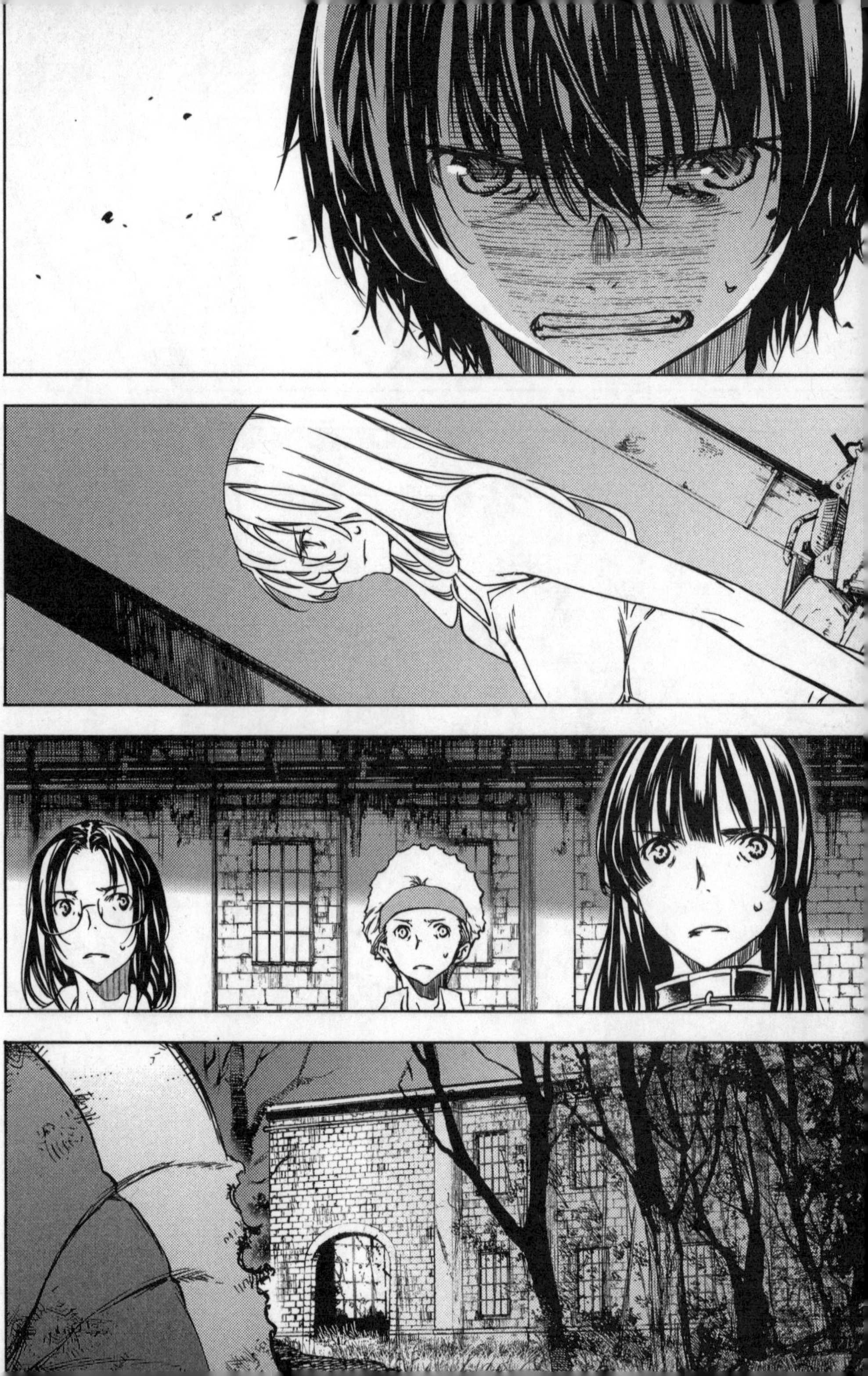

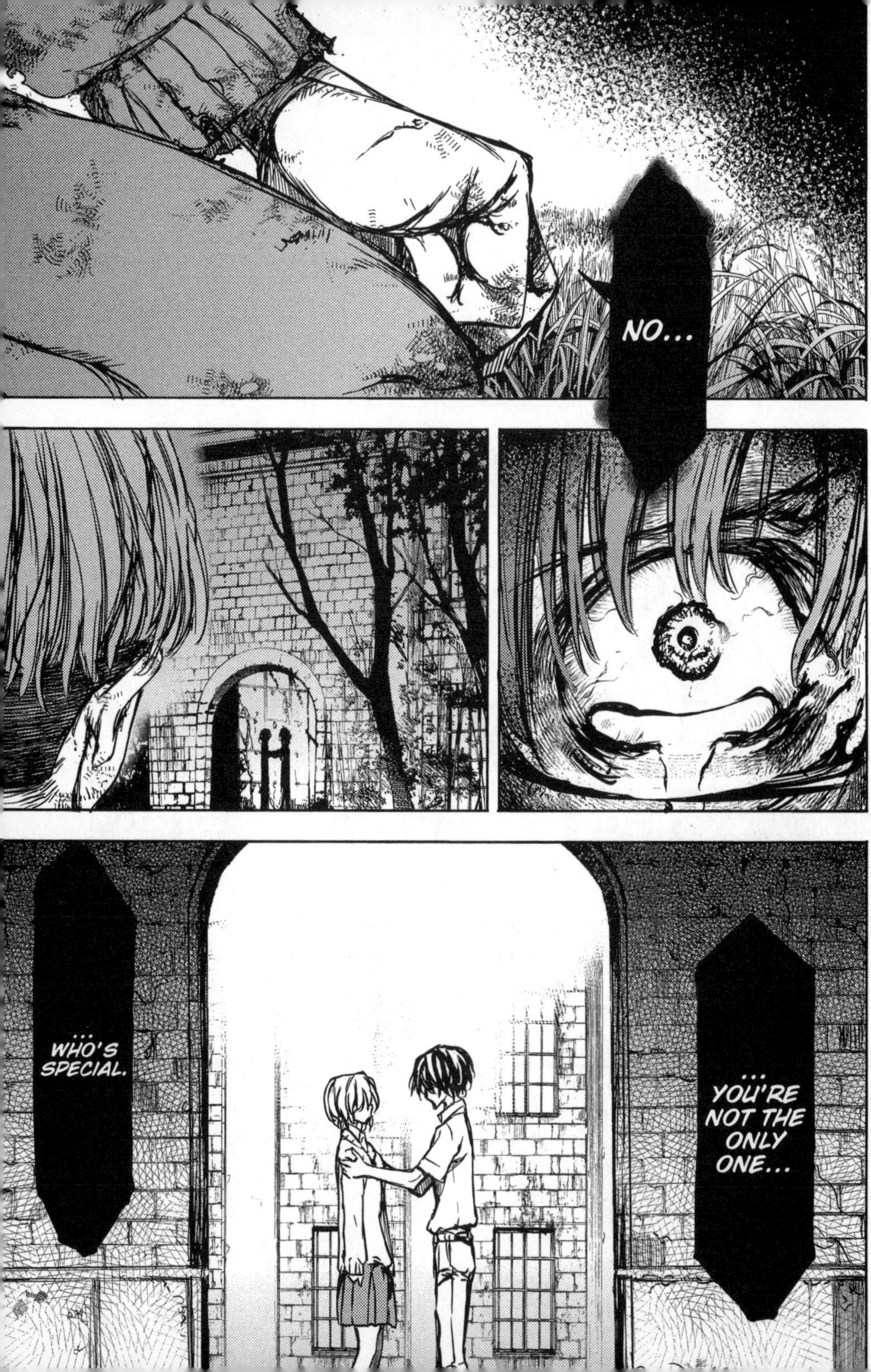
NO...
...YOU'RE NOT THE ONLY ONE...
...WHO'S SPECIAL.

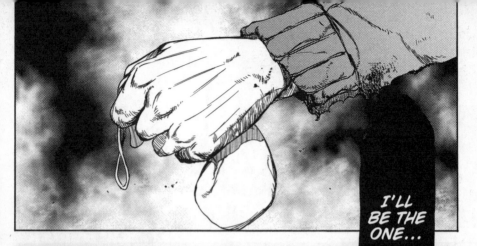

I'LL BE THE ONE...

...WHO SAVES YOSHIO-KA.

CONTINUED IN VOLUME 9

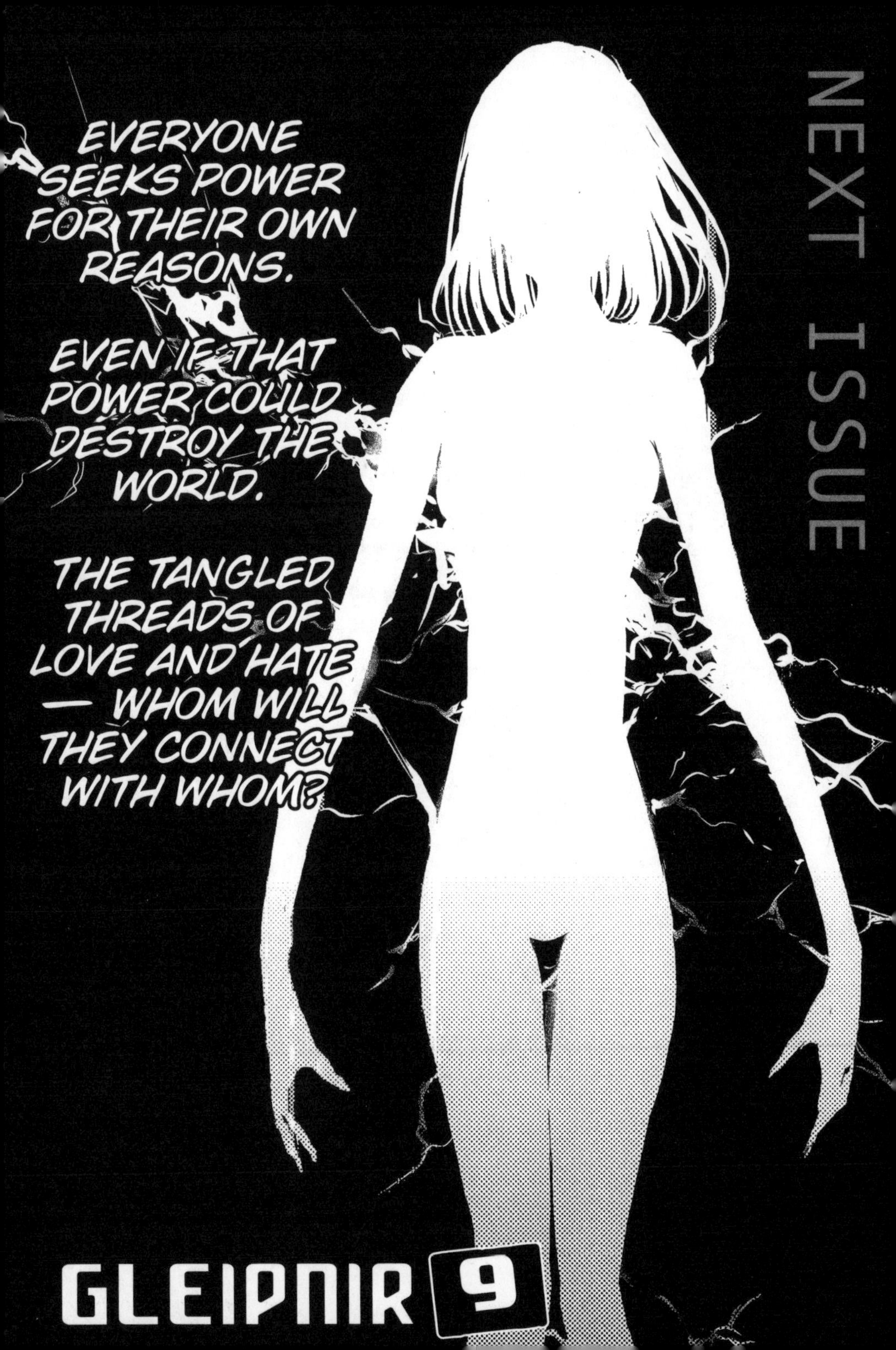
NEXT ISSUE
EVERYONE SEEKS POWER FOR THEIR OWN REASONS.
EVEN IF THAT POWER COULD DESTROY THE WORLD.
THE TANGLED THREADS OF LOVE AND HATE — WHOM WILL THEY CONNECT WITH WHOM?
GLEIPNIR 9

A Kodansha Comics Trade Paperback Original
Gleipnir 8 copyright © 2020 Sun Takeda
English translation copyright © 2020 Sun Takeda

Published in the United States by Kodansha Comics, an imprint of Kodansha USA Publishing, LLC, New York.

Publication rights for this English edition arranged through Kodansha Ltd., Tokyo.

First published in Japan in 2020 by Kodansha Ltd., Tokyo.
as *Gureipuniiru*, volume 8.

ISBN 978-1-64651-042-9

Printed in the United States of America.

www.kodanshacomics.com

9 8 7 6 5 4 3 2 1
Translation: ZephyrRZ
Lettering: Daniel C.Y.
Editing: Jordan Blanco
Kodansha Comics edition cover design by Phil Balsman

Publisher: Kiichiro Sugawara

Director of publishing services: Ben Applegate
Associate director of operations: Stephen Pakula
Publishing services managing editor: Noelle Webster
Assistant production manager: Emi Lotto, Angela Zurlo